Who is audience?

[T5]

Highlight good 'advice' (eg. mental calc)

Redundancy between chapters... each concept analysed at least twice (counting fractions...)

Mathematics Education
Models and Processes

+

Clean & well-structured story ... where all the parts fit together

✓ At least acknowledges source of knowledge is experience, not formal rules

✓ focuses on analogy as major mechanism

Unfortunately

① much of thinking is hence model accounts of domain under co... therefore it is not ... need to be explained ... ms of

Philosophical weakness: VanGlasserfeld Murez

a more general & comprehensive model (even if that model is not as tidy as we might like) non-objectivist model, constructivist, eg. cog. linguistic 'socio-cultural theory

[info. proc. model]

& well-ordered thought

all kinds of thinking social symbol constructivism 'concepts' are arguments

c, a set of prescriptions for teaching, which if followed will lead to error-free ing.

There are no children in this book — an edited volume or selection of original research reports would give a much better feeling for actual participants, settings, etc, as well as avoiding the implication that theory is fixed, settled.

Most recommendations are to do/teach exactly as is traditional, followed by prediction that errors ('should not') arise if students have ('correctly') ~~created mental map models~~ learned basis (cf p 182)

This is contradicted by research, and ignores growing body of results accounting for student errors/misconceptions.

Mathematics Education
Models and Processes

Lyn D. English
Queensland University of Technology,
Australia

Graeme S. Halford
The University of Queensland, Australia

1995

LAWRENCE ERLBAUM ASSOCIATES, PUBLISHERS
Mahwah, New Jersey
Hove, UK

Lawrence Erlbaum Associates, Inc., Publishers
10 Industrial Avenue
Mahwah, New Jersey 07430

Cover design by Jan Melchior

Library of Congress Cataloging-in-Publication Data

English, Lyn D.
    Mathematics education : models and processes / Lyn D. English,
Graeme S. Halford.
        p.   cm.
    Includes bibliographical references and indexes.
    ISBN 0-8058-1457-4 (alk. paper). -- ISBN 0-8058-1458-2 (pbk. :
  alk. paper)
    1. Mathematics--Study and teaching--Psychological aspects.
I. Halford, Graeme S. II. Title.
QA11.E675   1995
372.7'01'9--dc20   95-3959
                                                        CIP

Books published by Lawrence Erlbaum Associates are printed
on acid-free paper, and their bindings are chosen for strength
and durability

Printed in the United States of America
10 9 8 7 6 5 4 3 2 1

In appreciation of the support and encouragement provided by my parents, Brian and Denise English, and by my mentor in mathematics education, Dr. Graham A. Jones.

CONTENTS

Preface

This book is intended primarily for those interested in education, especially mathematics education, and also for those concerned with cognitive development and cognitive science. Our purpose in writing the book was to define better techniques of mathematics education by combining a knowledge of cognitive science with mathematics curriculum theory and research. Our concept of the human reasoning process has been changed fundamentally by cognitive science in the last two decades. The roles of memory retrieval, domain-specific and domain-general skills, analogy, and mental models are better understood now than previously. We believe cognitive science provides the most accurate account so far of the actual processes that people use in mathematics, and offers the best potential for genuine increases in efficiency. As we indicate, a cognitive science approach enables constructivist ideas to be analyzed and further developed in our search for greater understanding of children's mathematical learning.

The book is not simply an application of cognitive science, however. We provide a new perspective on mathematics education by examining the nature of mathematical concepts and processes, how and why we teach them, why certain approaches appear to be more effective than others, and how we might assist children to become more mathematically powerful. We use theories of analogy and knowledge representation, combined with research on teaching practice, to help children form links and correspondences between different concepts, and between the same concept in different contexts, so as to overcome problems associated with fragmented knowledge. In so doing, we capitalize on new insights into the values and limitations of using concrete teaching aids that can be analyzed in terms of analogy theory.

In addition to addressing the role of understanding, we analyze skill acquisition models in terms of their implications for the development of mathematical competence. We place a strong emphasis on the development of students' mathematical reasoning and problem-solving skills that we believe promote flexible use of knowledge. We indicate how children have at their disposal a number of general problem-solving skills that they can apply independently to the solution of novel problems and, in so doing, enhance their mathematical knowledge.

In writing the book, Lyn English took primary responsibility for chapters 1, 4, 5, 6, 7, 8, and 9, whereas Graeme Halford completed chapters 2 and 3. Overall, our aim has been to offer a foundation set of principles that can guide further development and research.

One of the most pleasant aspects of writing a book is to recall those people whose support and encouragement have contributed greatly to the book's development. Personnel from the Queensland University of Technology were most generous in providing Lyn English with a semester's leave from teaching duties to concentrate on the book. In particular, we are indebted to the vice-chancellor, Professor Dennis Gibson, the (then) deputy vice-chancellor, Professor Tom Dixon, and the dean of the faculty of education, Professor Alan Cumming, for granting this period of leave. Thanks must also go to Dr. Tom Cooper and Dr. Cam McRobbie (QUT) for adding their support. It was indeed a rare luxury to have such a concentrated period of time for writing.

There were several other personnel without whose assistance the book would not have been completed. We gratefully acknowledge the hard work of Lorraine English, Rebecca Haire, Martin Lambert, Lynn Burnett, Ann Heirdsfield, Clare Christensen, Kylie Rixon, Campbell Dickson, and Robert Dennys. We especially thank Rebecca Haire for preparing the figures for production. Lorraine English and the other research assistants from the Centre for Mathematics and Science Education gave freely of their time to help us gather the necessary reference materials. The encouraging and constructive comments of a reviewer at prepublication stage are also gratefully acknowledged.

Another major debt is owed to those people whose contributions to the literature have provided inspiration for, as well as the building blocks of, this work, and who are acknowledged, of course, in the citations. However, there have been others with whom we have shared intellectual stimulation, as well as support and encouragement. In particular, we would like to express our special appreciation to Graham Jones, Keith Holyoak, Gaea Leinhardt, Rochel Gelman, Dedre Gentner, Ed Silver, Lauren Resnick, Carol Thornton, Pat Cheng, Bob Davis, Carolyn Maher, Glen Evans, John Anderson, Lyn Reder, Kevin Collis, George Booker, Cal Irons, John Flavell, Bob Siegler, Robbie Case, and Leone Burton.

—*Lyn D. English*
—*Graeme S. Halford*

1

COGNITIVE PSYCHOLOGY AND MATHEMATICS EDUCATION

The discipline of psychology and, more recently, cognitive science has had a seminal influence on how mathematics is taught and learned (Kilpatrick, 1992). From the early part of the century, the teaching and learning of mathematics has received considerable attention from psychologists, as can be seen in E. L. Thorndike's (1922) book, *Psychology of Arithmetic*. Thorndike's work made a significant impact in many a classroom where the chanting of tables (reflecting Thorndike's "law of exercise") was a regular occurrence. Psychology has continued to show an interest in mathematics education, as can be seen from the large number of papers presenting a cognitive analysis of children's mathematical learning (e.g., J. S. Brown & VanLehn, 1982; Collis, 1974; R. B. Davis, 1984; Greeno, 1992; Halford, 1993; Siegler & Jenkins, 1989; Sweller, 1989). Mathematics has been a popular domain of psychological research largely because of its importance in the school curriculum and because its hierachical structure facilitates the construction of tasks of varying levels of difficulty (Kilpatrick, 1992). Mathematical knowledge also lends itself to representation in the computational models of cognitive science.

Changes in psychological thought over the century have been reflected in the major reform movements in mathematics education. These movements have been characterized by changes in the content of the curriculum as well as in the methods used to impart this knowledge. Thorndike's era, for example, was noted for its emphasis on arithmetic, with drill and practice activities reflecting Thorndike's primary laws of learning. Likewise, the current emphasis on problem solving and mathematical thinking processes, with children's active involvement in their own learning, reflects ideas from

1

the constructivist paradigm and from cognitive science, including information processing. In the first part of this chapter, we trace the main developments in psychological thought and their impact on mathematics education. These include the period of drill and practice, the period of meaningful learning, and the "new math" phase. We then review the psychological and societal forces that have shaped the current scene in mathematics education. We conclude with our views on a psychological theory of mathematics education and present an outline of the approach we adopt in this book.

HISTORICAL DEVELOPMENTS IN THE PSYCHOLOGY
OF MATHEMATICS EDUCATION

The Period of Drill and Practice

Arithmetic is . . . a set of rather specialized habits of behavior toward certain sorts of quantities and relations (Thorndike, 1922, p. 73) . . . learning arithmetic is like learning to typewrite . . . [it] is in some measure a game whose moves are motivated by the general set of the mind toward victory - winning right answers (pp. 283–284). Drill and practice was the primary focus of mathematics education during the first 30 years of this century. Edward Thorndike was the main proponent of this approach, with his theory variously termed, "connectionism," "associationism," and "S-R bond theory." Thorndike (1922) maintained that, by means of conditioning, specific responses are linked with specific stimuli. He believed that "almost everything in arithmetic should be taught as a habit that has connections with habits already acquired and will work in an organization with other habits to come" (p. 194). Instruction that focused on the formation of necessary bonds and habits was considered particularly important for elementary school children who were not thought to have the ability to deduce the rules of arithmetic from examples and previously learned rules.

Thorndike established three primary laws of learning: the law of exercise or repetition, the law of effect, and the law of readiness. The first law states that the greater the number of times a stimulus-induced response is elicited, the longer the response (i.e., learning) will be retained. This means that each S-R bond that is to be established requires many practice exercises. According to the law of effect, responses that are associated with satisfaction are strengthened and those associated with pain are weakened. Thorndike's third law, that of readiness, associates satisfaction or annoyance with action or inaction depending on a bond's readiness to act.

These laws led to a fragmentation of arithmetic into many small components of facts and skills to be taught and tested separately. Bonds were presented in a carefully programmed way so that the important bonds were practiced often, and the less important, less frequently. "Propaedeutic" bonds were used to promote the learning of new concepts and would be practiced temporarily but would subsequently fall away through lack of use. For example, to calculate four 2s, the child would be taught initially the propaedeutic bond for counting by 2s (i.e., 2, 4, 6, 8). This would be replaced later by the bond, "four 2s are 8." Because bonds were considered to have an effect on each other, Thorndike (1922) maintained that "every bond formed should be formed with due consideration of every other bond that has been or will be formed" (p. 140). It was not considered appropriate to teach closely related facts for fear of establishing incorrect bonds.

The teacher's role was to identify the bonds that comprised a particular body of mathematical content and then organize them so that learning the simpler bonds would assist the student in learning the more difficult bonds that occurred later in the teaching sequence. The teacher would then arrange for practice on each set of bonds, with this practice being just sufficient to avoid errors occurring when the next, more difficult set of bonds was introduced. Despite his strong empahsis on drill and practice, Thorndike nevertheless highlighted the importance of making arithmetic problems enjoyable and interesting for children and relevant to their everyday experiences. In this way, children would be more likely to make stronger connections and be better able to make the appropriate connections at the appropriate times. Applying a correct series of connections at the proper time indicated an ability to perceive the structure of a problem, to choose the appropriate series of connections, and to produce all of the connections in series (Nik Pa, 1986).

Thorndike's arithmetic texts reflected the drill sequences he recommended, however as Resnick and Ford (1984) noted, his rules for generating them were largely intuitive. Thorndike did not systematically address issues such as the amount of practice that is considered adequate for establishing a particular bond or the best way to organize practice on different kinds of bonds. Nevertheless, his theory had a big impact on mathematics education and is no doubt still alive in many classrooms today. Although Thorndike emphasized the content of specific subject matter, he had little to say about the nature or structure of thinking and learning (Resnick & Ford, 1984). This was left to members of the structural school of thought, which came into being during the progressive education era in the 1930s.

The Period of Meaningful Learning

The progressive education movement of the 1930s and 1940s emphasized "learning for living" (Kroll, 1989). There was a shift away from meaningless drill methods where speed and accuracy were the criteria for measuring learning, to a focus on developing mathematical concepts in a meaningful way. There were two schools of thought here. Some educators (e.g., Wheeler, 1935) stressed the social utility aspect of arithmetic learning where it was believed that children learn all the required mathematics through incidental experience rather than systematic instruction. Others however, did not consider such an approach to be the most effective and advocated teaching the structure of mathematics. William Brownell (1935, 1945) was one of the major proponents of this view.

William Brownell.   Brownell (1945) argued that "meaning is to be sought in the structure, the organization, the inner relationship of the subject itself" (p. 481). The aim was to impart to students the strucure of arithmetic, that is, the "ideas, principles, and processes" of mathematics. The test of learning was not "mere mechanical facility in 'figuring' but an intelligent grasp upon number relations and the ability to deal with arithmetical situations with proper comprehension of their mathematical as well as their practical significance" (Brownell, 1935, p. 19). For example, a child who promptly gave the answer "12" to the fact "7 + 5" would not be regarded as having demonstrated a knowledge of the combination unless she understood why 7 plus 5 equals 12 and could convince others of its correctness. This would require the child to have an understanding of the mathematical principles and patterns underlying computations, this being one of the four categories of arithmetic meanings identified by Brownell (1947).

It is worthwhile reviewing these categories because they are still relevant to today's curriculum. Brownell's first category comprises basic concepts such as the meaning of whole numbers, fractions, decimal fractions, and ratio and proportion. The second group of meanings includes an understanding of fundamental operations. Here, children must know when to add, subtract, multiply, and divide. They must also know what happens to the numbers used when a given operation is applied. Brownell's third category comprises the more significant principles, relationships, and generalizations of arithmetic such as, "the product of two abstract factors remains the same regardless of which factor is used as multiplier" (Brownell, 1947, p. 257). The final category pertains to an understanding of the decimal number system and its application in rationalizing computational procedures and algorithms.

The use of concrete materials and practical applications played an important role in Brownell's school. Drill and practice had a place but was to be utilized only after children had understood the ideas and processes that were to be reinforced. Without a meaningful understanding, drill activities would encourage students to view mathematics as a collection of unrelated ideas and independent facts. Investigating children's cognitive abilities was considered an essential aspect of curriculum and instruction, with adjustments to the curriculum being made to suit the child's mental capacities.

Henry Van Engen.   Another prominent advocate of meaningful arithmetic was Van Engen who belonged to the operational school. According to this school, arithmetic is concerned with the operations that can be performed on groups (1949). Van Engen expressed concern over the previous era, stressing that drill activities are only a means to an end, and that drill alone will do little more than teach children how to manipulate numbers. He advocated a change in curriculum content that was to be accompanied by an entirely different concept of instruction. An emphasis on the semantic meanings of arithmetic, in contrast to Brownell's strong syntactical focus, was considered essential. Van Engen argued that Brownell had not addressed meanings that involve associating a symbol with an operation, rather, he had concentrated on the syntactical meanings that involve the formation of relationships between operations. Van Engen's analysis of meaning was more advanced than Brownell's in that the child was seen to actively give meaning to symbols. The pupil acquired meaning by "reading into" a symbol, realizing that the symbol is a substitute for an object.

In contrast to Brownell, Van Engen did not consider the roots of arithmetical meaning to reside in the structure of the subject matter, rather he viewed physical or sensory-motor activity as its source (Nik Pa, 1986). Although Van Engen (1953) maintained that manipulative activities are of utmost importance in the development of children's number concepts, he nevertheless warned of the dangers of inappropriate use of visual aids. His advice is timely: "Too many visual aids in use today do not highlight the essential features of the concept they are supposed to teach. In many cases the essential features are too embedded in the total situation. In still others, it is merely a visual aid, there is no relevance to the development of the concept" (p. 93).

Van Engen's (1958/1993) emphasis on developing students' ability to recognize problem structure is also pertinent today. He believed that the schools of his time had failed to develop students' ability to detect patterns in similar and seemingly diverse situations and had been directing children to the wrong element in problem solving, namely the answer. Rather, the child should grasp the structure of a problem before she looks for the answer. Differences in ability to recognize structure were seen to distinguish good problem solvers from poor.

Gestalt Theory.   The Gestaltists also expressed concern for the development of the complex behaviors of problem solving and reasoning. The Gestalt or "field" theory grew out of a reaction against both the structuralist and connectionist doctrines (Dellarosa, 1988; Fehr, 1953). The German word *Gestalt* means an organized whole in contrast to a collection of parts. Learning, according to the Gestalt psychologists, is a process of identifying relationships and of developing insights. It is only when the relationship of a part of a situation to its whole is perceived that insight occurs and a solution to a problem can be produced. In contrast to Thorndike's approach, the Gestaltists would attempt from the outset to bring all the elements of a problem together.

The Gestaltists however, did not manage to overthrow their contemporaries' hold on psychological investigation. This was largely because they relied on the subconscious and failed to develop a comprehensive theory of behavior or cognition (Dellarosa, 1988; Schoenfeld, 1985b). Their body of work consisted mainly of descriptions of phenomena that did not serve as the basis for theory building but as evidence of the inadequacy of the connectionist and structuralist models. Nevertheless, the Gestaltists did make some significant contributions in the area of perception, problem solving, and thinking. For example, they pointed out how the qualitative aspect of an optical illusion could not be reduced to its components, supporting their view that "the whole is greater than the sum of its parts."

In the area of thinking and problem solving, the Gestaltists highlighted the active, constructive nature of the processes involved. The Gestalt "model" of problem solving involves (a) saturation, that is, working on a problem until one has reached the end of conscious resources; (b) incubation, where the problem is put aside while the subconscious mind works on it; (c) inspiration, in which the solution appears (the "Aha" experience); and (d) verification (Wallas, 1926). Because problem solving was considered to take place in the subconscious, the Gestalt model was not widely accepted. The Gestaltists could offer few suggestions as to how the teacher might foster students' problem-solving skills. Despite this, the Gestaltists did lay the foundation for some of the later work on problem solving and thinking. For example, Duncker (1945) used "think aloud" protocols of subjects solving problems to conclude that problem solving is a top-down, goal-oriented process rather than a bottom-up, stimulus-driven process of trial and error (Dellarosa, 1988).

Another prominent Gestaltist, Max Wertheimer, addressed the issue of productive thinking and provided useful suggestions for fostering such thinking in the classroom. In his classic text, *Productive Thinking*, Wertheimer (1959) distinguished between productive and reproductive thinking. A productive thinker grasps the structural relations in a given problem or situation and then combines these parts into a dynamic whole. A person who thinks reproductively fails to see relations among subparts and simply repeats learned responses to individual subparts. According to Wertheimer, productive thinking can be encouraged in the mathematics classroom by avoiding, where possible, the giving of ready-made steps.

A good example of fostering productive thinking is Wertheimer's approach to teaching area, in particular, the area of the parallelogram.

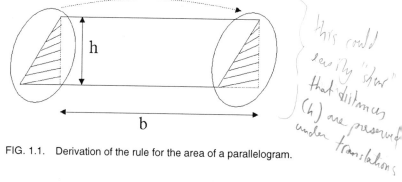

FIG. 1.1.   Derivation of the rule for the area of a parallelogram.

Wertheimer related the classroom example of how children who had been taught the standard rule had difficulty when presented with an "upside down" parallelogram. Because they did not understand the derivation of the rule, they could not apply it to this new situation. This understanding can be readily developed by making use of the functional equivalence between the parallelogram and the rectangle, as indicated in Fig.1.1 (Resnick & Ford, 1984).

Many of Wertheimer's ideas are directly relevant to mathematics education today. For example, students can be guided in deriving for themselves, the formulae for finding the area of the basic plane shapes rather than blindly following given rules. Once students know how to find the area of a rectangle, they can use this knowledge in generating the formulae for the square, triangle, circle, and parallelogram.

The Period of the "New Math"

The 1960s witnessed major changes to the mathematics curriculum. These changes were the result of severe criticism of the American education system in the postwar years. The restructuring of the mathematics curriculum followed the 1959 Woods Hole conference in which recommendations for reform were outlined. It was considered essential that students possess a knowledge of the fundamental structures of mathematics. This knowledge would enable students to reconstruct mathematical facts should they forget them.

The teaching of mathematical structure in the new math era tended to overemphasize the logical aspect (Ernest, 1985). This was evident in the explicit teaching of set theory and the laws of arithmetic, as well as in the teaching of traditional Euclidean geometry in the secondary mathematics curriculum. Numerous texts reflected this emphasis, with activities based on set theory, systems of numeration, and number theory. The explicit teaching of the notation and algebra of sets and the general laws of arithmetic were, by their very nature, abstract. The new math ideas were presented in a spiral format where previously taught concepts were revisited at higher grade levels and extended and elaborated upon. There were mixed reactions to the notion of introducing young children to mathematical topics that were formerly reserved for secondary school and college students. One strong supporter of this approach however, was Jerome Bruner (1960), whose text, *The Process of Education*, was widely acknowledged.

Jerome Bruner.   Bruner was one of several postwar psychologists who had an interest in the cognitive proceses involved in learning and thinking. He was particularly concerned with the ways in which children represent the concepts and ideas they are being taught. Building in part on the ideas of Piaget, he proposed that children move through three levels of representation as they learn: the enactive, the iconic, and the symbolic. These stages are considered to be developmental, with each mode building on the previous. In the enactive stage, the child directly manipulates objects. In the next stage, the child moves to the realm of mental imagery where she visualizes an operation or concrete manipulation. In the final phase, the child manipulates symbols rather than objects or images of these objects. Many advocates of the new math organized children's learning experiences according to these modes; that is, children were introduced to a new concept or procedure through the manipulation of concrete materials. The concept was then represented pictorially, and finally, in the symbolic form. This approach has been adopted by other theorists (e.g., Watson, Campbell, & Collis, 1993) and is still encouraged today, as we indicate in the remaining chapters of this volume.

Bruner was also an advocate of discovery learning and of introducing children to advanced concepts presented in simple forms. His ideas on children discovering new mathematical ideas were not widely accepted because this was considered an inefficient approach. Rather, the textbooks of the time adopted a guided discovery approach where examples and explanations were interspersed with leading questions such as, "Do you believe that . . . ?" or "Do you suppose it is true that . . . ?" (Kroll, 1989, p. 208).

Zoltan Dienes.   Another influential figure of this era was Zoltan Dienes, a collaborator of Bruner. Dienes (e.g., 1960, 1963) is best remembered for his development of concete materials and games in carefully structured learning experiences and for his psychological principles underlying the use of these aids. His best known materials are the multibase arithmetic blocks (MAB), which are sets of wooden blocks with each set representing a different base system. We review the MAB material in chapter 4.

Many of Dienes' instructional ideas are still applied today. He advocated a "learning cycle" (Dienes & Golding, 1971) in which children progress through a series of cyclic patterns, each comprising activities ranging from concrete to symbolic formats. The earliest learning phase in each cycle begins with plenty of free play where children manipulate structured materials to discover their key features. Following this, children's experiences are systematically structured using the concrete materials. Children are guided in discovering the inherent relations in the material and in abstracting the concept being represented. For the child to abstract mathematical concepts fully, the concepts should be presented in multiple embodiments that are as visually different as possible, according to Dienes' principle of perceptual variability. The embodiments should also display the full range of mathematical variables associated with a concept (Dienes' principle of mathematical variability). For example, his MAB material enabled children to manipulate numbers in different bases and experience the similar patterns of positional notation across the different systems.

The next step in Dienes' learning cycle is the transition from manipulative materials to more abstract representations such as pictorial models and graphs, and finally, to the mathematical symbols. The latter are introduced informally at first, with children developing their own symbols. In the final transition to the formal symbols, children should be able to readily map the new symbols onto their existing understanding of the concept, this understanding having been established through the rich set of experiences of the previous phases.

Jean Piaget.   Before leaving this new math era we need to consider briefly the impact of the developmental work of Jean Piaget. (For more in-depth reviews of his work, see, e.g., Copeland, 1974; Flavell, 1963, 1977; Halford, 1982; Kamii & DeClark, 1985; Resnick & Ford, 1984.) Piaget is best remembered for his extensive studies on the development of children's thinking where he emphasized their progress through stages. Each stage represents a distinctly different way of understanding the world. The first is the sensorimotor stage that lasts from birth to about 2 years of age. This is followed by the preoperational stage, which finishes at about 8 years. The stage of concrete operations lasts from 8 to about 13 years, and finally, the stage of formal operations represents the thinking of the adolescent and adult.

Piaget proposed that certain basic structures of thinking were inherent for human beings and that these developed through the individual's interaction with the social and physical environment. Piaget's notion of structure is more or less identical to the mathematician's definition. Piaget defined a structure as comprising a set of states (which a mathematician would call the state space or underlying set), a set of transformations (or mappings) between states, and a set of global laws governing the application of the transformations (Groen & Kieran, 1983). Because Piaget defined these structures in logical and mathematical form, the topics he chose for intensive study involved the use of basic logical structures. These included number, geometry, time, space, speed, and movement.

Piaget's (1971) theory was a theory of genetic epistemology, concerned with the development of knowledge in children, and based on the fundamental hypothesis that "there is a parallelism between the progress made in the logical and rational organization of knowledge and the corresponding formative psychological processes" (p. 13). However this was not the perspective used in earlier educational applications of Piaget's theory. Rather, the focus was on his developmental stages and the ways in which environments can be structured to facilitate children's movement through these stages. Several early childhood programs trained children on Piagetian tasks, such as conservation, and emphasized the attainment of developmental stages as approriate educational objectives (Williams, 1984). Concerns were expressed over this approach because of the gap between Piaget's tasks and those of school mathematics and also because the ages specified for transitions from one stage to another were among the least significant components of his theory. Piaget's theory provides no means for bridging the gap between his tasks and school mathematics, even though his stages might be considered to provide this means (Ginsburg, 1985; Groen & Kieran, 1983). Performance in school mathematics is not likely to be improved by explicitly teaching appropriate Piagetian tasks.

In the latter period of his life Piaget (1973) did comment on mathematics education, in particular, the processes used by the child in learning mathematics. He argued that the basic processes through which the structures underlying formal operations develop are the same as those that underlie the ability to think mathematically, these being the logicomathematical structures. These latter structures are said to develop through logicomathematical experience where the child engages in reflective abstraction, that is, the child learns from reflecting on her actions This is akin to the modern notion of metacognition, namely, thinking about one's thinking. We will return to the idea of reflective abstraction in the next section where we discuss a more recent extension of Piagetian thought, namely, constructivism.

CONTEMPORARY DEVELOPMENTS IN MATHEMATICS EDUCATION

Psychological Influences

Influences of the foregoing eras can be seen in mathematics classrooms today, with each era making important contributions to the teaching and learning of mathematics (Kroll, 1989). The associationist ideas of Thorndike play a role in children's learning of basic number combinations, for example. However the drill and practice activities of today are more refined and build on children's understanding of the facts to be learned. Several of the computer-based instructional packages also reflect Thorndike's principles. Material to be learned is presented in small units with activities designed to maximize the effectiveness of reinforcement. Our current emphasis on problem solving and reasoning is reminiscent of the Gestalts' concern for recognition of problem structure and the development of insight into the solution process. The era of meaningful learning and the new math period also showed us the importance of hands-on materials in real-world contexts and the need to develop students' understanding of mathematical structure. Today's mathematics programs are also strongly influenced by the constructivist paradigm and by cognitive science. These influences may be regarded as part of a knowledge base of children's learning, considered important in guiding current curriculum reform (Wang, Haertel, & Walberg, 1993).

Constructivism. The *Curriculum and Evaluation Standards for School Mathematics,* published by the National Council of Teachers of Mathematics (1989), highlights the importance of children being actively involved in their learning, that is, they should "construct, modify, and integrate ideas by interacting with the physical world, materials, and other children" (p. 17). The constructivist perspective, derived from the work of Piaget (e.g., 1970, 1980), asserts that conceptual knowledge cannot be transferred, carefully packaged, from one person to another. Rather, it must be constructed by each child solely on the basis of her own experience (Nik Pa, 1986). Children develop mathematical concepts as they engage in mathematical activity (Wood, Cobb, Yackel, & Dillon, 1993). This includes their attempts to make sense of the procedures and explanations they hear or see from others. Children should thus be provided with activities that are likely to generate genuine mathematical problems, ones that provide them with opportunities to reflect and reorganize their existing ways of thinking. According to Piaget (1980), a crucial component of the constructivist meaning of arithmetic is reflective abstraction because all new knowledge presupposes certain forms of abstraction. Many of the processes a child uses in solving a problem are unconscious. The child needs to become aware of these unconscious processes if mathematical thinking is to develop.

Like most psychological theories, constructivism has been subjected to misinterpretation and overinterpretation. The term, *constructivism,* refers to the Piagetian notion of the development of cognitive structures and does not suggest a theory of teaching or instruction (Kilpatrick, 1987b). However, it has frequently become a way of teaching that is characterized by one of two classroom approaches (Pirie & Kieren, 1992). Some teachers consider the use of manipulatives as sufficient for engaging in constructivist teaching.

Because children act on these materials, it is assumed that they are constructing mathematical ideas for themselves. However active participation within a meaningful context does not guarantee that children will acquire the desired understandings. Furthermore, although children's understanding depends on their experience, this does not necessarily have to be physical.

The other classroom approach that is often considered to be "constructivist" in nature is the use of group discussion. Although this technique can be a worthwhile means of developing students' mathematical understanding, it is not the only means. Children can actively learn a great deal of mathematics when it is presented in symbolic or diagrammatic form, without group interactions. As Pirie and Kieren (1992) commented, teachers' beliefs that these two approaches epitomize the constructivist perspective are indicative of a general underlying problem associated with the term, "constructivist teaching." It is the teacher's intentions, not any specific activities which might be performed or not performed, that determine the constructivist nature of the teaching.

Other writers who have attempted to interpret constructivism for the classroom have described the constructivist classroom as one that has moved away from directly transmitted content-based mathematics lessons to inquiry-oriented learner activites that promote meaningful and independent learning, as well as opportunities for learner reflection (e.g., Burton, 1993; Cobb, Wood, & Yackel, 1990; Confrey, 1990; von Glasersfeld, 1990). These authors view the mathematics classroom as a mathematical community in which there is negotiated discourse through collaborative group work. Students are expected to discuss, collaborate, challenge, reflect, negotiate, and renegotiate meanings. The teacher's role is to firstly acquire an adequate model of the students' understanding and then to assist them in structuring more appropriate and internally consistent understandings (Confrey, 1990).

It is worth noting though, that just because children are engaged in appropriate mathematical activities, we cannot automatically assume that they are performing "strong acts of construction" (Noddings, 1990, p. 14). Some students may engage in "weak acts" of construction when working in group situations, for example, by relying on others to supply answers. Conversely, traditional instruction does not necessarily imply "weak constructions" on the part of the students. The important point here is that teachers must probe deeply into students' responses to ascertain the nature and extent of their understandings and misunderstandings. This is where input from cognitive science can assist in the development of valid and meaningful models of students' mathematical learning.

Cognitive Science. One of the major goals of mathematics education is that students understand the mathematics they learn (Hiebert & Carpenter,

1992). The nature of understanding has been widely researched by cognitive scientists who have attempted to model the nature of knowledge representations (e.g., Anderson, 1990; Greeno, 1989; Halford, 1993; Ohlsson & Rees, 1988, 1991). Representation in mathematics learning has several roles (Kaput, 1985, 1987) including: (a) cognitive representation, that is, the internal representation of the individual's knowledge; (b) computer representation where computer programs embody hypothetical mental representations derived from observations of specific human behaviors; (c) explanatory representation, that is, the models and theories that psychologists pose to describe hypothesized cognitive structures and events; (d) mathematical representation where one mathematical structure is represented by another; and (e) symbolic representation, such as external mathematical notation.

The cognitive and explanatory representations are fundamental to cognitive science. Cognitive researchers have constructed models of the hypothesized knowledge structures and cognitive processes underlying the learning and application of mathematics (e.g., J. S. Brown & VanLehn, 1982; Gelman & Greeno, 1989; Greeno, Riley, & Gelman, 1984; Resnick & Singer, 1993; Siegler & Jenkins, 1989). They have also devised means of detecting and analyzing the representations and processes that underlie cognitive tasks (see Halford, 1993, chapter 2, for a summary).

As we indicate in chapter 2, cognitive processes entail operations on mental representations, which are internal mental structures that correspond to a segment of the world. Mental representations are often viewed in terms of networks of interrelated ideas, with the degree of understanding determined by the number and strength of the connections (Hiebert & Carpenter, 1992). As Hiebert and Carpenter remarked, the notion of connected representations of knowledge provides a useful means of thinking about mathematical understanding. It provides an effective link between theoretical cognitive issues and practical classroom issues. This is evident in contemporary curriculum documents, such as the *Curriculum and Evaluation Standards for School Mathematics* (National Council of Teachers of Mathematics, 1989), which calls for specific instructional activities designed to "connect ideas and procedures both among different mathematical topics and with other content areas" (p. 11). Interpretations of students' learning in terms of connections between mathematical ideas encourages us to critically analyze the structure of our curriculum and the instructional methods we employ. It is therefore important that we review some of the major forms of mental representations and the contributions they can make to mathematics education. We do this in chapters 2 and 3.

Cognitive science has also had a significant bearing on our knowledge of, and emphasis on, mathematical problem solving and reasoning. Most of the popular theories of problem solving are derived from the early information-processing models of human cognition, such as Newell and Simon (1972) and Simon (1978). Calls for reform in mathematics education place problem solving as one of the key curriculum outcomes (e.g., National Council of Teachers of Mathematics, 1989; National Research Council, 1990; Australian Education Council, 1990). These questions are considered in detail in chapter 8.

Cognitive studies of problem solving behavior encouraged mathematics educators to provide students with a repertoire of general problem-solving heuristics (in addition to a solid body of domain-specific knowledge). The classic work of Polya (1957) provided the framework for much of this development, as we discuss in chapter 8. However, simply providing students with these heuristics is of little value unless they know when, why and how to use them, and unless they make a conscious effort to monitor and reflect on their actions (Lester, 1989; Lester & Garofalo, 1982; Schoenfeld, 1985a, 1992). This is where metacognition comes into play. The seminal work of the eminent cognitive psychologist, John Flavell (1976) highlighted the important role of metacognitive processes in learning and development. These processes have since been recognized as a significant component of mathematical problem solving (e.g., Lester & Garofalo, 1982; Schoenfeld, 1992; Silver, 1985; Silver & Marshall, 1990).

In conjunction with this emphasis on problem solving, has been the call for the development of students' so-called higher order thinking skills, such as critical and creative thinking, and inductive and deductive reasoning. These skills have received a good deal of attention in the literature and are considered essential in all curriculum domains (e.g., Beyer, 1987; Fennema & Peterson, 1985; Halpern, 1992; Lesgold, 1988; Paul, 1990; Peterson, 1988; Resnick, 1987b; Resnick & Resnick, 1992).

Analogical reasoning plays a particularly important role in human cognition and has significant implications for children's mathematical learning, as we indicate throughout this book. Although the use of analogy has received considerable attention in the cognitive literature (Gentner, 1983, 1988; Halford, 1992, 1993; Holyoak & Koh, 1987; Holyoak & Thagard, 1989, 1995), it has not hitherto received as much attention in the context of children's mathematical learning.

Cognitive science has led to a greatly expanded knowledge of intelligence, both natural and artificial, and the field is progressing very rapidly. Its importance to mathematics education is that it provides the most detailed insights that are currently available into the way concepts are represented, and into the processes that are used in learning and reasoning. It provides the most scientific method yet devised for analyzing the real psychological processes that underlie mathematics. It offers great promise for increased efficiency in mathematics education, and it has been the single most important influence on the approach adopted in this book.

However, although the detailed models and data bases of cognitive science are a great benefit, the hypotheses it suggests for mathematics education are necessarily subject to verification by applied research, and by actual application in the classroom and in the home. The link between cognitive science and mathematics education is therefore bidirectional, because the feedback provided by the application of scientific principles in the classroom can help develop the science that generated those principles. Mathematics education and cognitive science can provide a useful stimulus to each other.

The current mathematics education scene has also been shaped by societal developments. These include improvements in technology, changes in world society and in international competitiveness, perceived declining standards in students' mathematical attainment, and changes in the mathematics and in society's need for the discipline (R. W. Howe, Blosser, & Warren, 1990). We address these developments in the next section.

Societal Influences

Technological Society. One of the main arguments for reform in our current mathematics education programs is that advances in technology and information systems have altered the needs of the future worker. School systems do not appear to be keeping up with these changes (Putnam, Lampert, & Peterson, 1990). Leaders in business and industry (e.g., Bernstein, 1988; Mayer Committee, 1992; Pollak, 1987) claim that future employees require more than the traditional basic arithmetical skills that were once adequate for jobs requiring repetitive and routine tasks. A higher level of mathematical knowledge and skills is now needed for daily living and for effective citizenship. We need to apply these skills in analyzing and interpreting the many mathematical concepts that permeate the mass media and that reside in a variety of data bases. We also need mathematical skills in making the numerous business and financial decisions that face us daily (R. W. Howe, Blosser, & Warren, 1990; National Research Council, 1989). New societal goals for education thus include the need for mathematically literate workers who are technologically competent, can adapt to change, can formulate and solve a variety of common and complex problems, can see the applicability of mathematical ideas to these problems, and who have the skills for effective life-long learning (National Council of Teachers of Mathematics, 1989; Howe et al., 1990; Pollak, 1987).

International Competitiveness. The past couple of decades have witnessed significant changes in world economic competition. Many countries are becoming more productive and are developing educational programs to accommodate these changes. Of concern to the larger nations such as the United States is recent data indicating that their students are not achieving as well in mathematics as their counterparts in other competing countries (Kouba et al., 1988; McKnight et al., 1987).

In the Second International Mathematics Study (Robitaille & Garden,

1989; Travers & Westbury, 1990), 12- and 13-year-olds were assessed on the topics of arithmetic, algebra, geometry, statistics, and measurement. Students across the nations found the test items rather difficult, with the Japanese students attaining the highest scores on all five areas. Although students' performance on items involving simple computation with whole numbers was satisfactory, their performance on items calling for higher level thinking skills was generally poor. So too, were students' responses to the rational number examples and to the basic computational items dealing with percent, ratio, and proportion. Analyses of these assessment data have indicated that the quantity and quality of the content covered by the teacher correlates positively with achievement, as do the depth of coverage of the subject and the amount of time allocated to it. Countries that have a more rapid pace of instruction, especially in the lower grades (e.g., Japan and China), tend to have higher achievement in mathematics.

The Third International Mathematics and Science Study is currently in progress, with more than 50 countries participating. The broad aim of the study is to characterize each country's provision of educational opportunity and to examine how that opportunity relates to educational achievement. The target populations are 9-year-olds, 13-year-olds, and students in their final year of secondary school. Curriculum and instructional practices, as well as student achievement, are being surveyed with the aim to identify the influence of curriculum on student learning. Analyses will focus on the intended curriculum, the implemented curriculum, and the attained curriculum.

Production of Curriculum Documents. In response to the national and international surveys of student achievement and to the broad changes in society, mathematics education communities have produced documents outlining desired curricula goals and how these might be achieved. In the United States, the *Curriculum and Evaluation Standards for School Mathematics* (National Council of Teachers of Mathematics, 1989) calls for major changes in both the content of school mathematics and in the form of mathematics instruction that, in turn, reflects changes in the underlying view of mathematics learning. For example, the *Standards* argues for a deemphasis on complex and tedious written calculations and on rote memorization of rules and procedures. It advocates an increased focus on conceptual development of the operations and on forming connections between ideas and procedures among different mathematical topics.

Reshaping School Mathematics (National Research Council, 1990) is another prominent U.S. document presenting a philosophy for teaching mathematics and a framework for curriculum design. Its recommendations include a greater breadth of mathematical sciences, an increased use of technology, more active learning, and an increased emphasis on higher order thinking skills.

In Australia, the *National Statement on Mathematics for Australian Schools* (Australian Education Council, 1990) was produced in response to the changing needs in business and community life. Its goals reflect those of the *Standards*, with an emphasis on developing students' capacity to use mathematics in solving problems, to communicate mathematically, to learn techniques and tools that reflect modern mathematics, and to experience the process through which mathematics develops.

The United Kingdom has implemented a national curriculum that provides programs of study, methods of assessment, and attainment targets for children at ages 7, 11, 14, and 16 years. Like the other documents, the national curriculum views mathematics as a means of communication, as a problem-solving and reasoning activity, and as a creative endeavor concerned with devising, testing, and justifying procedures for performing various operations. The fostering of positive attitudes towards mathematics is seen as a prime necessity and a key goal of the curriculum.

Japan also has a form of national curriculum (*Course of Study*) that must be taught uniformly in all schools (Miwa, 1992). Content is assigned to each grade level, with the requirement that all students complete the content. However, teaching methods and the number of hours devoted to specific content are left to the classroom teachers. Japanese mathematics programs value the importance of mathematical concepts, principles, and fundamental computational skills. Like other national programs, the Japanese system aims to develop students' ability to think mathematically, as well as their appreciation for mathematical thinking and its applications.

Nature of Mathematics.   The reforms advocated by these various national documents reflect underlying changes in the nature of mathematics and how it is perceived by society. As Dossey (1992) remarked, the way in which society perceives the nature and role of mathematics has a major influence on the development of school mathematics programs, instruction, and research. Currently, public attitudes towards mathematics are shifting from relative indifference and even hostility to a recognition of the important role it plays in society (National Research Council, 1990). As we noted earlier, the nature of the mathematical knowledge needed to meet professional and vocational goals is changing rapidly and is being seen in a much broader context.

Mathematics is typically portrayed in national documents as a dynamic, expanding field of study, in contrast to other views that define it as a static discipline, with a known set of concepts, principles, and skills (Dossey, 1992; C. Fisher, 1990). The documents highlight the patterns and relationships inherent in mathematics. To know and understand mathematics is to be able to detect patterns in complex and obscure contexts, to transform relations among patterns, to use the language of patterns, and to employ knowledge of patterns for various practical purposes (National Research Council, 1990).

It is interesting to note that nearly 40 years earlier, Van Engen (1958/1993) also viewed the structure of mathematics as the search for patterns, with this search involving the ability to abstract and generalize.

The classroom teacher's conception of mathematics has a powerful impact on the way in which mathematics is approached in the classroom (T. Cooney, 1985; Hersh, 1986). Cooney is of the opinion that the changes suggested by the national documents will be slow and difficult to implement because of teachers' beliefs about the nature of mathematics. The typical view is the existence of a formal, external body of knowledge that has to be transmitted to learners, rather than a dynamic, changing field in which students can explore, experiment, and experience the processes of mathematics. This view also reflects little knowledge of recent research on students' learning of mathematics. The current lack of a "genuine paradigm" for mathematics education (Fischbein, 1990) may be considered a contributing factor here.

TOWARD A PSYCHOLOGICAL THEORY OF MATHEMATICS EDUCATION

In his introduction to the monograph on mathematics and cognition by the International Group for the Psychology of Mathematics Education, Fischbein (1990) argued that mathematics education has "borrowed" the questions, concepts, theories, and techniques from psychology. However the mere application of psychological theories to the domain will not automatically produce results that can be readily translated into practice. We agree with Fischbein that mathematics education generates its own set of psychological problems that are foreign to the professional psychologist. The countless number of misconceptions evident in children's mathematical performance in school cannot be solved by simply applying some general psychological principles. We need to also address theories of mathematics curriculum development. A marriage of these two domains should go a considerable distance towards producing an effective psychological theory of mathematics education. Our book aims to develop such a theory.

As we indicate throughout this book, the essence of understanding a mathematical concept is to have a mental representation or mental model that faithfully reflects the structure of that concept. The important component of mental models, particularly for mathematical learning, is the relations they represent. As such, they have the power to deal with abstract ideas. The complexity of the relations that can be represented in parallel is very important in human reasoning, as we indicate in the next chapter. Being able to explicitly represent relations is often difficult for children (Halford, 1993); however this ability is critically important in mathematical thinking.

The nature of children's reasoning processes in dealing with mathematical ideas is of fundamental concern to both mathematics educators and psychologists. One such reasoning process, that of analogy, is a basic, yet powerful, mechanism for constructing new ideas from existing knowledge. It is generally accepted that learning is an active construction process that builds on previously acquired knowledge (Baroody & Ginsburg, 1990; Davis, Maher, & Noddings, 1990; Duit, 1991; von Glasersfeld, 1990). Throughout this book, we illustrate how analogical reasoning can assist children in their mathematical constructions.

In applying our psychological ideas to children's mathematical learning, we pay particular attention to the following issues:

1. The *cognitive complexity* of the mathematical concept, procedure, or process to be learned and the difficulties that can arise if instruction does not address this complexity;
2. The *mental models* and *processes* that we would like children to develop; we include here the various meanings that a particular mathematical concept might comprise, the prerequisite understandings children need in developing meaningful mental models and processes, the number of relations children must consider simultaneously in building a particular mental model, and the appropriateness of the analogs used in this development;
3. The nature of the *learning experiences* that might facilitate children's mathematical development.

OUTLINE OF THE BOOK

In the next chapter we provide an overview of some of the major components of cognition and cognitive development. We consider issues such as knowledge representation, relational complexity, processes of learning and understanding, reasoning, and transfer. In the third chapter, we apply these ideas to an analysis of mathematical learning and consider three main questions: what it means to understand mathematics, how understanding assists the child in developing procedures and strategies for performing mathematics, and how the complexity of mathematical concepts and tasks affects performance.

The remaining chapters analyze children's learning of specific topics in mathematics education and offer suggestions for developing mathematical understanding. Chapter 4 focuses on number and begins with a critical analysis of the analogs commonly used in the teaching of numerical concepts and procedures. The second part of the chapter examines children's learning of early number concepts, the numeration of whole numbers, rational numbers, and negative integers.

Chapters 5 and 6 address the development of elementary computational models and processes for whole numbers and fractions. Chapter 5 examines addition and subtraction, whereas chapter 6 deals with multiplication and division. In each chapter we present an overview of children's computational difficulties and suggest some reasons for these. We then consider the complexity of these computations and suggest ways in which the instructional process can accommodate this.

The advanced computational models students typically meet in their first few years of secondary school are examined in chapter 7. We focus specifically on the topics of algebra and proportional reasoning. The first part of the chapter analyzes the complexity of algebra and the sources of students' difficulties here. We offer some suggestions as to how these difficulties might be overcome. We also examine students' mental models of algebraic word problems. In the second part of the chapter we address the complex nature of proportional reasoning. We analyze students' approaches to solving proportional problems and consider children's growth in this domain.

Chapter 8 addresses problem solving, problem posing, and mathematical thinking. The chapter begins with a review of some of the different perspectives on the nature of these processes. The key cognitive factors involved in mathematical problem solving and problem posing are examined. To illustrate how these components may operate during problem solving, we consider some studies addressing children's solutions to novel combinatorial and deductive reasoning problems.

The final chapter reviews our main arguments on the development of children's mathematical models and processes. We consider the implications of our theory for mathematics education and offer some suggestions for structuring the curriculum to promote meaningful and productive learning.

2

COGNITION AND COGNITIVE DEVELOPMENT

This chapter provides an overview of those aspects of cognitive psychology and cognitive development that are most relevant to understanding mathematics education. These topics cannot be treated exhaustively here, and material in this chapter can be supplemented by more extended treatments, including Best (1992) and Halford (1993). Our aim is to provide the necessary insights into the way children understand, and operate with, mathematics.

KNOWLEDGE REPRESENTATION

Cognitive processes entail operations on mental representations, which are internal mental structures that correspond to the structure of a segment of the world (Halford, 1993, Halford & Wilson, 1980; Holland, Holyoak, Nisbett, & Thagard, 1986). The important feature of mental representations is structural correspondence, and representations are not simply pictures in the head. Representations, including those used in mathematics, can have different codes, the main ones being images and propositions.

Images are not simply copies of the external world, because there is evidence that images are active constructions (e.g., Shepard & Metzler, 1971), but they are content-specific representations. For example, an image of a house necessarily represents a specific house, so reason images are more readily used to represent concrete ideas, such as houses, than abstract ideas, such as justice (Paivio, 1971). On the other hand, a strength of images is that they can integrate large amounts of information. For example, an image of a scene can include many objects, together with their attributes and relations between them (Paivio, 1971). Also the concreteness of images does not preclude their use to represent abstract concepts, because analogical reasoning can utilise correspondences between representations with the same structure regardless of content, as we will see. Images may be the most primitive representations, because Premack (1983) argued that all animals have images, but only primates have abstract representations.

Propositions are the smallest units of knowledge that can have a truth value. For example "cat" is not a proposition because it cannot be true or false, but "cats purr" is a proposition, as also is "cats bark" because they have truth values, in the first case true and in the second false. Propositions have two components, predicate and argument(s). The predicate expresses a relation, and can be interpreted as an action or a state, so "purr" and "bark" are predicates. The argument(s) expresses the entity or entities that enter into the relation. Thus the argument of "purr" is "cats" in the proposition.

Propositions are normally written with the predicate first. Thus the propositions in the last sentence would be written as PURR(cats) and BARK(cats). Predicates may have more than one argument. For example, LARGER-THAN(horse, cat) signifies that horses are larger than cats. The predicate "LARGER-THAN" has two arguments, and is said to be a two-place predicate. A predicate such as "GIVE" has three arguments, representing giver, recipient, and given-object. For example, GIVE(Peter, Mary, ring) asserts that Peter gives Mary a ring.

Propositions are more abstract than images and they have a degree of content independence. Complex sentences or concepts can be represented by propositional networks, in which each proposition is represented by a node, with links to the relations and attributes. Propositional networks have been very successful in accounting for many aspects of cognition, including problem solving and sentence comprehension and they represent the linkages between ideas in a psychologically realistic way (Anderson, 1985, 1990; Best, 1992; Stillings et al., 1987). One important implication is that the links depend on association rather than on logic. Thus to achieve a coherent knowledge of a field such as mathematics, associations between ideas have to be strengthened by experience. They do not occur automatically just because they happen to be logical.

Theorists of cognition need ways of defining representations. Two important approaches are those based on condition–action rules or on neural nets.

Condition–action rules form the basis of *production systems*, which have been used to construct computer simulation models of many cognitive phenomena. Each condition–action rule has two major components: a condition and an action. The conditions specified on the action side must be fulfilled for the action to occur.

Production systems have mostly been used to represent *procedural knowledge*, commonly referred to as "knowing how." However condition–action rules can also be used to represent *declarative knowledge*, commonly referred to as "knowing that." It is knowledge that we can define or "declare." An example of a procedural condition–action rule would be: If a traffic light is red → Stop. The left side specifies a condition that is to be fulfilled; in this case that a traffic light is red. The right side specifies an action to be performed; in this case "stop." An example of a declarative condition–action rule would be: 3 + 4 → 7. Given the condition, in this case 3 + 4, the answer is 7. The action side can be thought of as a prediction about the world: If you have 3 things plus 4 things, you will have 7 things altogether. Declarative condition–action rules are an important way of representing relations in the world. Their use for knowledge representation has been explored by Holland et al. (1986) and Halford (1993).

Neural nets represent items of information in the form of a set of activation values over a set of neural units. The representation is commonly expressed as a vector. The representation is distributed over the units, which are activated in parallel. For example, a number, operation symbol, or relation symbol might be coded as a set of values, each of which can be thought of as an activation value on a neural unit. Alternatively, an object can be represented as a set of features: A car might be coded by the features four wheels, steel body, doors, seats, used for personal transport, and so on. Each feature can be represented by activation of a separate neural unit.

Neural net models are also called *parallel distributed processing* (PDP) models, or *connectionist* models. They are often seen as being closer to the way information is really represented and processed in the nervous system than are conventional computer models (McClelland & Rumelhart, 1986). They have one property that is important to the theory underlying this book, in that they provide a natural explanation for human capacity limitations, as we will see later in this chapter.

Schemata are organized bodies of knowledge that represents a category of things. For example we can have a schema for a room, a restaurant, a holiday, or for more abstract ideas such as permission. Schemata are also generative, in that they can be used predictively. For example, if we know that a certain establishment is a restautant, we can predict with fair confidence that it will serve food and drink, its staff will include chefs and waiters, and so on. Many schemata are induced from ordinary life experience and reflect our ability to detect regularities and commonalities in our experience. These stored regularities form the basis of the predictive function of schemata.

Mental models have been used with a variety of meanings depending on context, but in this book we will adopt Halford's (1993) definition: "Mental models are representations that are active while solving a particular prob-

lem and that provide the workspace for inference and mental operations"
(p. 23). Mental models tend to reflect the experience of an individual, and
are usually content specific. They tend to be used by analogy, rather than by
logical or mathematical rules. Mental models may be retrieved from memory,
or they may be constructed to meet the requirements of a particular task.
For example, Johnson-Laird (1983) has argued that in categorical syllogisms
people construct diagrams that are analogs of the problem. The concept of
mental models gives a more valid picture of the representations that people
use in understanding and reasoning than do scientific or logical categories
and rules. It is for this reason that we use these models in this book for
explaining children's mathematical understanding.

Implicit and Explicit Representations

The distinction between implicit and explicit knowledge has been made in a
number of contexts (Hayes & Broadbent, 1988; Karmiloff-Smith, 1986;
Norman, 1986; Reber, 1989). Implicit knowledge is normally identified with
ability to perform a task, but without the ability to explain the performance,
modify it without further experience, or relate it to other cognitive processes. Explicit knowledge on the other hand can usually be modified by the
performer without additional experience. It can be related to other cognitive
processes and can often be explained. Thus, although implicit knowledge is
often associated with effective performance, at least within restricted contexts, it tends to be automatic, not amenable to modification through the
operation of other cognitive processes, and cannot be explained. Explicit
knowledge on the other hand is more under the control of the performer.

An example of implicit knowledge would be a child who can add 305 to
497 but has no knowledge of place value. The child may even be quite skilled
in performing the task, but cannot modify it or relate it to other mathematical knowledge. She would be unable to see the relationship between this
task and subtraction; for example, she might not recognize that in both cases
the digits represent hundreds, tens, and ones. She may also fail to recognize
that any recomposition operations must preserve the value of numbers
involved.

The difference between implicit and explicit knowledge corresponds to
the difference between being subject to rules and being able to make rules.
Implicit knowledge is sufficient for performance that is consistent with rules,
even though the person might not be aware of the rules per se. An example
is knowledge of grammar in one's native language. Another way of expressing the difference is that implicit knowledge is ability to perform a task, but
explicit knowledge is required for autonomous modification of one's own
performance. Karmiloff-Smith (1990) argued that explicit knowledge occurs

through representational redescription, which entails creating a higher level representation of knowledge that already exists at a lower, implicit level.

Relational Complexity of Representations

The complexity of relations that can be represented at any one time (in parallel) is very important in human reasoning, and is probably the main limiting factor in higher cognitive processes. There is evidence that explicit representation of relations is difficult for children (Halford, 1993), for adults (Maybery, Bain, & Halford, 1986) and for the higher animals (Holyoak & Thagard, 1995). The difficulty of representing relations has a major impact on mathematical thinking, so we will devote a significant amount of space to this issue.

Relational complexity may be defined in terms of *dimensionality*; that is, the number of independent items of information entailed in the concept. Dimensionality is analogous to the idea of factors in an experimental design, and it corresponds to the number of aspects that are free to vary independently. The representation of concepts of different dimensionalities is shown in Fig. 2.1, together with the traditional Piagetian stage to which they can be approximately equated. There are four levels of relations: unary, binary, ternary, and quaternary. Each level of relation corresponds to a level of dimensionality, because each argument of a relation corresponds to an independent source of variation. Higher dimensional representations permit more complex relations to be computed; for example, with a ternary relation we can compute how one argument or factor varies as a function of either or both of the others. With a binary relation only the relation between one factor and another can be computed.

The four levels of dimensionality are analogous to four levels of experimental design; that is dimensionalities 1 to 4 correspond to experimental designs varying from two-way to five-way. Just as the complexity of interactions that can be computed increases with the number of factors in an experimental design, the complexity of relations that can be computed increases with the dimensionality of representations.

It has been shown elsewhere (Halford, 1993) that the four levels of dimensionality bear a broad correspondence to Piaget's (1950) major stages, as shown in Fig. 2.1. It has also been shown that representations of higher dimensionality impose higher processing loads (Halford, Maybery, & Bain, 1986; Maybery et al., 1986). The reason for this readily became apparent when attempts were made to model the representation of relations in neural net or Parallel Distributed Processing (PDP) architectures. Such models make it clear that representations of more complex relations impose a higher computational cost (see Halford, 1993, for a detailed exploration of this point).

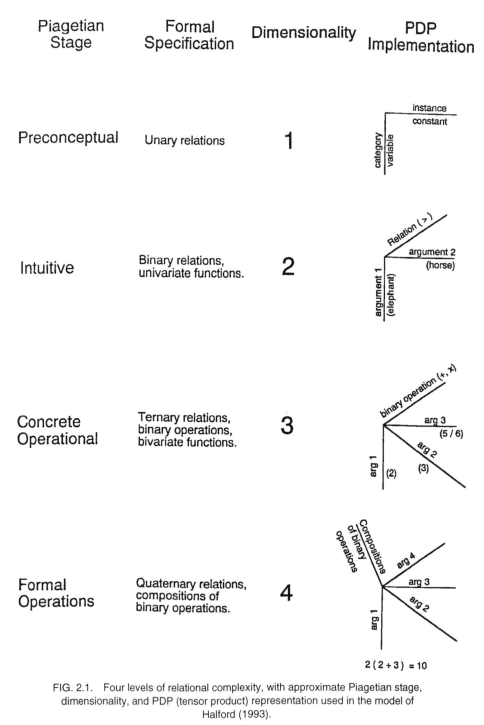

Piagetian Stage	Formal Specification	Dimensionality	PDP Implementation
Preconceptual	Unary relations	1	
Intuitive	Binary relations, univariate functions.	2	
Concrete Operational	Ternary relations, binary operations, bivariate functions.	3	
Formal Operations	Quaternary relations, compositions of binary operations.	4	

$2(2+3) = 10$

FIG. 2.1.   Four levels of relational complexity, with approximate Piagetian stage, dimensionality, and PDP (tensor product) representation used in the model of Halford (1993).

Now we will consider the four levels of relational complexity, from unary to quaternary, in more detail.

Unary relations include simple categories, defined by one attribute, such as the category of large things. They also include categories defined by a collection of attributes that can be represented as a single chunk, such as the category of dogs. A well-known phenomenon in infant cognition, the A not-B error, exemplifies unary relations. This most intriguing phenomenon in infant object constancy research can be thought of as requiring ability to treat hiding place as a variable. That is, when an infant has repeatedly retrieved an object from hiding place A, then continues to search for it at A despite having just seen it hidden at B, the infant is treating the hiding place as a constant. However if hiding place were represented as a variable this perseveration would be overcome. This requires a binding between the object and its location, and is equivalent to a unary relation.

The fact that children can represent category membership at about one year (Younger, 1993), and the A not-B error disappears about the same time, is consistent with ability to represent unary relations at that age. Thus Piaget's preconceptual stage appears to require this level of representation.

Binary relations are relations between two things, and include most of the commonly known relations such as LARGER-THAN, UNCLE-OF, RICHER-THAN, and so on. Univariate functions and unary operators also belong to this level because they are defined as sets of ordered pairs (Halford & Wilson, 1980; Halford et al., 1994). These are all two-dimensional concepts (given any two components, the third is determined). Based on an assessment of the cognitive development literature, Halford (1982, 1993) suggested they develop at approximately 2 years of age. They correspond to Piaget's observation that in the intuitive stage children process one binary relation at a time.

Ternary relations are relations between three things, and include everyday concepts such as "love-triangle" (a relation between three people), and middle (the middle element in a set of three). However, binary operations and bivariate functions also belong to this level, as they are defined as sets of ordered triples (Halford & Wilson, 1980; Halford et al., 1994). Ternary relations are three-dimensional, because there are three independent sources of variation (three ways of instantiating the arguments). Well-known examples include transitivity and class inclusion, but there are many other concepts that belong to this level, including conditional discrimination, the transverse pattern task, the negative pattern task, certain hypothesis-testing strategies (dimension checking in blank trials task), and many more (Halford, 1993). The familiar binary operations of addition and multiplication belong to this level.

Transitive inferences tend to be made by organizing premise information into an ordered set of three elements (Halford, 1993; Sternberg, 1980a, 1980b; Riley & Trabasso, 1974). For example, given the premises *Tom is taller than Harry*, and *John is taller than Tom*, we can construct the ordered triple, *John, Tom, Harry*, from which it is easy to infer that *John is taller than Harry*. This representation entails the ternary relation *transitively ordered-by-height (John, Tom, Harry)*. Class inclusion entails a relation between three classes, the superordinate, the first subordinate, and its complement (Halford, 1993).

All of these tasks are performed by about 5 years of age, but cause considerable difficulty below this age. In a broad sense, this level of processing corresponds to Piaget's concrete operational stage, which can be conceptualized as the ability to process binary operations or compositions of binary relations (Halford, 1982, 1993; Sheppard, 1978).

Quaternary relations are relations between four things. An everyday example is the balance scale, which comprises a beam on a pivot with pegs equally spaced from the fulcrum on each side. One or more weights can be placed on the pegs. The beam balances when the product of weight and distance on the left equals the product of weight and distance on the right; that is, when $W_l \times D_l = W_r \times D_r$. The balance scale concept, or principle of moments, is a relation between four variables, W_l, D_l, W_r, D_r. Quaternary relations also include ternary operations and compositions of binary operations. The concept of proportion, the psychological complexity of which is discussed in detail in chapter 3, is a quaternary relation. The proportion $\frac{a}{b} = \frac{c}{d}$ expresses a relation between four variables. In a broad sense, quaternary relations correspond to Piaget's formal operations stage, which entails relations between binary operations.

More complex relations impose higher processing loads, and this factor is an important component of the difficulty of concepts. The processing loads correspond to the computational cost of the representation, but it is a direct consequence of the dimensionality of the concept (Halford, 1993). The number of arguments of a relation defines the number of dimensions of variation in the relational structure. A unary relation has one argument, which can be instantiated in only one way at a time, so there is only one source of variation, and one dimension. A binary relation has two arguments, so two instantiations are possible at once, and there are two sources of variation. Similarly, a ternary relation has three arguments, hence three sources of variation and three dimensions, whereas a quaternary relation has four dimensions.

In general, concepts that require complex relations to be represented in parallel tend to be difficult. Relational complexity as defined here is a useful metric for scaling conceptual difficulty. Concepts that require quaternary relations to be represented are more difficult than those that require ternary relations, which in turn are more difficult than those that require binary or unary relations. Relational complexity, defined in this way, is an important component of conceptual difficulty in mathematics. More is said on this point in chapter 3 and elsewhere in this book.

REASONING PROCESSES

The processes people employ in reasoning are understood in much more detail now than in the 19th century. It has been traditional to think of humans as rational creatures, that being the most palpable way in which they differ from other animals. Logic was once regarded as being descriptive of human thought, so the British mathematician and logician, George Boole entitled his book, *An Investigation of the Laws of Thought* (Boole, 1854/1951). Research since then, and particularly in the 1970s and 1980s, has made it clear that people do not automatically apply logical rules, even implicitly (Johnson-Laird, 1983; Shaklee, 1979). Therefore we consider some of the major processes that have been found to underlie human inference.

Memory retrieval has been found to be the basis for a great deal of human inference and decision making. In a classical study, Kahneman and Tversky (1973) asked whether a particular letter, such as *k*, occurred more often as the first or the third letter of a word. The majority judgment was the first letter, though in fact it occurs more often in the third position. The reason is that people tried to retrieve instances of words with the relevant letter in the first position, and in the third position. First letters make better retrieval cues, so instances with the relevant letter in the first position were easier to retrieve. The results reflect a general tendency to judge frequency by availability in memory. Events that occur more frequently in our experience tend to be more available in memory. This heuristic is unlikely to be sanctioned in a standard logic text, yet it has a certain ecological validity. The ease with which items can be retrieved from memory is a reasonable guide to their frequency, occasional exceptions notwithstanding. There is an extensive research program of this kind that shows that memory retrieval plays a major role in human reasoning and decision making.

Rules are very useful units of analysis of cognitive processes, as production rule models (Klahr, 1984; Newell & Simon, 1972; Simon & Klahr, in press) and empirical analyses (Briars & Siegler, 1984; Scandura, 1970; Siegler, 1981) have shown. One implication of this research is that humans readily learn, and apply rules, which form the basis for much of our higher cognitive activity. There are certain distinctions between types of rules that we find useful.

Heuristics are rules that facilitate problem solving but do not guarantee solution. Examples include "hints" such as controlling the center of the board in a game of chess, and looking for analogies in mathematical problem solving.

Algorithms are rules that guarantee solution when correctly applied. Examples include computer programs, and procedures for performing arithmetic operations such as multiplication and division on multidigit numbers.

Strategies are sets of rules, together with higher order rules that specify when the rules should be applied. Strategies are a major component of reasoning and problem solving, and we discuss them on numerous occasions.

Analogy

Analogy appears to be one of the most important mechanisms underlying human thought, at least from the age of about 1 year, and there is evidence that it is also employed by monkeys and apes (Holyoak & Thagard, 1995). An analogy is a mapping from a base or source to a target (Gentner, 1983). In the simple analogy cat:kitten::mare:foal, shown in Fig. 2.2, cat:kitten is the base, and mare:foal is the target. Elements of the base are mapped into elements in the target in such a way that relations in base and target correspond. In this case the important relation is "mother of." Attributes of elements are not mapped; for example, the analogy in no way implies that the attribute "purrs" is mapped from cat to mare. Relations are mapped selectively, the selection being made according to the principle of systematicity (Gentner, 1983), which means that those relations that enter into a coherent structure are mapped.

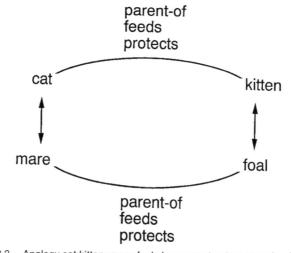

FIG. 2.2.   Analogy cat:kitten::mare:foal shown as structure mapping from base (cat:kitten) to target (mare:foal).

A structure mapping consists of a set of rules for assigning elements ot structure A to elements of structure B in such a way that the relations (functions, transformations) of structure A correspond to the relations (functions, transformations) of structure B. Systematicity may be defined in terms of higher order relations, which bind lower order relations together. A first-order relation has elements as arguments, whereas a higher order relation has relations as arguments. To illustrate, consider an analogy in which the base is "John hit Peter, making him cry" and the target is "Jenny thanks Mary, making her pleased." The validity of this analogy depends on a common higher order relation, which in this case is "cause." John's hitting Peter was the cause of his crying, just as Jenny thanking Mary was the cause of her being pleased. The arguments of "cause" are themselves relations. The base can be expressed as; cause(hit(John,Peter),cry(Peter)). The target can be expressed as; cause(thank(Jenny,Mary),pleased(Mary)). Base and target have the same structure, and can be mapped into one another, the validity of the mapping depending on the common higher order relation, cause.

Validity of mapping is defined in terms of two principles, uniqueness and correspondence. Uniqueness means that each element or relation in structure A is mapped into at most one element or relation in structure B. Correspondence means that if a relation R in structure A is mapped into a relation R in structure B, the arguments of R are mapped to the arguments of R' and vice versa.

It has been shown that levels of structure mapping can be distinguished by the complexity of the relations mapped (Halford, 1993), where complexity is defined according to dimensionality as discussed earlier. The more complex mappings occur later developmentally, impose higher processing loads, and support more abstract modes of thought. We briefly outline the four levels here.

Levels of Structure Mapping

The levels of structure mapping depend on the complexity of relations mapped in parallel. The four levels are element, relational, system, and multiple system mappings. They entail mapping structures based on unary, binary, ternary, and quaternary relations, respectively. The important factor is the information required to decide which elements and relations correspond in the two structures.

Element Mappings. These assign elements of structure A to elements of structure B according to one of three criteria, similarity, convention, or prior knowledge, the first two of which are illustrated in Fig. 2.3. According to the similarity criterion, an element in structure A can be mapped into an element in structure B to which it is similar. An image representing an object or event

FIG. 2.3. Element mapping based on image (A) or verbal label (B).

in the environment would be an example of a structure mapping based on similarity (see Fig. 2.3). An image typically resembles the thing it represents, so an image of a cat resembles a cat in some way. In this case structure A is a representational structure, and structure B is some kind of structure in the environment.

Alternatively, mappings may be based on a convention linking an element in structure A to an element in structure B. An example would be a word that is assigned to a referent by convention, as illustrated in Fig. 2.3. In this case a representational structure, linguistic in form, is mapped into a structure comprising a segment of the environment.

Relational Mappings.   Elements in structure A may be mapped into elements in structure B on the basis of similar relations between them. This is illustrated in Fig. 2.4, where two sticks of different lengths are used to represent the relation between a man and a boy. This mapping is not based on similarity between a stick and the person it represents, but on the fact that the relation between the sticks is similar to (at least) one relation between the man and the boy. That is, the size relation between the sticks is similar to the size relation between man and boy.

Relational mappings are independent of element similarity and convention, so they have a greater degree of flexibility and abstractness than element mappings. The price that is paid for this is that elements must be mapped in pairs. Whereas element mappings may be made considering one

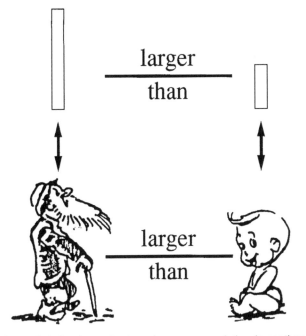

FIG. 2.4. Relational mapping based on common relation, larger than.

element from each structure at a time, with relational mappings, pairs of elements in structure A must be mapped into pairs of elements in structure B. That is, a binary relation must be processed in parallel. This means that relational mappings entail a higher degree of structural complexity than element mappings.

System Mappings.   These are independent of both element and relational similarity, and convention, and are based purely on structural correspondence. This is illustrated in Fig. 2.5, where the representation of a transitive inference problem is shown as a structure mapping. In this case there is no resemblance between the elements of structure A, the representation, and the elements of structure B, the problem. That is, "top" does not resemble Tom, nor "middle" Bill, and so on. Nor is the mapping based on similarity between the relations in the two structures. That is, any resemblance between "above" and "happier than" is unnecessary to validate the mapping. The mapping is based on the fact that relations in structure A consistently correspond to relations in structure B.

That is, "above" in structure A consistently corresponds to "happier than" in structure B, and to no other relation in structure B. Wherever "above" occurs between two elements in structure A, the relation "happier than" occurs between the elements into which they are mapped in structure

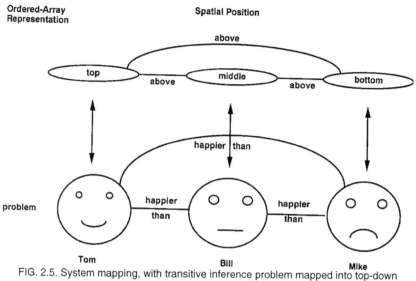

FIG. 2.5. System mapping, with transitive inference problem mapped into top-down ordering schema.

B. Therefore the correspondence between structures is consistent through-out. By contrast, the system mapping in Fig. 2.6 is inconsistent and invalid. The inconsistency arises from the fact that "above" corresponds to "happier than" on two occasions, and to "sadder than" on the third occasion.

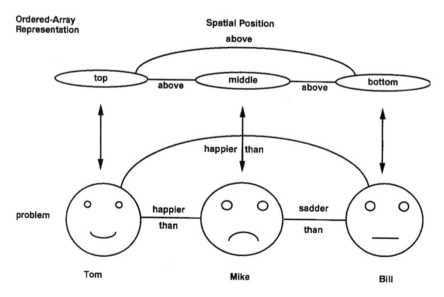

FIG. 2.6. Inconsistent system mapping.

System mappings have a higher degree of flexibility and abstractness than relational mappings. This is because they are independent of convention and similarity of elements and first-order relations. They depend on structural correspondence. The price paid for this is, once again, a higher processing load, because a structure based on a ternary relation must be processed in parallel. System mappings require a set of at least three elements in structure A to be mapped into at least three elements in structure B. The reason is that the structural correspondence criterion is only meaningful if at least two binary relations and three elements in one structure are mapped into corresponding elements and relations in the other structure. This is illustrated in Fig. 2.6, where the inconsistency is not apparent if only half of the figure is examined. If we examine only the left side of the figure, we simply see that "above" corresponds to "happier than," and no inconsistency is apparent. The same is true if we examine only the right half of the figure, because there is nothing inherently wrong with "above" corresponding to "sadder than." The inconsistency is only apparent if we examine the whole mapping, where it can be seen that above corresponds to two different relations, "happier than" and "sadder than." Therefore the structural correspondence rule, which is the basis of system mappings, depends on examining sets of three elements and two binary relations in each structure.

Multiple System Mappings.   This level of mapping is similar to system mappings, except that ternary relations, and/or binary operations, are mapped instead of binary relations. The example in Fig. 2.7 shows a structure mapping representation of an algebraic problem in which the task is to find two missing operations represented by the square brackets [ ]. That is, given the equation: (7 [ ] 3) [ ] 4 = 1, find the missing operations. The problem is that both operations must be found before it can be confirmed that either of them is correct. It is not possible to find the first operation, then turn our attention to the second.

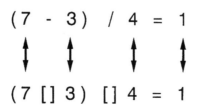

FIG. 2.7. Multiple system mapping in which problem with two unknown operations is mapped into arithmetic instantiation.

The structure mapping to which this problem corresponds is shown in Fig. 2.7. Each structure comprises four elements and two binary operations, subtraction (addition) and division (multiplication). Each structure is a quaternary relation and is four dimensional. The interpretation of the expression containing the missing operations is equivalent to a structure mapping. That is, the correct solution is one that creates a valid correspondence between the two structures (in this case the operations in the structures must correspond). This correspondence is more complex than in the case of system mappings, because it entails two binary operations, rather than two binary relations, and four elements are involved rather than three. Thus, whereas system mappings are a composition of two binary relations, such as "fairer than," a multiple system mapping is a composition of two binary operations, such as addition (subtraction) or multiplication (division). The greater complexity occurs because binary operations are three-dimensional concepts, whereas binary relations are two-dimensional concepts.

Criteria for Good Analogies

The features that make analogies useful in learning or thinking can also be expressed in structure-mapping terms. Gentner (1982) listed six features that can be used to evaluate analogies: base or source specificity, clarity, richness, systematicity, scope, and validity. We explain each of these in turn here and will revisit them in subsequent chapters of this book.

Source specificity is the degree to which the structure of the source is explicitly understood. For an analogy to be good, the user needs to have information about the objects and relations in the source stored in semantic memory. It will not be possible to map the source into the target, then use the source to generate inferences about the target, unless this information is available. We would add that because structure mapping imposes a processing load, the source information must be well enough known to make its retrieval effortless. Otherwise the analogy will be too difficult to use.

Clarity refers to absence of ambiguity in the mappings from source to target. High clarity means that each source node is mapped into one and only one target node and vice versa.

Richness is the number of predicates per node that can be mapped from source to target. It is equivalent to the density of attributes and relations that are mapped.

Systematicity was defined earlier, and refers to the conceptual coherence of an analogy, defined by the existence of higher order relations, that integrate lower order relations into a unified structure.

Scope refers to the number of different cases, or instances, to which the analogy can be applied. For example the analogy between cat/kitten and horse/foal in Fig. 2.2 has high scope because there are unlimited examples of parent–offspring relations.

Appropriateness (validity), as used by Gentner (1982), means that the analogy leads to valid inferences. "Motherhood is a career" might be considered an invalid analogy, if it were taken to imply that rewards such as pay, promotion, and retirement benefits that normally attach to certain careers also applied to motherhood. Because mothers are not normally paid in cash, are not promoted for good performance, and do not receive retirement benefits, it would not be valid to map these attributes from the source (career) into the target (motherhood).

Gentner's term *validity* is potentially confusable, in the context of this work, with the validity criteria for structure mappings given earlier. The term *validity*, as used in this book, is really closer to Gentner's concept of *clarity*, as mentioned earlier. Consequently we will substitute the term *appropriateness* for Gentner's term validity.

Expressive analogies are distinguished by Gentner from explanatory analogies. The former are mostly used in literature, whereas the latter are mostly used in science. An explanatory analogy should be high in clarity, scope, and systematicity, whereas richness tends to be more important for expressive analogies. Both types need source specificity and applicability. Gentner contrasts explanatory analogies such as the Rutherford analogy between the structure of the hydrogen atom and the structure of the solar system with expressive analogies such as used by Shakespeare and T. S. Elliot. The richness of allusion that is often one of the most salient attributes of a good poem tends to be accompanied by some ambiguity as to what refers to what; that is, the mappings can be ambiguous. This amounts to lack of clarity in terms of the criteria above. It can often increase the interest of a poem, but is frustrating and confusing in science.

Analogies in Reasoning

It has long been known that analogies are useful in reasoning, and Polya (1971) advised the use of analogies to facilitate problem solving. However, structure mapping is probably used much more extensively than is generally realized, as the following examples illustrate. Halford (1993) considered how an intelligent adult, who was untutored in symbolic logic, would tackle the following problem; a implies b, not a, therefore not b. Is this a valid inference? A logician would recognize it as the fallacy, denial of the antecedent, but how does a person who does not know that logical rule answer this question? One way is to map it into a familiar schema. Choice of a schema is likely to be idiosyncratic to some extent, but a suitable schema might be as shown in Fig. 2.8. We might call this the rain-cloud schema, and can be stated thus: rain implies clouds, no rain, therefore no clouds. Common experience

Mental Model **(source)**

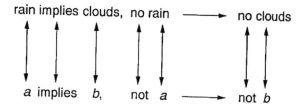

FIG. 2.8. Inference problem mapped into schema induced from everyday life.

tells this is false, because we often have clouds without rain. When the abstract version of the problem is mapped into this familiar schema, it is clear that it is false.

Throughout this book we apply the notion of analogy and analogical reasoning to analyses of children's mathematical learning.

WORKING MEMORY AND CAPACITY

Complex thought such as that entailed in mathematics is affected by limitations in the capacity of the human intellect. One of the major undertakings of cognitive psychology and cognitive science in the last three decades has been to understand the nature of these limitations. In this section we briefly review the implications of this work for mathematics education.

It is clear that there is more than one kind of capacity (Allport, 1980; Halford, 1993; Schneider & Detweiler, 1987; Wickens, 1974). Our capacity to process perceptual information considerably exceeds our capacity to represent information in thought, as we noted earlier, and motor information processing capacity also probably exceeds the processing capacity of thought. Furthermore, there are a number of different cognitive systems for processing information, and here we briefly review the most important of these.

Baddeley (1990) presented evidence that working memory has at least three components, which he called the phonological loop, the visuospatial scratchpad, and the central executive. The phonological loop is probably best known as the mechanism used to store a telephone number before dialing it. A number or other short string of items can be held in the phonological loop by rehearsal. There is evidence that it decays in about 2 seconds, so the number of items that can be held is the number that can be rehearsed in 2 seconds, which is about seven for digits (Baddeley, 1990). The visuospatial scratchpad is a visual short-term memory that can sometimes be used as an alternative for the phonological loop. If rehearsal is disrupted, items may be held in the visuospatial scratchpad rather than the phonological loop.

The central executive is where decisions are actually made. Whereas the phonological loop and the visuospatial scratchpad are primarily storage mechanisms, the central executive is concerned with processing information. In reasoning, information can sometimes be stored for later processing, but this is distinct from the information that is actually being processed. Consider, for example, mentally adding 368 to 597. We might add the 3 hundreds and 5 hundreds, yielding 8 hundreds. Now we have to retain the 8 hundreds while we add the 6 tens and 9 tens. While we are adding the 6 and 9, the 8 hundreds is in short-term store but is not being processed. The sum of 6 and 9 is not influenced by the 8 hundreds, so it is not processed while performing this addition. Extensive research on working memory (Baddeley, 1986, 1990; Halford, 1993) shows that storage and processing functions are at least partly distinct, and it is important not to confuse the two.

Resources, Load, and Capacity

The amount of information that can be processed can be understood in terms of the concept of resources, which are equivalent to the amount of mental energy that is available at any one time (Kahneman, 1973). Resources can be increased by effort, but there appears to be an upper limit to the amount of resources that any individual can make available, and this is the capacity of the individual (Halford, 1993).

Performance is positively related to resources invested in a task; the performance/resource function. *Processing load* (or demand) is defined by the slope of the performance/resource function. High load tasks have flatter slopes, because a greater increase in resources is required for any given improvement in performance.

It is essential to distinguish between processing load and difficulty. Difficulty can vary for many reasons besides processing load. There are tasks that impose low processing loads, but that are nevertheless difficult because of our lack of knowledge (e.g., recalling a forgotten telephone number). There are other tasks where we might have the required knowledge but have difficulty in processing all the information in parallel (e.g., interpreting three-way statistical interactions). It is important to keep this distinction in mind, because it has been common to commit the fallacy of assuming that all failures reflect capacity limitations.

Automaticity

The processing load imposed by a task can be reduced by making it automatic. This normally requires sustained practice with a task under reasonably constant conditions (Logan, 1979; Shiffrin & Schneider, 1977). Overlearning, that is, practice beyond mastery, may be required. However tasks that are performed automatically tend to be less modifiable, and less under the control of the performer, so automaticity is not a panacea for overcoming processing loads.

Complexity and Processing Load

One of the most difficult tasks of cognitive science has been to find a way of measuring complexity of concepts. It is essential of course if we are to decide when two concepts are of equivalent complexity, or which one is more complex. The concept of relational complexity, defined earlier, has been found very applicable to cognitive development (Halford, 1993), as well as to comparing tasks used for assessing animal intelligence (Holyoak & Thagard, 1995). It is also very useful in analysing mathematical concepts, as we will see.

Processing load varies as a function of dimensionality, as noted earlier. The important implication for mathematics education is that processing load will increase as the number of independent dimensions processed in parallel increases. We illustrate this argument by considering the dimensionality of some common mathematical concepts. A constant that is treated as a whole is zero dimensional, because there is no variation, and the representation is content specific. Thus the number 6 is a constant, as is the number 82,569, if treated as a whole, that is without regard to its place-value components.

The binding between a variable and a constant is one dimensional, because there is one source of variation. For example, given a variable such as height, a range of values can be assigned to it, each of which can be represented by height(1-meter), height(8.75-meters), and so on.

A binary relation, such as larger-than(5,3), univariate function, or unary operator are all cases of two-dimensional concepts. Univariate functions and unary operators are special cases of unary relations (Halford & Wilson, 1980; Halford et al., in press). The arguments of a binary relation can be instantiated in two ways at once: For example, >(5,3), >(6,2), . . . , >(18,12) etc. Each argument is a source of variation or dimension. Thus processing a binary relation entails processing in two-dimensional conceptual space.

A ternary relation, bivariate function, or binary operation are all three-dimensional, because there are three arguments, and three sources or variation. Bivariate functions and binary operations are special cases of ternary relations (Halford & Wilson, 1980; Halford et al., 1993). The fact that this concept is three dimensional is shown by the fact that, given any three components, the remainder can be determined. For example, given that the operation is multiplication, and that the product is 6 and one multiplicand is 2, we recognize "3" as the output. Alternatively, given that the inputs are 2, 3, 5 we see that the operation must be addition.

A quaternary relation, trivariate function, composition of binary operations, or ternary operation are all four dimensional. Trivariate functions and ternary operations are special cases of quaternary relations (Halford & Wilson, 1980; Halford et al., 1993). For example, $2(3 + 1) = 8$ is a relation between four entities, and is a quaternary relation.

Dimensionality of Mathematical Tasks

Now let us consider the dimensionality of some common examples of mathematical tasks. Comparison of two integers (e.g., Which is larger, 5 or 3?) is two dimensional. However comparison of two rational numbers, where numerator and denominator of both numbers have to be taken into account, is four dimensional; for example, which is larger $\frac{3}{8}$ or $\frac{7}{16}$? One reason why rational numbers are more difficult to understand is that each number entails two dimensions. This illustrates the point that the dimensionality metric captures differences in complexity between mathematical concepts. Gelman (1991) suggested that fractions are more difficult than whole numbers because we are innately endowed with enumeration processes based on whole numbers that conflict with use of fractions. Although the importance of innate enumeratation processes is recognized, it does not logically conflict with complexity as an explanation of children's difficulties.

Proportion, defined as $\frac{a}{b} = \frac{c}{d}$ is a quaternary relation, because it is a relationship between four variables, and it is therefore four dimensional. Consequently, it incurs a very high computational cost. Proportion has been a notoriously difficult concept, but this is understandable when its inherent complexity is recognized.

Processing Capacity in Children and Adults

One of the most difficult, but also most important problems of cognitive science has been to determine how much information humans can process in parallel. One of the earliest, but still one of the most famous, attempts to do this was Miller's (1956) proposal that humans process about seven items of information, or seven chunks, in parallel. A chunk is an independent unit of information of arbitrary size, so a digit, letter, or word can each constitute one chunk. More recent work has suggested, however, that the number may be nearer four (Broadbent, 1975; Fisher, D. L. 1984; Halford, 1993; Halford et al., 1994; Halford, Maybery, & Bain, 1988; Schneider & Detweiler, 1987). It has also been proposed (Halford, 1993; Halford et al., 1994) that chunks *makes it come out nicely — looking for a perfect fit (as are many connectionists — but nature is messy & not biological)*

can be identified with dimensions, because both are independent units of information of arbitrary size. Given that current evidence suggests that the number of chunks that can be processed in parallel is four, the number of dimensions that can be processed in parallel should also be four. Given that relational complexity is defined by dimensionality, as discussed earlier, this implies that quaternary relations are the most complex that can be processed in parallel.

The question of whether processing capacity changes with age has been the subject of much controversy (Case, 1985; Chapman, 1987; K. W. Fischer, 1987; Halford, 1982; J. Pascual-Leone, 1984). The theory offered by Halford and his collaborators (Halford, 1993; Halford et al., 1993) is that overall capacity remains constant, but that representations become differentiated with age, so more complex relations can be processed. This means that concepts of higher structural complexity can be understood. This is consistent with the well-established finding that differentiation increases with age (Werner, 1948). Halford (1987, 1993) has argued that children become capable of processing progressively higher levels of structure. Children are capable of wholistic representations at 4 to 5 months of age (Halford & Wilson, 1994). They can represent one dimensional concepts at a median age of 1 year, two dimensions at 2 years, 3 at 5 years, and 4 at 11 years (median ages). There are indications that this factor is at least partly maturational (see chapter 3, Halford, 1982), but more data are needed.

Chunking and Segmentation

Concepts that are too complex to be represented in parallel can be processed by either conceptual chunking or segmentation. *Conceptual chunking* entails recoding concepts of higher dimensionality into fewer dimensions; that is, it entails reducing multiple chunks to a single chunk. An example would be the relation between velocity, distance and time $v = \frac{d}{t}$. It is three dimensional. However it is also possible to think of velocity as a single dimension, such as the position of a pointer on a dial. It can then be combined with up to three other dimensions. The chunked representation of velocity can be used to define acceleration, which can be chunked in turn. It can then be combined with mass, yielding the concept of force, defined as the product of mass and acceleration. Conceptual chunking enables us to bootstrap our way up to concepts of higher and higher dimensionality without exceeding the number of dimensions that can be processed in parallel.

Though conceptual chunking is an important means of reducing processing loads, it is not a panacea because when representations are chunked, we temporarily lose the ability to recognize relations within the representation.

When velocity is represented as a single dimension, we can no longer compute the way velocity changes as a function of time, distance, or both. Similarly, we cannot compute what happens to time if distance is held constant, and velocity varies, and so on. In order to compute these we have to return to the three-dimensional representation, with its higher processing cost.

Segmentation entails developing serial processing strategies. In this case tasks are segmented into steps, each of which is small enough not to exceed the capacity to process information. Consider, for example, the problem $r = s + t$, $r + s + t = 30$. Here we have a complex set of relations, comprising a ternary relation and a quaternary relation, with the result that it is very difficult to think about the entire problem in parallel. A good strategy however is to substitute r for $s + t$, yielding $2r = 30$. We are now thinking only about one ternary relation, and it is easy to see that $r = 15$. This strategy breaks the task down into a series of steps each of which imposes quite a small processing load. Serial processing strategies are an important means of increasing processing effiency.

However serial processing strategies are not panaceas either, because it is not always possible to find an appropriate strategy. One particularly serious difficulty is that, as we see in chapter 3, autonomous strategy development requires a concept of the task, and this requires that there be sufficient processing capacity to represent the dimensions of the concept. Where children cannot represent sufficient dimensions for a particular concept, they will default to lower dimensionality representations, which will result in strategies that are partly correct, but that lead to errors on some variants of the task (Halford et al., 1992, 1995).

CAPACITY OVERLOAD

A child (or adult) who was unable to construct a representation of sufficient dimensionality for a task, and was unable to chunk or segment the task successfully, could default to a lower level representation. This typically results in performance that is partly correct, but will be invalid on telltale aspects of the tasks that depend on representing more complex relations. Much of the controversy that has dogged cognitive development (see Halford, 1989, and related commentaries) may be attributable to this situation. Advocates of precocious development can always point to those aspects of young children's performance that appear adequate. However advocates of capacity limitations can point to what they regard as telltale failures on more complex features of the tasks. Resolution of this polemic depends on more precise definition of competence in each domain.

LEARNING MECHANISMS

Theories of learning have come into disfavor to some extent in developmental psychology and education because they overemphasized passive, associationistic processes that were modelled on animal learning. However this situation has changed radically with the appearance of recent cognitive theories of learning (Holyoak, Koh, & Nisbett, 1989; Rescorla, 1988), theories of induction (Holland et al., 1986), and strategy development (Anderson, 1987; J. S. Brown & Van Lehn, 1982; Greeno, Riley, & Gelman, 1984; Halford et al., 1992, 1995). The implications of these theories for cognitive development have been considered elsewhere (Halford, 1993). In mathematics education it is clearly essential to understand the nature of the learning process, so we give an overview here that can be expanded in relation to specific topics in other parts of the book.

Basic Learning Processes

Human beings and other animals have the ability to acquire a prodigious quantity of information about their environments, and they do so without conscious effort. Because this information is acquired effortlessly and is not normally codified formally in books or elsewhere, it tends to be overlooked. It is of considerable importance, however, and should be considered in any account of learning. This basic learning includes the myriad contingencies of everyday life, such as that banks hold money, water is wet, restaurants provide food, and so on. Much of cognitive development depends on acquiring this information about the world, and some of that basic world knowledge provides a substrate for development of mathematical concepts.

Much of this knowledge is implicit and is acquired through associative processes. Implicit knowledge, both declarative and procedural, can be acquired through conditioning. Although conditioning was once interpreted in stimulus–response terms, Rescorla (1988) has shown that it can be interpreted as learning about relations among events in the environment. It is therefore an important means by which an organism is enabled to represent the structure of its world.

Implicit declarative knowledge comprises stored representations of relations between events in the world. It can be conceptualised as expectations or predictions of the form, given x, expect y. The acquisition of declarative knowledge is strengthened by confirmation, which differs from reinforcement because an event can be satisfying or reinforcing without confirming an expectation (Halford, 1993). Associations to redundant events are not learned, a phenomenon sometimes known as blocking (Kamin, 1968). That is, given that there is an association between x and y, a redundant association between x' and y will tend not to be learned. This principle can have important consequences for learning about scientific phenomena, as Holland et al. (1986) have shown. Because people learn certain kinds of relations between events in everyday life, they may be resistant to learn more scientific rules that relate to these same events. Thus a person who obtains regular apparent confirmation of the rule, "moving objects tend to slow down," may find it hard to learn the rules of Newtonian mechanics. Everyday observations are predicted by the rule that moving objects slow down, and the Newtonian laws of motion appear unnecessary and redundant. It is only when a wider range of phenomena is considered, perhaps including movements in space or in a vacuum, that the superior predictive power of Newtonian mechanics starts to become apparent.

Generalization and transfer of implicit knowledge depend on similarity. That is, to the extent that two situations comprise the same stimuli, they will tend to elicit the same responses or expectations. This mechanism provides appropriate generalization and discrimination within any one context. However it can also cause associative interference, because if two responses are associated with the same stimulus, they tend to interfere with each other. This can cause errors in mathematics. For example, given a sum, $3 + 4 = ?$, a common error is "5" (Briars & Siegler, 1984). This is a "counting-on" error, caused by the fact that 5 follows 4 in the counting sequence, so 4 becomes a stimulus that is associated with 5 as a response. Although associations can produce transfer between similar stimuli, they cannot mediate transfer from one domain to another. Such cross-domain transfer depends on analogical mapping.

Explicit knowledge is influenced by the same mechanisms as implicit knowledge, partly because explicit knowledge is sometimes developed from implicit knowledge through the process that Karmiloff-Smith (1990) called representational redescription. Explicit procedural knowledge is influenced by reinforcement, and explicit declarative knowledge is influenced by confirmation. However, there are other mechanisms that operate in the acquisition of explicit knowledge. These include construction of mental models, and development of strategies based on mental models.

Explicit Knowledge Based on Mental Models

Construction of a mental model can aid learning by enabling information to be predicted, thereby reducing the amount of learning that is needed. To illustrate, try learning the following triples; for example, for the stimulus pair (such as T,N) try to learn the response item (T).

$$T,N \rightarrow T$$
$$T,C \rightarrow R$$
$$T,A \rightarrow L$$

$$R,N \rightarrow R$$
$$R,C \rightarrow L$$
$$R,A \rightarrow T$$
$$L,N \rightarrow L$$
$$L,C \rightarrow T$$
$$L,A \rightarrow R$$

Although the task would seem to be simple on the surface, in that it entails learning only nine items, it is surprisingly difficult. One reason is associative interference. Each stimulus is equally associated with all three responses. That is, stimulus T is associated with responses T, R, L equally often. The same is true for each of N, C, and A. Therefore such a task is very difficult to learn by simple stimulus–response associations. This task is a case of what is sometimes called "configural learning" (Rudy, 1991; Squire, 1992), in which responses are associated with configurations of stimuli, rather than stimulus elements. Such tasks are notoriously difficult to learn by associative processes. It is amenable to learning by more explicit cognitive approaches, however.

Try constructing a mental model in the form of an equilateral triangle with the top vertex labeled as T (Top), the right vertex as R and the left vertex as L. Now think of N as null (no movement), C as one step clockwise, and A as one step anticlockwise. Now the answers are easy to generate; T,N means no movement, so the answer is T. T,C means move one step clockwise from the top, so the answer is R (right). No further effort is required, because all answers can be predicted. The slow process of associative learning is avoided. Learning based on a mental model is explicit in that the rules or relations are represented by the person. The mental model suggested above has rules like "move one step clockwise" which would not be present if the task were learned by associative processes. By contrast implicit procedural knowledge, based on stimulus–response associations, is inadequate in this task.

A second property of learning based on mental models is that it can be readily transferred, both within and between domains. For example the mental model constructed for this task could be applied to the cyclic 3-Group, or the Group of residue classes modulo 3, as shown in Table 2.1. (This can be done by substituting T,R,L for 0,1,2 respectively in the left column of Table 2.1, and N,C,A for 0,1,2 respectively in the top row of Table 2.1). In that context the elements are very different, yet the structures are identical. Transfer between these rather different contexts is possible because the rules that define the structure are known to the performer.

Mental models of this kind are essentially analogs. Such mental models may be constructed specifically for the task, though the components are

TABLE 2.1
Group of Residue Classes, Modulo 3

	0	1	2
0	0	1	2
1	1	2	0
2	2	0	1

normally transferred from other contexts. In the example just considered a mental model was constructed using an equilateral triangle learned in elementary geometry. In other contexts mental models may be transferred intact from another context. For example, a person learning about electricity might use water flowing down pipes as an analog (Gentner & Gentner, 1983).

Transfer Based on Understanding

Once an adequate mental model is constructed, it can produce efficient transfer even to quite different materials, or different domains. Consider the following task:

$$
\begin{aligned}
A,P &\rightarrow A \\
A,Q &\rightarrow B \\
A,R &\rightarrow C \\
B,P &\rightarrow B \\
B,Q &\rightarrow C \\
B,R &\rightarrow A \\
C,P &\rightarrow C \\
C,Q &\rightarrow A \\
C,R &\rightarrow B
\end{aligned}
$$

Having constructed the mental model based on an equilateral triangle discussed earlier, it is very easy to learn this task. However it would be as difficult as the original to learn by stimulus–response association. A good mental model mediates transfer across task isomorphs, based on different materials, but with the same structure.

In mathematics good mental models have the same effect. The example task is actually based on a mathematical concept, the cyclic 3-Group, as the reader may have recognized. Numerous examples are encountered in this book of correspondence between concepts being recognized by use of mental models. Good mental models facilitate recognition of concepts in different contexts.

MM ⇒ abstraction of structure

Objectivist

Mental Models and Understanding

contrast w/ A. Brown's (; other) defn.

This illustrates the point that understanding is essentially a matter of having a mental model. Halford (1993) proposed that "to understand a concept entails having an internal, cognitive representation or mental model that reflects the structure of that concept. The representation defines the workspace for problem solving and decision making with respect to the concept" (p. 7). Holland et al. (1986) also defined understanding as having a mental model. Mental models can vary of course in adequacy, and the adequacy of the mental models corresponds to the quality of understanding. Understanding has numerous advantages that are considered in more detail elsewhere (Halford, 1993), but one of them is that it permits development of strategies that are appropriate for a given task. Our next topic then is to consider how possession of a mental model can guide development of a strategy.

Learning Strategies Based on Mental Models

Mental models can guide the development of strategies and acquisition of cognitive skills. This is readily observable in everyday life, where for example knowledge of aircraft helps one to learn to fly, though the benefits tend to be greater in the early stages. The processes by which mental models guide strategy development have been modeled in considerable detail, reflecting the importance that is attached to them. Greeno, Riley and Gelman (1984) modeled the development of counting skills based on innate knowledge of counting principles, whereas Greeno and Johnson (1985) modeled the development of skills in arithmetic word problems. Halford et al. (1992, 1995) modeled the development of transitive inference strategies based on children's mental model of the concept of order. This model, called TRIMM (Transitive Inference Mapping Model) is also summarized elsewhere (Halford, 1993, chapter 4). VanLehn and Brown (1980) showed that the important properties of a performance are to be found, not in the surface form of a strategy, but in the way the strategy was planned, or developed from the person's concept of the task.

A major advantage of strategies and skills based on mental models is that they can be adapted to changing circumstances. For example a child who has an adequate mental model of counting can work out how to count in a number of different ways. If the conventional procedure of counting the first item in a row is precluded, the child can start with another item and return to the beginning of the row later, thereby counting in an unconventional, but correct, manner (Gelman & Gallistel, 1978). Skills based on understanding can be transferred from one context or domain to another. Mental models comprise explicit declarative knowledge, which can be transferred to other contexts and used to generate new strategies appropriate to that context.

If only it were that simple!

Declarative knowledge can be acquired in everyday life and used to develop strategies when they are required, even in unexpected contexts. The model of Halford et al. (1992) begins with experiences of ordered sets occurring in everyday life in early childhood. These include experiences with blocks that can be arranged in order of size, forming a "staircase", stories such as the three bears and the billygoats gruff that entail animals that vary in size or other attributes, and experience with different-aged siblings in the one family. These experiences are acquired in the course of everyday life, without conscious intent on the part of either child or mentor that they should be used for any subsequent learning. However they can be used to guide the development of strategies for unanticipated tasks. Suppose, for example, a child is presented with the following problem:

> *Tommy is taller than Michael.*
> *Johnny is taller than Tommy.*
> *Michael is taller than Peter.*
> *What is the order of these boys' heights?*

A child has presumably not been taught a strategy for this task, because there is no reason to anticipate a need for such a strategy. However, the model of Halford et al. (1992) shows that everyday knowledge, combined with basic cognitive skills such as means–end analysis and analogical reasoning, can be used to develop a strategy when it is required. The child maps the premises into a mental model of an ordered set experienced in everyday life in order to determine the correct ordering, then chooses an operator that will produce this order. The operator is then incorporated into a strategy, and on future occasions will be used where appropriate, without recourse to mapping into a mental model. In this case the most likely strategy entails transferring the first pair, Tommy, Michael to short-term memory. Then Johnny is placed at the front of the string, yielding Johnny, Tommy, Michael. Then Peter is appended, yielding the string Johnny, Tommy, Michael, Peter.

The development of strategies from declarative knowledge is cognitively effortful, because mapping into a mental model imposes high processing loads. Once the strategy is developed, however, this mapping is no longer required, and processing loads are considerably reduced. Thus the development of skills based on understanding can be expected to require allocation of high levels of resources. Application of the strategies once they are developed is much less effortful.

Strategy Development Without Mental Models

Glaser (1990) distinguished between self-regulatory skill acquisition and proceduralized skill acquisition. The former is based on understanding of the task, which we attribute to possession of a mental model. There is really no need to favor proceduralized or self-regulatory theories of skill acquisition, because both occur. Some learning does occur without understanding. For example, many people learn to drive a car without understanding how a car works. It is not possible to understand everything we learn, but the advantage of learning based on understanding is that it can be adapted and extended. The concepts we understand form building blocks in a developing knowledge structure, whereas performances that are not based on understanding tend to be restricted to the applications where they were acquired.

There are associative models of strategy development, the most notable in the context of mathematics being that of Siegler and Shipley (in press) and Siegler and Shrager (1984). We review this model in chapter 5 in our discussion on number fact learning. Although the model shows how much can be accomplished through associative strategy mechanisms, it does not incorporate any mechanisms whereby strategy development can be influenced by understanding of the task. Therefore it seems desirable that it should be combined with some metacognitive selection models that have successfully explained how strategies can be constrained by the performer's concept of the task.

Schema Induction

One of the most powerful and useful abilities in the human learning repertoire is schema induction. It is probably the main means by which the raw material of mental models is first obtained. It entails constructing a representation of the essential relations in a task or situation as a result of experience. Experimental work has shown that both humans and higher animals have this ability, so it is presumably a rather basic part of our cognitive equipment. Nevertheless, it does not occur easily or automatically. The question has been reviewed elsewhere in the context of so-called learning set acquisition and analogical transfer (Halford, 1993). Learning set research, which has traditionally been devoted to other animals and young children, entails training on a series of discrimination problems that have nothing in common except their structure. It is argued that learning set acquisition entails induction of a relational schema, which is transferred from problem to problem by analogical mapping. This suggests that humans and higher animals can spontaneously induce a schema that expresses the relations of a task. We consider the important principles of schema induction here.

Schemata will not be induced from a single experience with a task. They can be induced from two or more instantiations of a task, if help is given to encode the schema. This can be done, for example, by asking participants to state the similarities and differences between the instantiations (Gick & Holyoak, 1983). Schema induction can also occur if experience is given with a series of isomorphs of a task that differ in their surface characteristics. This enables participants to distinguish the structures that are common to the different instantiations from the properties that are coincidental to any one instantiation. This has been analyzed for "learning set" acquisition, or "learning to learn" by Halford (1993, pp. 223–227). A similar point has been made by Dienes (1964) under the principle of "multiple embodiment," meaning that a concept should be illustrated in more than one way.

Acquisition of Expertise

Expertise does not only require declarative and procedural knowledge as discussed previously, but also entails organizing and coding that knowledge. There is evidence that experts have much better organized knowledge than novices. They tend to code situations in terms of more powerful, overarching concepts and relations, and can see larger, more meaningful patterns than novices (Carey, 1985; Chi, Glaser, & Farr, 1988). Furthermore, as Holyoak (1991) pointed out, experts also have the ability to adapt knowledge, and expertise should be regarded as dynamic rather than static.

Acquisition of mathematics depends partly on development of expertise, and will therefore entail acquisition of integrated knowledge, including higher order relations and overarching concepts. Instruction is vital in helping the child to acquire this high-level conceptual knowledge.

Social Influences on Learning

As the section on basic learning mechanisms showed, children, like adults and other animals, can acquire prodigious amounts of information about their world quite spontaneously. It would therefore be a mistake to believe that children know only what they are taught. Furthermore, as we saw in the section on explicit knowledge and mental models, the child must actively construct her knowledge in the form of mental models of the world. A child's knowledge is not a gift from his or her mentors.

However the child's capacity for acquiring and organizing knowledge is not adequate for all purposes, and it would not be sufficient by itself for the acquisition of mathematical knowledge. Mathematics is a cultural achievement, and its acquisition requires cultural input. Vygotsky (1962) distinguished between spontaneous concepts, which develop mainly through the child's mental efforts, and nonspontaneous concepts, which are dependent on instruction. Vygotsky thought that these processes were related and constantly influenced each other. We believe this insight has important application in acquisition of mathematics.

Although the child's spontaneous efforts are undoubtedly important to mathematics, they are not sufficient, and instruction necessarily plays a vital role in acquisition of mathematics. Acquisition of mathematics requires an appropriate interaction of spontaneous and nonspontaneous processes. Spontaneous learning is insufficient, because no child could discover mathematics unaided, and because everyday life does not provide the experiences that are necessary for acquisition of many mathematical concepts. On the other hand instruction will be ineffective unless the child can integrate it with mental models that encode his own experience. Understanding and performance both require an experiential base, and instruction must relate clearly and unambiguously to this experience.

Instruction necessarily operates through the learning processes that are present in the child, but it can have a massive influence on the effectiveness of those processes. It does this through directing attention, maintaining motivation, providing feedback, and providing efficient ways of coding elements, classes, and relations. Furthermore, as Sigel (1984) has shown, parents and teachers help the child acquire "distancing" behaviors, which break space and time barriers, leading to broader, more flexible, less restricted conceptualization. In general, the teacher's questions and explanations help the child develop her mental models.

COGNITIVE GROWTH

A major issue in the theory of cognitive development has been whether it occurs in stages or is continuous. Piaget (1950) and the neo-Piagetian theorists, including Case (1985), Chapman (1990), and Pascual-Leone (1970), have argued that cognitive development passed through a series of discrete stages. Although Vygotsky (1962) was not a stage theorist, and was not specifically concerned with capacity, at least not as it is understood nowadays, he nevertheless argued for a zone of proximal development, which corresponds to the improvement that instruction can produce on the child's current knowledge stage. It implies that new knowledge can only extend a limited distance beyond existing knowledge. Other theorists such as Carey (1985), Chi (1978), Gelman (1990), Keil (1981), and Markman and Seibert (1976) argued that cognitive development depended on acquisition and reorganization of knowledge. There is an extensive literature on the stage question (e.g., Flavell, 1972, 1977, 1984; Brainerd, 1978; Halford, 1982, 1989, 1993).

A related question is whether cognitive development is capacity limited. Case (1985), Chapman (1990), Halford (1982, 1993), and Pascual-Leone (1970) have argued that growth in capacity has been an enabling factor in cognitive development. On the other hand Brainerd (1985), Goswami (1992), Howe and Rabinowitz (1990), Chi (1978), and Carey (1986, 1990) argued against a role for capacity. This issue has been considered in detail elsewhere

(Halford, 1993, chapter 3), and only the essential points are summarized here.

The basic processes of conceptualization and thought are the same at all ages. For example, the learning mechanisms discussed above are general throughout the lifespan. There is also evidence that even very young children can perform analogies, which are the core mechanism of thinking and novel problem solving (Goswami & Brown, 1990). The question of whether capacity grows with age is more complex, because there is more than one type of capacity, as noted earlier. We must therefore consider which aspects of processing capacity change with age.

There is very strong evidence that speed of processing changes with age. It has long been known that reaction time decreases with age (Halford, 1992), but Kail (1986, 1988, 1991) also produced evidence for a global processing speed factor that increases with age.

The capacity factor that has most significance for acquisition of mathematics is ability to represent complex relations. As discussed in the section on relational complexity of representations, there is evidence that the complexity of relations that children can represent increases with age, possibly due to differentiation of representations. As mentioned earlier, it would not increase overall capacity, but only the complexity of relations that could be explicitly represented. It is analogous to dividing an experiment into more independent variables. The number of cells or observations need not change, but the order of interactions that can be processed does change.

Attempts have been made to use Piagetian theory to predict children's capacity to understand concepts. For example it has sometimes been held that children cannot understand mathematics until they reach the concrete operations stage, as measured by tests such as conservation. These attempts can now be seen as misguided, primarily because both the theory and the measuring instruments were too imprecise. Although the issue will no doubt remain controversial for some time, it seems a fair summary that Piaget's theory and associated empirical work provided insights of great importance, and both were advanced in many ways relative to other approaches that existed at the time. On the other hand, whatever one's evaluation of Piaget, his contribution is now several decades old. This is not to denigrate scholarly study of Piaget, nor does it say we should not draw on his work where it has something to tell us, but we should not neglect the considerable advances that have been made in understanding of cognition in the last 30 years.

It has been argued elsewhere (Halford 1989, 1992, 1993) that many recent developments in cognitive science have yielded insights into the way information is represented and processed that give unexpected support to some of Piaget's observations. As noted earlier, the difficulty that children have in concrete operational concepts before age 5, and formal operational concepts before age 11, may be explicable in terms of the processing loads imposed by explicit representation of complex relations (Halford, 1993, chapter 6). It should be emphasized that these loads are not specific to children, but affect adults as well. They affect children more, partly because of their lower capacity for explicit representation of relations, partly because they are less efficient at conceptual chunking, and partly because they have less adequate serial processing strategies for avoiding the processing loads.

This way of conceptualizing children's ability to understand concepts is much more rigorous, and its implications more thoroughly understood, than Piagetian theory, simply because of the benefits provided by a few more decades of work on cognition. As we show in the next chapter, this approach can be used to predict what can be readily understood, and which concepts will cause difficulty, at each level. To allay fears that these predictions are pessimistic because they might imply barriers to children's understanding, we should point out that complexity analysis has often uncovered previously unrecognized potential to understand concepts. For example, Halford's (1993) analyses of complexity have suggested that young children should be more capable of understanding aspects of the balance scale and performing certain types of hypothesis testing and analogical reasoning than was previously recognized.

Growth in capacity to represent relational concepts is an enabling factor in cognitive development, but actual cognitive growth is experience driven and depends on the processes for acquiring information discussed earlier. It also depends on conceptual chunking, which reorganizes representations more efficeintly so they impose lower processing loads, thereby using the available capacity more efficiently. It also depends on acquisition of efficient strategies for processing complex tasks serially, so that capacity is not overloaded.

SUMMARY

The main points discussed in this chapter may be summarized as follows:

1. Relational complexity can be measured by the number of arguments of a relation. Human concepts appear to belong to one of four levels of complexity, corresponding to unary, binary, ternary, and quaternary relations. These correspond to concepts with one to four dimensions respectively. More complex relations impose a higher processing load, and tend to appear later developmentally.

2. Human reasoning processes depend more on memory retrieval and analogy than on application of formal logical rules. Rules that reflect the structure of the environment are readily learned and are employed in reasoning. Analogies are structure-preserving mappings from base to target.

Levels of analogy may be distinguished according to the complexity of relations that must be mapped in parallel. The four levels of structure mapping are element, relational, system and multiple-system mappings, in which unary to quaternary relations respectively are mapped.

3. Processing loads can be reduced by conceptual chunking (reducing the number of dimensions) and segmentation (using strategies for serial processing in small steps). However both entail costs as well as benefits, and neither is a panacea. Processing capacity is thought to increase with age because representations become differentiated into more dimensions, enabling more complex relations to be represented. Capacity overload does not lead to total breakdown, but to default to lower dimensional representations, which produce performances that are only partially correct.

4. Learning processes may be associative or metacognitive. Both can lead to either declarative or procedural knowledge, either of which can be implicit or explicit. Associative learning provides relatively effortless accumulation of large amounts of information, but it is subject to associative interference, and transfers only to similar contexts. Learning based on mental models, or concepts of the task, is more effortful but potentially more powerful, and can mediate cross-domain transfer. Schema induction provides the raw material of mental models. Learning a cultural domain such as mathematics depends on both spontaneous and nonspontaneous processes, the latter requiring social input.

[handwritten margin note: a bit too organized]

[handwritten note at bottom of page:]

Mechanistic, computational model with no adequate account of what (the content of) children 'know'; believe (? adults) intuitively.

Emphasis on correct MM (according to God's Eye view)

vs

adaptive, effective constructions of how the world is and what activity schemas/scripts work in it.

3

COGNITIVE MODELS AND PROCESSES IN MATHEMATICS EDUCATION

This chapter presents the cognitive processes that are involved in three aspects of mathematics. These are: the process of understanding, the way in which understanding assists the child in developing procedures and strategies for performing mathematics, and how the complexity of mathematical concepts and tasks affects performance.

UNDERSTANDING MATHEMATICS

The essence of understanding a concept is to have a mental representation or mental model that faithfully reflects the structure of that concept. Number is the core of mathematics, and to understand number is to have a mental model of it that includes all the essential relations of numbers, at least within the domain where the concept is used. A 5-year-old's concept of *number* is presumably much more restricted than that of a pure mathematician, but the 5-year-old may still have a representation of those number relations that are important within the particular domains in which she uses number. Our first purpose then is to consider what is involved in mental models of number.

A mental model is not normally based on formal definitions but rather on concrete properties that have been drawn from life experience. Mental models are typically analogs, and they comprise specific contents, but this does not necessarily restrict their power to deal with abstract concepts, as we will see. The important thing about mental models, especially in the context of mathematics, is the relations they represent. We will use diagrams to depict mental models for a variety of concepts, and it is important to keep in mind that any diagram, or even a non-diagrammatic representation that represents the same essential relations would be equally effective.

Mental models of number must represent two main kinds of relations: relations between the numbers and the sets they represent, and relations between numbers themselves. Numbers and the relations between them comprise the number system, of which the child must have some kind of mental model. Both types of relations are illustrated in Fig. 3.1, which could provide a possible basis for a mental model of elementary number.

Cardinal Value

In order to understand the cardinal value of a number, a child must recognize that it represents sets with a specific number of members. Mathematically, a cardinal number represents the set of all sets with a specific number of members: The number 2 represents the set of all sets containing two members. However an important way that mental models of number differ from formal definitions is that a mental model need not include the idea that a cardinal number represents the set of all sets with a specific number of members. Furthermore the formal definition of sets, and even the name set, need play no explicit role in a mental model. It is sufficient to know simply that a cardinal number represents the specific number of members in a set or collection.

This does not necessarily mean that mental models are imprecise. For example, even a very young child may clearly understand that *two* always represents exactly two things, but she probably has no explicit concept of set, and is even less likely to recognize the idea of a set of all sets of a given number of members. Thus, mental models can be quite precise within a limited range of contexts. They can also be enriched and refined progressively with experience.

Subitizing, or enumeration of small sets by direct apprehension, without explicit counting, may be a very basic and primitive process, requiring no explicit instruction, and possibly little or no experience. Experiments on subitizing indicate that both adults and children can subitize sets to about four elements, with no apparent improvement with age (Gelman & Gallistel, 1978). There is also evidence that nonhuman animals can quantify small sets (Gelman, 1991). One implication of this is that we may be innately equipped with representations of small, whole numbers, equivalent to the natural numbers 1–4. These probably provide the building blocks for a concept of number. One of the most important aspects of these primitive enumeration processes is that they orient us to the numerosities of sets we experience. Without this it may be difficult, if not impossible, to recognize numerosity as a property, because it is embedded in so many other features. Imagine, for example, our experiences of sets of two objects. We might see two cars, one

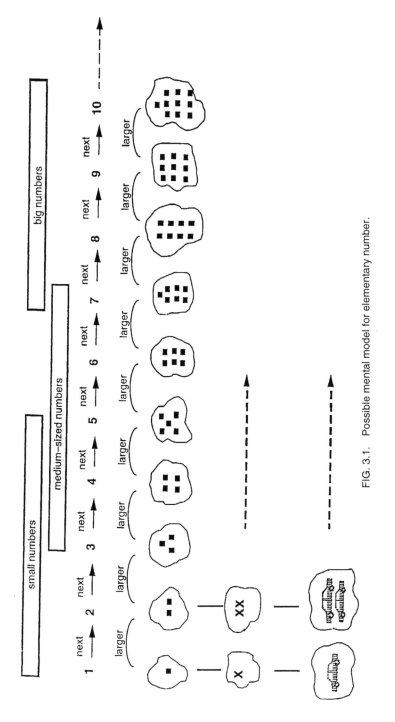

FIG. 3.1. Possible mental model for elementary number.

59

stationary, the other speeding away from us, each a different year, make, model, and color. Then we see an apple and a banana, a dog and a cat, two human beings, and so on. These experiences comprise an infinity of features, only one of which is that they are all sets of two objects. Extraction of the numerosity property would be difficult indeed without any innate constraints to orient us.

Subitizing is one of a number of primitive processes that appear to provide the basis for acquisition of the number concept. Others include what are often called "protoquantitative schemas," including "compare," and "increase/decrease." The former comprises the ability to compare numerosities of sets, and the latter the ability to understand that adding is an operator that increases the numerosity of a set, and removing members decreases the numerosity of a set. The protoquantitative increase/decrease schema appears to be present in infancy, and may be innate. Wynn (1992a), using the dishabituation technique that has been so successful with infants, showed that 4- to 5-month-olds recognized that adding an item inceased set size (from 1 to 2), whereas removing an item decreased set size. This suggests that children might be oriented to relevant set operations such as increase/decrease from an early age. This orientation may reflect an innate constraint (Keil, 1990).

Though acquisition of numerosity is probably assisted by innate constraints that orient us, nevertheless there is evidence that it is greatly aided by experience. For example, parents and siblings play games with young children in which they are taught the number of each type of body part. These games have the advantage that body parts are familiar and very regular in their numerosities. Such experiences enable children to acquire an understanding that numbers represent sets with a specific number of members. They assist children to build a mental model of number by defining the mappings between each number and the set of a given numerosity that it represents. In time, children can "call up" this model to create a re-representation of the number, regardless of the presence or absence of actual perceptual cues (Steffe & Cobb, 1988). Assignments of number names to sets are useful for early acquisition of number meanings, but number concepts gradually become independent of explicit set representations, as representations of the number systems become more autonomous.

Relations Between Numbers

The second major aspect of understanding numbers is to have a mental model of the relations between numbers themselves. This understanding can be aided by the fact that relations between numbers correspond to relations between sets of different magnitude, as shown in Fig. 3.1.

Acquisition of these relations probably begins with binary relations between numbers of different size. Children begin to recognize that one number is bigger or smaller than another, either because one number represents a larger set, or because one number succeeds another in the counting order. Resnick and Singer (1993) attributed this to the protoquantitative compare schema. Children also categorize numbers, so 9 might be considered "big," whereas 2 is considered "small," though these are usually fuzzy, overlapping categories (Siegler & Robinson, 1982).

The succession relation could be acquired partly through learning the number names in counting order. That is, children learn which number comes next after any given number by rote learning the order of the number names. However succession is not the same as difference in magnitude; for example, 7 > 3, but 7 is not the successor of 3. Furthermore, the rote learning of number names gives only a restricted meaning to succession. Succession becomes more meaningful when a child realizes that a successor always represents a set with one more member.

The meaning of both succession and relative magnitude might be learned partly by the use of protoquantitative increase/decrease schemas. If we add members to a set, we produce a bigger number (increase schema), and a smaller number results from removing members from a set (decrease schema). If we add one member to a set, we create a set that corresponds to the successor; if we have a set of 3, and add 1, we create a set of 4, and so on.

Though it seems eminently reasonable that protoquantitative schemas such as compare, and increase/decrease should play a role in mental models of elementary number, it is equally clear that they are not sufficient by themselves. If children are to acquire a mental model of number through experiences with sets, they must recognize the *correspondence* between set relations and number relations. Consider, for example, how a child might come to recognize that 3 represents a larger set than 2. The correspondences are shown in Fig. 3.2A.

There is the relation between the sets; the set with three members contains more than the set of two. The number 3 is assigned, or mapped, to the set of three members. This is the relation between the number 3 and (an instance of) the sets that it represents, discussed previously. Similarly, the number 2 is assigned to the set of two members. Finally, the number 3 is greater than the number 2. This relation corresponds to the relation between the sets. The set relations are really an analog of the number relations. An analogy was defined in chapter 2 as a mapping from a source to a target, such that the relations in base and target correspond. That is precisely what we have here: The relation MORE–MEMBERS(set-of-3,set-of-2) is the base. GREATER–MAGNITUDE(3,2) is the target. Therefore understanding that 3 > 2 because 3 represents sets with more members than 2 is an analogy between a source, which comprises the sets and the relations be-

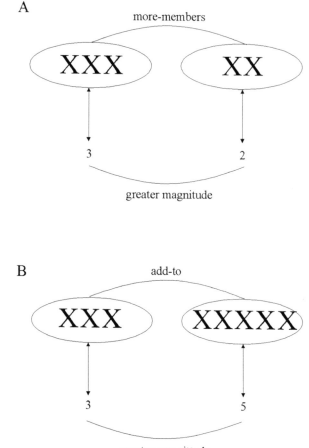

FIG. 3.2.   (A) Binary relation, 3 > 2, mapped into a set analog; (B) unary operator, add-to, mapped into a set analog.

tween them, and the target, comprising the numbers and the relations between them.

A similar analogy holds with increasing and decreasing sets, as shown in Fig. 3.2B. Suppose we have a set of three members, then we create a larger set, by adding two more members. The number representing the final set (5) is more than the number representing the starting set (3). The relation between the sets again corresponds to the relation between the numbers. This time however the relation between the sets is not "more-than," but "add-to." The relation is actually an operator, but it still corresponds to the relations between the relevant numbers. Thus the child's own activities, in adding to, or removing from sets, can be recognized as being in correspondence to number relations. In our current example, the number representing the final set (which results from adding) is more than the number representing the starting set.

Thus a mental model of elementary number can be built up by analogy with relations between sets of everyday objects. The protoquantitative schemas "compare" and "increase/decrease" are useful in enabling the child to recognize the set relations. For example, the "compare" schema permits the child to recognize the relation between the set of two and the set of three in Fig. 3.2A. However the protoquantitative schemas are not enough by themselves. They do not actually provide a mental model of number. This depends on recognizing the correspondence between the set relations and the number relations, and is a form of analogical reasoning. Such analogies help give meaning to number concepts. Once those meanings are learned however the analogies can be left behind, apart perhaps from an occasional retrospective check. It is not necessary to make continuous reference to the analog that gave the concept meaning originally. The analogy is valuable initially however in enriching the meaning of a concept.

A mental model such as that in Fig. 3.2. can be built up partly through the discovery of three kinds of simple relations: between numbers and sets, between sets, and the corresponding relations between numbers. However, even an elementary mental model of number depends on more than relations of "more than," and "less than." Some overarching relations are needed.

Higher Order Relations

Higher order relations are relations between relations, whereas first-order relations are relations between objects. Technically, they are relations whose arguments are relations, whereas first-order relations are relations whose arguments are objects. Examples of higher order relations include the fact that more-than is the opposite of less-than, and increase is the opposite of decrease: OPPOSITE($>$,$<$), and OPPOSITE(increase,decrease). These are higher order relations, because their arguments are relations.

Many higher order relations also can be acquired through experience with sets. It can be recognized that, for example, 4>3, 3>2, and 4>2, which is an instance of transitivity. There is a subtle difference, however, between recognizing these three relations as separate relations and recognizing an instance of transitivity. The latter requires the higher order relation: 4 > 3 and 3 > 2 *implies* 4 > 3. The first-order relations themselves become objects, or arguments, of a higher order relation.

There is probably an intermediate step before transitivity per se is explicitly recognized. This would entail recognizing that 4>3 and 3>2 are the same relation: that is, SAME-RELATION(4>3, 3>2). This can of course be extended to other cases; SAME-RELATION(4>3, 4>2), SAME-RELATION (3>2,4>2), and so on. If we recognize that these relations are the same and integrate them we can create the ternary relation, MONOTONIC-DECREASE (4,3,2). From this transitive inferences can be read off, because we can see that not only is 4>3 and 3>2, but 4>2. This is consistent with the processes that have been demonstrated in both adults' and children's transitive inferences (Halford et al., 1995; Sternberg, 1980a,1980b). Extending this process leads to recognition that there is a monotonic increase in magnitude as we progress through the numbers 1,2,3,4, . . . etc., and a monotonic decrease such as 9,8,7, . . . ,1.

Another example of a higher order relation is the relation between the periods in multidigit numbers. Consider the number 686,949. Within the ones period (949), the hundreds digit and the ones digit are related by 10^2. A similar relation holds within the thousands period (686) between the thousands and the hundred-thousands digits. Thus the same relations are repeated in the periods, so the relations in 949 are repeated in 686. The relations between periods are higher order relations, whose arguments are relations within periods.

The basis for some higher order relations is more subtle than it might at first appear. The idea that more-than is the opposite of less-than may seem sufficiently obvious to us, but on reflection we realize that it necessitates that numbers are ordered for magnitude. This in turn requires that the concept of order is understood. Mathematically, an ordered set is one on which an asymmetric, transitive, binary relation is defined. Such a formal definition is probably not psychologically realistic. The following features might, however, comprise a psychologically plausible mental model of the concept of order, as Halford et al. (1995) have proposed:

1. At least one binary relation, such as greater than, happier than, and so on, must be known;
2. It must be recognized that each element occurs once and only once;
3. It must be recognized that end elements have the same relation to all other elements; for example, in an ordered set (a,b,c,d), a has the same relation to all of b,c,d;
4. It must be recognized that the position of an element that is not at the end is defined by its relation to elements on each side of it; for example, b<a, b>c;
5. It must be recognized that the same relation exists between all pairs (this effectively provides the transitivity property of an ordered set).

All these properties can be instantiated in any ordered set of at least three elements. This has important implications, because it means that a child who knows a concrete instance of an ordered set of at least three elements has a potential basis for a concept of order. Furthermore a concrete instance of an ordered set can be used by analogical reasoning. It is used in this way to guide the development of transitive inference strategies in the model of Halford et al. (1995).

The idea of opposite relations between numbers really only has meaning when numbers are integrated into a coherent system, such as the ordering shown in Fig. 3.1. This however is a considerable conceptual achievement in itself, because it requires that all the component relations be organized in a manner that is consistent with the five features listed above.

Operations and Complex Relations

A mental model of elementary number also entails recognition of the operations, addition/subtraction and multiplication/division. These are really ternary relations, and are more complex relations than larger/smaller, increase/decrease. Their basis in set experiences is illustrated in Fig. 3.3. If (say) two objects are added to a set of three objects, the result is a set with five objects, as young children can readily verify once they have the set enumeration knowledge discussed above.

This example illustrates the important point that addition is really a ternary relation, or a relation between three things; addition is a relation between two addends and a sum, in this case between 3, 2, and 5. We could

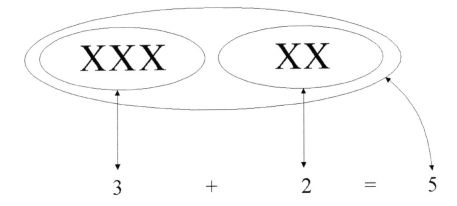

FIG. 3.3.   Binary operation (ternary relation), 3 + 2 = 5, mapped to set analog.

write it as ADDITION(3,2,5) or, more succinctly, as +(3,2,5); similarly, +(3,4,7), . . +(4,5,9), and so on. By contrast, increase was only a binary relation, between a set and a larger set. The magnitude of the increase is not specified. Magnitude difference is also a relation between two numbers or sets, with the size of the difference unspecified. We could write it as INCREASE(set-of-3, set-of-5), or (more succinctly) as >(5,3). These are binary relations, because they are relations between only two entities, one smaller and one larger. The magnitude of the increase, or the size difference, is not specified. By contrast, the operations of addition/subtraction, and multiplication/division, are ternary relations because they relate three things, or have three arguments. These binary operations are ternary relations, which gives them a complexity value in terms of our relational complexity metric. We consider binary operations in more detail in chapters 5 and 6. Magnitude comparisons are binary relations because they relate two things, and only have two arguments. This has important implications for the complexity of concepts, as we will see.

Set operations that correspond to multiplication are shown in Fig. 3.4. The multiplier is mapped to a set of sets (in this example, to the set of rows), and the multiplicand is mapped to the number of elements in each set (in this example to the rows). The product is mapped to the total number of elements in the array. Multiplication is three dimensional, like addition, but the sets to which it is mapped are harder to recognize, because one is a set of sets. More prior learning, and more chunking, is required to recognize the correspondence between multiplication and the set analog.

The analogical reasoning processes that were relevant to magnitude comparisons and increase/decrease also apply to the operations of addition/subtraction and multiplication/division, except that more complex relations are involved in base and target. They entail ternary relations, whereas magnitude comparison and increase/decrease only entail binary relations.

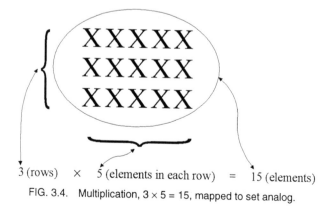

3 (rows)   ×   5 (elements in each row)   =   15 (elements)

FIG. 3.4.   Multiplication, 3 × 5 = 15, mapped to set analog.

Set operations underlie Whitehead and Russell's (1927) basis for number operations, but in order to use this approach as a basis for understanding, a child would not only have to master set operations but would also need to recognize the correspondence with arithmetic operations, which would necessitate that the latter too would need to be mastered. This is one of a number of cases where the axiomatic basis for a system of concepts may provide an elegant formal justification, but may not be a good basis for acquiring the concepts in question. A child who is acquiring an elementary understanding of number need not know explicitly the set operations that provide the formal justification. In our treatment here, union and intersection of small, disjoint sets are being used as analogs of number operations, rather than as formal justification. This is a very important shift. Analogies are a much more psychologically realistic basis for elementary number understanding than axiom systems, but they have their limitations, and no analog is fully adequate.

Children can learn valuable elementary knowledge using set analogs, but it is not practical for a child to learn all the relations that comprise the arithmetic operations by analogy with sets, however. For example, it would be cumbersome indeed to demonstrate, using concrete sets, that 8,974 + 487,278 = 496,252. In order to recognize such addition examples, children need some way of generalizing relations learned with small sets. This incorporates the place value of multidigit numbers, to be discussed in chapter 4. Simple practical operations on small sets can provide analogs that enable children to understand the meaning of basic arithmetic operations, which can then be generalized through more advanced number operations to indefinitely large numbers.

The part/whole schema, which is important in a number of arithmetic contexts, including counting and arithmetic word problems, also entails a ternary relation. It relates a whole and two component parts, as shown in Fig. 3.5. It can be interpreted either as an addition operation (e.g., 5 + 3 = 8)

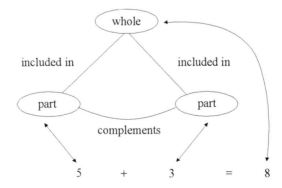

FIG. 3.5.   Addition, 3 + 5 = 8, mapped to part/whole schema.

or as part/whole; 5 and 3 are each parts of 8. The latter interpretation is likely to occur in arithmetic word problems; for example, John had 5 marbles, then Jane gave him 3 more, how many does he have altogether? We will address the part/whole schema in chapter 5.

Higher Order Relations Between Arithmetic Operations

There are higher order relations between arithmetic operations. For example addition and subtraction can be considered opposite processes, as can multiplication and division. The higher order relation between addition and subtraction is not as simple however, as that between increase/decrease. For example, although it may be true that $3 + 2 = 5$ is the opposite of $5 - 2 = 3$, this is really only a higher order relation between increase and decrease. It is really OPPOSITE(+2, −2). The relation between addition and subtraction amounts to accessing addition relations in a different way. If addition consists of mappings (facts) of the form $\{(3,2 \rightarrow 5), \ . \ . \ (4,3 \rightarrow 7). \ . \ \}$, then actually performing addition is a matter of accessing the two addends and deriving the sum, whereas performing subtraction is a matter of accessing one addend and the sum, and deriving the other addend. A similar argument is true for multiplication and division.

Some important relations between arithmetic operations are those contained in the principles of commutativity, associativity, and distributivity.

Commutativity applies to both addition and multiplication, that is, if a and b are any two integers, $a + b = b + a$, and $a \times b = b \times a$. It does not apply to subtraction or division, that is, $a - b \neq b - a$ and $\frac{a}{b} \neq \frac{b}{a}$. Commutativity can be illustrated using set analogs, as shown in Fig. 3.6.

Commutativity can also be recognized by calculating specific examples, then searching for counterexamples. For example, we can take as our mental model of commutativity of addition a number of instances such as $3 + 2 = 2 + 3$, $11 + 8 = 8 + 11$, $23 + 41 = 41 + 23$, and so on. We then check to see whether we can generate an instance where commutativity does not hold. We find (unless we make an error) that we cannot do so for addition, so we accept the commutativity principle as valid. This is consistent with Johnson-Laird's (1983) mental models approach to reasoning, where a

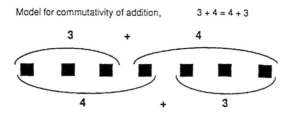

FIG. 3.6. Commutativity of addition illustrated by set analog.

mental model is first constructed, then an attempt is made to construct an alternative model that would generate a different conclusion. If no alternate model can be constructed, the conclusion is accepted as valid. Commutativity is revisited in chapter 5.

Associativity is also true of both addition and multiplication, but not of subtraction or division. That is, if a, b, and c are any integers, $a + (b + c) = (a + b) + c$, and $a(bc) = (ab)c$, but $a - (b - c) \neq (a - b) - c$, and $a/(b/c) \neq (a/b)/c$. As with commutativity, associativity can be acquired using a sets analog, or by using arithmetic examples as a mental model and checking for counterexamples. For example a child who has mastered elementary arithmetic operations, and also understands how to interpret parentheses, can verify that $2 + (3 + 1) = (2 + 3) + 1$, or that $8 + (5 + 4) = (8 + 5) + 4$, and so on. The process of checking for counterexamples is vital. Otherwise incorrect mental models might be adopted because they are confirmed by examples that happen to be correct by chance. For example, $1/(1/1) = (1/1)/1$, but other examples would show that division is not associative.

The *distributive property of multiplication* applies to both addition and subtraction, as shown: The distributive property of multiplication over addition: If a, b, and c are any integers, $a(b + c) = (ab) + (ac)$; The distributive property of multiplication over subtraction: If a, b, and c are any integers and b is greater than or equal to c, then $a(b - c) = ab - ac$.

An understanding of these properties can be acquired using a set analog, but is perhaps acquired more efficiently using arithmetic examples as mental models. A possible sequence for the acquisition of distributivity of multiplication over addition is discussed in Halford (1993, chapter 8).

Commutativity, associativity, and distributivity are really relations between ternary relations, and are equivalent to quaternary relations. An expression such as $a(b + c)$ can be evaluated to a result, d, thereby forming a quaternary relation between $a,b,c,$ and d. Similary, $(a + b) + c$ evaluates to a value, d, and a quaternary relation is formed.

Proportion is a higher order relation between two rational expressions, that is, $\frac{a}{b} = \frac{c}{d}$ and is of considerable importance, both mathematically and psychologically (Lesh, Post, & Behr, 1988). A number of ingenious concrete analogs have been devised, but a mental model based on specific arithmetic examples is also effective in developing an understanding of the concept. Proportion specifies a relation between four variables, $a,b,c,$ and d, and is another case of a quaternary relation. The complexity of the proportion concept is a major cause of difficulty however, as we will see later in this chapter and elsewhere. A further reason why proportion is difficult is that it requires an understanding of rational number, as discussed in chapter 7, in order to verify by arithmetic example that $\frac{a}{b} = \frac{c}{d}$. For example, even to recognize that $\frac{1}{2} = \frac{2}{4}$ it is necessary to understand the meaning of $\frac{1}{2}$ and also that it is equivalent to $\frac{2}{4}$.

Algebra and Abstract Number Concepts

In this section, we consider how children can begin to understand the nature of algebraic reasoning. Algebra has formal justification in terms of abstract structures such as groups, rings, and fields, but it is very unlikely that beginning algebra students could both understand these structures and relate them to the operations they routinely perform. The formal mathematical basis for algebra provides a synthesis for those who have already achieved significant mastery of the field, but it does not follow that it will make operations meaningful for the beginning student. By contrast, we suggest that understanding of algebra, as with other topics, depends on constructing appropriate mental models of the essential concepts. The question is how this can be done.

Whereas arithmetic is primarily concerned with relations between constants, algebra is primarily concerned with relations between variables. To understand algebra means to have a mental model of these relations, and be able to use this mental model to guide the development of appropriate operations and strategies.

Variables are normally represented by letters, rather than digits, so it is necessary that children understand how letters are used in mathematical expressions. Achieving this is only a preliminary step, however. For example, teaching a child that if $a + 4 = 7$, then $a = 3$, may help her understand that a letter can represent a number. However a is a constant in this example, and it does not teach the child anything about variables. If not used in conjunction with other appropriate activities it might even be counterproductive, because it could lead children to believe that letters are used to represent constants. The problem then is how variables can be understood.

A constant can be defined in several ways, as discussed in chapters 4 and 7. First it can be defined by cardinal reference, that is, by its relation to the sets that it represents. It can also be defined by ordinal reference, that is by reference to a particular ordinal position; 3 represents the third position in a series beginning at 1. However variables cannot be defined in either of these ways.

Variables must be defined either by number system reference or by expression reference. In the former case they are defined by their relations to other components of the number system. For example, deriving the meaning of a variable such as $\log_2 N$ is a matter of relating this variable to aspects of the number system, particularly those concerned with logarithms to the base 2. An example of defining a variable by expression reference is $x = 5y$, where the value of x is defined by its relation to y in this expression.

The important point that emerges from this analysis is that variables can only be understood in terms of their relations to other numbers, which may be either variables or constants. Where these relations are defined by convention, and are part of the number system, they will be relatively fixed. For example, the value of $\log_2 N$ will always have the same relation to the value of N, because of the way $\log_2 N$ is defined. However where the relation is defined by a specific expression, as with $x = 5y$, it is not fixed, and is not necessarily part of any predefined system. In such cases, interpretation of a variable symbol cannot be based on past experience with that particular symbol, but must be based on conventions used to interpret such expressions. Children who fail to understand this may try to relate the meaning of a variable to past experience, and believe that, for example, y must represent something like yachts, as discussed in chapter 7. Such failures, we suggest, are at least partly default reactions, and are attributable to lack of appropriate means of defining the meaning of the variable. The problem of how children can understand the meaning of variables is one of our major problems therefore, and we turn to it next.

The meaning of x in the expression $x = 5y$ is defined by its relation to y. Thus x is any number that is 5 times y. One way to achieve at least the beginnings of an understanding of this idea is by analogy with arithmetic. Just as relations between sets can be used as analogs of relations between constants, relations between constants can be used as analogs of relations between variables. Thus a mental model of $x = 5y$ can be formed through one or more arithmetic examples; $15 = 5 \times 3$, $30 = 5 \times 6$, $25 = 5 \times 5$, and so on. Recognition of the correspondence between each of these examples and the expression $x = 5y$ is a form of analogical reasoning, and may be represented as a structure mapping diagram as shown in Fig. 3.7. Children also need to recognize that there is an infinite set of ordered pairs that can be mapped into this expression. This does not imply that they must understand infinity per se, and it should be sufficient for them to realize that that any pair of numbers can be assigned to x and y, provided the first is 5 times the second.

Given that an elementary understanding of algebraic relations can be

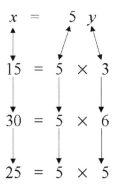

FIG. 3.7.   Structural correspondence between arithmetic examples and algebraic expression.

acquired by analogy with arithmetic relations, we can apply analogy theory to the problem. One point that emerges immediately is that the arithmetic relation is the source and the algebraic relation is the target. It follows that for the analogy to be effective, the arithmetic relation must be well learned. This is simply an application of the principle of source specificity, discussed in chapter 2. The important point that emerges from analogy theory is that learning algebra will depend crucially on how well arithmetic relations are learned, because arithmetic relations are the source for starting to understand algebraic relations (Booth, 1989a). Therefore more attention needs to be paid to ensuring that children understand arithmetic relations, as opposed to rote learning of arithmetic procedures. Understanding arithmetic relations has two major benefits. It gives children a rationale for the arithmetic procedures that they learn in their elementary years, and provides a basis for the more abstract understanding that is required in algebra. We elaborate on these points in chapter 7.

More complex relations that are important to algebra include commutativity, associativity, and distributivity, all of which were discussed earlier in the context of arithmetic. These complex relations can be acquired using an arithmetic analog (Halford, 1993; Halford & Boulton-Lewis, 1992). We refer the reader to Halford (1993, chapter 8) for an analysis of how arithmetic relations can provide a base for understanding these complex algebraic relations, using the distributive law as an example.

Understanding algebra does not end with arithmetic analogs. One reason is that, as discussed in chapter 7, there are some inconsistencies between arithmetic and algebra. One of the most important differences is that in arithmetic the answer to a problem is a specific constant, whereas in algebra the answer is itself a relation. The solution to an equation is usually a relation between one variable, on the left hand side, and an expression containing one or more constants and other variables on the right hand side.

Although differences between algebra and arithmetic are clearly important, it does not follow that arithmetic cannot be a useful analog for algebra. There are also important differences between sets and numbers, yet sets are a useful analog for understanding elementary number relations and operations. The value of analogies is partly that they transcend domains that may be very different apart from the relations they have in common. However, the most important thing about analogies in this context is that they are an excellent way of learning about relations, and they are a means by which relations that are learned in arithmetic can be transferred to algebra. The better this is done the more readily children can progress to more abstract understanding of algebra.

Another reason why understanding algebra does not remain tied to arithmetic analogs is that elementary algebraic relations can serve as mental models for more advanced relations. In this case an elementary relation serves as a source and the more advanced relation as the target. In other instances, an elementary relation in a conventional form can serve as the source for a more sophisticated form of the same relation. Both these uses of algebraic analogs will be illustrated later in this chapter, and in other chapters of this book.

Having learned to understand relations between variables using arithmetic examples as analogs, children can then progress to other mental models. For example, an effective way to represent the relation between two variables is by drawing a graph on cartesian coordinates. The expression $x = 5y$ can be represented easily as a straight line on x and y coordinates. Children can learn to do this by first calculating values of y for each of several values of x, then plotting the points obtained on the coordinates. Once this is done the type of curve that results can be inspected. It can be compared with the curve obtained for other equations, such as $x = y$, $x = 2y, \ldots, x = 10y, \ldots, x = 5y + 3$, and so on. From this, the concept of a linear function can be induced, together with concepts such as slope and intercept. From there the child can progress to finding curves for equations such as $x = 3y^2 + 4$, and can recognize curvilinear functions. These can be subsequently differentiated into quadratic, cubic, and so on. Graphs show the infinite range of possible ordered pairs, mentioned earlier. They also provide an image of the way one variable behaves with respect to another, and thereby enhance the mental model of this relation.

Notice two things about this process, however. The first is that it depends initially on the use of arithmetic, not only to plot the curves, but also to make them meaningful. The linear function $x = 5y$ is only meaningful if one has a mental model of cases where one number is 5 times another number. In essence, such a function is ultimately made meaningful by reference to number relations. Second, mental models in the form of functions plotted on coordinates are analogs. This illustrates the point that analogy plays a very important role in the thinking of even sophisticated mathematicians. However it needs to be noted that graphical analogs do present a number of difficulties for children and hence careful guidance in their construction and application is needed (C. Kieran & Chalouh, 1993).

The significance of analogy in mathematical thought was well recognized by Polya (1954), and its use in mathematical problem solving appears to be ubiquitous. Consider the following two expressions:

$$fg = c$$
$$j(N + x) = s$$

If we substitute g for $(N + x)$, the expressions are essentially the same. The fact that different symbols are used is irrelevant. This correspondence is due to common relations in the two expressions; specifically, one variable is expressed as the product of two others. Therefore recognition of the correspondence between the expressions is essentially the same kind of process as

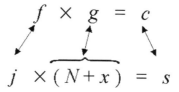

FIG. 3.8.   Structural correspondence between two algebraic expressions.

is involved in analogical reasoning. It can be represented as a structure mapping, as shown in Fig. 3.8. So recognition of common relations in different expressions is really a form of analogical reasoning.

This process is commonly used when deciding how to solve a problem, such as factoring the expression;

$$x^2 + pMx \pm p^2N \tag{1}$$

Mathematicians would recognize this as a case of the equation;

$$x^2 + Mx \pm N \tag{2}$$

These are both quadratics, having linear factors with integer coefficients ("factoring twins;" Minor, 1988).

Recognition of Equation 1 as a case of Equation 2 is really a form of analogy, in which Equation 2 is the source and Equation 1 is the target. Once recognized, it is clear what procedure to adopt. Mathematicians normally have "reference examples" for particular types of expressions, and each reference example is associated with a known procedure. Knowledge of these reference examples, and the procedures associated with them, is a significnant component of expertise. Each reference example might be thought of as a mental model for a particular concept, or class of expressions, and the use of reference examples in this way is essentially a case of analogical reasoning.

Higher order relations are also important in understanding algebra. This can be illustrated even with very simple expressions, such as $a + b = 10$. This equation constrains a and b so that, as one increases, the other decreases. This can be expressed as: OPPOSITE(change-a,change-b). OPPOSITE is a second-order relation, because its arguments, change-a and change-b are relations.

Generalized arithmetic is not the same as algebra of course, and the use of arithmetic analogs to make algebraic relations meaningful does not imply that this distinction is not important. The equation $a + b = 10$ might be thought of by some children in terms of one or more pairs of numbers, as discussed in chapter 7. Children might think the solution is $a = 4$ and $b = 6$. This misses the point that the equation holds for any pair of numbers, and therefore expresses the higher order relation mentioned in the previous paragraph. Such simplistic understanding is in no way a result of using content-specific mental models as an analog for the relation. Recall that sophisticated use of mental models entails looking for alternative models. The expression $4 + 6 = 10$ is a legitimate instantiation of $a + b = 10$, but so is $1 + 9 = 10, .., 7 + 3 = 10, .., 3.1416 + 6.8584 = 10, .., (-18) + 28 = 10$, and so on. Children should be encouraged to find alternate mental models, and then to induce the relation that is common to each of the instantiations generated.

Bad analogs are also possible of course. One example is where children solve $3x + 4$ as $7x$. This is by an inappropriate analogy with arithmetic, as discussed in chapter 7. The inappropriate analog is shown in Fig. 3.9A. The

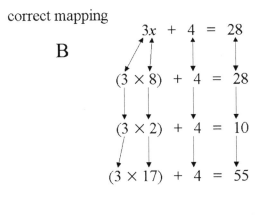

FIG. 3.9. Structural correspondence between algebraic expression and arithmetic instantiations: (A) incorrect mapping, (B) correct mapping, (C) analog to show why mapping in A is incorrect.

expression $3x + 4$ is mapped into $3 + 4$, treating it as an ordinary arithmetic sum, ignoring the variable x, which is then concatenated to the 7. The way this is done suggests the expression $3x$ is interpreted as a concatenation of 3 and x ignoring the meaning of the product. The true meaning of the expression can be shown by an appropriate arithmetic analogy, or set of analogies, in Fig. 3.9B. These analogs make it clear that $3x$ refers to the product of 3 and x. The analog in Fig. 3.9C makes it clear why the equation $3x + 4 = 7x$ represents an inappropriate interpretation of the expression. It is analogous to adding the product of 3 and 8 to 4 and obtaining 7×8, or 56, which children who are familiar with arithmetic relations should readily recognize as incorrect. Thus analogs, if well used, can actually make it easier to understand why certain procedures are incorrect.

Are Analogs and Mental Models Desirable?

This chapter so far has included a few cases where we show that analogs can assist children in acquiring understanding of mathematical relations. Two caveats are appropriate, however. The first is that the structure mapping diagrams that are used to represent the analogies are not intended as pedagogical tools. They are part of the theory of analogies, and it would be a misconception to think that use of analogy in mathematics education requires children to master analogy theory. The strength of analogs as pedagogical tools is that analogical reasoning is something that both children and adults do naturally, provided certain provisos, such as familiarity with the source, avoidance of excessive processing load, and so on, are met. Our concern has been to specify these provisos. The use of analogy does not mean that children need to master analogy theory, any more than they need to master set theory or education theory. Structure mapping diagrams are used in this book as a convenient shorthand way of representing the correspondences that children must recognize between different sets of relations. However, the child does not need to draw structure mapping diagrams, and having them do so may even be counter-productive, because it could distract them from important relations between numbers.

The second caveat is that analogs should be used to promote understanding, or acquisition of mental models of relations, rather than as aids in calculation. The diagram in Fig. 3.3, for example, indicates that the relation $3 + 2 = 5$ can be understood using set union as an analog. The purpose of the analog is to give meaning to the addition operation, especially early in acquisition. It does not imply that children should construct set analogs for every addition they perform thereafter. Understanding can be enhanced with suitable, appropriately used analogs, and it makes acquisition of number competence more efficient. It is still necessary, however, to learn the appropriate relations; the child must eventually learn that $3 + 2 = 5$, and so on. Thus analogs are an aid to understanding, which promotes more efficient acquisition, transfer, and utilization of knowledge. Analogs are not a panacea. They can aid acquisition of mathematical knowledge, but they are not a substitute for mathematical knowledge.

It might be argued that concrete analogs are restrictive because they lock children into concrete concepts of number and prevent them from understanding abstractions. Actually such fears are misplaced, and analogies, if well chosen and well used, are likely to have precisely the opposite effect. The reason is that if they assist children in recognizing number relations, they will actually make it easier to acquire abstract meanings. As we have seen, and show in more detail later, learning algebra depends largely on understanding number relations. If appropriately used analogs promote understanding of number relations, they will make it easier to acquire algebra. Thus there is a paradox in that appropriate concrete experiences may actually promote long-term acquisition of abstractions. The most important thing is for children to acquire an adequate understanding of number relations. This has often been neglected, because we tend to test for mastery of mathematical procedures and do not test whether children understand mathematical relations.

DEVELOPMENT OF PROCEDURES

One benefit of understanding is that it can guide the development of appropriate strategies and procedures, and we will now consider how this can occur for some elementary mathematical tasks. Not all procedures are learned with understanding of course, because it is possible, as discussed in chapter 2, to acquire skills such as car driving with very little understanding of the process. In mathematics strategies can also be selected on the basis of their past record of success or failure in a particular context, without resort to the cognitively demanding process of understanding the relevant concepts. The associative strategy selection models of Siegler and his colleagues (Siegler & Shipley, in press) have demonstrated the effectiveness and applicability of this process, as discussed in chapter 2 and elsewhere in this book. The TRIMM model (Halford et al., 1995) of strategy development in transitive inference blends metacognitive and associative strategy development mechanisms. Associative mechanisms are the first resort because of their low demand, and metacognitive mechanisms are resorted to only when no existing strategy is sufficient for the current situation.

This model will be taken as the basis for our treatment of mathematical procedures in this section. A procedure that has been used successfully in the past will tend to have high strength and will therefore be applied where the appropriate conditions apply. When a set of conditions occurs for which no strategy exists, or where none of the existing strategies has a strength above threshold, then understanding will be used to develop a new strategy. Strategies will almost never be built "from the ground up," and new strategies will either be modifications of old ones, or will be composed of components of previously used strategies. The appropriateness of the strategies that are developed will depend on degree of understanding. Where understanding is adequate, strategies will tend be effective, but where understanding is inadequate, "malrules" and error-prone strategies will result.

Understanding of concepts influences both the selection of procedures and the monitoring of performances. Children can only select an appropriate procedure if they have an adequate mental model of the relevant concept. Such a mental model also provides a yardstick for performance. A person cannot know whether her performance is adequate unless she has a mental model of the concept that underlies the task. We illustrate these processes with the mathematical concepts of counting, arithmetic operations, algebraic manipulations, and operations on fractions.

The essence of strategy development based on a mental model is shown in Fig. 3.10. First, the current situation is interpreted (*coded* is the conventional term in cognitive psychology). Then a search is made for a procedure that is applicable to the situation. In the TRIMM model of Halford et al. (1995), this entails finding a condition-action (production) rule with a condition side that matches the current situation. If a procedure is found, it is applied. Suppose, for example, the current situation was that the following problem had just been presented:

$$236$$
$$\underline{+194}$$

To an educated person, this is immediately recognizeable as an addition problem, and a conventional addition algorithm would be applied. Because a procedure with high strength (or confidence rating) is available, recourse to a mental model of addition is unnecessary, and the decision to apply the addition algorithm would be relatively automatic.

After the procedure has been applied, the result can be checked. This can take a number of forms. These include obtaining external feedback, such as asking someone else to check the answer, checking it with a calculator, or using estimating skills to see that it is reasonable. Following feedback, either external or internal, strength of (or confidence in) the procedure is increased if the procedure was successful and decreased if it was not.

If no procedure with strength (confidence) above threshold matches the current situation, then a procedure must be developed. This is where the person's understanding of the situation is invoked. The first step is to search for a mental model of the task. The relations in this mental model are then matched to the current situation, the criterion of a good match being consistency (Halford, 1993; Halford et al., 1994). This will be illustrated in

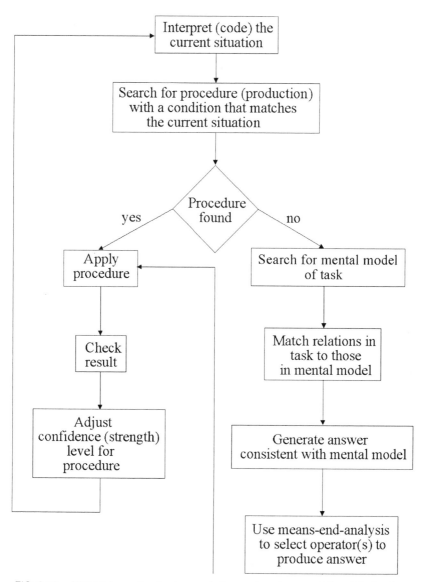

FIG. 3.10.   Basic schema for development of procedure from mental model of task.

more detail in the following sections. This application of the mental model to the current situation can be used to generate an expected answer to the problem. This is equivalent to a specification or guideline for the appropriate answer, and provides a goal for the problem-solving activity that is to follow.

The next step is to find a procedure that will generate an appropriate answer. One way of doing this for a novel problem is means–end analysis, which proceeds as follows:

1. Assess the difference between the current state and the goal.
2. Search for an operator or action to remove this difference.
3. If no operator can be found, set a subgoal, then return to (1).

Means–end analysis will result in a procedure, involving one or more steps, each guided by a goal or subgoal, for performing the task in a way that is consistent with the mental model. Once this procedure is devised, it is applied, the result is checked, and strength is adjusted. Thus procedures that are developed under the guidance of a mental model are subject to checks on their adequacy after they are applied. Procedures that yield inadequate performance are weakened and will eventually cease to be used. Practice with successful procedures strengthens the associations involved in their performance and makes them faster and less effortful. Thus the initial appearance of procedures can be heavily influenced by mental models, but both the survival and the long-term efficiency of procedures depends on associative processes.

This generalized account of procedure development, and the specific examples of it to be considered in the following sections, do not constitute formal models. On the other hand they do provide a set of principles that can be incorporated into formal models. TRIMM is a formal model that works according to these principles, and provides an "existence proof" of their validity, because it demonstrates that a model which works this way can develop effective strategies, the output of which matches human data.

This model makes it clear that although understanding can guide the development of procedures, it is not a panacea. Understanding confers definite benefits, in that it enables children both to generate and to generalize appropriate procedures, but mastery requires practice of these procedures. There is no cognitive "magic" that produces appropriate performance automatically. Good mental models can make learning both more enjoyable and more efficient, greatly reduce learning effort, facilitate seeing relations between concepts, and promote abstract reasoning, but our performance also has an associative component, which brings efficiency through practice. With this caveat in mind, we will consider how this conception of strategy development can be applied to selected mathematical tasks.

Counting

The principles of counting were defined by Gelman and Gallistel (1978) as follows:

1. One-to-one: There is one and only one number tag for each object.
2. Stable order: The number tags are used in a fixed order (1,2,3, . . , etc.).
3. Cardinal number: The last number tag used is the cardinal value of the set.
4. Abstraction: Attributes of objects other than their set membership are irrelevant.
5. Order irrelevance: The count is the same irrespective of the order in which objects are counted.

These are essentially formal specifications for counting, and Gelman and Gallistel suggested young children would know them implicitly rather than explicitly. However these principles can be instantiated in a mental model as shown in Fig. 3.11A. This is based on the accumulator model of counting,

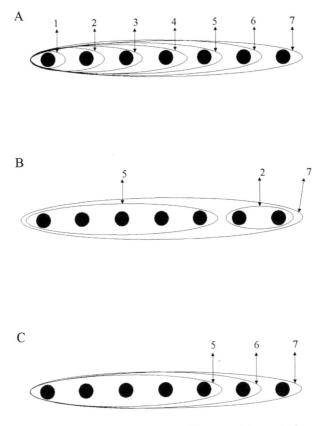

FIG. 3.11.   Mental models based on sets: (A) accumulator model for counting, (B) model of elementary addition, (C) for counting-on.

adapted from some ideas by Wynn (1992b), which is discussed in more detail in the next chapter. The mental model expresses the following ideas:

1. Each counting number is mapped to a set.
2. The numbers occur in a fixed sequence.
3. The sets to which the numbers are mapped increase in magnitude by one element with each successive number.
4. Each set is included in the next larger set.
5. Counting continues until all objects are assigned to a counted set.

The abstraction principle of counting is taken into account by the fact that the mental model is a mapping between two structures each of which is defined by a set of relations. As with other analogical mappings, the attributes of the elements in each structure have no necessary influence, the mappings being based on common relations. This mental model captures the counting principles defined by Gelman and Gallistel, but represents them in a more psychologically realistic way. G+G account for actually seen errors

Now let us consider how this mental model can guide a child in counting a set of objects. The child wants to find out how many objects there are in a set. The child knows the sequence of number names through frequent repetition, perhaps guided by siblings and parents. The child also knows that each number stands for a set. As each number is spoken, it is assigned to a set of objects. It is important that it is assigned to a set of objects, not to an individual object. This is the main way in which the model differs from one of the major alternatives, as we will see. The set to which the number is assigned corresponds to the set that has been counted. When the last object is counted, all objects have been assigned to this set, and the last number mentioned is mapped to this set of counted objects. Note that this is a natural consequence of the fact that numbers are assigned to sets, not to objects, and the set corresponding to each number includes the sets corresponding to all earlier numbers (see Fig. 3.11A). It is a direct, and critically important, consequence of this model that the last number represents the set of all objects that have been counted, and therefore represents the cardinal value of the set.

Notice how the principles of counting are incorporated in a content-specific mental model, as shown in Fig. 3.11A. Counting procedures that are consistent with these principles are generated by mapping them to the mental model. This mapping is based on the uniqueness and correspondence principles (Halford, 1993) defined in chapter 2. In the current counting example, this means that each number is assigned to one and only one set, and relations between numbers correspond to relations between sets. Notice that the principles of counting actually overlap to a considerable extent with the principles of analogy. This is no surprise because analogies are formally similar to representations (Halford, 1993; Holland et al., 1986), and counting, like other kinds of measurement, is really a form of representation (Coombs, Dawes, & Tversky, 1970; Halford & Wilson, 1980; Suppes, 1965).

Now let us contrast the effects of this mental model with the successor or standard counting model shown in Fig. 3.12.

The essential difference is that in the successor model, numbers are assigned to objects rather than to sets, and the relation between successive objects is simply "next." The successor mental model therefore does not capture properties 1, 3, 4 or 5 of the accumulator model in Fig. 3.11A. Given that, according to the successor mental model, a child is assigning numbers to objects, it would hardly be surprising if the child did not recognize that the last number represents the cardinal value of the set. In the successor mental model, numbers only represent sets of one!

However, we considered evidence earlier that young children and even nonhuman animals can enumerate small sets. It therefore seems likely that young children do recognize that the first few numbers represent sets, when taken individually. For example, if shown a set of two elements they can recognize that it is 2, without counting. Therefore they can apply one number to each set, for the smallest sets. What they cannot do is recognize the relations between sets of different numbers of members, and map these relations to the relations between numbers. Their quantification skills are fragmented, and amount to assigning each number to a single set. They do not have a quantification system, except for very small numbers.

When these primitive quantification skills are combined with the successor mental model in Fig. 3.12, conflict would be expected. With primitive quantification, numbers are assigned to sets, but with the successor mental model, they are assigned to objects. The result that can be predicted from this would be some confusion as to what numbers do represent. This could

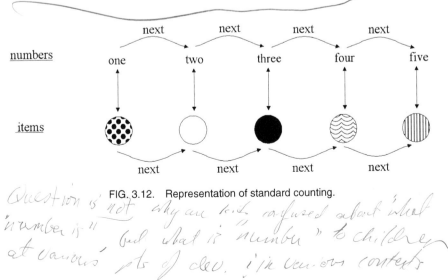

FIG. 3.12.   Representation of standard counting.

Question is not why are kids confused about what "number is", but what is "number" to children at various pts of dev. in various contexts

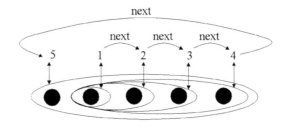

FIG. 3.13.   Accumulator mental model of counting, applied to nonstandard count.

explain the paradox that, on the one hand, even very young children know numbers represent sets within the subitizing range, yet they apparently do not know that, when counting, the last number represents the cardinal value of the set.

Now let us consider how the mental model in Fig. 3.11A can guide an unusual count. This is shown in Fig. 3.13 for one of the cases used by Gelman and Gallistel (1978), that in which counting begins with the second object in a row. The number 1 is assigned to the set containing that object, the number 2 to the set containing that object and the next . . . and the number 4 to the set containing the fifth object in the row. The child then turns to the first object, which is included in a set with the other four. Thus the accumulator model is consistent with, and can guide the development of, both conventional and unconventional correct counting procedures.

Arithmetic Operations

More than one strategy is normally available for arithmetic operations, as we have indicated with reference to Siegler's associative model of strategy selection (Siegler & Campbell, 1990; Siegler & Jenkins, 1989; Siegler & Shipley, in press). Siegler et al. have shown that, where children cannot perform (say) an addition example by fact retrieval, they resort to a series of backup strategies. One of these is the *sum* strategy, and entails counting through both sets. The *min* strategy is more advanced, and amounts to counting the smaller of the addends. For example, given 5 + 2 = ?, the sum strategy amounts to counting through both 5 and 2, whereas the min strategy amounts to counting on from 5, that is, "5, 6, 7."

The ASC-EM (pronounced "ask 'em") model of strategy selection (Siegler & Shipley, in press) provides a very good fit to the data on such problems, but the question remains as to how children recognize, usually around the first grade, that the min strategy is optimal. We will consider how the mental models of addition, shown in Fig. 3.3, and the accumulator model of counting shown in Fig. 3.11A, might guide a child to recognize the value of the min strategy.

Models of a models for ?

From the mental model of addition in Fig. 3.3, a child can recognize that addition entails combining a number representing one addend set with a number representing another (disjoint) addend set, and then finding a number to represent the sum set (union of the disjoint addend sets). A similar mental model is shown in Fig. 3.11B for comparison. The accumulator model of counting, in Fig. 3.11A, includes recognition that counting assigns a number to a set. In combination, these imply that counting is a way of assigning numbers to the addend sets and to the sum set. A composite mental model that makes this clear is shown in Fig. 3.11C.

It is a simple inference that the sum set can be quantified by simply counting it. It is more complicated to recognize that one of the addends does not need to be counted, because a number is already assigned to it. However this inference is possible from the mental model for addition, because as Fig. 3.3 and Fig. 3.11B make clear, a number is already assigned to each addend set. The essential insight is that this number can substitute for the number obtained by counting one of the addend sets, as shown in Fig. 3.11C.

However the min strategy requires recognition that only the smaller addend set should be counted. It seems reasonable to assume that children learn from experience that it takes longer, and requires more effort, to count a larger set. We could call this meta-counting knowledge. It is well established that set sizes can be estimated approximately without counting (Payne & Huinker, 1993). Together these items of information should enable a child to recognize that counting the smaller set will require less effort. Combined with the information from the mental model discussed above, this should be sufficient to guide the child to adopt counting of the smaller addend set in order to quantify the sum set.

This argument is designed to provide a psychologically plausible account of the way understanding of addition and of counting can guide the child to adopt the min strategy. We have not provided a computational model of this strategy development, but it is consistent with the principles embodied in the computational model of Halford et al. (1995), discussed earlier. A computational model that worked in accord with these principles should be capable of developing the min strategy.

Fractions

Arithmetic operations on fractions have proved difficult for children, and we consider how mental models can guide children to appropriate procedures in this domain. We only present general principles here and expand on these in chapter 5. We consider the problem of how a child recognizes that $\frac{1}{4} + \frac{1}{8} = \frac{3}{8}$.

An effective mental model for fractions may be derived from the area construct, as discussed in detail in chapters 4 and 5. The fraction, $\frac{1}{4}$, is

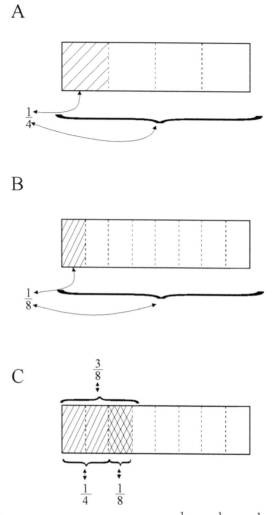

FIG. 3.14.   Area model for fractions, (A) $\frac{1}{4}$, (B) $\frac{1}{8}$, (C) $\frac{1}{4} + \frac{1}{8}$.

represented in Fig. 3.14A by a rectangular area, divided into four equal parts. The numerator, 1, is mapped to one of the parts, and the denominator, 4, is mapped to the whole area, that is, to the four parts.

A similar representation is shown for $\frac{1}{8}$ in Fig. 3.14B. Here the area model is divided into eight equal parts, the numerator is again mapped to one part, and the denominator to all eight parts, as before. The representation for the addition of these fractions is shown in Fig. 3.14C. We have an area model divided into eight equal parts. The fraction $\frac{1}{4}$ is mapped to two of those parts. Similarly, the fraction $\frac{1}{8}$ is mapped to one of these parts. The sum of the parts, represented by the three parts together, is mapped to the fraction $\frac{3}{8}$. This representation is eventually formalized as follows:

$$
\begin{array}{c}
\frac{1}{4} \\
+\ \frac{1}{8} \\
\hline
\end{array}
\quad \rightarrow \quad
\begin{array}{c}
\frac{2}{8} \\
+\ \frac{1}{8} \\
\hline
\frac{3}{8}
\end{array}
$$

(not usually written this way, often this way)

Of course, children will need guidance in acquiring a meaningful mental model of this formalized procedure that includes an understanding of equivalent fractions, as we discuss in chapter 5. The point we wish to make here is that understanding influences both selection of procedures and monitoring of performances. The child's mental model of the addition procedure, derived from the area representation, can help her see how the formal procedure yields an appropriate answer and can also serve as a checking device. The mental model thus plays a useful monitoring role.

A further point we wish to emphasize is that learning with understanding is not synonymous with discovery learning. Learning is partly a matter of constructing mental models and linking these mental models to procedures, as we have illustrated in this section. However this construction process needs guidance, and that guidance needs to be skillful. Therefore, we see again that understanding is not a panacea. Just as understanding does not remove the need for associative learning, it does not remove the need for skilled guidance. Promoting understanding is an important part, but only a part, of good pedagogy. It certainly can promote the child's own discoveries, but it does not make pedagogical guidance unnecessary. This example illustrates that learning with understanding is guided discovery.

Algebra

Mental models can influence algebraic procedures by analogical mapping. We saw earlier in this chapter how arithmetic relations can provide mental models for early understanding of algebraic relations, but elementary algebraic relations can also provide mental models for understanding of more advanced algebraic relations. This is illustrated in Fig. 3.15 for a number of instances of the distributive law.

We assume a child has reached the point where the distributive law is understood in some conventional form, such as $a(b + c) = ab + ac$. We also assume, for the present example, that this form of the distributive law is well enough understood to serve as a mental model, and to be used as a source in analogical mappings of the type shown in Fig. 3.15. Recognition that $3(x^2 - 2) = 3x^2 - (3 \times 2) = 3x^2 - 6$ can be obtained by seeing

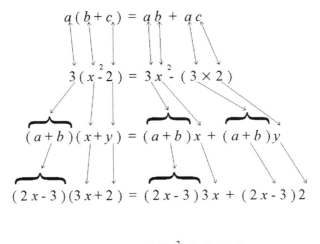

FIG. 3.15.   Structural correspondence between prototypical distributive law and some algebraic examples.

the correspondence with the distributive law, $a(b + c) = ab + ac$. This is shown as a structure mapping in Fig. 3.15. Recognition of this correspondence is a form of analogical reasoning, because it is a mapping of one representation into another on the basis of structural correspondence. Recognition of this structural correspondence necessitates a coding that is sophisticated enough to realize that addition in the expression $a(b + c)$ corresponds to subtraction in the expression $3(x^2-2)$. This in turn requires recognition that multiplication and division have corresponding roles (being different ways of accessing the same mathematical operation), as also do addition and subtraction.

Although it might not seem a good example of analogy as the term is understood in everyday usage, it is perfectly appropriate to treat it as analogy, for two reasons. First, it conforms fully to the definition of analogy given in chapter 2, as a structure-preserving map between source and target representations. Second, it has long been recognized that algebraic reasoning entails analogies in this way (Polya, 1954).

The expression $3x^2 - 6$ can be factored by recognizing its correspondence to the conventional form of the distributive law, provided the factoring relation has also been learned, as discussed earlier. It then becomes possible to see that $3x^2 - 6 = 3(x^2 - 2)$.

The expression $(a + b)(x + y)$ can also be mapped into $a(b + c)$, as shown into Fig. 3.15. This makes it possible to see that $(a + b)(x + y) = (a + b)x + (a + b)y$. The reverse of this relation amounts to recognition of factoring $(a + b)x + (a + b)y$ to yield $(a + b)(x + y)$. This can be further processed by $(a + b)x = x(a + b) = xa + xb$, and so on. The expression $(2x - 3)(3x + 2)$ can be processed in a similar way. The expression $(2x - 3)$ maps to the a term in $a(b + c)$, whereas $3x$ and 2 map to the b and c terms respectively, as shown in Fig. 3.15.

These examples illustrate the point that mapping algebraic expressions into mental models of known algebraic relations can guide the adoption of appropriate procedures. These examples illustrate how appropriate mental models enable recognition that, for example, factoring is a possibility in certain expressions. This is a specific case of the more general point that appropriate mental models can guide the adoption of effective procedures in a wide variety of mathematical tasks.

COMPLEXITY OF MATHEMATICAL CONCEPTS

Mathematics is often regarded as a difficult subject, and much of this book is devoted to ways of reducing this difficulty. However to do this effectively, we must ourselves understand the underlying causes of the difficulty. In this section we explore the role of complexity as a factor in mathematical difficulty. It turns out that the reason why some concepts are difficult is that they are inherently complex concepts. This can only be recognized, however, if a valid means of assessing complexity is available. It is important therefore to analyze the nature of this complexity, which in turn can help us to find ways of dealing with it.

Complexity is defined by the number of related components, as explained in chapter 2. This corresponds to the number of arguments of a relation, which in turn corresponds to the number of dimensions in the space on which the relation is defined. Recall also from chapter 2 that a unary relation is defined on one dimension, a binary relation on two dimensions, a ternary relation on three dimensions, and so on. Our purpose here will be to define the relational complexity of basic mathematical concepts.

Unary relations include such mathematical concepts as the *cardinal value* of a set. Cardinal value is an assignment of a constant to the variable *cardinal value*. For example, the cardinal value of the set of fingers on a typical human can be defined as: CARDINAL–VALUE–FINGERS(10). The cardinal value of a set may also be thought of as a mapping from the set to a number, and corresponds to an element mapping. As noted in chapter 2, there is evidence that unary relations can be explicitly represented at approximately one year. It follows that children should be capable in principle of explicitly representing the cardinal value of sets at 1 year.

Binary relations relate two objects and include everyday examples such as larger-than, "uncle-of," and so on. Important mathematical concepts that are binary relations are:

Size-relation between numbers. The fact that $4 > 3$, $4 > 2$, $3 > 2$, and so on, are all instances of the binary relation, larger-than. *Succession* is also a binary relation; 2 succeeds 1, 3 succeeds 2, and so on.

Unary operators are also binary relations (Halford & Wilson, 1980). These include *change sign*, which may be defined as CHANGE-SIGN(x.-x). The change sign operator relates two things, one a positive number and one a negative number, and is thus a binary relation. Note that, in general, operators and transformations are relations. Technically, they are simply a way of interpreting relations. Increase and decrease are also unary operators. Increase has two arguments, a number and a larger number; INCREASE(number,larger-number). Similarly decrease may be defined as DECREASE(number,smaller-number).

In simple successor counting models, the size relation between numbers and the size relation between sets amounts to a correspondence between binary relations (see Fig. 3.1). It is a relational mapping, as defined in chapter 2. The correspondence between the succession relation between numbers and the size-relation between sets differing in magnitude by one element is also a relational mapping. The accumulator model of counting entails ternary relations however, as we will see.

Ternary relations relate three objects, and include the concept of middle, and the concept of love-triangle.

The binary operations of arithmetical addition and multiplication are both ternary relations. Addition is the set of ordered triples such that the third element is the sum of the first two. Arithmetic addition may be defined as the set of ordered triples; $\{(1,2,3), \ldots, (2,7,9), \ldots, (8,7,15), \ldots\}$. It can also be defined as the ternary relation +(a,b,c) where the c is the sum of a and b.

Notice that addition is not the same as increase, because the latter has only two arguments, corresponding to the initial and final number. Addition has three arguments, which correspond to the two addends and the sum. For comparison with increase, we can think of addition as having the arguments of initial number, increase, and final number.

Multiplication may be defined as the ternary relation $x(a,b,c)$ where c is the product of a and b. *Part/whole* is also a ternary relation, and has a minimum of three arguments, the whole, a part, and a complementary part.

The higher order relation, same-relation($(a>b)(b>c)$) requires a set of (at least) three elements. Thus the higher order relation between two binary relations requires a ternary relation to be represented.

Counting by the accumulator model (see Fig. 3.11A) entails a ternary relation, because it depends on inclusion. The properties of the mental model discussed earlier show that counting entails assigning a number to a set that (apart from the first set) includes the sets to which previous numbers are assigned. Thus 5 is assigned to a set that includes the set of 4, plus the additional element assigned to the 5 set (See Fig. 3.11A).

It follows that counting by the accumulator model is more complex than counting by the successor model, because the latter entails only binary relations, whereas the accumulator model entails ternary relations. This means the dimensionality of the accumulator counting model is higher, and processing loads in reasoning about the counting process will therefore be higher. The accumulator model nevertheless entails significant benefits however, as noted earlier.

Quaternary relations have four arguments and relate four objects. Perhaps the most important mathematical concept that belongs to this level is *proportion*, which may be defined as $\frac{a}{b} = \frac{c}{d}$. Here we have four sources of variations, or four dimensions, *a,b,c,d*. To get some feel for the complexity this entails, consider the following expressions:

$$\frac{1}{2} = \frac{3}{6} \tag{3}$$

$$\frac{1}{2} < \frac{4}{6} \tag{4}$$

$$\frac{1}{3} < \frac{3}{6} \tag{5}$$

$$\frac{5}{7} > \frac{5}{8} \tag{6}$$

These examples illustrate the point that to determine the relation between two rational numbers, both numerators and both denominators must be considered. Comparing (3) and (4), we note that increasing the numerator of the second fraction destroys the equality, and we no longer have a proportion. The same effect is achieved by increasing the denominator in (5). Then in (6) equality is destroyed by increasing the denominator of the second fraction (or reducing the denominator of the first fraction). These examples are sufficient to illustrate the point that dealing with relations between fractions can entail considering all four numbers. This means four sources of variation, or four dimensions must be related to one another.

Research in processing capacity, outlined briefly in chapter 2, shows that relating four dimensions imposes a very high processing load, and may be at the limit of processing capacity even for adults. This is the fundamental reason why proportion, and any other tasks that entail reasoning about relations between fractions, will be difficult. As we noted earlier, relations between fractions are entailed in operations on fractions, such as addition and multiplication. Small wonder then that these are major sources of difficulty in children's mathematics. We will consider the implications of this in the next section.

Implications of Complexity and Capacity

It might be argued that fractions are not necessarily complex because children can be taught fractions easily in familiar or interesting contexts. For example, even very young children have no difficulty understanding what half a pie means. However this argument is based on a misconception about the reason for capacity limitations. Because it is a common misconception, we consider it in some detail.

Capacity theory does not deny the importance of knowledge, nor does it fail to recognize that children, like adults and other animals, generally tend to perform better in familiar or interesting contexts. Furthermore, capacity theory does not say that young children cannot understand anything about fractions. If the previous argument was followed carefully it will be clear that difficulties will be encountered only where children have to think in a high dimensional space. Those tasks that require children to relate four dimensions, as when they must relate two numerators and two denominators, will impose high processing loads, for both children and adults. The loads will tend to have more effect on children's performance, partly because their processing capacity is less, but also because they have less advanced techniques such as chunking and segmentation for circumventing the loads.

However, understanding half a pie does not entail four dimensions. Indeed, it is only necessary to consider two components, the pie and the half; this may be expressed as an ordered pair (part,whole). This concept is two dimensional, so demonstrating that it can be understood by young children has no theoretical implications at all. It certainly does not invalidate the proposition that young children have difficulty with four dimensional concepts. As the reader will recognize, it is irrelevant to that proposition.

There is an important general point that is illustrated in this example, namely, that dimensionality depends on what is being processed. Thus it is not correct to put simplistic labels on concepts, as occurs in statements such as "fractions are four dimensional." Only tasks that require all four variables a,b,c,d to be taken into account, as when numerators and denominators of both fractions must be considered to make comparisons, are four dimensional. Therefore correct application of relational complexity theory must take account of what is being processed and how. This sometimes requires sophisticated techniques to analyze the cognitive processes entailed. Such analyses should not be bypassed, because superficial judgments can be quite misleading.

Another common counterargument is that supposed limitations in children's understanding have often been overcome in the past, either by training or by child-appropriate testing. Cases that are often cited include work using the transitive inference paradigm of Bryant and Trabasso (1971), work on inclusion by McGarrigle, Grieve and Hughes (1978), or Markman and Seibert (1976), work on conservation by P. E. Bryant (1972), or McGarrigle and Donaldson (1975), and so on. The extensive literature on this topic has been considered elsewhere (Bryant, 1989; K. W. Fischer, 1987, Grieve & Garton, 1981; Halford, 1984, 1989, 1993; Halford & Boyle, 1985; Halford & Leitch, 1989; Kallio, 1982). We simply summarize the main points here.

Many of the claimed improvements have been found not to withstand careful scrutiny. For example, it has been common to claim chance or below chance performances as positive results, as has been pointed out elsewhere (Halford, 1989, 1993). In other cases it has been possible to show that the task could be performed by using an alternate simpler, concept, or that children were given undue help in performance. These cases have been considered elsewhere (Halford, 1989, 1993). In still other cases it has been shown that the gains apply only in very restricted conditions, and are not typical of performance at the relevant age (K. W. Fischer, 1987; Halford, 1993).

In some cases gains have been made. For example, McGarrigle and Donaldson (1975) showed that children performed better in conservation if the transformation appeared to be accidental. This effect was replicated by Halford and Boyle (1985) but the performance with 3- to 4-year-old children was still not better than chance. Above-chance performance on conservation seems to have been demonstrated mainly with children of 5 and over. This is in fact quite a typical finding: Improvements are found in children who are at or slightly above the transition age. It is usually overlooked that these improvements are marginal at best and do not remove the major age differences (Halford, 1989).

It would be a fair summary to say that precocious performance in relationally complex tasks has involved gains that are minimal, marginal, partial, and restricted. The important age differences have certainly not been removed. There is nothing wrong with trying to improve children's performance of course and it is always possible that genuine improvements may be achieved in the future. What is detrimental is to emphasize factors that have a dubious and marginal effect, to the exclusion of those that have a major impact. Relational complexity accounts for huge age differences, whereas most of the alternatives, even when validly demonstrated, tend to account for marginal differences.

Greater gains are to be made by recognizing the true causes of children's difficulties. We should not forget that children's difficulties are qualitatively the same as those of adults, even though children's capacity appears, on present evidence, to be less in a quantitative sense. It follows that children, like adults, can perform very well despite these limitations. Taking this into account gives us some very important insights into the way cognitive tasks are actually performed. That is the topic of the next section.

Reducing Processing Loads

It is possible to reduce processing loads of complex concepts by chunking and segmentation, as noted in chapter 2. Recall that conceptual chunking entails recoding high dimensional concepts into fewer dimensions. Segmentation entails using serial strategies to process a task a little at a time, so processing capacity is never overloaded at any one time.

In the example of the distributive law discussed earlier, $(a + b)(x + y) = (a + b)x + (a + b)y$, $(a + b)$ is treated as a chunk. It is treated as a single variable when it is considered as an example of the distributive law. While dimensions are chunked, relations within the chunk cannot be processed. Therefore, while $(a + b)$ is being treated as a chunk, the addition operation $(a + b)$ cannot be processed. However once the distributive law has been applied as above, the chunk $(a + b)$ can be unpacked, and then processing is possible. To do this, however, requires a serial processing strategy. That is, one operation must be processed first, then the second is unchunked and processed. In this way the number of relations processed in parallel never exceeds the capacity limit.

Adults have strategies for performing complex tasks in such a way that their capacity is not normally overloaded. Children also can learn chunking and serial processing strategies, but some caveats are necessary.

Chunking depends on knowing the structure of the material. It utilizes redundancies or other relations within the material, and it is therefore dependent on prior knowledge of the particular content. It is often difficult to find the appropriate basis for a chunk in new material. One reason why experts outperform novices is that they are much more adept at recognizing chunks. In the example we have just considered, a mathematician would immediately recognize that $(a + b)$ can be taken as a unit in an application of the distributive law. Children are less likely to recognize such a chunk. Enabling them to do this is one of the goals of mathematics education.

Another caveat is that the planning process is critically dependent on ability to represent the relevant relations. We saw in an earlier section how mental models, which include the crucial relations, can guide the development of appropriate procedures. The procedures entail serial processing, but planning the procedures requires the essential relations of the task to be represented in parallel. Where the child's representation of the task is inadequate, strategies will also be inadequate. They can of course be taught strategies without understanding, that is, without a mental model of the task relations, but they will be restricted to using such strategies in stereotyped formats.

On the other hand there is no reason why children cannot be taught partial concepts, or precursor concepts. For example, arithmetic addition and multiplication are ternary relations, and their complete understanding appears unlikely to be attainable before a median age of 5 years. We noted, however, that increase and decrease are unary operators, and are within the scope of children from a median age of 2 years. Similarly, although counting with the accumulator model is evidently a ternary relation, assigning number names to individual sets is a unary relation, and should be attainable from age 1. Again, although full understanding of proportion entails quaternary relations, there are some limited concepts of fractions that are reducible to ternary or even binary relations.

There is no reason why children should not be taught those concepts that are within their reach. It would be a complete misconstrual of the present theory to suggest that children should be taught nothing about, for example, counting until they are 5, or about fractions until they are 11. It is important however not to mistake partial knowledge for complete knowledge (a very common error in both developmental and educational psychology). For a child who knows what half a pie means has not mastered fractions, any more than a child who knows what one and two mean has mastered counting.

Finally, it is important to conduct accurate and valid assessments of conceptual complexity. Without this, many of the true causes of difficulty will not be understood, and therefore will not be truly overcome. At the present time this is very much a task for the specialist cognitive scientist, but the results of these analyses can be communicated to researchers and practitioners who are more directly concerned with developmental and educational psychology. This simply emphasizes the need for a team approach in mathematics education.

SUMMARY

The main points discussed in this chapter may be summarized as follows:

1. Initial understanding of number relations and operations can be acquired using sets of discrete items as analogs. This utilizes protoquantitative schemas such as compare, but also necessitates recognition of the correspondence between set relations and number relations.

2. Algebra entails relations between variables, which differ from constants in that their meanings cannot be defined by relations to sets, but must be defined by number system reference or expression reference. Algebra therefore depends on understanding of relations between numbers, which can be understood using arithmetic relations as analogs.

3. The accumulator mental model embodies the principles of counting, can guide development of counting procedures and, together with a mental model of addition, can guide acquisition of the min strategy. The area model can guide development of operations on fractions.

4. Development of procedures is guided by appropriate mental models, but associative processes are necessary for selective strengthening of successful procedures.

5. Cardinal value is a unary relation, whereas size relations, unary operators and increase-decrease schemas are binary relations. Binary operations, addition and multiplication, and part/whole, are ternary relations. Counting by the accumulator model also entails ternary relations. Proportion is a quaternary relation.

4

NUMERICAL MODELS AND PROCESSES

This chapter is concerned with how children acquire an understanding of number. Such understanding depends on the development of mental models that represent the relevant numerical relations. In the early stages, it is important that children experience concrete analogs of number such as sets of discrete items and can understand the relations between sets. Because these analogs provide an experiential base for understanding numerical concepts and processes, we begin this chapter with a review of some commonly used analogs. We propose a number of principles for learning through analogy and apply these to a critical analysis of these analogs. The remainder of the chapter concerns children's learning of early number concepts, the numeration of whole numbers, rational numbers, and negative integers.

MATHEMATICAL ANALOGS

Manipulative materials are a significant and powerful representational system in the learning of mathematics. They have little meaning per se, but feature inherent relationships and operations that can mirror mathematical concepts and procedures (Lesh, Post, & Behr, 1987). Pictorial and diagrammatic representations serve a similar function although they are usually more abstract. All of these materials serve basically in an analogical capacity (Halford, 1993; Halford & Boulton-Lewis, 1992). Recall that an analogy can be defined as a mapping from one structure, the base or source, to another, the target (Gentner, 1983). In the case of mathematical analogs, the concrete or pictorial representation is the source and the concept to be acquired is the

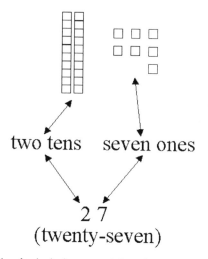

two tens   seven ones

2 7
(twenty-seven)

FIG. 4.1.   Analogical representation of a two-digit number.

target. The value of these analogs is that they can mirror the structure of the concept and thus enable the child to use the structure of the representation to construct a mental model of the concept. This is illustrated in Fig. 4.1 where base-ten blocks are used to illustrate the meaning of a two-digit numeral, *27*. Here, the two ten-blocks represent the digit *2* in the tens place of the numeral. This representation is shown by a mapping from the source, the two ten-blocks, to the target, the digit *2*. The seven single blocks represent the *7* in the ones place of the numeral (a mapping from the source, the set of seven blocks, to the target, the digit *7*). We address this form of representation in greater detail in the next section.

How Effective are Mathematical Analogs?

It is generally accepted that manipulative materials can facilitate learning in a number of ways (Dienes, 1960; Fuson, Fraivillig, & Burghardt, 1992; Grover, Hojnacki, Paulson, & Matern, 1994; Halford & Boulton-Lewis, 1992; Kennedy, 1986; McCoy, 1990; National Council of Teachers of Mathematics, 1989; Sowder, 1989; Sowell, 1989). They can help children understand the meaning of mathematical ideas and their applications, can increase flexibility of thinking, can be used generatively to predict unknown information, and can reduce children's anxiety towards mathematics.

There are a number of false assumptions however, regarding the use of concrete analogs. Firstly, analogs in and of themselves cannot impart meaning. Mathematical truths cannot be directly "seen" through the use of these materials; mathematical ideas do not actually reside within wooden and plastic models (Ball, 1992; Wearne & Hiebert, 1985). Secondly, we cannot automatically assume that children will make the appropriate mapping from the concrete representation to the abstract form, particularly when some of the materials themselves are abstract (Halford & Boulton-Lewis, 1992; Onslow, 1991). Associated with this last point, is the problem of the processing load entailed in mapping a concept into an analog (Halford, 1993; Halford, Maybery, & Bain, 1986; Maybery, Bain, & Halford, 1986). We will revisit this last issue in our assessment of mathematical analogs.

Despite their significance in the mathematics curriculum, there has been little open debate on the appropriate roles and uses of manipulative materials (Ball, 1992). Furthermore, as Thompson (1992, 1994) pointed out, the research findings on their effectiveness have been equivocal. Some studies (e.g., Labinowicz, 1985; Resnick & Omanson, 1987) found little impact of the base-ten blocks on children's facility with algorithms. Other studies (e.g., Wearne & Hiebert, 1988b; Fuson & Briars, 1990), reported a positive effect of these materials on children's understanding of, and skill with, decimal numeration and multidigit addition and subtraction. Still other studies (e.g., Gilbert & Bush, 1988) have indicated that concrete materials are not widely used, with their overall use decreasing as grade level and length of teaching experience increase.

Given these varied findings, we need to examine more closely the structure of the common analogs with a view to identifying why we sometimes get positive outcomes, and at other times, negative ones. However, this will only give us part of the story. We need to keep in mind two other significant factors, namely, the appropriateness of the accompanying "mapping language" and the "mapping procedures" used in manipulating the analogs. Irrespective of an analog's potential for representing a particular concept, it will fail miserably if the accompanying explanation is unclear and if the manner in which it is manipulated does not mirror the target concept or procedure. As noted by several researchers, children need clear rules on the use of manipulatives (Nesher, 1989), as well as assistance in building relationships between physical, pictorial, verbal, and symbolical representations (Ball, 1992; Bednarz & Janvier, 1982; Fuson & Briars, 1990; Hiebert & Wearne, 1992; Janvier, 1987; Lesh et al., 1987; Thompson, 1992). We return to these points in later discussion. We turn now to an analysis of the structural complexity of some of the more common analogs and assess their appropriateness for conveying significant mathematical ideas.

Assessing Mathematical Analogs

It is fairly obvious that the analogs we choose must make sense to children and must help them form a meaningful link between what they know (their concrete everyday world) and what they are to learn (the abstract world of mathematics). However, this is easier said than done. As Ball (1992) commented, adults can overestimate the value of concrete materials because they can more readily "see" the concepts being represented. This is not such an easy matter for children. Some manipulatives, as we later indicate, can be distracting, ambiguous, and open to misinterpretation. In addition, the use of multiple embodiments of the one concept can result in some children seeing as many different concepts as there are representations (Dufour-Janvier, Bednarz, & Belanger, 1987). Unfortunately, teachers are not given a great deal of assistance in selecting among alternative analogs and, furthermore, are offered little advice on how to assist students in making connections among different representations of the one concept or procedure (Ball, 1992; Baroody, 1990; Hiebert & Wearne, 1992; Kaput, 1987). It is understandable, then, why teachers often fail to consider carefully the analogs they are using when trying to help children resolve difficulties in their learning (Dufour-Janvier, Bednarz, & Belanger, 1987).

It is important that we assess the suitability of a particular analog before we decide to use it. To assist us here, we have developed a set of principles for learning by analogy. Although the principles we cite here are applied to an analysis of concrete and pictorial analogs, they are not confined to analogs of this type. They are applicable also to the more abstract analogs, namely, previously established mental models that serve as the base for a new target concept or procedure. In proposing these principles, we draw upon some of Gentner's (1982) criteria for effective analogs that we examined in chapter 2.

Principles of Learning by Analogy

Clarity of Source Principle: The structure of the source should be clearly displayed and explicitly understood by the child. For an analogy to be effective, children need to know and understand the objects and relations in the source. It is particularly important that the child abstracts the structural properties of the source, not its superficial surface details. It will not be possible to map the source into the target, then use the source to generate inferences about the target, unless this understanding has been acquired and is readily available. Because structure mapping imposes a processing load, the source information must be well enough known to make its retrieval effortless. Otherwise the analogy will be too difficult to use.

Clarity of Mappings Principle: There should be an absence of ambiguity in the mappings from base to target. The child should be able to recognize clearly this correspondence between base and target. When a base has to be recalled from memory, it should be retrieved in terms of its generalizable structure rather than in terms of particular surface details (Gholson, Morgan, Dattel, & Pierce,1990). This is particularly important in the development of abstractions, as was indicated in chapter 3. These are formed from mappings in which the source itself is an abstract relational structure, with few or no attributes. Hence if children are to form meaningful abstractions, they must learn the structure of the examples they experience. Good analogs can assist here because mapping between an analog and a target example encourages children to focus on the corresponding relations in the two structures.

Principle of Conceptual Coherence: The relations that are mapped from base to target should form a cohesive conceptual structure, that is, a higher order structure. According to Gentner's (1983) systematicity principle, relations are mapped selectively, that is, only those that enter into a higher order structure are mapped. For example, in the number analog in Fig. 4.1, the relation between the sizes of the blocks (tens blocks are 10 times longer than ones blocks) is mapped into the relation between the tens place and the ones place (i.e., the tens place is ten times greater than the ones place). However, other attributes of the blocks, such as color, are not mapped, because they do not form part of a coherent structure in this analog.

Principle of Scope: An analogy should be applicable to a range of instances. Analogies with high scope can help children form meaningful connections between mathematical situations. For example, the "sharing" analogy in teaching the division concept can be applied readily to both whole numbers and fractions. Likewise, the area model can effectively demonstrate a range of fraction concepts and procedures, as we indicate in this chapter.

We now apply these principles to an assessment of the concrete and pictorial analogs used in children's mathematical learning. Given the range available, we can only assess the structural suitability of some of the more common analogs. To assist us here, we have classified them into three categories: unstructured, semistructured, and structured analogs. As we indicate in our analysis of these, some analogs may be structurally simple, yet prove to be complex learning aids when applied to target concepts that comprise inherently complex relations. This places an additional processing load on children as they attempt to interpret the arbitrary structure that has been imposed on the concrete analog to mirror the structure of the target concept. This can result in a failure to acquire the concept.

Unstructured Analogs

Materials in this category refer to discrete items such as counters and other simple environmental items typically used in the study of basic number and computation. These materials do not possess inherent structure, that is, they

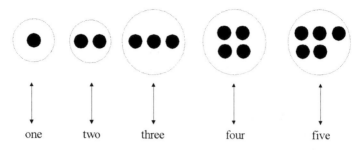

FIG. 4.2.   Using counters to represent single-digit numbers.

do not display in-built numerical relationships; the structure has to be provided in the way the materials are arranged or manipulated. The sets of dots shown in Fig. 4.2 have no inherent structure, because there are no relations intrinsic to the dots. However, this unstructured analog can effectively demonstrate the cardinality of the single-digit numbers because the dots are arranged into sets with a specific number of elements. In this instance there is just one mapping from the source (each set of counters) to the target (the number names).

When applied to the learning of basic number concepts, these unstructured analogs score highly on clarity of source structure and mappings, as shown in Fig. 4.2. Because children's initial number experiences are with discrete, everyday items, these analogs are most suitable for early number activities. When used with the appropriate explanation and manipulative

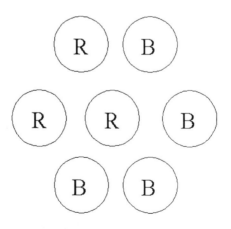

FIG. 4.3.   Using counters to represent a fraction of a set.

procedures, these analogs can promote a cohesive understanding of single-digit numbers and of the elementary number operations.

At this point, it is worth examining another common use of these unstructured analogs, namely, their application in the study of fractions. This is shown in Fig. 4.3, where counters serve to illustrate a fraction of a set.

The use of counters in this context involves more complex mappings. To interpret the above example as "three sevenths of the counters are red," the child must initially conceive of the set as a whole entity to determine the name of the fraction being considered (seven counters→ sevenths). An added difficulty here is that the items do not have to be the same size or shape (in contrast to an area model, which comprises equal-sized parts, as we indicate later). Hence the child must see the items of the set as equal parts of a whole, even if the items themselves are unequal. While keeping the whole set in mind, the child must then identify all the red counters (three red counters) and conceive of them as a fraction of the whole set, that is, "three out of seven counters, hence, three sevenths." This part/whole construct, which we referred to in chapter 3 and revisit later in this chapter, can be difficult to perceive with this set analog. Ascertaining the whole and the parts requires more or less simultaneous mapping processes and hence, it is not uncommon for children to treat the red and blue counters as discrete entities and interpret the fraction in terms of a ratio (i.e., three parts to four parts, giving the fraction three fourths; Behr, Wachsmuth, & Post, 1988; Lesh, 1991; Novillis, 1976).

The difficulty of recognizing the display in Fig. 4.3 as the fraction, "three sevenths" is an instance of the processing load imposed by ternary relations. It is a relation between three sets; red counters, blue counters, and round counters. Round counters include red and blue counters, so it is another case of the inclusion concept, and is isomorphic to the part/whole schema. One reason why children may default to treating the analog as the ratio, three parts to four parts, is that this involves a simpler, binary relation. It is a relation between two sets, red counters and blue counters. As discussed in chapter 2, processing load depends on dimensionality, and ternary relations are three dimensional, whereas binary relations are two dimensional. Ternary relations therefore impose the higher processing load. The load could be obviated by ignoring blue counters and simply attending to the relation between red and round counters. This is difficult, however, because blue counters are more salient than round counters; that is, the attribute blue is more salient than the attribute round in this situation. The set of round counters tends to be noticed because it corresponds to the union of red and blue counters, which entails the ternary relation mentioned above. The area analog, discussed later, may be preferable because the total area is a more salient cue.

Semistructured Analogs

Included in this category are materials such as bundling sticks, unifix cubes, and colored chips. Although these are basically unstructured materials, we would classify them as semistructured because they are used with an imposed or implied structure. We illustrate this with an analysis of colored chips or counters when they are used to convey place-value ideas.

In this role, colored chips represent an abstract learning aid because they adopt an arbitrary structure in order to mirror the structure of the target and, as such, the mappings between the source and target become quite sophisticated. This implied structure is of a grouping nature where groups of counters or chips of one color are traded for a chip of a different color to represent a new group. This single chip represents a number of objects rather than a single object (LeBlanc, 1976). The analog thus becomes an abstract representation because the value of a chip is determined only by its color, which is arbitrary, and not by its size. As shown in Fig. 4.4 there is no obvious indication of each chip's value, that is, there is no apparent power relation between the red, blue, and green colors. There is not a clear mapping from the base material to its corresponding target numeral. In fact, there is a two-stage mapping process involved, namely, from chip to color, then from color to value. That is, the child must first identify the color of the chip and then remember the value that has been assigned to that color. This naturally places an additional processing load on the child, especially if she does not readily recall this value. Given the lack of clarity in its source structure and the multiple mappings required, this material does not seem an appropriate analog for introducing grouping and place-value ideas. It appears more suitable for enrichment work.

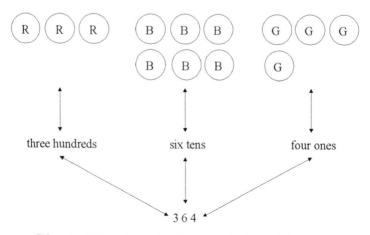

FIG. 4.4.   Using colored chips to represent a three-digit number.

Structured Analogs

In this category, we place materials such as the base-ten blocks, the place-value chart, the abacus, the Cuisenaire rods, money, the number line, and area or region models for representing fractions. Structured analogs, as the name implies, have an in-built structure designed to reflect specific numerical relationships and properties. We illustrate this with an analysis of the base-ten blocks, the place-value chart, the abacus, money, and the area model for representing fractions. (We refer the reader to Halford, 1993, for an analysis of the Cuisenaire rods and, for a review of the number line, to Dufour-Janvier, Bednarz, & Belanger, 1987; Bright, Behr, Post, & Wachsmuth, 1988; Hiebert, Wearne, & Taber, 1991.)

Base-Ten Blocks.   The base-ten blocks, along with the place-value chart (which we examine next), are probably the most commonly used analogs in the teaching of numeration and computation. Dienes (1960) is normally credited with the introduction of these blocks, having designed them in a range of bases; hence their name, multibase arithmetic blocks (MAB). As shown in Fig. 4.5, the size relations between the bocks reflect the magnitude relations between the quantities being represented. These relations are highlighted when 10 blocks of one value are swapped for one block of the next higher value. The indentations on the blocks facilitate this trading process and also clearly show the base-ten relationships of our number system. As an analog then, the base-ten blocks display clarity of source structure and clear mappings to the target concepts, as was indicated in Fig. 4.1. The analog also demonstrates high scope because it can be applied to a range of instances, such as the renaming and regrouping of numbers, and hence can foster conceptual coherence of our numeration system.

The base-ten blocks in Fig. 4.5 provide a further illustration of the

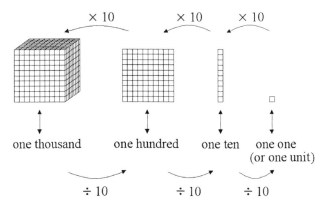

FIG. 4.5.   Relationships inherent in the base-ten blocks.

principle of systematicity mentioned earlier. The same relation exists between the thousands, hundreds, tens, and ones blocks because they are all related to one another by powers of ten; that is, the tens blocks is 10 times the ones block, the hundreds block is 10 times the tens block, and so on. That is, the blocks represent 10^0, 10^1, 10^2, and so on. The relation between each pair of blocks is part of a system of relations. We could express this by a higher order relation, as follows: SAME-RELATION (10-times-greater(10,1), 10-times-greater(100,10). That is, the same relation occurs between 10 and 1 as between 100 and 10. SAME-RELATION is a higher order relation, because its arguments are relations. Thus relations between thousands, hundreds, tens and units blocks are bound by a higher order relation, and thereby have the systematicity property as defined by Gentner (1983).

Although the blocks represent a highly appropriate analog, their effectiveness will be limited if children do not form the correct mappings between the analog representations and the target concepts and between their manipulations with the analog and the target procedures. This can happen if the blocks are not arranged in accordance with the positional scheme of our number system or if sets of blocks are combined in any order, beginning with any size block and moving back and forth to trade for another size when necessary (Hiebert, 1992). Children's failure to form connections between the analog representation and the target ideas has been reported in several studies (Baroody, 1990; R. B. Davis, 1984; Resnick & Omanson, 1987). Findings from other studies have shown that the nature of the teacher's explanations during the learning sequence is a crucial component in this process, with appropriate and frequent verbal explanations seen to enhance learning (Fuson, 1992b; Leinhardt, 1987; Stigler & Baranes, 1988). The importance of children's verbal explanations, with an emphasis on the quantities they are manipulating, has also been highlighted (Resnick & Omanson, 1987). We return to these points in subsequent sections.

Whereas the base-ten blocks serve as an effective analog for whole numbers, they take on an added complexity when representing decimal fractions. Changing the values of the blocks to accommodate decimal fractions poses a higher processing load for the child. For whole numbers, the values assigned to the blocks normally remain fixed and children associate a given block with its whole number value. When the blocks take on new values, children are faced with additional mapping processes. For example, if the flat block is assigned the value, one unit (or one one), the long block is equal to one tenth and the mini, one hundredth. This means that, to interpret the representation shown in Fig. 4.6, children must firstly identify the flat block as representing one whole unit. They must then recall that the flat block is equivalent to 10 long blocks as well as 100 mini blocks. Next, children have to perceive the long block as equivalent to one tenth and the

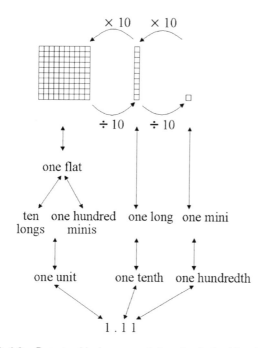

FIG. 4.6.   Base-ten block representation of a decimal fraction.

mini, one hundredth, of the flat block. This process itself involves an application of the fraction concept. Once the respective values of the blocks have been established, children must interpret the decimal fraction being represented. If children do not make all of the mappings required, there is the danger that they will interpret the decimal fraction as a whole number, record it as such, and simply insert a decimal point.

The complexity of the mapping processes involved here means that the base-ten blocks can lose clarity of both source structure and mappings when used as an analog for the initial representation of decimal fractions. Because children have to apply an understanding of fractions in interpreting this analog, it would seem more appropriate to employ less complex analogs, such as partitioned region models, in introducing decimal fractions and reserve the base-ten blocks for subsequent application activities.

Place-Value Chart.   The place-value chart serves as a bridge between the concrete Representation of a number and its abstract, symbolic form. It acts as a form of bridging analogy, which is an intermediate third case between source and target that shares features with both of these (Clement, 1993). The place-value chart is designed to develop the understanding that the value of

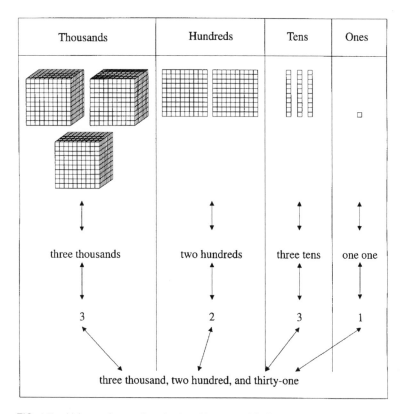

FIG. 4.7.   Using a place-value chart and base-ten blocks to represent a multidigit whole number.

a digit in a multidigit numeral depends on its position in the numeral. For example, the digit 5 in the numeral 3,546 has a value of five hundreds, whereas in the numeral, 5,624, its value is five thousands. When used in conjunction with the base-ten blocks, the chart facilitates a clear mapping from the source, that is, the concrete representation, to the target, the written numeral, as indicated in Fig. 4.7.

The versatility of the place-value chart means it can show the value of any multidigit number, including decimal fractions, and can also highlight the relationships between the places in our numeration system, as indicated in Fig. 4.8.

The scope afforded by the place-value chart is also evident when it is applied to the understanding of metric measurements, as indicated in Fig. 4.9 (Baturo & English, 1985). Interpreting a measurement such as 5.2 meters requires children to map their knowledge of length relationships (i.e., 1

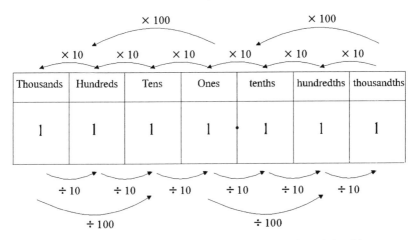

FIG. 4.8.   Using a place-value chart to show place-value relationships.

meter is equivalent to 10 decimeters, 100 centimeters, and 1,000 millimeters) onto their knowledge of decimal number positional relationships (i.e., 1 unit is equivalent to 10 tenths, 100 hundredths, and 1,000 thousandths). The metric unit, meter, is then mapped onto the ones or units place, decimeter is mapped onto the tenths place, and so on.

The Abacus.   A typical classroom abacus consists of 9 beads on each of several vertical wires that designate the places in our number system. There are no more than nine beads in any one column since 10 is represented by one bead in the column immediately to the left (reflecting the Egyptian

Tens	Ones or Units	tenths	hundredths	thousandths
	↕ meters	↕ decimeters	↕ centimeters	↕ millimeters
	↕ 5	↕ • 2	↕ 0	↕ 0

five meters and two decimeters
five meters and twenty centimeters
five meters and two hundred millimeters

FIG. 4.9.   Using a place-value chart to interpret a metric measurement.

system). Because 9 (not 10) beads on one wire are swapped for a single bead on the next wire, it is more difficult for the child to see the intended correspondence between the source and the target place-value ideas. Although all the beads are identical, except perhaps in color, they adopt different numerical values depending on the position of the wire. The new single bead has a value 10 times greater than a single bead to its right; however, this relation is implicit.

In interpreting a number on the abacus, the child must undergo a three-stage mapping process, namely, from the number of beads on a particular wire to the wire's position, then to the value of this position, and finally, to the target numeral. This poses quite a high processing load for the child. Given these complexities, the abacus is not an appropriate analog for introducing grouping and place-value concepts. In fact, the child must apply a prior understanding of these concepts when representing numbers on this device. Hence the abacus is more appropriately used when the child has acquired this knowledge.

Money. At first glance, money might seem an appropriate and appealing analog. It certainly has the desirable features of being real world and "hands-on" for the child. However, this does not automatically qualify it as a suitable analog for teaching number concepts and operations. Money is not unlike the colored chip material in that the relationships between the denominations are not immediately discernible. More importantly, relations between coins do not clearly correspond to relations between numbers, which is an essential property of a good analog. For example, in the United States, the dime (10 cents) is smaller than the nickel (5 cents); in Australia, the $2 coin is smaller than the $1 coin. Thus the size relations between coins do not correspond consistently to the relations between the numbers represented. There is also the problem of some coins not fitting nicely within the "10-for-1" trades of our decimal system, for example, the U.S. nickel and quarter (Fuson, 1990b).

Because the base-ten feature of decimal currencies is not explicit in the material, the use of money to illustrate grouping and place-value concepts presents complex mapping processes for the child. This is particularly the case when money is used to illustrate decimal fractions. Children have difficulty in seeing a particular coin as being a fraction of another, particularly because the relative sizes of the coins do not suggest a fractional relationship. Furthermore, through their everyday transactions with money, children (and adults) come to see a particular denomination as an entity in its own right, not as a fraction of some other denomination. For children to see 45 cents as 45 hundredths of a dollar, for example, they must first identify the four 10-cent coins as equivalent to 40 cents and the one 5-cent coin as equivalent to 5 pennies. Second, children must identify the $1 coin (or note) as one whole unit comprising 100 cents. There is no visual indication, of course, that this is the case. Finally, children must apply their understanding of the part/whole fraction concept to the recognition that 45 cents is 45 hundredths of a dollar. Again, there are no visual cues that this is the case (that is, the child cannot place the 45 cents on top of the $1 to see that it "covers" only 45 hundredths of the dollar). Because the use of money for this purpose entails several mappings, it can place a considerable cognitive load on the child. As such, we argue that money is not a suitable analog for establishing decimal fraction concepts and consider it to be more appropriate for application activities.

Area Models for Representing Fractions.   The manipulative aids most frequently used for illustrating fraction concepts are the area, region or measurement models (sometimes called continuous models), and the set (discrete) models (Behr et al., 1988). We have already addressed the complexity of the set analog and focus here on the former model.

The area model comprises a geometric shape, most commonly a square, rectangle, or circle, that can be partitioned to illustrate equal parts of a whole. The model is very versatile in that various shapes and partitionings can be used to develop a broader understanding of fractions as "equal parts of a whole" (Pothier & Swada, 1983). Activities with this analog include paper folding and cutting (the fractional parts can be superimposed on the original shape) and the shading of designated fractional parts of a pre-partitioned shape. The identification of the part/whole relationship can be enhanced by highlighting the perimeter of the shape and using broken lines to indicate the partitioning, as shown in Fig. 4.10. The use of broken lines can help avoid the danger of children treating each part as though it were an independent unit or whole number (Kieren, 1988; Mack, 1990, 1993).

Fractions are necessarily defined as a relation between numerator and denominator, and must be at least binary relations, with a minimum of two dimensions. Analogs may have more than two dimensions, and the sets analog in Fig. 4.3 has three dimensions, as noted earlier, because it is a relation between red, blue, and round counters. The area analog is preferable because the total area is a more salient cue, enabling the analog to be coded as a relation between shaded area and total area. This is a binary

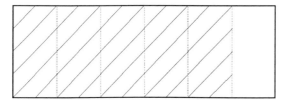

FIG. 4.10.   The area model as a fraction analog.

relation and is simpler than the ternary relation that tends to be involved in the sets analog. Perhaps the most important point, however, is that because fractions are two dimensional, whereas integers are one dimensional, fractions are necessarily more complex, and this makes efficient analogs all the more necessary.

We revisit the use of the area analog later in this chapter and turn now to a consideration of how children develop numerical ideas and how the analogs we have examined can contribute to this development.

EARLY NUMBER

in what sense a mm?

In the previous chapter, we reviewed children's acquisition of counting skills. We considered the notion of counting principles and considered a mental model of counting based on the accumulator model (Wynn, 1992b). In this section, we examine these points in greater detail and extend our discussion to include children's learning of the formal symbol system.

For children to understand the counting system, they must first know that a number word refers to a numerosity. Second, they must know the precise numerosity a number word designates. To learn the cardinal meanings of all the number words, the child must realize that a word's position in the number word list determines the numerosity to which it refers and must understand how this numerosity is derived (Fuson, 1988a; Gelman & Greeno, 1989; Meck & Church, 1983; Wynn, 1989, 1992b). Although very young children have some concept of numerosity (Gelman, 1977; Starkey, Spelke, & Gelman, 1990), the problem they face is that of mapping these number concepts onto words.

As we noted in chapter 3, one of the difficulties here is that the number words do not refer to individual objects or to properties of individual objects, but to properties of sets of objects (Wynn, 1992b). Yet our counting routine assigns a number word to each item, so that the child sees an individual item labeled *one*, another labeled *two*, another *three*, and so on. To learn that our number words refer to properties of sets of items, not individual items, is quite a complex task for young children. We return to this point.

Models of Counting: Innate Versus Acquired Principles

Extensive research has been conducted on children's counting skills, with considerable debate over whether these skills reflect domain-specific knowledge of number or some general cognitive capacities (e.g. Frye, Braisby, Lowe, Maroudas, & Nicholls, 1989; Fuson, 1988a, 1988b; Greeno, 1991; Gelman & Greeno, 1989; Wynn, 1989). A related issue is whether under-

Can't they co-emerge?

standing precedes counting skill (innate principles) or whether it follows skill acquisition (acquired principles). Gelman and her associates (e.g., Gelman & Gallistell, 1978; Gelman & Meck, 1986) have adopted a principles-first position that claims there are a number of innate, number-specific principles that underlie children's ability to count. According to their theory, preschoolers have preexisting implicit knowledge of these principles that guide their early counting as well as developments in that skill. We cited these "how-to-count" principles in the previous chapter.

The innate-principles theory predicts that children will learn the cardinal meaning of each number word relatively easily once they have identified the word's place in the number word sequence. Greeno (1991) suggested that children's innate counting skills are easily developed because order and correspondence are direct correlates of spatial and spatial/temporal properties. The ability to construct mental models of number would therefore seem relatively easy for children because they can identify sets of objects according to a simple spatial principle.

The other school of thought, the acquired principles theory (e.g., Bialystock, 1992; Briars & Siegler, 1984; Fuson, 1988a, 1988b; Wynn, 1989) claims that children first learn to count as a routine activity that is modeled for them by others. With experience, children learn to count in different contexts, such as counting claps or counting items arranged in a circle (for a discussion on children's counting types in different contexts, the reader is referred to Steffe & Cobb, 1988). Once they have developed procedures for these various contexts, children are able to identify their commonalities and draw some generalizations, resulting in their acquisition of the counting principles. Only after this has taken place are children considered to have principled knowledge.

Wynn (1990, 1992b) presented convincing evidence that children do not begin the counting process with unlearned counting principles that lead them to the meanings of the number words and guide their acquisition of counting skills. She maintained that children must learn how to count and must learn the meanings of the number words through some means other than their correspondence to a set of mental counting tags. She demonstrated that by about $3\frac{1}{2}$ years children understand how the counting system determines numerosity and have acquired the cardinal meanings of all the number words within their counting range. However there seem to be several steps on the way to this knowledge. Children appear to learn sequentially the cardinal meanings of smaller number words before learning the meanings of larger number words within their counting range. Children who can give the cardinal meanings of smaller numbers (prior to being able to give larger numbers) rarely use counting to do so. It seems they directly map smaller numerosities onto their correct number words and thus succeed in giving the required numerosities. Wynn claimed that once children learn the way in which counting determines the numerosity of a set of items, they acquire the cardinal meanings of the remaining number words within their counting range; they can then give any number of items they are asked for.

The interesting issue here is how children actually map their own concept of number onto the counting system. As Wynn (1992b) commented, this would seem to be a straightforward process given that the linguistic counting system embodies a representation of number that is very similar in form to that which children are assumed to possess innately. However Wynn's research has indicated that, once children have learned that the number words refer to numerosities, it still takes about a year before they learn how the counting system represents numerosity. This suggests that children may have difficulty in mapping their own representation of numerosity onto the counting activity because they perceive number differently.

The "Accumulator" Theory of Counting

A plausible explanation for this difficulty can be found in the "accumulator" theory of counting (Meck & Church, 1983; Wynn, 1992b). The theory proposes that infants possess the same mechanism for determining numerosity as that proposed to explain other animals' numerical abilities (e.g., Gallistel, 1990). This accumulator theory is likened to a mechanism that fills up in equal increments, one for each entity that is counted. Number is thus represented in quite a different way to that of the standard counting system. It is the entire fullness of the accumulator, not the final increment alone, that represents the numerosity of the items counted (Wynn, 1992b). Fig. 4.11 provides a model of this accumulator number representation.

In chapter 3, we listed a number of key ideas featured in the accumulator model. Whereas the "next" relation is evident in these features, as indicated by the fact that numbers occur in a fixed sequence, it is the relation "one more" that is highlighted. That is, one more item is accumulated with each count. However the "next" relation would have been emphasized in the child's acquisition of the number word list (e.g., 5, next comes 6, next comes 7. . .). This relation also features strongly in the standard model of counting

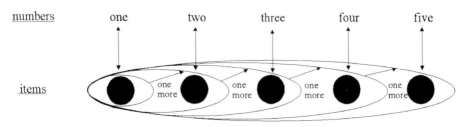

FIG. 4.11.   The accumulator model of counting.

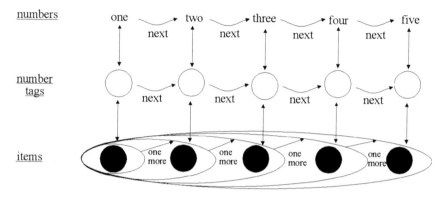

FIG. 4.12.   Mapping processes in children's initial counting.

where there is a one-to-one correspondence between single items (not sets of items) and the number name. Hence in counting a set of objects, the child must map her accumulated set model (emphasizing accumulated sets of items and the relation, "one more") onto the standard counting model (involving single items and the relation, "next"), and finally, onto the corresponding number name. This is clearly a complex process for the young child, as it involves a two-stage mapping, as shown in Fig. 4.12. It is understandable, then, why it takes considerable time for children to learn the counting system.

An additional source of complexity is that the accumulator model entails the inclusion concept, because each set includes the next smaller set, plus the item currently being counted. Inclusion is a ternary relation, and is three dimensional, which would increase processing load. The standard count or successor model is simpler, because it entails only binary relations, such as "next" and "larger." However it can never give an adequate mental model of counting because it has numbers mapped to objects rather than to sets.

At this point, it is worth considering why children have initial difficulty with a seemingly straightforward skill of identifying the number that comes immediately before or after a given number in the counting word list. If young children conceive of our number system in terms of accumulated sets rather than tagged items, then it is understandable that the concepts of *just before* and *just after* present difficulties. The item "just before" is contained in a set that is a subset of the current item, which in turn is included in the set that also includes the item "just after." Again, a ternary relation is entailed here, and it is more complex than the simple binary relation of "successor." Similarly, the concepts of *more than* and *fewer than* should be less difficult for children to grasp, because they are only binary relations, as discussed in chapter 3. Research findings lend support here (e.g., Michie, 1985; Fuson, 1988a, 1988b; Fuson & Hall, 1983; Fuson, Richards, & Briars, 1982).

The final issue we consider in children's elementary number understanding is their recognition of the formal symbol system. Although this is obviously an important component in the learning process, symbol recognition per se does not indicate an understanding of number.

Symbol Recognition

The reading of the standard numerals is a basic associative learning task for the child, that is, the child sees the numeral and recalls its number word (Fuson, 1988a, 1988b). Bialystok (1992) referred to symbol recognition as the second step in a three-step progression in children's development of a symbolic representation for number, the first step being the recitation of the correct name for each element in the number sequence. During the symbol recognition phase, children can recognize, produce, and name the written notations. They mentally represent the written numbers as objects with particular visual characteristics but not as symbols that stand for meanings. It is not until the third step that they understand the meaning of the individual symbolic forms. This third step signifies symbolic representation where the child is able to associate the written form of a number with the quantity it denotes. This actually involves a two-step mapping, firstly from the base numeral, for example, 8, to the oral number name, "eight," and then to a model of eight, be it a mental, physical, or pictorial representation. These mapping processes are illustrated in Fig. 4.13.

Once children acquire meaningful symbol recognition, they need practice transferring from one representation to the other (Post, Cramer, Behr, Lesh, & Harel, 1993). For example, given a set of five counters, children should be able to count the number in the set, state orally its cardinal value, and identify and write the corresponding written numeral (and subsequently, the written word, *eight*). Conversely, when shown the symbol, 8, children

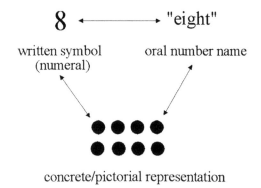

concrete/pictorial representation

FIG. 4.13.   Mapping processes in meaningful symbolic representation of number.

should be able to state the number name (eight) and show this amount with counters. Extensions of these activities include identifying the set of 8 items from pictorial representations of various sets and identifying the corresponding written numeral from a list of different numerals (selecting numerals on the calculator is an effective activity here). It is not the intention of this book to provide a range of such activities, however it is important to highlight the importance of developing children's facility with all representations of number. The concrete, pictorial, and oral representations can be easily neglected once the written forms have been established.

PLACE VALUE OF WHOLE NUMBERS

Children's progression to the two-digit numbers involves a totally new dimension, namely that of place value. The two-digit numbers should already be within the child's counting repertoire, that is, the child should be able to recite the counting sequence to 99 and should be able to count sets of objects comprising more than 10 items. The introduction of place-value ideas means that children must progress from counting where *one* is the iterable unit to counting where *ten* is the iterable unit (Fuson, 1990b; Gray, 1991; G. A. Jones, Thornton, & Putt, 1994; Miura, Okamoto, Kim, Steere, & Fayol, 1993; Steffe & Cobb, 1988). This is not a simple task, as the two-digit numbers feature a number of irregularities that present an added complexity for the child. As we demonstrate in this section, these irregularities necessitate a careful analysis of our number system and of the instructional approaches we adopt. Exploring the two-digit numbers in a mathematically logical way, that is, in a sequential manner from 11 to 99, is not the most cognitively appropriate path.

To understand place value, children must have an implicit understanding of the basic properties of our base-ten numeration system (Hiebert, 1992; S. H. Ross, 1989). These include:

1. Positional properties. The value of an individual digit in a numeral is determined by the position or place it holds in the whole numeral.
2. Base-ten property. The values of the places in a numeral increase in powers of ten from right to left (and decrease in powers of ten from left to right).
3. Multiplicative property. The value of an individual digit is obtained by multiplying the face value of the digit (0 through 9) by the value assigned to its position. This is known as the canonical value of the digit, that is, the value in terms of the number of units of quantity (Hiebert, 1992)
4. Additive property. The value of the whole numeral is the sum of the

values represented by the individual digits. For example, the value of 382 is $(3 \times 100) + (8 \times 10) + (2 \times 1)$.

A child who understands place value not only knows that the numeral *65* can refer to a set of 65 items (its cardinal value), but also that the digit on the right represents five of these items whereas the digit on the left represents 60 (six groups of ten). An understanding of place value is essential if children are to deal meaningfully with multidigit numbers and algorithms. The development of this understanding is a complex process, involving the construction of multiunit conceptual structures (Fuson, 1990a, 1990b; Steffe & Cobb, 1988) and the formation of connections between these structures and the corresponding number name and written symbol (Hiebert & Wearne, 1992). As we illustrate, there is not always a direct correspondence between the number name and the written notation (e.g., *thirteen* and *13*). However, with the appropriate use of physical materials to highlight the grouping structures, we can assist children in establishing these important connections and thus help them acquire a more coherent understanding of place value (Hiebert & Wearne, 1992).

Given the significance of place value in children's mathematical learning, it is of considerable concern that children are not acquiring these concepts adequately and are not applying them in their algorithmic work (Baroody, 1990; Fuson, 1990a, 1990b; G. A. Jones & Thornton, 1993; C. Kamii & Joseph, 1988; Kouba et al., 1988; Lindquist, 1989; Resnick & Omanson, 1987; Ross, 1989). A major contributing factor is the linguistic complexity of our place-value system for English-speaking students.

The Linguistic Complexity of Place Value

Our English number naming system is made more difficult for our children because we do not explicitly name "tens" (e.g., we say, "sixty," not "six tens") and we have irregularities in our number names that cause added problems (e.g., we say "twelve" for one ten and two ones). In contrast, Asian children speak a number language that is not only a totally regular system but also includes explicit reference to tens (e.g., "12" is read as "ten two," "67" is read as "six ten seven"). The particular difficulties posed by the irregularities in our English number words have been well documented (e.g., Fuson, 1990a, 1990b, 1993; Miura, Okamoto, Kim, Steere, & Fayol (1993). We review some of these irregularities to highlight the problems they present for children.

The numbers between 10 and 20 pose particular problems. First, there are the arbitrary names, "eleven" and "twelve," for one ten and one one, and one ten and two ones, respectively. These names give no indication of the composition of the numbers. Of the remaining teen numbers, "thirteen" and

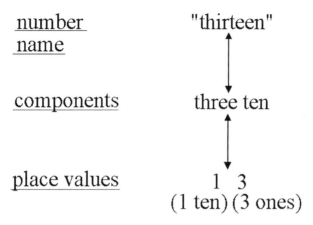

FIG. 4.14.   Interpreting "thirteen" from a place-value perspective.

"fifteen" are irregular in that they do not conform to the "digit-teen" pattern (Fuson, 1990b). That is, we say "*thir*teen" rather than "*three*teen" (in contrast to a regular teen such as "sixteen"). Probably the greatest difficulty with the teens is the reversal in their names. In contrast to the remaining two-digit numbers, the teens are read in the opposite way to which they are written. For example, "19" is read as "nineteen" not, "ten nine." The tens digit is said *after* the ones digit, yet is written *prior* to the ones digit. It is easy to see why children would write "91" for "nineteen" and why they would confuse teen names with similar sounding decade words, for example, "fourteen" and "forty" (Behr, 1976). In addition, the name, "teen," is a modification of "ten" and does not clearly indicate the value of ten. Acquiring a mental model of the teen numbers is thus quite a complex process for the child. This is evident in interpreting the number, "thirteen," for example. Here, the child must identify the tens and ones components by mapping the name, "thir," onto "three" and the name, "teen," onto "ten." The components, "three and "ten," must then be mapped onto their respective place-value positions, "1 (ten) 3 (ones)," as illustrated in Fig. 4.14. Given that a two-stage mapping process is involved here, it is understandable that children find the teen numbers difficult.

Although the remaining two-digit numbers present fewer difficulties (e.g., they are read and written in a consistent manner), they nevertheless feature some irregularities. First, the suffix, "ty," in the number names does not clearly indicate a value of ten (a similar situation to the teens). Secondly, there are irregularities in some of the decade names, namely, "twenty" (not "twoty"), "thirty," and "fifty." This makes it difficult for children to see how these decade number names are related to the single-digit number names, that is, there is not a direct mapping from the number names, "two," "three," and "five," to the names, "twenty," "thirty," and "fifty" (compare this with the mapping from "six" to "sixty"). These cases give the child little choice but to memorize the irregular decade names, as well as the teen names. For many children, this memorization process extends to the learning of the corresponding symbolic forms with the result that they only ever acquire unitary structures for these numbers; they fail to recognize the inherent relations (Fuson & Briars, 1990; S. H. Ross, 1986).

Cross-Cultural Comparisons of Place-Value Understanding

In contrast to the linguistic complexity of the English system, the Asian number words clearly convey place-value ideas. For example, the teen numbers are formed by affixing the tens name to a ones name so that 11, 12, 13 . . . are spoken as "ten-one," "ten-two," "ten-three," and so on (Miura et al., 1993). The number "20" is read as "two-ten(s)." Since the spoken numbers in Japanese correspond directly to their written form, it would not be surprising to find that Japanese students develop a better understanding of place-value ideas. Miura et al. (1993) found that Asian students in first grade showed a preference for a canonical base-ten construction when asked to represent numbers concretely. That is, they used 4 ten blocks and 2 ones blocks, rather than 42 single ones blocks, to show the number, "forty-two." The non-Asian children, by comparison, preferred the latter represen-tation, that is, 42 loose blocks. Miura et al. argued that, if the block representations are assumed to reflect the child's mental image of number, then the Japanese and Korean children view numbers as organized struc-tures of tens and ones, with place value an inherent feature of these repre-sentations. In contrast, the non-Asian students' preference for representing numbers with a collection of ones blocks suggests that they do not readily interpret numbers in terms of tens and ones but rather, as single units. It has thus been argued that learning to count in an Asian language enables students to construct an image of number that is congruent with the tradi-tional base-ten system (Fuson & Kwon, 1992; Miura et al., 1993).

Although not denying the important role of language in children's num-ber learning, it would seem inappropriate to cite linguisitic differences as the sole factor responsible for the superior performance of the Asian students. It hardly seems plausible that Asian students would naturally choose ca-nonical base ten constructions if they had not been encouraged to do so in their classroom experiences. There are, in fact, several other factors contrib-uting to these cross-cultural differences.

Stigler and Baranes (1988) reported that Asian teachers devote more quality time to mathematics, offer more verbal explanations and discussion sessions, make more effective use of manipulatives, and incorporate more problem-solving scenarios in their lessons than their U.S. counterparts. Of particular importance is their finding that the Asian teachers use manipulatives in different ways to the U.S. teachers. Whereas the American teachers were found to employ a wide variety of manipulatives (such as bundling sticks, base-ten blocks, cuisennaire rods, etc.), the Japanese teachers used a limited number of materials but employed them repeatedly for different instructional purposes. The Japanese teachers were also observed to give a greater frequency of verbal explanation while using the materials. In contrast, the U.S. teachers did not use increased explanation with these materials. As Stigler and Baranes aptly commented, " In the presence of concrete referents, Japanese teachers use the objects as a topic of discussion, whereas American teachers tend to use the objects as a substitute for discussion" (p. 297).

There are clearly more effective ways of helping children understand place-value ideas than learning a foreign language. We devote the next section to this issue.

Developing Mental Models of Place Value

In this section, we consider how we might foster the development of children's mental models of place value. In so doing, we apply some further principles for learning by analogy. These principles refer not only to the use of concrete analogs but also to the more abstract analogs, namely, previously established mental models that serve as the base for a new target concept or procedure. We use the term *mapping* to refer to the process of associating the salient relations in the base with the corresponding relations in the target.

Principle of Reduced Mappings. The number of mappings required for the abstraction of a concept or procedure should be the minimum possible for the formation of the desired mental model.

Clarity of Source Principle. The mappings to be made from the base to the targeted concept/procedure should be clear and direct. Where an established mental model serves as the base, children need to explicitly recognize the correspondence between this model (e.g., the "hundreds, tens, ones" pattern in a three-digit number) and the targeted concept (e.g., the parallel pattern in the thousands period of a multidigit number).

Principle of Prerequisite Mappings. All necessary prerequisite mappings should be in place prior to the introduction of a new mapping.

Principle of Uniformity of Mapping Procedures. There should be uniformity in the manner in which an analog is manipulated or transformed and the cognitive processes required in the formation of the desired mental model.

ten ones   one ten

1. The child bundles and trades *ten ones for one ten* and *one ten for ten ones.*

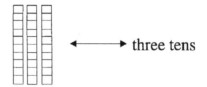

← → three tens

2. The child constructs two tens, three tens . . . nine tens (without single ones remaining) and identifies the groups as *"n tens."*

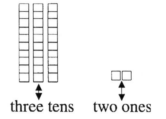

three tens   two ones

3. The child constructs groups of ten with single ones remaining and identifies the amount as *"x tens y ones."*

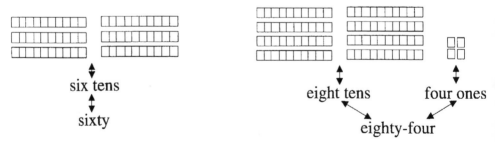

six tens

sixty

eight tens   four ones

eighty-four

4. The child associates the *formal number names* with the "regular" decades by mapping *"x tens"* to *"x ty."* This is done initially with tens only, then with tens and single ones.

FIG. 4.15.   (Continued)

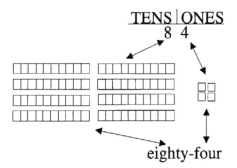

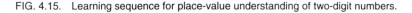

eighty-four

5. The child records the *formal symbols* for the above on a place-value chart, recording tens and ones initially (e.g., "84") then tens only (e.g., "60").
6. The child revisits the previous two stages with the irregular decades, namely, "twenty," "thirty," and "fifty."

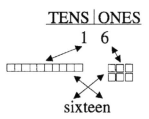

sixteen

7. The child explores the *teen numbers* as special cases of the multi-decade numbers. Using parallel activities to the above, the child investigates the regular teens (e.g., "sixteen") and then the irregular teens (e.g., "thirteen"), leaving the most difficult numbers, "eleven" and "twelve" until last.

FIG. 4.15.   Learning sequence for place-value understanding of two-digit numbers.

Principle of Uniformity of Mapping Language. Appropriate "mapping language" should accompany the manipulation or transformation of an analog; such language should facilitate the development of the desired mental model.

We now draw upon some of these principles in making recommendations for the teaching of place value. Our aim here is not to examine all components of place value in detail, but to address some of the key issues in facilitating the development of desired mental models.

We draw attention to the first two principles. If we wish to reduce the number of mappings the child must make from base to target and want to ensure that these mappings are clear and direct, then we need to carefully sequence the introduction of each new place-value idea. We present a suggested sequence for teaching the place value of two-digit numbers in Fig. 4.15. As the figure is self-explanatory, we highlight only some of the key features and refer to the remaining principles in doing so.

First, each step in the sequence involves only one new mapping and builds on previously established mappings. For example, in step 5, there is just one new mapping, namely, from the number name to the formal recording. The prerequisite mappings should already have been established, including the mappings from the concrete representations to the number components (x tens y ones) and to the number names ("x ty"). It is worth noting here that the recording of both tens and ones (e.g., 84) prior to the recording of tens only (e.g., 60) is more effective in highlighting the positional property of our place-value system. If the latter case (e.g., 60) is introduced in the first instance, it can encourage the common error of recording the cardinal value of the tens (that is, recording *804* for *84*).

Uniformity of mapping procedures and mapping language can be achieved by ensuring that the verbal explanation accompanying the use of the analog maps directly onto the concept being targeted. For example, in step 2, the number represented by the blocks is best referred to as "three tens" not "thirty," because it is grouping by tens that is being emphasized. The latter term, "thirty," highlights the cardinal rather than the place-value aspect of number and furthermore introduces an additional mapping process for the child (from 3 tens to thirty). Uniformity of mapping procedures is evident in step 5 with the introduction of a place-value chart. Here, the tens blocks are placed to the left of the ones blocks in the respective columns of the chart. This facilitates a direct mapping between the analog representation, the number name, and the symbolic recording.

Children who have developed a meaningful mental model of place value should be able to apply their knowledge to a range of number activities. For example, they should be able to explain the counting sequences they use in terms of place-value models and should be able to apply this knowledge when comparing numbers (e.g., 62 is greater than 59 because it has 6 tens, whereas 59 has only 5 tens). This knowledge is also crucial in developing an understanding of the regrouping process, that is, x tens y ones is equivalent to $(x - 1)$ tens and $(y + 10)$ ones (e.g., 45 = 3 tens 15 ones). Experience in partioning numbers in various ways also helps children develop flexibility in representing and understanding multidigit numbers (Jones et al., 1994). We return to these points when examining computational models in the next chapter.

The points we have raised regarding children's learning of the two-digit numbers apply equally to their study of the three-digit numbers and beyond. It is important that the introduction of these new numbers builds on children's existing place-value knowledge. Uniformity in analog use, including consistent application of language and procedures, will facilitate this process. For example, using the base-ten blocks and place-value chart, children can map the procedure of grouping and trading ten tens for one hundred onto the known procedure of grouping and trading ten ones for one

Millions Period			Thousands Period			Ones Period		
H	T	O	H	T	O	H	T	O
Hundreds	Tens	Ones	Hundreds	Tens	Ones	Hundreds	Tens	Ones

FIG. 4.16. The periods within our number system.

ten. As with the two-digit numbers, we recommend that the three-digit block representation be read initially as "x hundreds, y tens, and z ones" to highlight the place-value, rather than the cardinal, aspect of number. Because the hundreds number names do not comprise irregularities, the learning of this new place should involve relatively straightforward mapping processes from the analog representation to the number name and formal recording.

A direct mapping from the analog to the formal symbol can be ensured by having children initially record numbers comprising hundreds, tens, and ones (e.g., 562) prior to examples involving hundreds and tens only (e.g., 560) and hundreds only (e.g., 500). As with the two-digit numbers, if children's initial experiences involve recording hundreds only, they can end up recording the cardinal value of each digit when presented with numbers comprising hundreds, tens, and ones, for example, recording "562" as "50062" or worse, still, as "500602." In these instances, children attempt to make the written recording parallel the oral name (Fuson et al., 1992).

Children's understanding of three-digit numeration provides the base for the learning of four-digit numbers and beyond. The introduction of larger multidigit numbers presents a new concept for the child, namely, the periods within our number system (Baturo & English, 1985). These periods comprise repeated groups of three digits with each group containing hundreds, tens, and ones places, as shown in Fig. 4.16. Interpreting a number such as 348,749 would entail identifying each group of three digits, assigning the appropriate period names (i.e., the thousands period and the ones period), and then mapping a mental model of the "hundreds, tens, ones" pattern onto each period (i.e., "three hundred and forty-eight *thousands*, seven hundred and forty-nine *ones*").

An explicit recognition and understanding of the relationships between and within the periods of our number system is essential if children are to deal meaningfully and flexibly with larger numbers. When equipped with this understanding, children can readily identify the value of any digit within

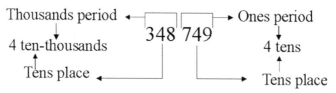

FIG. 4.17.   Identifying the value of a digit in a multidigit numeral.

a multidigit number, as indicated in Fig. 4.17. They can also identify equivalent values of a given digit, for example, the digit 5 in the numeral 453,496 not only has a value of five ten-thousands but also fifty *thousands,* five hundred *hundreds,* five thousand *tens,* and fifty thousand *ones.* This understanding is important in multidigit subtraction.

RATIONAL NUMBER

We now examine a domain that continues to present major learning obstacles for children, that of rational number. A rational number may be defined as "a pair of integers $\frac{a}{b}$ that satisfy the equation, $bx = a$" (Kieren, 1993, p. 53). By this definition, rational numbers are qoutients. They can be expressed in common fraction form (e.g., $\frac{3}{4}$) or in decimal fraction form (e.g., 0.75). The set of rational numbers includes the set of integers that, in turn, comprises negative integers and whole numbers, as shown in Fig. 4.18.

Although students have a substantial body of informal knowledge about the basic principles underlying rational number, they nevertheless have difficulty in mastering the domain. Numerous studies have reported on the

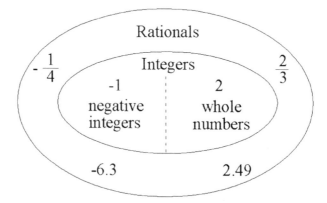

FIG. 4.18.   The rational number system.

complexity of rational number and the difficulties it presents children (Behr, Harel, Post, & Lesh, 1992; Bigelow, Davis, & Hunting, 1989; Carpenter, Fennema, & Romberg, 1993; Freudenthal, 1983; Gelman, 1991; Hope & Owens, 1987; Kieren, 1976, 1980, 1988, 1992; Leinhardt, 1988; Mack, 1990, 1993; Ohlsson, 1988; Steffe, 1989; Vergnaud, 1988; Wearne, 1990). Indeed, it has been reported that many elementary teachers tend not to develop a deep understanding of rational number and fail to see how it fits into the broader mathematical domain (Leinhardt, 1988). As a consequence, many of the learning experiences these teachers provide children (and were subjected to themselves) display numerous deficiencies, resulting in misconceptions such as "multiplication makes bigger" and "division makes smaller" (Behr et al., 1992). If we analyze the complexity of rational number, we can begin to see why it is a difficult area to both teach and learn.

The Complexity of Rational Number

Two major sources of difficulty in the learning of rational numbers are first, the need to consider a number of relations jointly, and second, the existence of various meanings that can be assigned to a fraction. We address the first issue by considering the common fraction $\frac{3}{4}$. This representation involves relationships between pairs of numbers. It has been noted in the mathematics education literature that children must simultaneously coordinate two unrelated ideas to interpret the fraction (Davydov & Tsvetkovich, 1991; Hope & Owens, 1987). That is, the meaning of the fraction is determined by considering the numerator and denominator in relation to one another, for example, "three parts out of four equal parts" (part/whole construct). Although the digits *3* and *4* have specific referents (i.e., parts or components), they are not meaningful in isolation. That is, neither "three parts" nor "four parts" alone gives us an idea of the fraction in question. Furthermore, the value of a fraction changes whenever one of its components changes, for example, changing the denominator in the fraction, $\frac{3}{4}$, while retaining the numerator, results in different fractional amounts: $\frac{3}{4} > \frac{3}{8} < \frac{3}{2}$. This is actually a specific instance of the general principle that complexity is measured by dimensionality, as was discussed in previous chapters. Integers are one dimensional, whereas rational numbers are two dimensional, and their complexity is correspondingly greater.

Because of their one-dimensional nature, the digits in whole numbers hold meaning on their own and do so because of their position within the numeral. For example, the digit *3* in the numeral, 349, has a value of 3 hundreds because it is in the hundreds place; furthermore, it is always worth 3 hundreds whenever it is in this position, irrespective of the other digits surrounding it. Unfortunately, many children perceive fractions in this manner, that is, as isolated digits, with the numerator and denominator as separate entities to be operated on independently (Behr, Wachsmuth, Post, & Lesh, 1984; Gelman, 1991). As a consequence, students' understanding of fractions frequently comprises a knowledge of rote procedures (often incorrect) rather than the concepts underlying the procedures (Mack, 1990).

The second source of difficulty arises from the numerous meanings that can be assigned to a fraction (Kieren, 1983, 1988; Leinhardt, 1988; Ohlsson, 1988). The more common of these are the part/whole construct, decimals, ratios, quotients, operators, and measures (Kieren, 1976; 1980). These different meanings add a new perspective to children's interpretation of number. Up until now, children have experienced numbers with "fixed meanings." That is, the digit, "3," in the numeral 349 has a fixed value of 3 hundreds. Its value would only change if it were placed in another position within a numeral (e.g., 439). With rational numbers however, the meaning of the component digits is not fixed. For example, the fraction, $\frac{3}{4}$, can take on any of the following meanings:

1. Three parts out of four equal parts (part/whole construct);
2. 3 divided by 4 (quotient construct; the decimal representation, 0.75, is derived from this division);
3. Three quarters of a number, object, or set (this is the operator construct, where the numerator, 3, extends the amount being operated on while the denominator, 4, contracts it; Behr et al., 1992);
4. Three parts to four parts, 3 wholes to 4 wholes (ratio);
5. As a point on a number line between 0 and 1 (the measure construct).

We now examine the complexity of some of these constructs. We begin our discussion with the part/whole notion as we consider this to be the major unifying model for establishing rational number understanding. This is not denying the importance however, of the other constructs in completing this understanding (Kieren, 1988); we return to these later.

Part/Whole Construct.   Children are typically introduced to rational number via the part/whole construct. This interpretation requires an ability to partition either a continuous quantity or a set of discrete objects into equal-sized subparts or sets (Behr, Lesh, Post, & Silver, 1983). The two most commonly used analogs for establishing this idea are the area or measurement model and the set model that we examined earlier. Although the part/whole construct is the easiest for children to grasp, it nevertheless presents some degree of complexity for children. As we show in Fig. 4.19A and B, the child must consider a number of relations jointly in order to interpret the fraction represented by the analog. In essence, this involves a system mapping process.

We consider the area or region model first (Fig. 4.19A), as this is the less

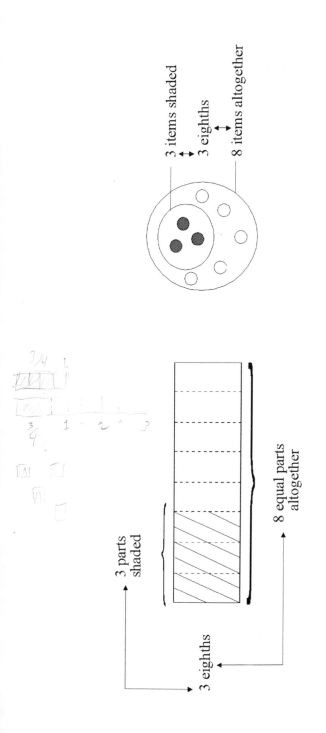

(A) area or region model　　　　(B) set model

FIG. 4.19.　Mapping processes involved in interpreting the part/whole construct.

129

complex analog for illustrating the part/whole construct. Before children can determine the fraction represented by the shaded portion of the model, they must first recognize that the parts are equal. They must then identify the total number of parts and map this number onto the name of the fraction (eight equal parts → eighths). The number of parts shaded must then be identified (three). Determining the fraction that is shaded involves coordinating both items of information to yield the fraction, three eighths. The mappings are shown in Fig. 4.19A. The concept of *inclusion* is entailed here because the shaded parts, together with the unshaded parts, are included in the whole, which corresponds to the set of equal parts. However, the salience of the whole in this analog means the unshaded parts will tend to be ignored, which would effectively reduce the analog to a relational mapping. The symbolic recording of the fraction involves further mappings that we address later.

Interpreting the set model (Fig. 4.19B) is more difficult for children, as we indicated earlier. Here, the child must conceive of the set of discrete items as a whole entity. Furthermore, these items do not have to be the same size or shape. Hence the child must see the items as equal parts of a whole, even if the items themselves are unequal. Because it is more difficult to ascertain the whole and the parts in the set model, it is not uncommon for children to treat the shaded and unshaded items as discrete entities and interpret the fraction as a ratio (i.e., "three parts to five parts"). It is for this reason that the set model appears inappropriate for introducing the part/whole construct (Hope & Owens, 1987).

Quotient Construct.   The quotient construct represents quite a different fraction idea for the child and involves more complex mappings than the part/whole construct. It refers to solutions to equations of the form, $ax = b$ where a and b are integers and a is not equal to zero (Kieren, 1980, p. 72). Behr, Harel, Post, and Lesh (1993) defined this construct in procedural terms, namely, "One (a) starts with two quantities, (b) treats one of them as a divisor and the other as the dividend, and (c) by the process of partitive or quotitive division, obtains a single quantity result (pp. 43–44).

This division process also serves to introduce the conversion from common fraction to decimal fraction form. To illustrate the mapping processes involved here, we consider a common analog for introducing this division idea, namely, the sharing of pizzas among a given number of people (partitive division). The processes involved in sharing three pizzas among four people are illustrated in Fig. 4.20.

This analog builds on children's previous knowledge of the sharing process. However children's prior experiences would have involved the sharing of whole items, rather than fractional parts. This new analog requires children to recognize first, the nature of the sharing situation (i.e., three

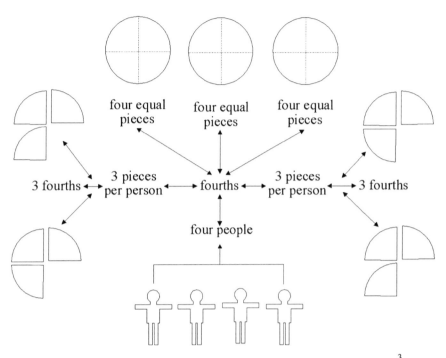

FIG. 4.20.   Mapping processes involved in modeling the quotient construct for $\frac{3}{4}$.

items shared among four, not four items shared among three). Children must then realize that, because four people are sharing, each person will receive one fourth of the items.

In contrast to the part/whole construct where the fraction name is derived from the number of equal parts comprising the whole, the name of the fraction in this model is derived from a number of wholes, that is, from the people sharing the items (not the items themselves). This means that there is a mapping from the number of people (four) to the fraction name, fourths. Children must then apply their understanding of the part/whole construct to the partitioning of the pizzas. This involves a mapping from the fraction name (fourths) to the number of pieces into which each pizza must be subdivided (four). Notice that the emphasis here is from fraction name to number of pieces, in contrast to the part/whole construct where the initial emphasis was from number of parts to fraction name. However the nature of the mapping process itself indicates that children should be able to move freely between source and target. Once each pizza has been partitioned into four equal parts, the parts must be apportioned accordingly amongst the four people. Each person receives three pieces of pizza. Because each piece represents one fourth of a pizza, each person's share is equivalent to three fourths of a pizza. *referring again to 3 out of 4 pieces*

Overall, this sharing analog for the quotient construct presents quite complex processes for children, even though it is "real world" and can be readily modeled with hands-on materials. The number of simultaneous mapping processes involved in its application need to be taken into account in the instructional process.

Operator Construct.   The operator construct of rational number adopts an algebraic interpretation (Behr et al., 1983). For example, $\frac{m}{n}$ can be thought of as a function that transforms a given set into another set with $\frac{m}{n}$ times as many elements. It may also be viewed as a function that transforms geometric figures into similar figures $\frac{m}{n}$ times as large. This operator notion is often embodied in a function machine, an "*m* for *n*" machine, where an input of length or cardinality *n* produces an output of length or cardinality *m*.

Behr et al. (1993) interpreted the operator construct in terms of "duplicator/partition-reducer" and "stretcher/shrinker" notions. These both operate on an operand as an "exchange function." For example, given the fraction $\frac{3}{4}$, the duplicator/partition-reducer exchanges every set of 4 units with a set of 3 units of the same size. The stretcher/shrinker, on the other hand, exchanges every 4-unit with a 3-unit, thereby maintaining the number of units in the operand constant but reducing the size of each. We revisit the operator construct in our discussion on fraction multiplication in chapter 6.

Ratio.   Ratio is a real-world application of mathematics, yet it is a complex notion for children and adults (Hart, 1984). A ratio involves a comparison between two quantities of the same kind, for example, two teachers to 40 children. Here, the comparison is between two distinct wholes, however it can also be between two parts comprising a whole, such as a cement mixture comprising two parts sand and three parts cement. In this last example, the total number of parts is five, but the ratio is 2:3. When recorded in common fraction form, $\frac{2}{3}$, there is potential for confusion between the ratio and part/whole constructs, that is, $\frac{2}{3}$ can be misinterpreted as "two parts out of 3 parts." The use of the ratio symbol (:), in preference to the common fraction symbol (–) helps to avoid this confusion. The latter symbol would only be appropriate if the ratio involved a comparison between a part and whole, such as, the ratio of the number of chocolate ice-blocks sold to the number of ice-blocks sold altogether. Although ratio is a commonly accepted rational number construct, its inclusion within the fraction strand of the school curriculum appears inappropriate. The basic part/whole fraction idea does not provide an adequate foundation for the introduction of ratio and, furthermore, can lead to misconceptions.

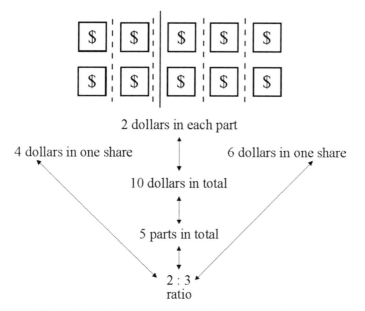

FIG. 4.21. Mapping processes involved in solving a ratio problem.

Summarizing the previous points, we see that the complexity of the ratio construct lies largely in its different referents, namely, it can refer to a comparison between parts, between wholes, or between parts and a whole. Recognizing which of these referents is being addressed is the first step in solving a problem such as, "Share $10 in the ratio of 2:3." This example demands not only an application of ratio but also an understanding of both the part/whole and the operator constructs of rational number. Proportional reasoning is also involved in transforming the ratios into fractions (Lesh, Post, & Behr, 1988). The complex mapping processes involved here are illustrated in Fig. 4.21.

The first mapping required in solving this problem is from the ratio (2:3) to the total number of parts represented in the ratio (5). The next mapping associates the total number of parts with the set of 10 dollars and leads to the operation of division to find the number of dollars in each part. Because there are five parts in all and 10 dollars in the set, then each part comprises 2 dollars. The problem is not solved yet, however. A mapping is now required from the original ratio, two parts to three parts, to the subdivided set of 10 dollars. Two parts of the set represent 2 lots of 2 dollars, that is, 4 dollars, whereas three parts comprise 3 lots of 2 dollars. Hence the solution to the problem is 4 dollars in one share and 6 dollars in the other share.

Decimal Fractions.   In many ways, decimal fractions appear less complex than common fractions because they represent an extension of the whole number system and are thus introduced in the context of "potentially supportive prior knowledge" (Wearne & Hiebert, 1988b). Decimal fractions exhibit many of the properties of whole numbers, such as place value. That is, the right-to-left increase by factors of 10 (and conversely, left-to-right decrease by factors of 10) holds for both decimal fractions and whole numbers. This has both advantages and disadvantages for children's learning of decimal fractions. Although whole-number relationships and processes can serve as analogs for the learning of decimal fractions, children can focus too strongly on the whole-number components and ignore the special features of decimal fractions. This is understandable, given that the symbols used in decimal notation look like whole numbers yet represent quantities that are fractions (Hiebert, 1992). As a result, children make the common error of comparing decimal fractions as if they were whole numbers. For example, they would claim that 0.46 is greater than 0.5 because 46 is greater than 5. Reading decimal fractions as whole numbers, such as, "point four six" (or worse still, "point forty-six") rather than, "forty-six hundredths," contributes to this error (Wearne & Hiebert, 1985).

Although decimal fractions have parallel features to whole numbers, they also display unique characteristics. They can represent both discrete and continuous quantities (e.g., length); however, in written computations, they often appear as though they represent discrete constructs only (Hiebert, Wearne, & Taber, 1991). Unlike whole numbers, decimal fractions display a continuous feature in that between any two decimal numbers a third decimal can always be inserted (Hiebert et al., 1991, 1992), for example, a decimal that would fall between 0.42 and 0.43 is 0.422. Of course, there are an infinite number of these. Another feature of the continuous quantity of decimal fractions is that digits can be adjoined to the right of a numeral without end and, in so doing, add less and less to the size of the number (Hiebert, 1992).

Although decimal fractions would appear to present fewer complexities for children than other fraction constructs, they nevertheless pose significant problems. A common finding is that children lack a conceptual knowledge of decimal fractions and, as for common fractions, resort to memorization of rules and procedures that they frequently apply erroneously (Fischbein, Deri, Nello, & Marino, 1985; Hiebert & Wearne, 1986, 1988; Hiebert et al., 1991; Resnick et al., 1989; Wearne, 1990; Wearne & Hiebert, 1985). In one such study, Hiebert and Wearne (1986) observed that elementary school children recognized few, if any, connections between their conceptual knowledge of decimals and the symbol manipulation procedures they applied to decimal problems. In fact, this lack of connection was so extensive that the two kinds of knowledge appeared to characterize two distinct mental models.

Developing Mental Models of Rational Number

Given the complexity of the rational number domain and the difficulties it presents children, it is clear that we need to consider carefully the nature of the instructional experiences we design for children. The analogs we use should enable children to readily integrate new ideas and procedures, to apply these to related situations, and to develop both precision and flexibility in their dealings with these numbers. As previously mentioned, we advocate the part/whole construct, represented by an area or region representation, as the major unifying model for introducing and establishing rational number concepts and processes.

We now give consideration to developing this model, drawing upon the principles we proposed earlier. We firstly address the introduction of the concept, including the formal fraction names. Because we derive common and decimal fractions from this same construct, we treat their development jointly. However, once we consider the symbolic representations, we examine the two fraction forms separately and highlight their unique features.

Developing the Part/Whole Schema. Children's initial activities with the area model would focus on "real-world" situations, with the child subdividing various shapes into equal parts and re-assembling them to form the whole unit. As the emphasis in this introductory stage is on the concept of "equal parts" and subsequently, "*x* equal parts," it is important that children be able to distinguish between shapes that are subdivided into equal parts and those that are subdivided into unequal parts. Once children can identify the number of equal parts forming the whole region they can consider the number of shaded parts within this region, as was indicated in Fig. 4.19A.

Reading the fractional amount as "three parts out of eight equal parts" can help children understand that the shaded parts represent a fraction of the whole. The notion of "*x* parts out of *y* equal parts" not only reinforces the part/whole construct but also prepares the child for the later introduction of the formal symbols. At this stage, the formal fraction name such as "eighths" only adds an unnecessary mapping and is best left until later. These early activities need to also include simple comparison activities, such as, "Which covers more, five out of your eight pieces or three out of your eight pieces? How do you know? How can you show that you're correct?" It is particularly important that these preliminary activities include units divided into 10 equal parts so that children develop one cohesive mental model for both decimal and common fractions, not two unrelated models. Although not denying the obviously unique features of these two fraction forms, it is unfortunate that they are treated as quite separate entities in schools and reported as such in the literature.

The introduction of the formal fraction names should involve only one new mapping process for the child (e.g., eight equal pieces → eighths), as was indicated in Fig. 4.19A. This can be achieved by introducing the regular fraction names (e.g., "fourths," "sixths," "tenths") prior to the irregular names ("halves," "thirds," "quarters," "fifths"). Because there is not a direct mapping from the analog representation (e.g., three equal pieces) to the irregular fraction name (e.g., "thirds"), the learning of these names involves a memorization process. However children's familiarity with these irregular names from their informal experiences and also from their ordinal number activities would assist here.

Formalizing the Part/Whole Construct. The next major process for the child is to map her knowledge of the fraction names and referents to the formal symbols (Wearne & Hiebert, 1988b, refer to this as the "connecting process"). The formal recording of the part/whole construct can be of two formats, namely, common fraction and decimal fraction. Although derived from the same part/whole construct, common and decimal fractions take on unique features once in symbolic form. For example, decimal fractions incorporate place-value properties that enable them to be readily compared, sequenced, and operated on. In contrast, common fractions do not lend themselves as easily to these processes because they do not possess place-value characteristics. Fractions with unlike denominators (e.g., eighths and sixths) must be converted to equivalent fractions before these processes can be applied.

Because children commonly perceive written symbols and procedures as unrelated to their concrete representations (Wearne & Hiebert, 1988a, 1988b), it is imperative that there be a clear and direct mapping between the fraction analog, the fraction name, and the formal symbol. We give initial consideration to the recording of decimal fractions and the processes of comparing and ordering. We follow this with a brief discussion on the recording of common fractions and then devote a section to the development of children's mental model of equivalence.

Formalizing and Consolidating the Decimal Fraction Construct. The recording of decimal fractions represents an extension of whole-number recording. That is, we extend the place-value relationships (decreasing by a factor of 10 from left to right) beyond the ones place to incorporate the partitioning of ones into tenths, and later, tenths into hundredths, and hundredths into thousandths. The use of concrete or pictorial referents on a place-value chart can assist in developing this understanding, as indicated in Fig. 4.22. Interpreting the fraction as "two and three tenths," rather than as "two point three," reinforces the meaning of the decimal fraction and helps reduce children's tendency to interpret it as a whole number. This also applies to the initial reading of fractions comprising hundredths and thousandths

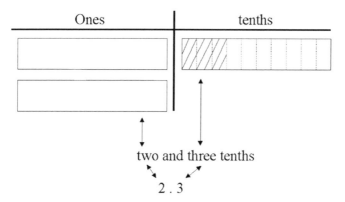

FIG. 4.22. Mapping processes involved in the recording of the decimal fraction form.

(e.g., "two and thirty-four hundredths" rather than "two point three four"). Although the decimal point has been included in Fig. 4.22, we recommend that it be omitted in the initial recording phase as it only creates an additional mapping process for the child. A vertical line separating the ones and tenths on the place-value chart can be used instead. Children can later see the need for the decimal point when the line is removed. It is important that children understand that it is the ones place, not the decimal point, that is the pivotal point on the chart. That is, the grouping process (increasing by a factor of 10) begins with the ones and develops the whole numbers (tens, hundreds, etc.). The partitioning process leading into the decimal fractions also begins with the ones. The inclusion of both ones and tenths, not simply tenths, in the initial symbolization phase reinforces this understanding.

The area model lends itself readily to the learning of hundredths and thousandths. Children's understanding of a whole unit partitioned into ten tenths can be extended to incorporate the partitioning of the ten parts into one hundred equal parts, that is, one hundred hundredths, as indicated in Fig. 4.23. The shaded portion represents 37 parts out of 100 equal parts, that is, thirty-seven hundredths. The analog also illustrates the equivalence of ten hundredths and one tenth (a clear template of the unit partitioned into ten tenths can highlight this equivalence). The shaded portion can now be interpreted as both "thirty-seven hundredths," and "three tenths seven hundredths."

We conclude this section by mentioning a few points on the reading and symbolization of more complex decimal fractions and on the comparing and ordering of these numbers. One of the difficulties with the recording of hundredths and thousandths is the difference in the way they are read and written. When we read a decimal fraction, such as 4.387, we only say the last place name (e.g., "four, and three hundred and eighty-seven thousandths").

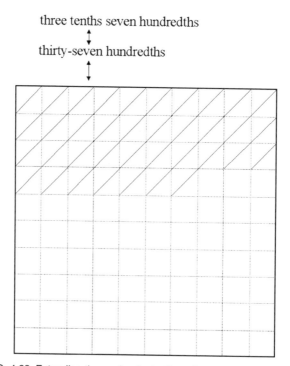

three tenths seven hundredths

thirty-seven hundredths

FIG. 4.23. Extending the analog for tenths to incorporate hundredths.

Yet we use all places in the recording of the number, that is, 3 tenths, 8 hundredths, 7 thousandths. Furthermore, as Hiebert (1992) noted, there is a mismatch between the digit names that we say (e.g., "three hundred") and their positional value (e.g., tenths). That is, the word, "hundred," is used with the digit, *3,* in the tenths' place. The mismatch changes as more digits are added to the numeral. It is thus important that the child develops a sound place-value understanding of decimal fractions and can rename one place in terms of another (e.g., 3 hundred thousandths is equivalent to 3 tenths).

The recording of numbers comprising zeros (e.g., 3.002, 4.607, and 3.025) can present particular problems for children and hence are best introduced after the recording of all nonzero examples (e.g., 5.465). With the former examples, the mapping from the reading to the recording is even less direct. Hence, an example such as 3.025, read as, "three and twenty-five thousandths," can be erroneously recorded as, "3.25."

Children who lack a conceptual understanding of decimal fractions will have difficulty comparing and ordering these numbers. As mentioned earlier, children frequently state that 0.436 is greater than 0.59 "because 436 is greater than 59." They are clearly treating the decimal fractions as if they

were whole numbers. These misconceptions can be overcome with appropriate development of the decimal fraction ideas, as discussed previously,
and with a few simple comparison procedures such as comparing the places
of greatest value first.

Formalizing and Consolidating the Common Fraction Construct.   Recall
our earlier discussion on establishing an understanding of "*x* parts out of *y*
equal parts" in developing the part/whole idea. This schema leads directly
into the symbolic recording of the common fraction form, $\frac{x}{y}$. Here, there is
a direct mapping from "*x* parts" to the numerator of the fraction (*x*) and from
"*y* parts" to the denominator (*y*). Furthermore, there is a direct mapping from
the notion of "out of" to the fraction bar or vinculum, as shown in Fig. 4.24.
This latter mapping gives meaning (albeit a "part/whole" meaning) to this
abstract fraction symbol. Once this recording has been established children
should be able to translate readily between the symbolic form, the corresponding analog representation, and the fraction name. Activities involving
these translations can encompass proper fractions (e.g., 5 sixths), improper
fractions (e.g., 7 sixths) and mixed numbers (e.g., 1 and 3 sevenths).

The processes of comparing and ordering are more complex for common
fractions than for decimal fractions, especially when fractions with unlike
denominators are involved (e.g., thirds and fifths). It is at this point that we
need to address equivalent fractions.

Developing a Mental Model of Equivalent Fractions

One of the common errors children make in identifying the larger or smaller
of two fractions with unlike denominators is comparing the denominators as
if they were whole numbers (Behr et al., 1984; Mack, 1990). Without appro-

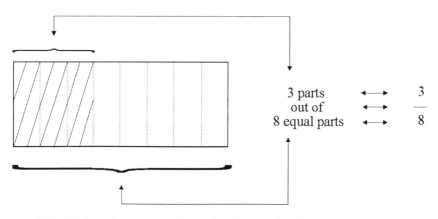

FIG. 4.24. Mapping processes involved in the recording of the common fraction
format.

priate intervention, we see children misapplying the same schemas to the addition and subtraction of fractions, erroneously concluding that, for example, 3 quarters + 2 thirds = 5 sevenths. One of the key understandings here is the compensatory relation between the size and number of equal parts in a partitioned unit (Behr et al., 1984). In their preliminary activites with cutting and folding of shapes, children's attention needs to be drawn to the fact that the greater the number of parts into which the unit has been partitioned, the smaller the fraction size, and vice versa.

In these initial activities, children can readily compare and order fractions with like, then unlike, denominators by directly comparing cutouts of variously sized fractional pieces of a whole unit. Eventually, children need to appreciate the need for equivalent fractions when comparing fractions with unlike denominators. This is made more difficult when none of the denominators being compared can serve as a common denominator (e.g., $\frac{2}{3}$ and $\frac{3}{4}$). Given that our ultimate aim in teaching equivalent fractions is to help the child become progressively independent of concrete embodiments (Post, Wachsmuth, Lesh, & Behr, 1985), we need to consider a way in which this might be achieved.

Activities with paper folding are particularly suitable here as they are easily manipulated and constitute a well-known referent for children (Leinhardt, 1988). Children's familiarity with both the structure and associated language of the part/whole region model makes it easier for children to map their existing knowledge onto the new ideas of equivalence. To assist this process, we need to apply the same language and same sequence of steps in the paper-folding activities as we used in our introductory activities. We can then lead the child to an understanding of equivalence by introducing one new mapping at a time. An appropriate activity might involve children in, first, shading two parts of a region that has been divided into six equal parts. After identifying the fraction shaded (2 sixths), children can fold the region in half and identify the new number of shaded parts (four) as well as the new total number of parts (12). The new fraction shaded can then be identified (4 twelfths). Children can then see that the fractions, 2 sixths and 4 twelfths, are equivalent because the total area has not changed. Additional equivalent fractions can be generated with further folding.

Children's actions with the paper-folding activity lead easily into the formalization process, as shown below. Given that this process involves a multiple-system mapping, it is particularly important that children experience the concrete activity first.

Number of shaded parts is multiplied by $2 \leftrightarrow \underline{2 \times 2}$
Total number of parts is multiplied by $2 \leftrightarrow \overline{6 \times 2}$

It is also important here for children to realize that $\frac{2}{6}$ retains its value since it is being multiplied by one ($\frac{2}{2}$), the identity element for multiplication. Children can easily generate further equivalent fractions by multiplying the original fraction by $\frac{3}{3}$, $\frac{4}{4}$, etc. At this point, it is worth mentioning briefly the notion of "cancelling" of fractions. This involves the reverse of the procedure for generating equivalent fractions. For example, $\frac{6}{9}$ can be reduced to its lowest terms by factorizing it into its prime factors ($\frac{3}{3} \times \frac{2}{3}$) and then "cancelling out" the factors common to the numerator and denominator ($\frac{3}{3}$). This again involves the identity element for multiplication.

The set model does not lend itself readily to the discovery of equivalent fractions nor to the generation of the formal procedure. In fact, the child has to apply an understanding of equivalence (and proportion) to identify the equivalent fractions. For example, if children were presented with a set of six counters comprising five black and one red, would they know to increase the black and red counters by the same amount to produce the equivalent fraction, $\frac{10}{12}$, if they had not been taught to do so? It is difficult to perceive the equivalence of the two fractions because there is a visible increase in the numbers of counters. It is not the area that remains constant here (although this could be achieved by placing the new counters underneath the old), but the ratios between the corresponding numerators and denominators (5:10 = 6:12). When we realize that this process involves an understanding of proportion (Lesh et al., 1988), we can begin to appreciate the complexities this model presents.

NEGATIVE INTEGERS

We conclude this chapter with a brief consideration of negative integers. Although these numbers are basically an extension of the set of positive numbers and of the structures operating on positives (Schwarz, Kohn, & Resnick, 1992), they are nevertheless abstract entities and form the first component of the core of higher level mathematics (Schwarz, Kohn, & Resnick, in press). According to Schwarz et al. (1992, in press), the central idea about the nature of negative numbers is that of extension. More specifically, negative integers represent an extension of:

- The state of quantity and number to another kind of magnitude, namely, directed magnitudes;
- The domain of application for operations defined a priori on positives. For example, the operation "+" can be used in the expression "(–3) + (–4) = (–7);"
- Operations to a new realm of what is operable on numbers, for example, the operation "– –" can be applied, as in "4 – – 2 = 6;"
- The relation of order as defined on positives, for example, –3 < – 1.

Larger

-3 -2 -1   0 +1 +2 +3

FIG. 4.25. The "continuous number line" representation of negative numbers.

Negative numbers are more difficult to perceive than positive integers because they are not rooted directly in children's everyday experiences. Despite this, children seem to have some preinstructional intuitions about these numbers (Peled, Mukhopadhyay, & Resnick, 1988). In their study of children's mental models of negative integers, Peled et al. identified a progression from a model of number in which negative numbers do not exist to a model in which all of the integers (positive and negative) are ordered in a "mental number line," with numbers organized symmetrically around zero. The children's responses suggested that there are two forms of number-line representation. In the most sophisticated representation, namely, a continuous number line, children order the numbers along a single continuum from smaller (the negatives) to larger (the positives), as shown in Fig. 4.25

A less advanced model joins two symmetric strings of numbers at zero and emphasizes movements toward and away from zero rather than simply up and down. Peled et al. (1988) referred to this as the "divided number line" model, as shown in Fig. 4.26. Unlike the previous model, the divided number line requires special rules for crossing zero when performing computations. Typically, a child would partition the number to be added or subtracted into the amount needed to reach zero and then continue counting off the remaining amount on the other side of zero. This suggests that children are applying their understanding of additive composition (Resnick, 1986) to produce this partitioning strategy. Peled et al. concluded that children develop preinstructional intuitions about these abstract entities by elaborating on previously developed ideas about number, in particular, additive composition and partitioning. These ideas are grounded in physical experience and, through practice, become so familiar that they become "intuitions in their own right" (p. 7).

Smaller   Larger

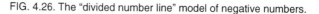

-3 -2 -1   0   +1 +2 +3

FIG. 4.26. The "divided number line" model of negative numbers.

SUMMARY

In this chapter we examined children's acquisition of numerical models and processes. Our main points may be summarized as follows:

1. Children's early learning involves experience with concrete analogs that mirror important numerical relations. Not all analogs clearly convey the intended mathematical ideas. Some analogs may be structurally simple yet prove to be complex learning aids when applied to target concepts that comprise inherently complex relations.

2. There are two major schools of thought on how children develop early counting skills, namely, through innate counting principles or through acquired understandings. The accumulator theory provides a plausible account of the latter.

3. To ensure that children develop a meaningful canonical base-ten representation of multidigit numbers, the introduction of place-value ideas needs to be carefully sequenced to enable a clear and direct mapping from the analog representation to the target concept. Appropriate explanations must accompany these mapping processes. An explicit recognition and understanding of the relationships inherent in our number system is essential if children are to deal meaningfully with larger numbers.

4. The introduction of rational number presents difficulties for children, largely because a number of relations must be considered jointly. The various meanings that can be assigned to a fraction also pose problems. These meanings include part/whole, quotient, operator, ratio, and measure. Children are usually introduced to rational number via the part/whole notion. The area or region model can effectively demonstrate this idea, whereas the set model presents more complex relations for the child. The part/whole construct can help children form a cohesive mental model of decimal and common fractions.

5. Negative numbers are abstract entities for children because they are not rooted directly in experience. Children nevertheless have some informal understanding of these numbers, in the form of mental number line-models where the positive and negative integers are organized systematically around zero.

5

ELEMENTARY COMPUTATIONAL MODELS AND PROCESSES: ADDITION AND SUBTRACTION

In this chapter and the next, we examine the development of elementary computational models and processes for whole numbers and fractions. This chapter focuses on addition and subtraction whereas chapter 6 addresses multiplication and division. We begin this chapter with a brief discussion on children's computational performance. Because children's difficulties appear to stem largely from a failure to form connections among important mathematical ideas, we give consideration to the links that must be established among the various representations for number and computation. We then examine some conceptual and procedural models of addition and subtraction, for both whole numbers and fractions, and offer some suggestions for developing children's understanding of these.

CHILDREN'S COMPUTATIONAL PERFORMANCE

Several studies have indicated that young children bring to school a substantial body of knowledge about number and informal computational processes (e.g., Ginsburg & Baron, 1993; Resnick, 1992; Resnick & Greeno, 1990; Resnick, Bill, & Lesgold, 1992). Kindergarten children can successfully solve a range of computational problems by directly representing or modeling the actions or relationships described in the problem (Carpenter, Ansell, et al., 1993). Because they can draw upon their real-world knowledge in solving problems in the early school years, these young children have some idea of whether or not their solutions make sense. However, as they progress through the grade levels, their perception of mathematics appears to deteriorate (Wearne & Hiebert, 1985). They tend not to see mathematics as meaningful and relevant to their world, rather, they see it as a domain that calls for meaningless manipulations of symbols, rules, and procedures (Greeno, 1988; Onslow, 1991). They find it difficult to link what they already know and understand about mathematics to the symbols and rules they use. The middle years appear to be the time when mathematics loses meaning for many students, a time when symbols take on a life of their own with little attachment to conceptual models (Wearne & Hiebert, 1988b). In essence then, we see students' losing their grip on any mental models they might have developed in the early years; they have little option but to turn to memorized rules and procedures. It is little wonder that they seldom consider whether their answers are sensible. Because they fail to recognize correspondences between problems, they will not realize that they have produced two different answers for variations of the same problem.

The importance of helping students form connections between mathematical concepts, facts, and procedures has long been advocated in the mathematics education literature (e.g., Brownell, 1935; Fehr, 1953; Van Engen, 1949). Research reports and curriculum documents have offered numerous suggestions for achieving this (e.g., Australian Education Council, 1990; National Council of Teachers of Mathematics, 1989, 1991). Yet despite their efforts, children are still failing to form the connections we desire and, hence, failing to construct appropriate mental models. In an effort to determine why this is happening, we give consideration to the various connections children need to form among the representations they encounter for number and computation. Making these links should entail efficient use of cognitive resources, with the connections being appropriate, unambiguous, and meaningful. In the next section, we consider the types of connections to be formed among external representations (concrete, pictoral/diagrammatic, symbolic) and among internal representations (mental models).

Forming Connections Among External Representations

The connections children form among external representations of computational concepts and procedures form the basis of their construction of internal computational models (cf. Hiebert & Carpenter's, 1992, argument). We show these connections in the matrix of Fig. 5.1. The external representations listed in the matrix include the concrete, pictorial/diagrammatic, and symbolic elements. Each representation comprises four key components, namely, design, format, actions, and explanation. We address each component in turn, and then examine the connections to be formed between corresponding components.

The first component, that of *design*, refers to the way in which the

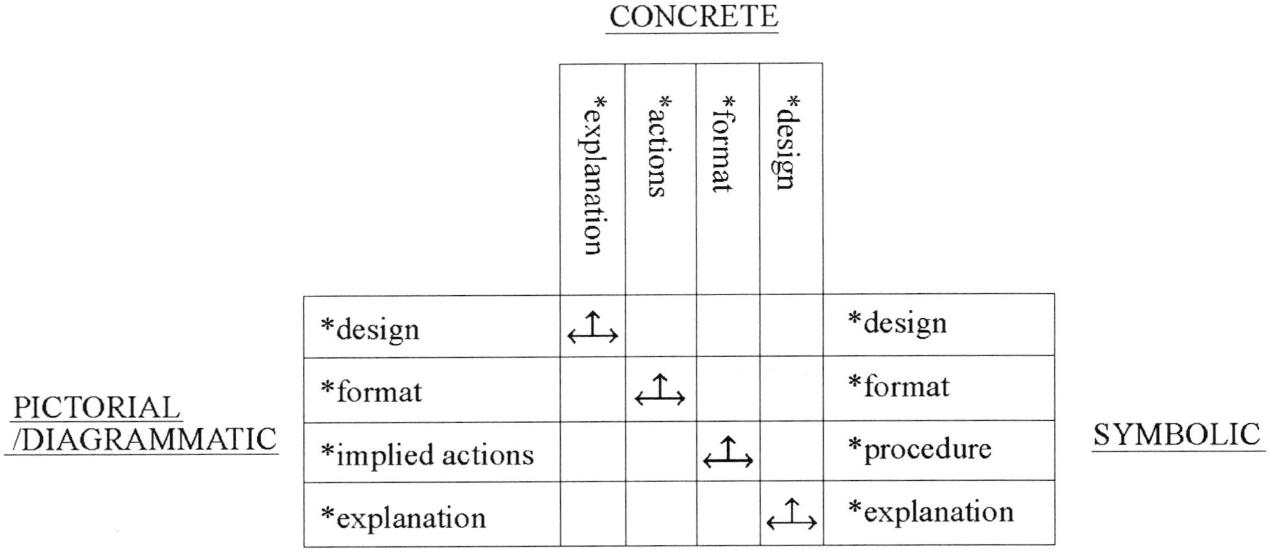

CONCRETE

	*design	*format	*actions	*explanation
*design				↕
*format			↕	
*implied actions		↕		
*explanation	↕			

PICTORIAL /DIAGRAMMATIC

SYMBOLIC

*design	
*format	
*procedure	↕
*explanation	

FIG. 5.1.   Matrix of representational connections.

representation is structured. For example, the base-ten blocks comprise pieces of wood that are structured in terms of ones, tens, hundreds, and thousands. Their properties thus simulate both the properties of our number system and the effects of operations on the numbers represented by the blocks (Greeno, 1991). Included in the structure of these external representations is the appropriateness of the representation for the concept or process being developed. The next component, that of *format*, refers to the layout or arrangement of the external representation. This includes the way in which concrete and pictorial materials are arranged, such as the tens blocks to the left of the ones blocks in a base-ten representation of a two-digit number. The component designating how the materials or symbols are manipulated is referred to here as, *actions* (for the concrete representation), *implied actions* (pictorial representation), and *procedures* (symbols). The final component, that of explanation, is the verbalization (of both teacher and child) that accompanies the implementation of the other components.

As shown in the matrix, there is a direct connection between corresponding components of each representation, such as between the format of the concrete representation, the format of the symbolic representation, and the format of the pictorial representation. This gives a three-way connection across all representations. A written computation will only be meaningful to children if they can map their mental model of the symbolic procedures onto their mental model of the corresponding procedures with the concrete and pictorial embodiments (Hiebert & Carpenter, 1992). To illustrate this point, we consider the addition example, 34 + 19, and the corresponding formats of the base-ten representation and the symbolic representation. If we were to place the tens and ones blocks randomly in one set and the symbolic representation in a horizontal format (34 + 19), there clearly would not be a direct connection between the two formats. To establish a clear link, the three tens blocks are best placed below the one tens block and the four ones blocks below the nine ones blocks on a place-value chart, with the symbolic recording adopting a vertical format. This would then enable the additive actions on the blocks to mirror the additive procedures performed with the symbols. We elaborate on these points in subsequent discussion and turn now to a consideration of the connections between mental models.

Forming Connections Among Internal Representations

A failure to make the appropriate connections between external representations of computational concepts and procedures is not the only cause of children's poor mental models. Their difficulties may also stem from their inability to see the links between related computational procedures, as well as between these procedures and the underlying numeration concepts. More specifically, children can experience difficulty in forming connections between:

- Inverse computational processes (e.g., addition and subtraction);
- Computational procedures (e.g., the subtraction algorithm) and numeration concepts and processes (e.g., place value and regrouping);
- Computational procedures involving whole numbers and the corresponding procedures involving fractions;
- Early computational processes (e.g., "take-away" subtraction involving the removal of items from a set) and later, more advanced procedures (e.g., multidigit subtraction involving removal of blocks from a base-ten representation); and
- Known understandings and procedures (e.g., adding multidigit numbers without regrouping) and new procedures (e.g., adding multidigit numbers with regrouping).

We will return to these points during the course of this chapter and turn our attention now to the development of the conceptual models of addition and subtraction. We initially consider the various meanings of these operations and how children might conceptualize and proceduralize them. We include here an analysis of the more complex computational word problems and the particular difficulties they present for children.

CONCEPTUAL MODELS OF WHOLE NUMBER ADDITION AND SUBTRACTION

Schwartz (1988) defined addition and subtraction as "referent preserving compositions," because two like quantities are composed to produce a third like quantity (p. 41). Extensive research has been conducted on children's learning of these operations (e.g., Baroody, 1984; Baroody & Ginsburg, 1986; Bergeron & Herscovics, 1990; Carpenter, 1985; Carpenter & Moser, 1984; Carpenter, Hiebert, & Moser, 1981; Carpenter, Moser, & Romberg, 1982; Fuson, 1988a, 1992a, 1992b). Although there is a decreased emphasis on detailed paper-and-pencil calculations (e.g., National Council of Teachers of Mathematics, 1989; Shuard, 1991) and a greater emphasis on mental computation and computational estimation (e.g., Beishuizen, 1993; Sowder, 1988; Sowder & Kelin, 1993), children still require an understanding of basic computational processes.

In chapter 3, we referred to children's early experiences with real-world situations involving increasing and decreasing sets of items. Children's development of "protoquantitative *increase/decrease* schema," which involves reasoning about quantity without measurement or exact numerical quantification, lays the foundation for an understanding of addition and subtraction (Resnick et al., 1992, p. 216). Resnick et al. identifed two other types of protoquantitative schemata, namely, *compare* and *part/whole.* The compare schema allows the child to make comparative judgments of given amounts, initially in a perceptual way ("greater than/smaller than"), then later using numerical comparisons. With a part/whole schema, children can reason about the ways in which familiar materials come together and break apart. This is a particularly important schema as it enables children to make judgments about various relationships between parts and wholes and thus provides the foundation for binary addition and subtraction, as well as important mathematical principles (e.g., commutativity).

These schemata can also assist children in solving some of the different types of addition and subtraction situations they meet in their everyday world and which are subsequently formalized as word problems in the classroom. These situations have been variously defined in the literature, with earlier descriptions incorporating a distinction between static and active cases (Briars & Larkin, 1984; Carpenter & Moser, 1982, 1983; Fuson, 1992a; M. S. Riley & Greeno, 1988).

More recent category systems frequently collapse this static/active distinction into a binary/unary classification (Fuson, 1992b). Fuson (1992b) identified four basic situations that incorporate this classification. These are *compare, combine, change-add-to,* and *change-take-from* situations (hyphens added). Compare and combine situations involve operations on two numbers to produce a third; they are termed binary operations. Change-add-to and change-take-from are considered to be unary operations because they involve adding to, or taking from, one quantity to produce a unique third number. It is not our intention to address each of these categories and their subcategories in detail. A comprehensive coverage of these can be found in Fuson (1992a, 1992b) and M. S. Riley and Greeno, (1988). For our present purposes, we will examine the following categories of problems: (a) change-by-adding and change-by-subtracting; and (b) combine and separate (part–part–whole), compare and equalize.

We initially consider the less complex of these, namely, the change-by-adding and change-by-subtracting cases and the operations of combine and separate. With these problems, there is a clear mapping between the given problem situation and the operation required to solve it. We then examine the remaining operations of compare and equalize. These involve more complex models, as there is not always a clear mapping between the problem situation and the required operation.

Change-by-Adding, Combine, Change-by-Subtracting, and Separate Problems

Children's early experiences with addition and subtraction involve direct modeling of a real-world problem situation using physical embodiments (Bergeron & Herscovics, 1990; Carpenter & Moser, 1984; Fuson, 1992a,

Change-by-adding

Jane had 6 marbles. Jo gave her 3 more marbles.

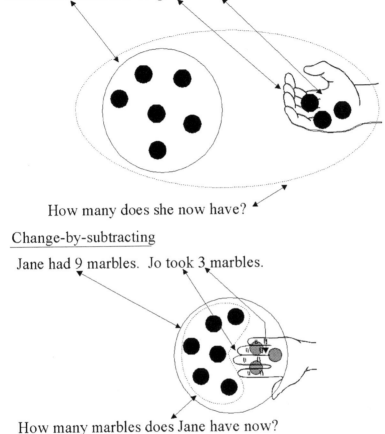

How many does she now have?

Change-by-subtracting

Jane had 9 marbles. Jo took 3 marbles.

How many marbles does Jane have now?

FIG. 5.2.   Modeling of change-by-adding and change-by-subtracting problems.

1992b; Gray, 1991). Figure 5.2 illustrates this modeling with a change-by-adding and change-by-subtracting situation. Here, there is a direct mapping between the concrete representation and the items in the problem. There is also a mapping between the actions or relationships stated in the verbal problem and those performed on the materials.

Change-by-Adding.   We consider the addition example first. Recall in the last chapter we referred to the accumulator model for determining numerosity, where the entire fullness of the accumulator, not the final increment alone, represented the numerosity of the items counted. In the present example, children would construct a set of six items to represent the six marbles. As they add three more items to the set (for the three additional marbles), they must switch from their accumulator model to a counting-sequence model (cf. Fuson's, 1992b, cardinal-to-count transition, p. 248). That is, they must count out, one, two, three, as they add the required number of items to their existing set of six items. To determine the solution to the problem, children would initially count all of the items in the total set (counting-all strategy, Carpenter & Moser, 1984). The accumulator model would be invoked as the set is counted, representing a switch from a counting-sequence model back to an accumulator model. An alternative solution procedure, however, is to count on from the set of six items (i.e., "six, *seven, eight, nine*"), however this is a more sophisticated strategy as we will indicate.

Combine.   Additive problems of the combine type involve similar processes for the child, although they entail actions or implied actions on two distinct quantities, for example, *"Sue has 8 green pencils and 3 blue pencils. She puts them all in her pencil case. How many pencils does she have altogether?"* These problems are effectively modeled using a part–part–whole approach (Resnick, 1983; Resnick et al., 1992). One part, the eight green pencils, is mapped onto a set of eight counters, while the other part, the three blue pencils, is mapped onto a set of three counters. The whole is represented by the two parts taken together (refer to Fig. 5.3); for a discussion on the ways in which the parts may be arranged, see Bergeron and Herscovics (1990). As before, the child can determine the whole amount by counting all items or by beginning with the cardinal value of one of the original parts.

An important conceptual development associated with the latter proce-

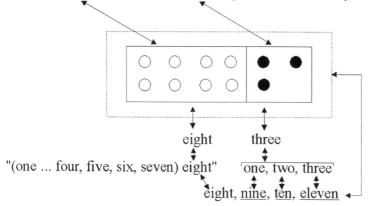

FIG. 5.3.   Solving a combine problem by counting-on.

dure is what Fuson (1992b) termed, "embedded integration" for both addends. That is, the two parts and the whole can be considered simultaneously by embedding the parts within the whole. This means the child is able to abstract the cardinal value of one of the parts (e.g., "eight") and does not need to re-count its items in determining the whole. In preparation for adding on the second addend, the child must map the cardinal amount of the first addend onto a counting-sequence model. This latter model may be viewed in terms of "an abbreviation of the actual counting of the objects for the first addend, a summary of this counting act" (Secada, Fuson, & Hall (1983, p. 49). The cardinal value of the second addend must then be mapped onto a counting-sequence model (*one, two, three*) and seen as the beginning (cf. Secada et al.) of the counting-on process. This process does not involve a direct mapping for the child, however. As indicated in Fig. 5.3, each number in the counting-sequence model of the second addend (i.e., *one, two, three*) must be mapped onto each corresponding number in the count of the new whole set (i.e., *nine, ten, eleven*). This means the child has to shift from perceiving the items within the parts as belonging only to two disjoint sets, to seeing them also as members of the whole sum set (Secada et al., 1983). When we consider the complexities of this task, we can see why children's transition to the counting-on process is not a rapid one (Baroody, 1987; Siegler & Jenkins, 1989).

Change-by-Subtracting.   Returning to the change-by-subtracting example of Fig. 5.2, we can see that the child models the problem by initially forming a set of nine counters. Because the problem involves the removal of three marbles, the child must take away three of her counters. Note here that we have a take-away situation that serves as the model for subsequent multidigit subtractions of whole numbers and fractions. We now consider this take-away process in greater detail. As for the corresponding addition example, the child must switch from an accumulator model of the total set to a counting-sequence model. That is, the child has to count, *one, two, three,* as she removes each of the required number of items. She then returns to her accumulator model as she counts the number in the remaining set to determine the solution to the problem.

The part–part–whole model also lends itself well to take-away situations involving separating a subset from a whole set. It can readily show the inverse relationship of addition and subtraction (i.e., separating one part from the whole leaves one part; combining the two parts makes the whole). It is also particularly useful in promoting the embedded integration process in which the whole set and the two separated parts are considered simultaneously. This facilitates children's transition to a more sophisticated solution strategy, that of counting down from the initial set. The need to consider the parts and the whole simultaneously is clearly evident here. We illustrate

Sally had 8 marbles. She lost 3 marbles. How many has she now?

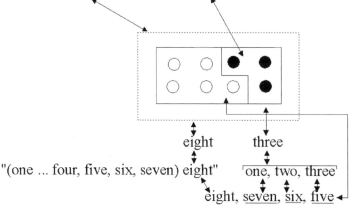

FIG. 5.4.   Solving a separate problem by counting down.

this with the example, "*Sally had 8 marbles. She lost 3 marbles. How many has she now?*" (refer to Fig. 5.4).

The subtraction process begins with the cardinal value of the whole (original) set (eight); this value is then decremented by the required amount (three) to produce two parts. The whole set retains its "wholeness" during the decrementing process because it serves as the reference point for the formation of the parts. In decrementing the whole set, the child must switch from an accumulator model of the set to a counting-sequence model. The amount by which the set has to be decremented (three) also has to be converted to a counting-sequence model. However, as for addition, there is not a direct mapping between this counting-sequence model and that of the original set. An additional mapping is required here, as shown in Fig. 5.4. That is, the child must firstly, map a counting sequence model, *one, two, three*, onto the cardinal value "three" of the subtrahend of the original problem. The counting-sequence model of the whole set, (*eight*), *seven, six, five*, must then be mapped onto this former counting sequence (i.e., seven is mapped onto one, indicating that when one counter has been removed there are seven remaining, six is mapped onto two, indicating that the removal of two counters leaves six, and so on). However there is an added complexity here. The point at which the mapping process begins is not "eight," but "seven." Considerable modeling of this counting-down process with concrete items is needed to avoid the error of beginning the count at "eight," that is, at the "abbreviation" (Secada et al., 1983) of the counting of the objects in the whole set.

Formalizing Children's Computational Procedures.   To this point, we have focused on children's modeling of these elementary addition and subtraction examples. Children also need the opportunity to record their procedures. Initially, children's written records will be of an informal nature, chosen by them as their way of documenting their actions. However, at some point these procedures need to be formalized. Their progression to more formal methods must be a meaningful one for them. Clear links must be established between their actions on physical materials, their drawings of these, their informal numerical recordings, and the new formalized procedures. In other words, children must see that "teacher-imposed" ways of recording problem situations are simply alternative means of documenting their existing understandings. Earlier in this chapter, we addressed the importance of establishing appropriate connections between the different representations (refer to Fig. 5.1). We now apply this to the formalization of children's solution procedures to these elementary examples.

The formal recording of addition and subtraction problems can adopt a horizontal format, for example, $3 + 4 = 7$, or a vertical format

$$\begin{array}{r} 3 \\ +4 \\ \hline 7 \end{array}$$

We would argue that the latter form is a more appropriate one for children to meet initially. The vertical format is not complicated by the equals sign and is also the usual format adopted for the addition and subtraction of multidigit numbers. It is important that children see the analogy between their modeling of the problem and the formal recording of it, as shown in Fig. 5.5. A take-away interpretation of the subtraction symbol is used in this example as it is the most meaningful to children in the introductory stages. However, it is important that children see the symbol as representing other situations as they gain more experience with the subtraction domain. In Fig. 5.5, we recommend that the written operation be read as, "seven take away three." This mirrors the modeling process more directly than other interpretations, such as, "three from seven," or "seven minus three" and hence is the preferred format at this point.

In connection with this recording it is worth noting the difficulty presented by the pictorial representation of take-away subtraction, as shown in Fig. 5.5. Because it is difficult to perceive both the original set and the set being separated, there is not as clear a mapping from this representation to the recording. There is the tendency for children to interpret the diagram as, "four take away three," rather than as, "seven take away three." In this instance, children are perceiving the situation as a comparison of sets. This is an example of the part/whole schema, which is isomorphic to class inclusion, and is a ternary relation, as discussed in chapter 3. The set of seven is the whole, and includes the set of three and the set of four. When children see it as "four take away three" they are in effect defaulting to a binary relation,

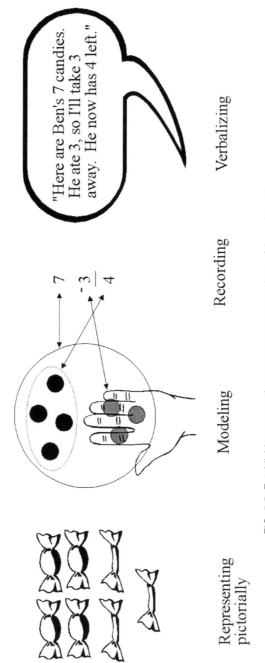

Ben had 7 pieces of candy. He ate 3 pieces.
How many pieces has he now?

Representing
pictorially

Modeling

Recording

Verbalizing

"Here are Ben's 7 candies.
He ate 3, so I'll take 3
away. He now has 4 left."

7
− 3
___
4

FIG. 5.5. Establishing connections across representations of the subtraction process.

between the set of four and the set of three. The higher processing load imposed by the ternary relation between the set of seven, the set of three and the set of four, is presumably a factor in the difficulty of dealing with this concept.

Compare and Equalize Problems.   Once children have mastered these basic addition and subtraction models, they need experience in solving the more difficult compare and equalize problems. In solving these types, children often obtain the right answers for the wrong reasons. For example, they can simply focus on the numbers involved and ignore the words (De Corte & Verschaffel, 1987). This is exacerbated by the situation in many texts where there are several pages of word problems of the one type that encourage blind application of procedures (Stigler, Fuson, Ham, & Kim, 1986). Alternatively, children can focus on key words as a clue to the operation (e.g., "fewer" as indicating subtraction; Schoenfeld, 1982; Stern, 1993). These inappropriate responses are especially likely to occur with compare problems (Cummins, Kintsch, Reusser, & Weimer, 1988; Lewis, 1989; Lewis & Mayer, 1987; Mayer, Lewis, & Hegarty, 1992; Stern, 1993). One of the major difficulties here is that there is not a clear mapping between a given problem situation and the operation required to find the unknown quantity (cf. Fuson's, 1992b, argument). For example, consider the following two compare problems:

Sally has 6 goldfish. She has 3 more goldfish than Samantha. How many goldfish does Samantha have?

Bill has 6 marbles. He has 3 fewer than Martin. How many marbles does Martin have?

Both of these problems have an unknown reference set and are considerably more difficult than those with an unknown compare set, such as, "*John has 5 marbles. Peter has 2 marbles fewer than John. How many marbles does Peter have?*" (Stern, 1993). The unknown reference set examples are difficult for children because the comparison sentence cues the opposite operation. For example, the sentence, "*She has 3 more goldfish than Samantha,*" suggests that an addition operation is needed. Similarly, the sentence, "*He has 3 fewer than Martin,*" implies subtraction. There are less difficult compare problems, however. These involve an unknown difference set, such as, "*Sue has 7 cherries. Penny has 4 cherries. How many more cherries does Sue have than Penny?*" These are not as complex for children because they can solve them by building a one-to-one correspondence between the two sets and then counting the remaining objects.

Equalize problems are sometimes referred to as "missing-addend" problems (e.g., "*Sue has 9 marbles. Jenny has 6 marbles. How many more marbles*

158

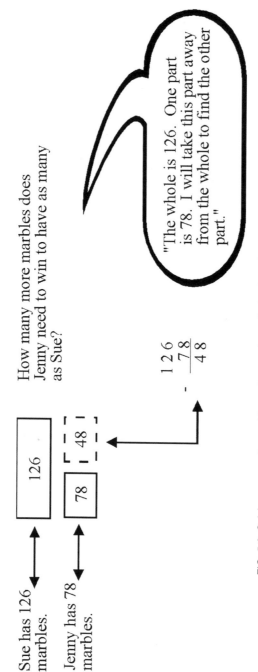

FIG. 5.6. Solving an equalize problem using a schematic drawing of the part–part–whole construct.

does Jenny need to win to have as many as Sue?"). Children can solve these by applying an adding-on strategy. This entails modeling the known addend, adding on more items until the sum has been reached, and then counting the added-on items to get the unknown addend. Although this strategy can be used with small numbers, it is impractical for larger numbers. Here, children need to identify the formal operation required. This can be difficult because the wording of equalize problems frequently suggests the opposite operation (e.g., *"How many more?"*). In this case, children need to be able to map the problem information onto a meaningful representation. The part–part–whole construct, represented by a schematic drawing (Fuson & Willis, 1989) can be effective here, as we indicate in Fig. 5.6.

Problem-Solving Models

We now consider some problem-solving models that attempt to explain the mental models and processes involved in solving computational word problems. In addressing these models, we focus on the equalize and compare problems because of the special difficulties they present children. When children attempt to solve these problems, they need to understand specific linguistic terms (e.g., "fewer than"), interpret the described situation, identify the appropriate operation, and finally, compute an answer (Stern, 1993). Numerous problem-solving models have attempted to address these skills, with different levels proposed for conceptualizing and solving word problems (e.g., Cummins et al., 1988; Kintsch, 1986; Kintsch & Greeno, 1985; Reusser, 1990; M. S. Riley & Greeno, 1988; Silver, Mukhopadhyay & Gabriele, 1992; Silver, Shapiro, & Deutsch, 1993; van Dijk & Kintsch, 1983).

We propose a three-pronged schematic system for the solving of computational problems. The system draws upon the ideas of Kintsch (1986), Nesher (1992), van Dijk & Kintsch (1983), Silver et al. (1992), and Silver et al. (1993). Its three components are the problem-text model, the problem-situation model, and the mathematical model, as shown in Fig. 5.7. We contend that the appropriate mapping between and among these components plays a crucial role in children's interpretation and subsequent solving of word problems.

The problem-text model is similar to Kintsch's (1986) "textbase," which he defines as the "mental representation of the text that a reader or listener constructs in the process of comprehension." For our purposes, it refers to the mental model the child constructs from an initial analysis of the verbal formulation (spoken or written) of the given problem. This involves identifying what Nesher (1992) termed, the logical *conditions and semantic relations* that constitute a well-structured problem (p. 202).

The second component, the problem-situation model, is akin to Kintsch's (1986, p. 88) *situation model*, which he defined as a "mental representation

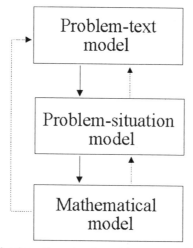

FIG. 5.7. A schematic system for solving computational problems.

of the situation described by the text." However our model does not include Kintsch's derivation of an arithmetic structure; this is the role of the third component. Our problem-situation model is the mental model the child forms by mapping her problem-text model onto an analogous familiar situation. The development of this mental model is crucial to effective problem solving and tends to be neglected in several problem-solving models. Indeed, the problem-situation model forms the meaningful link between the problem-text model and the remaining component, the mathematical model. This latter component comprises the formal mathematical expression that represents the solution to the problem and is akin to the "problem model" advanced in a later study by Nathan, Kintsch, and Young (1992). The mathematical model is formed by mapping the required mathematical operation onto the problem-situation schema to generate a solution. The child should also be able to map this mathematical model onto the initial problem-text model. Because these three models are interdependent, children will have difficulty in solving a problem if any one model is incorrect or incomplete. For example, if children have difficulty in interpreting the problem text then they will have difficulty in forming an appropriate mental model of the problem situation. Consequently, they will be unable to form the desired mathematical model or will end up adopting an erroneous one.

There are two key factors that tend to be highlighted in the problem-solving models presented in the literature, namely, mathematical knowledge and linguistic processes. The problem models of Briars and Larkin (1984) and M. S. Riley and Greeno (1988) emphasize the application of mathematical knowledge in solving word problems. In particular, they emphasize the development of the part/whole schema (or the "part–part–whole schema" we use here to emphasize the addition/subtraction situations; Fuson, 1992b). This schema is considered especially useful for solving problems that cannot be readily solved by using one-to-one correspondence between sets or by applying the "counting-all" and "separate" strategies (Carpenter & Moser, 1983). These include problems involving an unknown reference set (e.g., *"Sue has 6 cakes; She has 2 more cakes than Sally. How many cakes does Sally have?"*).

According to M. S. Riley and Greeno (1988), these more difficult problems can be solved by mapping the textual information given in the word problem onto the appropriate part–part–whole schema. However, this first entails the use of a mathematical transformation strategy where the sets represented in the problem are mapped onto one of the part–part–whole relations involved in the comparison of sets (e.g., "small set = large set – difference set"; Stern, 1993). Hence, to solve the foregoing problem, the child has to infer from the second sentence whether the set mentioned in the first sentence is the small set or large set, and on the basis of this, decide whether to add or subtract according to the appropriate part–part–whole relation. In this instance, we have 6 as the large set and 2 as the difference set and hence, can apply the appropriate equation, "small set = large set – difference set," to obtain the answer of 4.

This process is clearly a complex one for children. For a start, they have to understand the comparison of sets, that is, children must know that three sets are involved. They must then be able to identify these sets within the context of the problem, that is, they must identify the compare set (the set being compared to another), the reference set (this other set), and the difference set. Before the child can do anything with this information, she must recall that the mathematical relations between the three sets depend on whether the compare set is the small set and the reference set is the large set or vice versa (Stern, 1993). She must then map the information gleaned from the problem statements (i.e., the problem-text model) onto her knowledge of these mathematical relations. Once these sets have been identified and the child knows which particular set is the unknown, she must map this knowledge onto one of the three part–part–whole relations. This requires the child to have an existing mental model of these part–part–whole relations.

It is questionable whether these part–part–whole relations would serve as an effective problem-situation model for the child. There is the danger that they could become just a collection of rotely learned rules, particularly because the child's previous application of the part–part–whole construct for combining and separating sets involved numbers that were interpreted as the cardinal values of sets. However, in this new application of the part–part–whole construct, the numbers involved in the set differences must be understood as a *relation* between sets or between the cardinalities of two sets (M. S. Riley & Greeno, 1988).

The previous problem-solving model becomes even more complex when we consider the linguisitic processes involved. Even before the child can identify the three sets he must comprehend the text of the problem. Several problem-solving models, including the one we propose, underscore the significance of these linguisitic processes (e.g., Cummins, 1991; Cummins et al., 1988; Kintsch, 1986; Reusser (1990). It is argued that children's comprehension is influenced by the nature of the language used in the problem text. They frequently misinterpret the linguistic forms of a problem (e.g., "How many more X's than Y's?") and misinterpret them in certain ways. Their faulty problem-text model thus inhibits access to the part–part–whole "superschema" that guides children's comprehension of these problems. They are then unable to form an appropriate problem-situation model.

Certain verbal formats, however, allow contact to made with this schema whereas others do not (Carpenter, Hiebert, & Moser, 1981; De Corte, Verschaffel, & De Win, 1985; Greeno, 1988; Hudson, 1983). For example, Hudson (1983) found that young children performed poorly on the problem, *"There are 5 birds and 3 worms. How many more birds are there than worms?"* However there was a dramatic improvement when the last sentence was changed to, *"How many birds will not get a worm?"* This modified wording could well induce a simpler schema. The original version of the problem tends to encourage a part–part–whole schema, whereas the simplified version tends to induce a comparison of two sets; the birds set (five) is compared with the worms set (three). This is an easier schema than the part–part–whole schema.

Developing Children's Understanding of Compare Problems.   The foregoing discussion brings us to the question of how we can best assist children in interpreting these more difficult compare problems. We would argue that, although the part–part–whole schema serves as a unifying and versatile problem-situation model for many types of addition and subtraction situations, it is not suitable when complex mapping processes are involved. This is particularly the case when it is applied to unknown reference set problems, as we have just illustrated. Other research supports our concerns (e.g., De Corte & Verschaffel, 1987; Wolters, 1983). Furthermore, Stern's (1989) research has shown that good problem solvers only use an abstract representation of a problem when they think it is most helpful; they tend to prefer more familiar action-based procedures. Hence, if children do not find the part–part–whole schema useful or find it labor intensive, they will resort to other, less taxing procedures.

We recommend introducing children to a linguisitic restructuring strategy to help them construct an appropriate problem-text model (Lewis &

Mayer, 1987; Stern, 1993). This procedure involves transforming these difficult unknown reference set problems into the easier unknown compare set problems. For example, the unknown reference set problem, *"John has 6 marbles. He has 2 marbles fewer than Sam. How many marbles does Sam have?"* can be transformed into an unknown compare set problem by changing the second sentence to, *"Sam has 2 more marbles than John."* There is now a direct mapping between the linguistic structure of the first sentence and that of the second sentence. That is, both the known variable in the first sentence and the unknown variable in the second sentence are subjects. Prior to the transformation, the unknown variable was the *object* of the sentence. According to Lewis and Mayer (1987), children and adults prefer this consistency in language and mentally rearrange the information in the manner described. This would suggest an application of metacognitive knowledge, namely that it is easier to deal with two cases of one comparative than two different comparatives (cf. transitive inference as well as use of the "min" strategy, as discussed in chapter 3).

However, as Stern (1993) emphasized, this linguistic restructuring requires flexibility in the use of language describing quantitative comparison. Stern's studies have indicated that a large proportion of first graders lack a knowledge about the symmetry of language concerning quantitative comparison. For these children, the relations of "x fewer than y" and "y more than x" appear quite independent of each other, with the activation of one concept inhibiting the activation of the other. This is because they do not understand that the higher order relation "x fewer than y" is OPPOSITE-OF "y more than x." Stern found a relation between an understanding of this symmetrical comparison and the solving of unknown reference set problems, with children's difficulties due to their failure to acquire a mental model of symmetrical comparison. Stern's findings highlight the importance of including the reciprocal nature of addition and subtraction in the development of children's computational schemas. This understanding is also important in children's mastery of the basic number fact combinations, to which we now turn.

PROCEDURAL MODELS OF ADDITION AND SUBTRACTION: NUMBER FACT STRATEGIES

In the previous section, we focused on the conceptual models of addition and subtraction. In this section, we consider some procedural models for these operations. Our emphasis here is on children's mastery of the addition and subtraction number facts. These include all of the basic whole number addition combinations from 0 + 0 through to 9 + 9, together with the corresponding subtraction combinations.

Chronometric Analysis

A large component of the research in this area has involved chronometric analysis where reaction times for producing different combinations have been used to infer the processes people use or the way they organize these combinations in memory (e.g., Ashcraft, 1990; Ashcraft, Donley, Halas, & Vakali, 1992; Groen & Parkman, 1972; Kaye, deWinstanley, Chen, & Bonnefil, 1989; Resnick, 1983; Siegler & Campbell, 1990; Widaman & Little, 1992). The results of these studies are now well documented, including children's use of a "min" strategy (Groen & Parkman, 1972) to solve simple number facts such as 4 + 3. This is like the counting-on strategy we reviewed earlier. Here, the value of the maximum addend (4) is registered into a mental counter and then incremented by ones the number of times specified by the minimum ("min") addend (i.e., "five, six, seven"). Other findings have shown that the "doubles" facts (e.g., 3 + 3) are much easier to learn than others, that combinations with larger addends take longer to complete than those with smaller addends, and that older children and adults use automated recall in preference to other strategies. Not surprisingly, the findings also show that the predominant strategy for performing mental arithmetic changes across development, from "min-based" counting to recall (Ashcraft, 1990; Siegler & Shipley, in press; Siegler & Shrager, 1984).

One of the well-documented models of children's progression from the earliest counting-all procedures to the final fact retrieval is that of Siegler and his colleagues (Siegler & Shipley, in press; Siegler & Jenkins, 1989; Siegler & Schrager, 1984). Siegler's basic tenet is that children use more than one strategy for a task. The selection of strategies is based on the child's confidence that the strategy will yield the answer. Memory retrieval is tried first because, in the child's experience, it has a good record of providing answers to addition problems quickly and reasonably reliably. When it fails, the strategy with the next best record is tried, then the next best and so on. The selection is based on the child's stored knowledge about how good the answer provided by the strategy is. If the strategy can be relied upon to provide a good answer, it is retained, otherwise it is replaced.

Derived Fact Strategies

Although Siegler's model provides a cohesive account of children's (and adults') long-term memory network for arithmetic knowledge, it does not seem to represent the most economical use of resources (Baroody & Ginsburg, 1986). For example, if each basic addition combination were associated with five responses, this would mean that a child has stored in long-term memory 500 mostly incorrect, specific numerical associations. In contrast, a model that draws upon existing number-fact knowledge to generate answers to unknown facts would be less cognitively demanding because relationships, rather than numerous specific numerical associations, would be retained.

Unfortunately, many classrooms focus on direct fact recall without first providing children with meaningful and effective strategies for generating answers to unknown facts (Baroody & Ginsburg, 1986; Thornton, 1990). This is not helped by the fact that only a few studies have addressed children's use of derived fact strategies, the conceptual structures these strategies require, and children's transition from these strategies to automatic recall (Baroody & Ginsburg, 1986; Fuson & Kwon, 1992; Gray, 1991; Steinberg, 1985; Thornton, 1990; Thornton, Jones, & Toohey, 1983).

By derived fact strategies we refer to procedures in which the numbers in the given fact are redistributed to become numbers whose sum or difference is already known (Fuson, 1992b). For example, 7 + 8 can be simplified by decomposing the numbers to generate a doubles fact ([7+ 7] + 1) and then solved by using a knowledge of doubles (i.e., "double seven is 14, and one more makes 15"). Because these strategies build on the structure and relationships among the basic combinations, they enable children to move away from a reliance on inefficient counting procedures to more effective generative procedures. They also facilitate recall and equip children with fall-back mechanisms for when they are unable to retrieve a fact from memory (Putnam, deBettencourt, & Leinhardt, 1990; Steinberg, 1985).

It is worth noting that these derived fact strategies do not reflect a *logical* mathematical learning sequence, rather, a *psychological* learning sequence. In other words, the number facts are not learned in a mathematical sequence, such as facts comprising addends of one, then two, then three, and so on, nor are they arranged according to a given sum, such as the number facts to 10. This latter sequence has been typically used in the teaching of basic facts (e.g., Gray, 1991). In contrast, with the derived fact strategies, the basic facts are clustered according to meaningful semantic relationships such as doubles (e.g., 4 + 4) and near-doubles facts (e.g., 4 + 5). In this way, children can develop flexible thinking in using numbers (Steinberg, 1985), as well as acquire an organizational framework for learning and applying these facts (Rathmell, 1978). The role of these strategies in children's transition to basic fact retrieval is also evident (Steinberg, 1985). Because the strategies are designed to assist children in making connections among the different facts, they can establish the types of associations that were featured in Siegler's model. These associations are not formed from repeated exposure to random facts but rather, from an understanding of the semantic relationships among the facts. They can thus influence how the basic facts are represented in, and retrieved from, long-term memory (Steinberg, 1985).

Children should be introduced to these derived fact strategies only after they have acquired a mental model of the particular operation. Their initial attempts at solving unknown facts would have entailed the counting procedures we reviewed earlier, namely, counting-all, counting-up, and counting-back. The counting-on and counting-back strategies are appropriate for generating answers to examples that involve adding or subtracting 1, 2, or 3 (e.g., 4 + 3; 6 – 2). Indeed, the count-on strategy alone can generate answers to 64 of the 100 addition facts (this includes the use of the commutative principle to which we will return).

Because we examined the counting-on and counting-back procedures in previous sections, we will not revisit them here. However, it is worth mentioning that children need experience in discriminating when it is more appropriate to count up than to count down. For example, counting-up is not appropriate for solving examples where there is a large difference between the subtrahend and minuend (e.g., 9 – 2). Counting-back is more efficient here. It is particularly important that children apply such metacognitive decisions when using any of the derived fact strategies. We will return to this point.

The derived fact strategies have been variously defined in the literature. For our present purposes, we refer to the "doubles," the "near doubles," and the "build-to-10" strategies for addition. Collectively, these strategies, along with application of the commutative principle, generate all of the remaining addition facts. For subtraction, the most appropriate strategy is to identify the corresponding addition fact (e.g., knowing that 8 + 5 = 13 can help solve 13 – 5).

Children find doubles facts ($a + a$) easier to remember than most other facts. This would be due largely to the ease with which children can meaningfully associate these facts in memory. It is likely that such a model would have been established early in children's informal number experiences. The use of visual mnemonics (e.g., eight spider legs for "double four") can assist children in forming meaningful associations and hence stimulate recall of the doubles facts (Thornton & Toohey, 1985).

Once children know these doubles facts they can use them to derive answers to unknown related facts. For example, to solve 6 + 7, the child can recall the related doubles fact, 6 + 6, and then add on one more. This process is not as easy as it might appear. First, the child has to realize that she can use a known doubles fact to generate the answer. The child then has to identify which doubles fact is the appropriate one to apply. This entails applying an understanding of the associative principle and decomposing the existing numbers to expose a double (e.g., decomposing 6 + 7 as 6 + 6 + 1, or 7 + 7 – 1). Tied in with this is an appreciation of conservation of number, that is, the value of the fact does not alter when the addends are decomposed and then recombined. Attention needs to be given to these understandings in the instructional process.

The remaining addition strategy, build-to-10, is appropriate for those facts where one of the addends is 9, such as, 9 + 6. This strategy draws upon children's place-value knowledge, as well as their understanding of the associative principle. Here, the fact is decomposed and then reconstituted to make 10 as one of the addends, for example, 9 + 6 becomes 9 + 5 + 1 and then, 10 + 5. Children may also apply this strategy to facts comprising 8 as one of the addends.

The major strategy for generating answers to subtraction facts, namely, "think-of-the-addition-fact," is best introduced after children have mastered the corresponding set of addition facts. Children cannot use this strategy to solve subtraction facts involving doubles if they do not know the addition doubles. Children need considerable time to consolidate newly learned addition facts before attempting to apply them to obtain solutions for subtraction (Thornton, 1990).

In advocating the use of these strategies, we wish to highlight a number of instructional issues. Firstly, we believe the strategies need to be specifically taught (Rathmell, 1978; Suydam, 1984) and should be done so through meaningful and enjoyable activities that utilize a number of senses (e.g., Thornton, Jones, & Toohey, 1983). Although children should not be discouraged from developing and applying their own, individually created, procedures for generating number facts, they do need to be exposed to these more efficient generative strategies. Indeed, we believe children should play a major role in the development of these, with the teacher providing the appropriate guidance and assistance. If children cannot see the relevance or utility of these strategies, they will be reluctant to draw upon them and will resort to some other, usually less efficient procedures. It is doubtful whether such procedures would form the associations we desire in long-term memory.

The second point we wish to stress is the role of mathematical principles and relationships in children's mastery of the basic facts. In particular, children need to be familiar with the commutative law of addition, $a + b = b + a$, and the associative law, $a + (b + c) = (a + b) + c$. They do not have to know the formal names of these principles, however. Children also require an understanding of the inverse relationship between addition and subtraction, as well as a knowledge of the identity element under addition ($a + 0 = a$; $0 + a = a$). These principles and relationships can be readily illustrated with sets of concrete materials. Research suggests that young children regularly use the commutative principle to shortcut computational effort and that they have learned to do so through their informal experiences (Baroody, Ginsburg, & Waxman, 1983; Resnick, 1992). An understanding of these principles and relationships will promote children's flexibility with number, an integral component of their development of number sense (Sowder, 1988, 1990, 1992).

The third point we wish to highlight is the importance of children's metacognitive processes in applying these strategies. Children should not only know how to apply a particular strategy, but also *when* to apply it. Because there are several facts that can be solved by more than one strategy, children must decide which strategy is the most appropriate or the most convenient for them to use. Activities in which children have to discriminate between those facts they can retrieve from memory and those requiring application of a newly learned strategy can assist here. Encouraging children to justify their choice of strategy can further promote these metacognitive processes.

Our final point pertains to children's transition to automatic fact recall. Ashcraft (1990) and Steinberg (1985) suggested that children's mastery of the derived fact strategies eventually becomes automatic and develops into a retrieval process where the strategies are used unconsciously. Steinberg, Baroody, and Fuson (1984) have also put forward the hypothesis that children and adults may not memorize many of the number facts but generate them rapidly from rules or principles. However, generation is costly in terms of cognitive load. Although it is important to have a mental model that can generate strategies and number facts, efficient performance requires that at least the frequently used ones become automatic. This requires practice. The value of understanding is that it obviates wasteful practice, makes the acquisition process more efficient, and makes the knowledge acquired more durable and adaptable. It is important that we engage children in enjoyable and relevant practice activities to consolidate each new set of facts. It is clear, however, that we do need more research on children's transition from the deliberate use of strategies to automatic retrieval.

PROCEDURAL MODELS OF ADDITION AND SUBTRACTION: MULTIDIGIT WHOLE NUMBERS

In this section, we examine the development of computational models of mutidigit addition and subtraction. We firstly give consideration to children's informal mental strategies for solving these examples and then turn to the formal written algorithms. We illustrate the complexities of these formal procedures by providing an initial analysis of the subtraction algorithm. We then consider a number of teaching and learning issues, including the importance of forming meaningful connections between children's manipulations with concrete analogs and their symbolized procedures.

Development of Mental Computation

When children are faced with a novel problem, that is, one for which they do not have an immediate solution procedure, they invent a number of interesting strategies (Burton, 1992; Cobb, Yackel, & Wood, 1988; DeLoache,

Sugarman, & Brown, 1985; English, 1992a; Kouba & Franklin, 1993; Resnick, 1992). These informal procedures often display principle-based mathematical reasoning, as Resnick (1992) showed in her account of 7-year-old Pitt's creative approach to counting a large disorderly pile of Monopoly money.

Children's creative responses form the basis of effective mental computation where an arithmetic calculation is performed without any external aids. Mental computation has received increased attention in recent years as a viable alternative to other computational models and as a significant means of developing mathematical thinking and powerful estimation techniques (e.g., Reys, 1992; Sowder, 1990; Sowder & Kelin, 1993). Efficient mental computation necessarily utilizes different algorithms from those usually associated with paper-and-pencil calculations (Sowder, 1988). For example, 68 + 26 could be solved by performing a series of calculations such as, 60 + 20, 8 + 6, 80 + 10, 90 + 4. Alternatively, 68 could be incremented to 70 and 26 decremented to 24, to produce the simple sum, 70 + 24. The written algorithms are not appropriate for mental computation because they utilize too many cognitive resources in the absence of pen and paper and furthermore, they do not correspond to the ways people calculate mentally (such as working from left to right and operating holistically rather than on individual digits).

Effective mental strategies enable children to be creative and flexible, developing an algorithm on the spot to suit the problem at hand (Sowder & Kelin, 1993). However skilful mental computation requires an understanding of numeration concepts and processes, as well as important number properties. Sowder (1988, p. 185) illustrated this in her discussion on the key questions children need to consider (either consciously or not) when faced with a mental calculation. These include: (a) How can I rearrange the numbers to produce basic fact questions? and (b) How will I then proceed as a result of re-expressing the numbers?

Responding to the first question requires a knowledge of basic facts, an understanding of place value, an ability to express numbers in different ways, and an ability to operate with multiples and powers of 10 (e.g., knowing that 90 is 9 tens and 40 is 4 tens enables children to map this knowlege onto the known fact, 9 (tens) – 4 (tens). Question b also requires the ability to operate with powers of 10, as well as skills in regrouping terms using associative and commutative properties of addition [e.g., (40 + 6) – (20 + 3) = (40 – 20) + (6 – 3)]. An ability to use the distributive property is also needed [e.g., 4 × (20 + 4) = (4 × 20) +(4 × 4)]. Responding to these questions also requires the application of metacognitive processes. For example, children need to decide if one strategy is more effective than another for solving a particular problem. They also need to monitor their mental calculations and determine a means of keeping track of their totals.

The difficulty with mental calculation is that it is cognitively demanding and, hence, strategies need to be selected to help reduce the load on working memory. Because these strategies can be cognitively taxing themselves, it is important that the mental procedures children develop are efficient as well as meaningful. In Hope and Sherrill's (1987) study of skilled and unskilled mental calculators in Grades 11 and 12, the skilled students not only applied a comprehensive knowledge of number properties but also demonstrated a number of strategies to reduce memory load. These included:

1. Eliminating the need for a "carry operation" (i.e., renaming and regrouping);
2. Proceeding in a left-to-right manner, because fewer errors should result from dealing with the most significant digits first; and
3. Progressively incorporating each interim calculation into a single result (1987, p. 108).

The unskilled students, however, did not use these strategies nor did they apply any number properties. Rather, they employed a pencil-and-paper mental analogue, that is, they attempted to work the written algorithm mentally.

Given that the strategies employed in mental computation are different to those of the conventional algorithm, the issue arises as to whether the formal procedures should be taught at all. It has been suggested that pen-and-paper algorithms are unnecessary and that children's formal recording procedures should be restricted to informal child-chosen ones (Shuard, 1991). Furthermore, research has shown that the conventional algorithms can restrict children's mental calculation strategies and that unschooled children use various spontaneous strategies that schooled children are reluctant to use (Ginsburg, Posner, & Russell, 1981; Petitto & Ginsburg, 1981; Saxe, 1991; Sowder, 1990). On the other hand, the children who have been cited as skilled mental calculators either have a predisposition towards exploring number and number patterns or else reside in a domain that calls on these skills (e.g., street sellers; Hope, 1987; Ginsburg, Posner, & Russell, 1981; Saxe, 1991). They thus have an advantage over other children who have little opportunity to hone their mental calculation skills. When children lack these skills they have little choice but to rely on the conventional procedures they have been taught. Although children will have picked up some informal knowledge of mathematical principles (e.g., knowing that numbers can be decomposed in many ways), they will need guidance in explicating this knowledge and in utilizing it to develop effective mental strategies.

These mental strategies can assist children in exploring alternative ways of working the conventional algorithms. We would argue that children still need a knowledge of these formal algorithms, despite the availability of technology. It was shown in a British study (Foxman, Ruddock, McCallum, & Schager, 1991) that children who were calculator dependent had great difficulty in explaining the errors in a multidigit computation, whereas their calculator-independent counterparts were able to do so. Although we strongly support technology in children's mathematical learning, we also believe we cannot deny children the right of access to other powerful computational systems, namley, the conventional algorithms. Once children have a knowledge of these systems, they can then decide whether or not to use them in a given computational situation. We need to ask children how they prefer to do a given calculation and give them the option of computing mentally or applying a written algorithm (Reys, 1992).

We now turn our attention to these conventional algorithms and highlight their complexity for children. We illustrate this with reference to the subtraction algorithm. We then offer some suggestions as to how instruction might promote a meaningful mastery of this algorithm.

The Complexity of the Subtraction Algorithm

Children's difficulties with this algorithm have been well documented (C. A. Brown et al., 1989; Hiebert & Wearne, 1992; National Assessment of Educational Progress, 1983; Stigler, Lee, & Stevenson, 1990). As we mentioned earlier, one of the major reasons for children's poor performance here is their failure to abstract the appropriate mental models of computation from the external representations. Furthermore, they fail to make the connections across different representations of the one abstraction. Their inability to link important place-value ideas with computational procedures is also a significant weakness.

In analyzing the complexity of the subtraction algorithm, we will refer to the "decomposition" method, in contrast to the "equal additions" method (Brownell & Moser, 1949). The decomposition method, as the name implies, involves decomposing the minuend to enable the subtrahend to be subtracted (e.g., to solve $400 - 178$, we must regroup 400 as 39 tens 10 ones).

Solving a multidigit subtraction of this nature demands the application of several major concepts and processes. We consider first, the processes of renaming and regrouping. These terms refer to the two distinct, but related, procedures involved in the decomposition of the minuend. The renaming of place values is a quantity-conserving change where any place can be renamed as another, for example, x hundreds can be renamed as $10x$ tens and $100x$ ones; similarly, y tens can be renamed as $10y$ ones. Regrouping is also a quantity-conserving change involving the recomposing of numbers, for example, x hundreds y tens can be regrouped as $(x - 1)$ hundreds $(10 + y)$ tens, and y tens z ones can be regrouped as $(y - 1)$ tens $(10 + z)$ ones. An understanding of these renaming and regrouping processes is an essential component of children's mastery of the subtraction algorithm and should develop from a comprehensive mental model of place value. It is not sufficient though, for children just to master these procedures; they must also appreciate the need to apply them and know when to apply them. Furthermore, they must see them as quantity-conserving changes and recognize that the same set of relations holds for their representation in concrete analog form and in abstract symbolism.

The subtraction algorithm also utilizes a number of other conceptual models and procedures that we revisit in the next section. These include:

- the change-by-subtracting and separate forms of subtraction;
- the combine form of addition;
- the right-to-left progession of the subtraction algorithm and the uniformity of each subtraction process, that is, the same process is applied to the ones, tens, hundreds, and so on;
- basic addition and subtraction number facts.

Developing a Mental Model of Multidigit Subtraction

Recall that at the beginning of this chapter we stressed the importance of children forming the appropriate representational connections in their mastery of computational models. These include the connections across the concrete, pictorial, and symbolic representations of a computation. We also emphasized the need for children to form connections between computational procedures and the associated numeration models and processes (e.g., place value and regrouping), and between initial computational processes and subsequent, more advanced procedures. The teacher plays a significant role here (Fuson et al., 1992). In particular, the teacher's explanations during the learning sequence are important in promoting these links (Leinhardt, 1987). At the same time, children need to verbalize their actions, with an emphasis on the quantities they are manipulating (Resnick & Omanson, 1987). This can help avoid the situation where students know how to set up the concrete representation but do not use it to guide them meaningfully through the algorithms; their procedures are akin to those used with the calculator (R. B. Davis, 1983).

We now look at how we might apply our ideas in developing children's understanding of the subtraction algorithm. Our approach is designed to exemplify our principles of learning and does not rule out other approaches to developing the algorithms, such as those of Fuson (1992b). With further research, improvements will no doubt be made on our ideas. One of the advantages of establishing a sound set of psychological principles is that they can be used to generate potentially worthwhile instructional techniques. We illustrate our approach with the example, 443 – 157, as shown in Fig. 5.8 (A–D). This example would be best couched within a meaningful real-world context.

In addressing this example, we make use of base-ten blocks on a place-value chart, as indicated in Fig. 5.8. This representation emphasizes the subtracting of like places (ones with ones, tens with tens, etc.). Children would begin with the modeling of the minuend only, in accord with their earlier modeling of single-digit take-away situations. Modeling only the minuend highlights the original amount and distinguishes it from the amount that has to be subtracted. Interpreting the example as "443 subtract 157," rather than "take 157 from 443" helps to reinforce this distinction. The modeling of the minuend entails a two-stage mapping process, namely, from each block representation (e.g., four flats) to its value (4 hundreds) and then to its recorded form (443) (the limitations of space prevent the display of all mapping processes in Fig. 5.8). It is important that children make this link between the concrete analog and the recorded form from the outset (Fuson & Burghardt, 1993). The analog representation can be read in a number of ways (e.g., "four hundreds, four tens, three ones," "four hundred and forty-three ones," etc.). This not only helps avoid the problem of treating the multidigit numbers as isolated single digits, but also contributes to children's development of number sense (Sowder, 1992).

To subtract the amount indicated by the subtrahend (157), the child has to appreciate that each place is considered in turn and that because we are dealing with a formal pen-and-paper algorithm, it is easier to begin the operation with the ones place (this can be contrasted with the left-to-right strategy used in mental computation). The fact that we can proceed column-by-column is due to our number system "permitting" us to calculate by partition (Resnick, 1992). As Resnick explained, in performing a calculation, it is permissible to divide the quantities being operated on into any convenient parts, to operate on these parts, and to accumulate partial results. However this partitioning is subject to a number of constraints. In particular, the child needs to appreciate that each part in the subtrahend must be subtracted from its corresponding part in the minuend and each subtrahend part may be subtracted only once.

Because there are only 3 ones available in the minuend, the child must recognize that the 7 ones cannot be subtracted until more ones can be obtained. This requires the child to apply her understanding of the numeration processes of renaming and regrouping, and the "separate" model of subtraction (this model is applied in the actual renaming/regrouping process). This represents quite a complex task for the child, because she must first switch from thinking about the 7 ones that have to be removed and the insufficient number of ones currently available, to a consideration of the number of tens available (i.e., the 4 tens displayed in the minuend). To

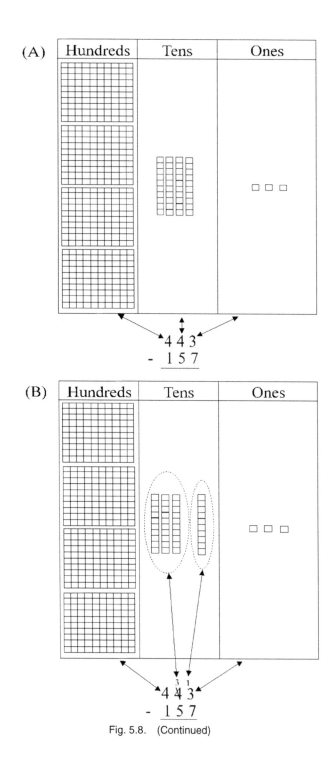

Fig. 5.8. (Continued)

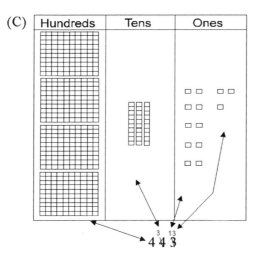

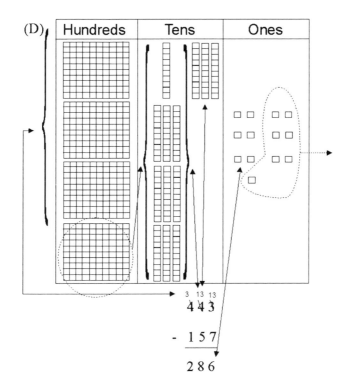

FIG. 5.8. Concrete analog and symbolic representation for multidigit subtraction with regrouping.

utilize these tens, the child must separate the 4 tens blocks into two sets, one set comprising 1 tens block and the other set, 3 tens blocks.

Note the two important understandings here, first, the tens blocks must be separated in preparation for the renaming process, and secondly, the separation procedure must produce one set of 1 ten. It is important the child records this procedure, as shown in Fig. 5.8B, and can explain the symbolic and analog connections. The next step is to rename the 1 ten as 10 ones by trading the set of 1 tens block for 10 ones blocks, as shown in Fig. 5.8C. This represents a quantity-conserving change from 4 tens (and 0 ones) to 3 tens 10 ones and is the first stage of the renaming/regrouping process. The second stage, the regrouping component, involves combining the 10 ones with the existing 3 ones blocks (applying the "combine" model of addition). The child has now completed the quantity-conserving change from 4 tens 3 ones to 3 tens 13 ones and will have recorded it as indicated in Fig. 5.8C.

After having completed all of this, the child is now at the stage of subtracting the ones. This is completed by removing 7 of the ones blocks from the combined set of 13 ones. The amount remaining can then be recorded, as shown in Fig. 5.8D. The previous steps must now be repeated with the 4 hundreds and 3 tens of the minuend to enable the 5 tens to be subtracted. That is, the 4 hundreds blocks must be separated into a set of 1 hundreds block and a set of 3 hundreds blocks, with the former subsequently traded for 10 tens blocks. This represents the quantity-conserving change, 4 hundreds to 3 hundreds 10 tens. The regrouping component follows next, with the 10 tens being combined with the existing 3 tens, resulting in a change from 4 hundreds 3 tens to 3 hundreds 13 tens, as indicated in Fig. 5.8D. The corresponding recording is also shown. Subtraction of the 5 tens and 1 hundred, respectively, can now take place.

In sum, the subtraction algorithm with regrouping requires the child to coordinate a comprehensive set of conceptual models and processes. If children lack these components, they can develop meaningless and frequently erroneous computational procedures.

Instructional Issues

Given the complexity of the renaming/regrouping processes, we recommend that children have prior experiences with these in their exploration of number. This reduces the demands placed on them as they attempt to apply this knowledge to the algorithm. Here, children need to know not only *how* to apply these procedures to the algorithm, but also *when* to apply them and *why* they are applying them. The verbal interactions between the teacher and children and amongst the children themselves as they implement these procedures play a significant role here (Hiebert & Wearne, 1993).

In connection with the regrouping process, it is worth addressing the issue of whether all necessary regroupings should be completed on the minuend prior to subtracting, or whether each place should be considered in turn. Fuson (1992a) argued that regrouping the entire minuend eliminates switching between unitary and multiunit conceptual structures when subtracting and trading each column. She also claimed that, because this form of "low-stress" algorithm (Hutchings, 1975) "fixes" the minuend, children are free to subtract the digits from either direction or in any order. However, we would argue that this procedure is both cumbersome and confusing for the child, especially in concrete analog form where the child would be faced simultaneously with large collections of traded blocks (e.g., a set of 13 ones and a set of 13 tens). Furthermore, this alternative procedure could be conducive to children automatically regrouping all digits in the minuend, whether or not this is required. As a consequence, children may end up viewing the regrouping and subtraction procedures as distinct, unrelated entities. Hence, the approach we recommend here is one in which children consider each place in turn, make a reasoned decision as to whether regrouping is required, and then complete the subtraction for that particular place.

Another issue pertains to the order in which examples with and without renaming/regrouping should be introduced. There has been considerable debate on this point (e.g., Ashlock, Johnson, Wilson, & Jones, 1983; Engelhardt & Usnick, 1991; Fuson, 1992a, 1992b; Reys, Suydam, & Lindquist, 1984). The traditional school of thought is that examples without regrouping should be introduced prior to examples with regrouping, because the former are less complex. Other schools argue for regrouping examples to be introduced first (e.g., Engelhardt & Usnick, 1991), or for both types to be introduced simultaneously, with all possible combinations of trading being done from the beginning (e.g., Fuson, 1990b). We contend that, from the outset, children need to acquire a mental model that provides the scaffolding for the subsquent introduction of more complex examples. That is, children need to develop a conceptual framework that will effectively support and integrate the introduction of each new algorithmic procedure. This is best established with nonregrouping examples since the initial development of such a scaffolded model will require considerable processing capacity. When children are introduced subsequently to examples involving regrouping, they will have both the conceptual structures and the processing ability to accommodate the new learnings. Children's metacognitive processes, involving decision-making at each stage of the algorithm, play a significant role in this development. (The research of Carr & Jessup, 1993, adds support here.)

Instructional sequences also need to take into account the complexity of examples involving internal zeros, such as 4002 – 1367. Children's mental model of less complex examples (e.g., 4352 – 1367) provides the base for these more difficult cases where the use of a concrete analog is both unnec-

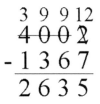

$$
\begin{array}{r}
3\ \ 9\ \ 9\ \ 12 \\
4\ 0\ 0\ 2 \\
-\ 1\ 3\ 6\ 7 \\
\hline
2\ 6\ 3\ 5
\end{array}
$$

FIG. 5.9. "Chunking" the renaming/regrouping process.

essary and inappropriate. These complex examples draw heavily on children's understanding of place value and renaming. We can show children how, in examples such as, 4002 − 1367, we can chunk all of the renaming/regrouping processes into one. That is, the 4 thousands can be renamed as 400 tens; the 400 tens 2 ones can then be regrouped as 399 tens 12 ones, as shown in Fig. 5.9.

It is also worth commenting on the role of basic fact knowledge in children's completion of the algorithms. We would argue that children should have sound mastery of the number facts contained in a given algorithm. This does not mean that they need to know all of the number facts, however, before they meet an algorithm. Rather, they can be given examples that utilize the particular facts that they know. A high processing load is imposed when children have to retrieve poorly learned facts and attempt to generate the answers to these, and, at the same time, contend with the processes involved in the algorithm itself (cf. Kaye's, 1986 argument). Furthermore, children do not need to rely on the concrete analog to supply them with the answer, that is, they should not have to count the items resulting from an additive or subtractive action. The analog's role is to model the algorithmic processes, not to serve as a calculating device.

It takes considerable time to develop these computational models. Children will not acquire them in one or two lessons, as is evident from the research in this area (e.g., Resnick & Omanson, 1987; Thompson, 1992). As Fuson et al. (1992, p. 106) noted, children's mastery of the algorithms entails "a slow process of interiorization" resulting from prolonged linking of the concrete analog with the corresponding verbal and written representations. Initially, strong connections are established between all three representations, followed by a phase in which the recording is completed without the concrete analog. Here, the accompanying explanation replaces the analog. Finally, the recording is employed without any external aids. At this point, the child's mental model of the algorithm should provide meaning to the symbolic representation and should also guide the child in solving nonroutine cases.

The points we have raised in this section have been based on a set of principles that are sufficiently sound and sufficiently general to be applied to computations with fractions. We turn to this domain now.

DEVELOPING COMPUTATIONAL MODELS FOR THE
ADDITION AND SUBTRACTION OF FRACTIONS

In this section, we address the development of computational models for the addition and subtraction of decimal and common fractions. We offer some suggestions as to how instruction might overcome the inherent complexity of these operations.

The difficulties children experience here have been well documented (e.g., Bezuk & Bieck, 1993; Hiebert, 1992; Hiebert & Wearne, 1986; C. Kieren, 1992; Nesher & Peled, 1986; Wearne, 1990). These may be attributed largely to the way fractions are presented in many school texts, that is, children are shown how to apply rules to the written symbols to produce correct answers (Hiebert, 1992). Little attention is given to helping children form connections between their symbolic procedures and their manipulations with the concrete analogs. As a result, children frequently view the actions they perform on the concrete analog and those they complete with paper and pencil as quite different procedures (Hiebert & Wearne, 1985).

This lack of conceptual understanding means that students become inflexible in their rule application and develop a procedural competence that outstrips, and therefore is no longer guided by, their conceptual competence. Because these powerful syntactic procedures allow students to move beyond their level of understanding, students are unable to monitor their own performance and can only check an answer by re-executing a rule. They thus have no idea of the reasonableness of a solution (Wearne & Hiebert, 1988b).

The first step in helping children develop mental models of these computations is to establish an understanding of the concept of a fraction, including the symbolic notation for decimal and common forms. We addressed this issue in the last chapter. We can then progress to the next step where we can build children's mastery of the computations on their intuitive understanding of fractions and base this on their actions with concrete analogs (Ball, 1993; Mack, 1993; Bezuk & Bieck, 1993; Kieren, 1988; Streefland, 1985). Only after this has been achieved can we proceed to the third step where we help children practice and routinize their procedures (Wearne & Hiebert, 1988b). In this way, children are more likely to develop meaningful mental models, that is, they can link their symbolic manipulations to real-world referents and have an appreciation of the appropriateness of their procedures and the reasonableness of their results.

In their initial computational experiences, children need assistance in mapping their manipulations with the fraction analogs onto their existing mental models of whole number addition and subtraction. Real-life problems that draw on children's informal knowledge assist them in making this mapping. These problems also help children make the connections between their informal knowledge and the subsequent symbolic representations

(Mack, 1993). We illustrate these points with reference to the following examples:

Jenny has 3 quarters of an apple. If she gives 2 quarters of it to the possum, how much will she have left?

For a mid-morning snack, Martin's Mom gave him 3 tenths of a whole chocolate bar. In the afternoon, she gave him another 5 tenths of the chocolate bar. How much of the chocolate bar did Martin eat altogether?

These problems involve familiar change-by-subtracting and change-by-adding situations that can be modeled with fractional parts of real objects or with cut-out parts of region models. In interpreting these problems, children should see them as analogous to previous whole-number examples they have encountered and map these new situations onto their existing mental models of whole number addition and subtraction. That is, they need to identify the commencing amount in each case (e.g., 3 quarters, 3 tenths) and decide what action is being addressed (i.e., taking away, adding on). This beginning amount can be displayed with a concrete analog and the required amount then added or subtracted. Of course, if children do not have a sound understanding of the fraction concept, they will not be able to form meaningful representations of these problems.

As children model these problems, they can be encouraged to discuss their actions and justify their solutions by relating them back to their original problems. It is important that children develop one mental model of elementary addition and subtraction, whether this involves operating on whole numbers, common fractions, or decimal fractions (including measurements). Difficulties arise when children adopt a separate mental model each time an operation with a new number system is introduced. We can prevent this by establishing uniform procedures for operating with both whole numbers and fractions, including the manipulation of materials, the renaming and regrouping of amounts, and the recording of results.

Children's recording of these early problem-solving experiences should be directly linked to their actions on the materials and the related symbolic procedures (Hiebert, 1992; Wearne & Hiebert, 1985). The modeling and recording of these initial examples provide the base for the introduction of more complex cases. To illustrate how these latter cases map onto children's exisiting schemata, we examine the procedures involved in solving the examples in Fig. 5.10.

Notice how the recorded format for each of the examples in Fig. 5.10 maps onto the format for whole number operations. This not only creates uniform recording procedures but also helps avoid the error of adding

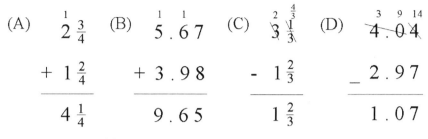

FIG. 5.10. Addition and subtraction of fractions.

numerators and denominators in common fraction examples, an error that is exacerbated by the procedures used in the multiplication of fractions. In each of these examples, children need to appreciate that digits with like values are aligned and that the most efficient method is to begin adding/subtracting with the column of least value.

In the case of the addition examples (A and B), the child initially combines the 3 quarters and 2 quarters and the 7 hundredths and 8 hundredths respectively, and annotates this procedure, as shown. As for whole number addition, constraints apply to the amount that can be recorded in each column. In the common fraction example (A), the 5 quarters must be renamed as 1 whole unit (or 1 one), with the remaining 1 quarter being recorded in the fractions column; likewise for the decimal fraction example B. Whether or not renaming is necessary, we recommend that children apply the same metacognitive strategies as before where they question whether there are sufficient quarters or hundredths to rename as 1 unit or 1 tenth. Note that the renamed amount is recorded at the top of the next column in accord with whole number addition.

The decomposition method used in the subtraction of whole numbers applies also to fractions, as indicated in the foregoing examples. Indeed, the equal additions method is inappropriate for common fractions and many measurement examples (e.g., subtracting time periods). As for whole-number subtraction, the child must identify the commencing amount (minuend) and decide whether it is in a form that will permit the subtraction process to take place. The present examples will not allow subtraction of the subtrahend (2 thirds in example C and 7 hundredths in example D) until renaming/regrouping processes are applied. In example C, one of the whole units must be renamed as 3 thirds, resulting in the quantity-conserving change, 3 units to 2 units 3 thirds. The 3 thirds is then combined with the existing 1 third to produce the quantity-conserving change (regrouping), 3 units 1 third to 2 units 4 thirds. The renaming/regrouping of example D involves a "chunking" process where the 4 ones are renamed firstly as 40 tenths and then as 39 tenths 10 hundredths (a quantity-conserving change of 4 ones to 39 tenths 10 hundredths). This is then combined with the existing 4 hundredths to produce the quantity-conserving change, 4 ones 4 hundredths to 39 tenths 14 hundredths. Using whole-number decomposition processes as the base for these fraction cases helps children develop a consistent and cohesive model of the decomposition procedure. Prior experiences with the renaming/regrouping of fractions with concrete analogs assist in this development. These experiences enable the renaming/regrouping procedure to become embedded within the subtraction process, thus avoiding additional processing loads.

Because we wish to reduce the number of mappings the child has to make in completing these fraction operations, we recommend that examples be carefully sequenced and that children be given sufficient time to internalize the procedures with the concrete analogs (Thompson, 1992) prior to working solely with the abstract forms. There is no need for children to work with unrealistic fractions nor to complete unnecessarily complex calculations (National Council of Teachers of Mathematics, 1989). In the case of decimal fractions, we advocate the use of "nonragged" examples first (e.g., 3.24 + 4.12) prior to "ragged" examples (e.g., 3.24 + 1.3), without renaming or regrouping procedures. However, if children's initial mental models incorporate the understanding that like place values are added/subtracted, then the "ragged" examples should not prove a problem. The subsequent introduction of more difficult decimal examples can entail one renaming/regrouping at a time, as for whole numbers. These, of course, demand a thorough understanding of place value, as was evident in our previous decimal fraction example. Once again, we need to ensure that children know when to apply these renaming/regrouping processes, how to apply them, and why they are doing so.

In the case of common fractions, children's initial experiences involve the addition and subtraction of like fractions, again without renaming or regrouping (e.g., $2\frac{1}{4} + 3\frac{2}{4}$). Children can then progress to examples that require these processes. Once children are proficient with these, they can meet examples that involve equivalence. Children have particular difficulties here (Howard, 1991; Peck & Jencks, 1981) and require experiences with equivalence prior to applying their understanding to computational examples. Initially, children can work examples in which one of the existing fractions provides the common referent (e.g., quarters and eighths), prior to cases where an external referent is needed (e.g., thirds and quarters). Children will need guidance in identifying a suitable referent. This can be achieved through exploring equivalent concrete analogs (Bezuk & Bieck, 1993) or by generating equivalent fractions using more formal methods such as multiplying each of the fractions by $\frac{2}{2}$, $\frac{3}{3}$, $\frac{4}{4}$, and so on. We recommend that the application of equivalence be introduced without the added complexity of the renaming/regrouping processes. These processes can be applied at a later stage.

The limitations of space prevent us from addressing the range of misconceptions children display in addition and subtraction computations. We refer the reader to the well-documented accounts of these in the literature (e.g., Ashlock, 1992; J. S. Brown & Burton, 1978; J. S. Brown & VanLehn, 1980, 1982; Resnick, 1983, 1987a; Resnick & Omanson, 1987; VanLehn, 1990). The important issue in overcoming these misconceptions is to identify their underlying causes and to design appropriately sequenced learning experiences that will target these basic deficiencies.

SUMMARY

The key points addressed in this chapter may be summarized as follows:

1. Children's difficulties with addition and subtraction stem largely from their failure to form meaningful and appropriate connections among external and internal representations. They also fail to link computational procedures with numeration understandings, and earlier computational processes with more advanced computational models.

2. The foundation for children's understanding of whole-number addition and subtraction lies in their early experiences in increasing and decreasing sets of items, as well as in their activities with comparison and part/whole ideas.

3. The types of addition and subtraction problems children meet may be classified in terms of the change-by-adding and change-by-subtracting situations, together with the operations of combine and separate (part–part–whole) and compare and equalize. The last two types can present particular difficulties for children because their wording can often suggest the opposite operation.

4. One schematic system that attempts to explain the solving of computational word problems incorporates a problem-text model, a problem-situation model, and a mathematical model. The appropriate mapping between and among these components plays a crucial role in children's interpretation and subsequent solving of word problems.

5. Children's mathematical models should include a knowledge of the basic addition and subtraction number facts to 9 + 9. The use of derived fact strategies can enhance children's mastery of these facts.

6. Effective mental computational strategies enable children to be creative and flexible in their calculations. Skilful mental computation requires an understanding of numeration concepts and processes, as well as important number properties. Children's mental strategies can assist them in exploring alternative ways of working the formal written algorithms.

7. Children's understanding of the algorithms depends on their abstracting the appropriate mental models from the external representations. They

must also link their understanding of place value and renaming/regrouping processes to their computational procedures. Children's learning of the algorithms needs to be consistent with their earlier computational experiences.

8. In operating with fractions, it is important that children make the connections between their symbolic procedures and their manipulations with the concrete analogs. Children need assistance in mapping their manipulations with the fraction analogs onto their existing mental models of whole number addition and subtraction.

9. It is important to sequence the introduction of computational examples, particularly those involving renaming/regrouping or unlike denominators. In this way, children will have time to internalize each new procedure, thus reducing the number of new mappings they have to make in working these examples. This is particularly important in common fraction cases involving unlike denominators where an understanding of equivalent fractions is required.

6

ELEMENTARY COMPUTATIONAL
MODELS AND PROCESSES:
MULTIPLICATION AND DIVISION

The introduction of the multiplication and division operations represents a significant change in children's dealings with number, that is, children must now contend with a change in the nature of the unit. As children progress from additive to multiplicative situations they experience two major unit-related changes, namely, changes in what the numbers are and changes in what they are about (Hiebert & Behr, 1988). We begin this chapter by considering some of the major types of multiplication and division situations and the approaches adopted in analyzing these. We then consider how we might best assist children in acquiring meaningful and comprehensive mental models of these situations. Here, we revisit our three-pronged schematic system for the solving of computational word problems. The second part of the chapter addresses procedural models of multiplication and division, including the learning of basic number facts and the development of multidigit multiplication and division.

The onset of multiplication is characterized by a shift from operating with single units to operating with composite units (Steffe, 1988). There is also a change in the referents of numbers. With addition and subtraction operations, two like quantities are composed to produce a third like quantity. With multiplication and division however, two either like or unlike quantities are composed to produce a third quantity that is generally unlike the two original quantities (Schwartz, 1988). Schwartz referred to the multiplication and division operations as "referent transforming compositions" (p. 41). With additive situations, children deal with "extensive quantities" that they derive from their environment and quantify by counting or measuring (e.g., five toys). However, for a proper understanding of multiplicative situations, children must deal with what Schwartz (1988) termed, *intensive quantities.* These involve relationships between relationships and are generated through the process of division (e.g., a bag of cookies weighing 1.2 kg, costing $7.00 → $5.00 per kg). We will return to this notion of intensive quantities.

The complexity of these new ideas places a number of cognitive demands on the child, as is evidenced by reports of children's difficulties with these operations, particularly in story problem format (e.g., Bell, Greer, Grimison, & Mangan, 1989; Graeber & Tanenhaus, 1993; Kouba et al., 1988; Nesher, 1992; Quintero, 1985). Children's (and adults') limited understanding of these operations is also reflected in their belief that "multiplication always makes bigger," "division always makes smaller," and "the divisor must be smaller than the dividend" (Bell, Fischbein, & Greer, 1984; Graeber & Tirosh, 1988; Graeber & Baker, 1991; Graeber, Tirosh, & Glover, 1989; Greer, 1992; Tirosh & Graeber, 1990). We return to these points.

MULTIPLICATION AND DIVISION MODELS

In this section we review some of the major types of multiplication and division situations that have been identified in the literature. Analyses of these problem situations have been taken from three main perspectives (Nesher, 1992). The first approach involves an analysis of the semantic factors in the problems, that is, an analysis of the problem text itself (Greer, 1992; Kouba, 1989; Nesher, 1989, 1992). The second adopts the notion of implicit primitive psychological models (Bell, Greer, Mangan, & Grimison, 1989), whereas the third approach uses a dimensional analysis (Vergnaud, 1983; 1988; Schwartz, 1988). We review each of these in turn.

Semantic Analysis.   Kouba (1989, p. 148) identified two major semantic factors that can serve to distinguish multiplication and division word problems and that may have a bearing on children's solution strategies. These are the nature of the quantities used and the quantity that serves as the unknown. We consider the former factor first. Differences in the nature of the quantities give rise to four main types of problems (Kouba specifies three types; however we have added a fourth type, rectangular area, cited by Greer, 1992). These categories are as follows (alternative labels appear in parentheses).

1. Common equivalent set problems (equal groups): *Four children have 3 balloons each. How many balloons do they have altogether?*

These involve situations in which there is a number of groups of objects with the same number in each group. Equivalent set problems can also be expressed in terms of a rate, for example, "If there are 3 balloons per child, how many balloons do 4 children have?" In both of these cases, the number per group (the multiplicand) is multiplied by the number of groups (the multiplier) to find the total number (product; Greer, 1992). Because these two factors are assigned different roles (i.e., the multiplier and multiplicand), problems involving equivalent sets may be classified as asymmetrical situations, in contrast to symmetrical situations where the roles of the two factors are clearly interchangeable, such as in cross-product examples (Bell, Fischbein, & Greer, 1984; De Corte, Verschaffel, & Van Coillie, 1988).

Equivalent set problems usually comprise the child's first multiplicative encounters where repeated addition is used to find the total (i.e., 3×5 would be interpreted as $5 + 5 + 5$ or $3 + 3 + 3 + 3 + 3$). Fischbein, Deri, Nello, and Marino (1985) considered this repeated addition model to be the "primitive intuitive model" for multiplication (p. 4). It can tacitly affect the way in which multiplication is interpreted and used. We revisit these models in a later section.

2. Scalar problems (multiplicative comparison): *Penny has 3 times as many cars as John. John has 4 cars. How many cars does Penny have?*

Problems of this type adopt the general form, "*x* times as many as," and may also be classified as asymmetrical situations (Bell et al., 1984). Children find scalar problems more difficult than the equivalent set type because they have trouble interpreting the phrase, "*x* times as many as . . ." (Kouba & Franklin, 1993).

3. Cross product problems (Cartesian products): *Sue has 3 different blouses and 4 different skirts. How many different outfits can she make?*

This type of problem corresponds to the formal defintion of $m \times n$ in terms of the number of distinct ordered pairs that can be formed when the first member of each pair belongs to a set with m members and the second to a set with n members (Greer, 1992). Cross-product problems are symmetrical cases because the roles of the two factors are easily interchangeable (Bell et al., 1984). This structure can sometimes lead children to view these problems as additive cases because there is no verbal cue for multiplication (Nesher, 1992).

Situations of this nature also represent a component of the domain of combinatorics involving the selection and arrangement of objects in a finite set. That is, the cross product of two sets m and n, may be viewed as the set of combinations obtained by systematically pairing each member of set m in turn with each member of set n.

4. Rectangular area (cf. an array model).

This fourth category refers to rectangular area where the sides of the rectangle are integral (e.g., $3 \text{ cm} \times 2 \text{ cm}$). This is another example of Bell et al.'s (1984) symmetrical situations. Because the rectangle can be divided into squares of side 1 cm to highlight its dimensions (and hence, its area of 12 cm^2), it is clearly analogous to the physical arrangement of $m \times n$ objects in a rectangular array with m rows and n columns (Greer, 1992). As we indicate later, the array model is particularly useful in demonstrating the multiplication concept and its associated properties, such as commutativity.

Division Situations.   The second major semantic factor identified by Kouba (1989), namely, the quantity that serves as the unkown in the problem, also gives rise to three broad categories of problems, namely, multiplication (product unknown), partitive division (number in each set unknown), and measurement or quotitive division (number of sets unknown). Partitive division corresponds to the common practice of forming equal shares and hence is usually referred to as a sharing approach. Here, an object or set of objects is divided into a number of equal subsets or shares, as illustrated below (the word *share,* however, need not be explicitly stated).

> *Mrs. Baker has 12 chocolates and will share these among her 3 children. How many will each child receive?*

These partitive problems may be defined in general terms as division by the multiplier (Greer, 1992). The dividend must be larger than the divisor (or operator), which, itself, must be a whole number (Fischbein et al., 1985). The partition model is seen as the intuitive primitive model for division, with the quotitive model being acquired later through instruction (Fischbein et al., 1985). This view is supported by studies in which an overwhelming number of subjects have written a partitive division word problem for a division example such as, "12 divided by 3" (Af Ekenstam & Greger, 1983; Bell, Fischbein, & Greer, 1984; Graeber & Tirosh, 1988).

In quotitive division one determines how many times a given quantity is contained in a larger quantity, for example:

> *Tom baked 12 cakes for the fair. He wishes to sell them in boxes of two. How many boxes will he need?*

Quotition may be defined as division by the multiplicand (Greer, 1992). The only constraint here is that the dividend must be larger than the divisor. If the quotient is a whole number, the model can be conceived of as repeated subtraction (Fischbein et al., 1985).

Research (e.g., S. Brown, 1992) has shown that prior to any formal instruction on division, children can solve some division problems. Brown's research, in accord with that of Zweng (1964), and Sato (1984), found that quotitive problems are easier for young children to solve than partitive examples. Mulligan (1992), however, did not find much difference in the difficulty levels of the two problem types. It is interesting that the children in Brown's study used a grouping-by-multiples strategy far more frequently than a sharing strategy, even when the grouping strategy did not correctly model the partitive division problem. Here, a correct solution could still be obtained despite the formation of an inappropriate problem-situation model. For example, in the partitive problem involving the sharing of 12 chocolates among three children, a grouping strategy where four groups of three are removed from a set of 12 items would be an incorrect representation of the problem because the number of groups would not correspond with the number of children. We would argue that the reason children found the quotitive problems less difficult was that these examples are a little easier to model than the partitive problems, that is, a grouping-by-multiples strategy maps readily onto the semantic structure of a quotitive problem. We return to this issue in a later section.

Implicit Psychological Models.   The second approach to analyzing multiplication and division situations addresses children's implicit psychological models. Fischbein et al. (1985) claimed that children's implicitly held models account for their performance on multiplication and division problems. They hypothesized that "each fundamental operation of arithmetic generally remains linked to an implicit, unconscious, and primitive intuitive model" (p. 4). These intuitive models can hinder, divert, or even prevent a solution because conflicts arise between formal algorithmic structures and these implicitly held models. The basis of their hypothesis was the finding that children have difficulty in solving problems in which the multiplier is a decimal fraction and hence not readily interpreted as "lots of" or "times." Other investigations have also shown that the distinct roles of multiplier and multiplicand have an effect on children's performance (e.g., De Corte et al., 1988; Graeber & Tirosh, 1988; Greer, 1988). It appears that the kind of numbers in the multiplier position, rather than in the multiplicand position, strongly influences children's ability to identify the correct operation. For example, problems with an integer as the multiplier appear significantly easier for children than when the multiplier is a decimal fraction greater than one. The most difficult are problems where the multiplier is less than one.

These implict models are assumed to arise from the way in which children are introduced to the multiplication and division concepts. That is, the equivalent set model (interpreted as repeated addition) and the partitive model (interpreted as sharing) are normally the first representations children meet and thus tend to become strongly entrenched as mental models. A second explanation for the enduring and influential effects of these models is that they correspond to the natural and basic features of human cognition (Fischbein et al., 1985). That is, people tend to naturally interpret facts and ideas in terms of models that are meaningful to them. Because these early multiplication and division models are assumed to be meaningful to the child, they tend to remain active and overshadow any new conceptual models.

If this hypothesis is correct, then, teachers are faced with a basic didactical dilemma. That is, should these intuitive models that relate easily to the child's world be established initially, with the possible danger that they will hinder more formal learning, or should other, more comprehensive models that will be less "real world," but will encompass the different multiplication and division constructs, be the first models children meet? We would argue that meaningful models can be introduced to children in their initial multiplicative experiences without hindering future learning. We agree with Nesher's (1988) argument that the phenomenon described by Fischbein et al. (1985) is not necessarily related to intuitive implicit models but is explicitly created by our teaching methods. We will return to this point in our discussion on developing children's multiplicative mental models.

Dimensional Analysis.   We review here the final approach to analyzing multiplication and division situations, namely, the theoretical perspectives of Schwartz (1988) and Vergnaud (1983, 1988). Both adopted a broader view of multiplication and division, regarding them as part of a larger multiplicative conceptual field including vector spaces, rational numbers, ratio, and so on. Their emphasis was on the dimensions and unit structures of these problem types. Vergnaud argued that the development of this conceptual field takes considerable time, in fact, up to adulthood. Within multiplicative structures, Vergnaud (1983) identified three main classes of problems, namely, isomorphism of measures, product of measures, and multiple proportions. Isomorphism of measures refers to situations in which there is a direct proportion between two measure spaces (e.g., "four apples per child; how many for three children?"). The quantities within each measure space can be integers, fractions, or decimals. The first two categories of problems that we identified earlier (equivalent set and scalar problems) are subsumable within this class. The foregoing example (four apples per child/three children) is regarded as a four-place relation since there are two basic dimensions, M1 (children) and M2 (apples), with each dimension comprising two numbers, as shown:

Children (M1)	Apples (M2)
1	4
3	?

Vergnaud refers to a mapping function between the two dimensions, M1 and M2, which maintains a constant ratio (i.e., 1:4 and 3:?). There is also a scalar increase or decrease within each dimension (i.e., between 1 and 3 or 4 and ?).

Vergnaud's second major class of problems, namely, product of measures, covers examples where two measure spaces, M1 and M2, are mapped onto a third, M3. This category subsumes both the cross product and the rectangular area problems that we identified earlier. In the example, "*What is the area (M3) of a floor of length 4 meters (M1) and width 2 meters (M2)?*" the child has to contend with three measures, one of them being proportional to each of the others when all other variables remain constant; the child must thus deal with double proportions. In Vergnaud's third category, namely, the multiple proportion problems, a measure, M3, is proportional to two different independent measures, M1 and M2 (e.g., "*If one chihuahua eats 150 grams of food per day, how many grams will 4 chihuahuas eat in 3 days?*").

Schwartz's (1988) dimensional analysis distinguishes between intensive and extensive quantities, which we defined earlier. Schwartz drew attention to the dangers of children only conceiving of multiplication as repeated addition and of division as sharing and argued that a proper understanding of these operations can only be obtained through a knowledge of these intensive quantities. Such a quantity is usually not counted or measured directly, such as the price per kilogram of coffee; it is a descriptor of a "quality" of the coffee, not the amount of coffee. Mathematical intensive quantities can usually be recognized by the word "per" although, as Schwartz pointed out, this may be implicit in the unit measure (as in the case of the "knot"). In essence, an intensive quantity is a statement of a constant multiplicative relationship between two quantities. It is thus inappropriate to model these situations with repeated addition or partitive models.

Nesher (1988, 1992) reported on an instructional study by Mechmandarov (1987) in which children underwent special instruction aimed at freeing them from the repeated addition model by introducing a mapping table incorporating Vergnaud's (1983) dimensional model. Although Nesher (1992) highlighted the benefits of this approach, the study's findings did show that only 10% of children voluntarily used the mapping table when not directed to do so. When students did use the table voluntarily, it was usually for the more difficult examples. Given that the mapping table is an abstract representation and is not suitable for all problem types, we do not consider it appropriate for children's initial multiplicative experiences.

Developing Mental Models of Multiplication Situations

We now turn to the difficult task of determining how we might assist children in acquiring meaningful and comprehensive mental models of multiplication and division situations. In so doing, we draw upon our three-pronged schematic system for the solving of computational word problems that we introduced in the last chapter. Recall that the three components of this system are the problem-text model, the problem-situation model, and the mathematical model. Because the three models are interdependent, children will have difficulty solving a problem if any one model is incorrect or incomplete. The research we have cited points to the important role of the problem-situation model in children's learning. For example, children who have difficulty producing concrete or pictorial representations from verbal descriptions of equivalent set problems (Graeber & Tanenhaus, 1993) would lack a meaningful problem-situation model. Children who interpret multiplicative situations in terms of repeated addition develop a limited problem-situation model. This hinders the production of the corresponding mathematical model, particularly when the problems are not of the equivalent set type (cf. Fischbein et al.'s, 1985, argument).

Difficulties can also arise when children form a mathematical model directly from their problem-text model without developing a problem-situation model. Although proficient problem solvers may not need to form such a model (at least for simple problems), less proficient solvers tend to avoid reading problem texts and try to solve word problems by attending solely to the numbers in the problems (Bell et al., 1984, 1989; Mulligan, 1993). In this case, they would have an incorrect or incomplete problem-text model and hence would likely generate an erroneous mathematical model, such as dividing when an operand is less than one (De Corte et al., 1988).

Given the points we have raised, we contend that a number of modifications need to be made to some current classroom practices. First, we would argue that the common practice of using a repeated addition approach to interpret multiplicative situations reflects a fundamental misunderstanding of its role. That is, it appears that repeated addition is used both as a representation of the problem situation as well as the corresponding mathematical model (e.g., $4 + 4 + 4$). We contend that if repeated addition is to be used at all, it should serve only as a means of generating the answer to a multiplicative operation that has resulted from an appropriate modeling process. About all that repeated addition does is highlight the equivalence of the groups in an equivalent set problem. It does not emphasize the multiplicative structure of the problem situation and severely restricts children's interpretation of multiplication per se. The presence of addition symbols in the recorded form is potentially confusing for children because they will eventually have to replace several familiar signs with just one, new symbol, that of multiplication. When repeated addition is used in this manner, it is questionable whether children ever come to see multiplicative situations in terms of multiplication. We thus recommend that repeated addition only be used as a means of calculating the answer to a multiplication statement.

The second modification we advocate is a greater emphasis on the semantic complexity of these word problems and an increased repertoire of problem situations to challenge and expand children's existing mental models. Nesher's (1988) research indicated that it is not the type of problem that is the major source of difficulty for children, rather, it is other factors within the particular type, such as the presence of contextual cues. Nesher found that children are able to solve simple cases within a range of problem types. We recommend that children's early multiplicative experiences include examples drawn from the categories of equivalent set, cross product, and rectangular array with later examples involving scalar (multiplicative comparison) problems. We make this recommendation based on our research that has shown that young children can handle cross product examples and that they find these easier than scalar problems where the terminology ("x times as many as") presents difficulties (English, 1990a, 1992a, 1994). We will now offer a suggested approach to developing children's facility with multiplicative word problems, based on our three-component referential model. We will use the following equivalent set problem as an example.

Kathy has 3 shelves of toys in her room. On each shelf there are 4 toys. How many toys altogether has she on her shelves?

To solve such a problem, children initially need to develop a meaningful text-base model. This requires them to analyze the verbal information to identify the relevant data and the logical conditions and relationships (cf. Nesher, 1992). Children will need guidance in identifying the following text components:

1. The *pair of referents* in question, that is, the toys and shelves;
2. The *relationship* between the members of the referent pair, that is, four toys to one shelf.
3. The *role* of each referent. Since this problem is asymmetrical, the multiplier and multiplicand can be identified. The number of toys (4) is the multiplicand while the number of shelves (3) is the multiplier. While children initially do not need to know the formal terms, *multiplier* and *multiplicand*, they do need to distinguish between the number per group and the number of groups in the asymmetrical problems.
4. The problem *goal,* including the *referent* that is being addressed, that is, the total number of toys.

The identification of these problem-text components is essential to the formation of a meaningful problem-situation model. Children's initial development of this situation model can involve representing the problem with concrete materials, followed later by corresponding pictorial models. The structure of the concrete/pictorial model and the accompanying language is crucial here. Because the array model clearly illustrates the multiplicative structure, $m \times n$, as well as commutativity, we recommend that it be introduced to children in their early activities. The array can be used in conjunction with a grouping (sets) model because we use the same language for both. In time, children can experience a range of representations, including tree diagrams, charts, and measurement models (Kaput, 1989). To help children map these concrete and pictorial representations onto their problem-text models, we need to direct them to the salient text components. The following dialogue illustrates one way in which this might be achieved with our equivalent set example. Such a dialogue would take place initially in child-dominated child-to-teacher discussion and then subsequently in child-to-child discussion (Kouba & Franklin, 1993).

Suggested questioning sequence:
What items are we considering in Kathy's room?
What do we have to find out?
Let's start by looking at her shelves. How many shelves has she?
Let's make her three shelves. (These can be drawn or modeled with
   pieces of string, as shown in Fig.6.1)
Does she have toys on each shelf? Does she have the same number
   of toys on each shelf? How many on each shelf?
Place four of your counters on each of the shelves (refer to Fig. 6.1).
Check to see that you have exactly four toys/counters on each shelf.
Now check that you do have three shelves.

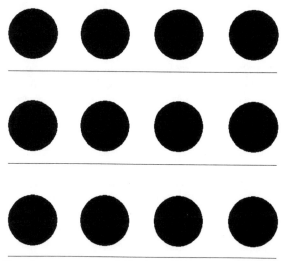

FIG. 6.1.   Use of an array representation to model an asymmetrical multiplicative
problem.

We have 4 toys on each shelf and we have three shelves.

We can say this another way. We can say we have "four toys on each shelf by three shelves." (Children can indicate this on their model.)

How could we find out how many toys Kathy has altogether?

Have we solved the problem? How do you know?

Note in the dialogue that repeated addition was not used as the basis for modeling the problem. Children may, however, employ repeated addition or counting to help them calculate the total number. We recommend that they be encouraged to find more than one way of calculating the total and to verify their results each time (the reader is referred to Anghileri, 1989, and Kouba, 1989, for a discussion on children's various solution strategies).

Children's formal recording of their actions involves mapping the mathematical model onto their problem-situation model. They should then be able to map this symbolic model onto the original problem text. The formal modeling however, should only occur after children have had considerable experience in forming problem-situation models (cf. Kouba & Franklin, 1993). Initially the term, *by*, can be used in the mathematical model instead of the formal multiplication symbol (×), with the mathematical model read as, "four by three," then later as "four multiplied by three," as shown in Example 1:

$$
\begin{array}{rl}
4 & \leftarrow \quad \text{four (toys on each shelf)} \\
\underline{\text{by } (\times)\ 3} & \leftarrow \quad \text{by three (shelves)} \\
12 & \leftarrow \quad \text{twelve (toys altogether)}
\end{array}
$$

Once children understand commutativity, they can also read the statement from "bottom to top," that is, as "three fours." Reading the multiplication statement from both directions is consistent with the problem-situation model (3 sets of 4). If the statement were to be read as, "four threes" or "four times three," it would not match the problem situation (i.e., there are not four shelves with three toys on each). We prefer to use the mathematically "correct" term, *by* or multiplied by, because it conforms with the conventions for the other operations (Anghileri, 1989) and furthermore, is applicable to a range of multiplicative situations. Although the term, *times*, is commonly used, it implies a repeated addition construct and may thus contribute to the "implicit model" difficulties we cited earlier. Note that we have used a vertical recording format because it lays the foundation (or scaffolding) for multidigit multiplication. In this way children are less likely to conceive of the multiplication algorithm as unrelated to these initial multiplicative models.

In addition to meeting a range of multiplicative situations and models, children also need to expand their multiplicative language (e.g., the rate term, *per*) (Kouba & Franklin, 1993; National Council of Teachers of Mathematics, 1989). Other terms that warrant attention include factor, multiple, product, and quotient. Children can be introduced to these informally through investigative activities, such as finding the factors of a number using an array of tiles or graph paper. This can lead to an exploration of prime numbers (comprising only two factors, 1 and the number itself), composite numbers (more than two factors), and square numbers (which can be expressed in the form of two equal factors) (National Council of Teachers of Mathematics, 1989). Children can also explore the principle of commutativity when using an array model (e.g., by rotating an array of counters on a sheet of paper).

Developing Mental Models of Division Situations

We now turn to children's interpretation of division problems. As we mentioned earlier, there are two types of division situations that can be derived from asymmetrical multiplicative problems, namely, partition and quotition. Recall that partitive division occurs when the multiplicand is unknown, that is, the number of members in a group (or set, row, rate) has to be found. Quotitive or measurement division has the multiplier as the unknown, that is, the number of groups has to be determined.

Although quotitive problems may be easier for children to model, as was evident in S. Brown's (1992) research, they are not necessarily more meaningful. We maintain that partitive situations occur more naturally and more frequently in children's lives than quotitive examples and, hence, are likely to be more meaningful. Indeed, research (e.g., Graeber & Tirosh, 1988) has shown that people clearly favor partitive situations when asked to provide a word problem to match a given division statement. A partitive approach is also more suitable for modeling the division algorithm (whole numbers and decimal fractions) and some common fraction examples, as we indicate later. By continuing this model through to the more complex calculations children are less likely to see these new examples as unrelated to their earlier learning. Given these arguments, we feel that partitive problems should form a significant component of children's initial experiences with the division concept. However we are aware of the danger in overexposing children to this model, to the neglect of the quotitive model. Because we want children to acquire a comprehensive mental model of division, we need to ensure that both situations are included in the curriculum. We now turn to a consideration of how we might foster children's understanding of these division types. Given the limitations of space, we will only examine a partitive case. We refer to the following problem:

Mrs. Baker has 12 chocolates and will share these among her 3 children. How many will each child receive?

In forming a problem-text model, children will need guidance in identifying the text components discussed previously (i.e., the pair of referents, the relationship between the referents, the role of each referent, and the problem goal). Once children have identified these components and have a model of the problem text, they can proceed to develop a model of the problem situation. Initially this can be accomplished by directing children to act out the problem with concrete materials; this can be replaced later by pictorial representations. Once again, the structure of the concrete/pictorial model and the accompanying language is particularly important in helping children form a meaningful representation of the problem text. We offer one suggested approach to developing this modeling process in accord with the learning principles we are advocating.

Suggested questioning sequence:
What is happening in this problem?
How many chocolates has Mrs. Baker?
Let's show these chocolates with our counters.
What is Mrs. Baker going to do with these chocolates?
Will she give each child the same number of chocolates? How do you
    know?
Before we share out our counters, we need to check that we have
    three children. Do you have three of your friends with you?
What are some ways in which you could share your counters?
Now share out your counters amongst your three friends.
Tell your friends how you shared your counters.
How can you be sure that you gave each friend an equal share?
Let's look back over our problem (children can be guided in deriving
    the following statements).
We started with 12 chocolates and we shared or divided these
    amongst three friends. Each friend received four chocolates.
    Another way we can say this is, "12 divided by three is four."
We can think about what we've made in another way. Do you see
    that we have made three groups of chocolates with four choco-
    lates in each group? How many does that give us altogether? Is
    this the amount we started with?

Notice how children are encouraged to find their own ways of sharing the counters in the previous activity. There are various such strategies that have been identified from children's actions in these situations, such as trial and error, systematic one-to-one dealing, and so on (Davis & Pepper, 1992; Hunting, 1991; Kouba, 1989; Kouba & Franklin, 1993; Mulligan, 1992). Notice also how the last statement is designed to highlight the inverse property of division and multiplication.

The symbolism and language used to express division situations is more varied and subtle than that used for multiplication, for example, "12 divided by 3" is entirely different from "12 divided into 3." This highlights the importance of children forming a meaningful problem-situation model where they clearly understand the roles of the dividend, divisor, and quotient (Graeber & Tanenhaus, 1993). We recommend that children interpret division situations as "x divided by y," rather than as "y goes into x," or "y divided into x," because the latter do not reflect the modeling of the problem situation. When we finally guide children in formally recording their mathematical model, we can choose from three symbolic representations, namely, $y\overline{)x}$, $x \div y$, and $\frac{x}{y}$. The first example clearly separates the dividend from the divisor and is the format used in the recording of the algorithm. Provided children are taught to interpret this correctly, it can be used as an initial form of recording. Alternatively, the second representation may be employed since it maps directly onto the problem-situation model. Children can familiarize themselves with this symbol by recording their division situations on a calculator. The third representation is the most abstract and offers a potential connection between the operation of division and the rational numbers (Graeber & Tanenhaus, 1993). It can thus be introduced at a later stage.

If children are given a variety of problem-situation modeling experiences prior to recording the mathematical models, they should have less chance of developing misconceptions about the nature of division. One such misconception is the belief that "x divided by y" is the same as "y divided by x." This represents an overgeneralization of the commutative properties of addition and multiplication, compounded by confusion as to how to read division statements (Graeber & Tanenhaus, 1993).

The problems we have addressed to date have not included remainders. Indeed, children's experiences with division situations should include cases where first, a nonzero remainder can be ignored and the quotient gives the required answer (a "quotient-only" problem) and second, the remainder must be taken into account and the quotient increased by one to answer the problem (an augmented-quotient problem) (Mulligan, 1992; Silver et al., 1992; Silver et al., 1993). Children's difficulties with these cases, especially the augmented-quotient type, were evident in children's responses to the "bus problem" on the Third National Assessment of Educational Progress (1983). Only 24% of 13 year-olds chose the correct response to the problem, "An army bus holds 36 soldiers. If 1,128 soldiers are being bused to their training site, how many buses are needed?"

Problems of this nature highlight the importance of a meaningful problem-situation model because correct computation alone, cannot ensure a successful solution (Silver et al., 1993). Silver et al. (1993) further investigated children's responses to problems of this type by asking them to show all of their work and to explain their answer in writing (the NAEP study involved multiple-choice responses only). It was found that 60% of students in Grades 6, 7, and 8 were able to execute their computation correctly, but only 45% responded with the augmented quotient or were able to give an appropriate interpretation for an alternative answer. Overall, their findings showed that it was not the computational requirements of the problem that were the major barrier to students obtaining a correct solution, rather, their unsuccessful solutions were more often due to a failure to interpret their computational results. This was compounded by two important mediational factors, namely, the school performance context (i.e., children's dissociation of school mathematics requirements from more "real-world" ways of thinking and reasoning) and the difficulty of providing a written explanation.

Developing Procedural Models of Multiplication and Division: Number Fact Strategies

The application of a known multiplication or division fact in the solving of a problem represents a substantial step in children's abstraction of these operations (Anghileri, 1989). After children have developed meaningful mental models of multiplication and division, they can begin to develop mastery of the basic facts (0×0 through to 9×9 and related division facts). We reviewed some approaches to number-fact mastery in our discussion on the addition and subtraction facts in the last chapter. We will extend some of those ideas to our present discussion.

Research on children's mastery of the multiplication and division facts has not been extensive (J. B. Cooney, Swanson, & Ladd, 1988). According to Anghileri's (1989) research, children are reluctant to use multiplication facts to solve multiplication problems. They prefer to use number patterns, even when the application of a single number fact would be a more economical solution. Anghileri suggested that children's difficulty in progressing from a counting or number pattern strategy to the use of a number fact may be tied in with the development required for the transition from unary to binary operations. This is in line with Vergnaud's (1983, 1988) argument that young children do not use a binary operation for multiplication but a unary operation using either a scalar or function operator. To encourage children to move away from this reliance on a number pattern, we need to help them see the benefits of acquiring a mastery of the basic facts.

As for the addition and subtraction facts, we recommend introducing children to derived fact strategies that emphasize thinking patterns based on special groups of related facts. These strategies provide children with meaningful models for generating all of the multiplication and division facts. We review these briefly here and refer the reader to other sources, such as Booker, Briggs, Davey, and Nisbet (1992).

The thinking strategies for the twos' and fives' facts are the least complex

$$\frac{\begin{array}{c}9\\2\end{array}}{18} \quad \frac{\begin{array}{c}9\\5\end{array}}{45} \quad \frac{\begin{array}{c}9\\6\end{array}}{34} \quad \frac{\begin{array}{c}9\\8\end{array}}{72} \quad \frac{\begin{array}{c}9\\3\end{array}}{27}$$ less than 30
so 2 — how much less?
one 3, so **27**

because they can be related readily to children's existing knowledge. Children can use their knowledge of the addition doubles facts as a base for deriving the twos' facts. For example, using an array model, children can verify that 2 threes is the same as double three and can also see the equivalence of the commutative pairs ($2 \times 3 = 3 \times 2$). Recognizing these pairs reduces the number of individual facts the child has to learn for each cluster of facts. The thinking strategies children use in simple number and counting activities can be applied to the fives' facts.

The thinking strategies for the next cluster of facts, the nines' facts, involve recognizing the particular patterns displayed by these numbers. That is, the tens' digit of the product is always one less than the second factor because the first factor, nine, is close to 10. Furthermore, the ones' digit and the tens' digit of the product always total nine. For example, in the fact, $9 \times 6 = 54$, the sum of the digits in the product (54) is nine and the tens' digit (5) is one less than the second factor (6). Children can explore these patterns for the facts to 9×9 and then see how the pattern changes for nines' facts beyond 9×9. A calculator can be used to generate the products of these higher facts so that children can focus on the patterns without the extra load of complex calculations. Children can then predict the product of a multiplication such as 9×36 and check their response with a calculator.

The next cluster of facts, the zeros' and ones' facts would normally be the first sets of facts studied under the traditional approach. However these present difficulties because children often do not understand multiplication by zero and one, and division by one, and tend to rely on rotely learned rules (J. B. Cooney et al., 1988; Campbell & Graham, 1985). Because the array model is inappropriate here, a sets analog is needed to develop the required understanding (e.g., three plates, each with one counter, or three plates each without a counter).

The thinking strategies for the final two clusters of facts are more difficult. These facts include the "squares" and the remaining threes, fours, and sixes facts. Although the "squares" facts are more difficult than the previous examples, they can be displayed clearly with the array model and their identical factors highlighted. Children can generate the remaining cluster of facts by adding on to known facts. For example, to determine the answer to "3 sevens," children can think "2 sevens are 14, and one more seven makes 21."

Children's mastery of each cluster of multiplication facts provides the basis for the generation of the division facts. Provided children have explored the inverse relationship of multiplication and division, they can use their knowledge of the corresponding multiplication fact to answer a given division fact. The main strategy for generating the division facts is thus, "think of the multiplication fact" (Booker et al., 1992; Suydam, 1984; see Booker et al. for activities designed to develop this strategy).

The points we made regarding the teaching of the thinking strategies for addition and subtraction apply also to the present operations. We will not revisit these except to say that children should play a major role in developing these strategies (Heege, 1985) and should know not only how to apply them but also when to apply them. It is advisable for children to have mastered a particular strategy and be able to recall the associated facts (without reliance on the strategy) prior to embarking on a new strategy. It is important here that children make use of the fact that, for every single combination they recall, they can also recall three related facts. Automatic recall of these facts means children will use fewer processing resources and hence will have greater processing capacity to deal with the next cluster of facts. Furthermore, a well-established knowledge of one cluster provides children with a base for new learnings and also helps reduce the problem of interference. Because interference can occur when a new strategy is developed from those previously learned, it is important that children be given the opportunity to discriminate one strategy from another, as we noted in our earlier discussion on the addition and subtraction facts. The problem of interference is a difficult one, as noted by Campbell and Graham (1985) and J. B. Cooney et al. (1988).

Developing Procedural Models of Multiplication and Division: Multidigit Whole Numbers

In this section we give initial thought to children's use of informal computational strategies. Because we addressed this in detail in the last chapter, we give it only brief consideration here. In conjunction with this, we cite a number of mathematical principles that underlie both informal and formal multidigit multiplication and division. We then consider different approaches to the teaching of these operations and offer some instructional suggestions.

Students tend to view multidigit multiplication and division as simply rules to be followed, and persist in thinking of the numbers involved as single units rather than as grouped amounts. This prevents them from using numbers to show relationships between quantities, and to reason proportionally between the dividend and the quotient in division situations (Behr et al., 1983; Fischbein et al., 1985; Graeber & Tanenhaus, 1993; K. Hart, 1981; Lampert, 1992). Several researchers thus advocated that children be actively involved in devising their own algorithms by applying their understanding of estimation, place value, and relevant mathematical principles (e.g., Lampert, 1986, 1992; Stanic & McKillip, 1989). We addressed the importance of children's invented strategies in our discussion on addition and subtraction. The points we raised also apply here.

We consider it beneficial for children to develop efficient mental computational strategies prior to being introduced to the conventional algorithms. Delaying mental computation until after the formal written algorithms have been mastered can be conducive to children applying the paper-and-pencil procedures to mental calculations (Sowder, 1990). Furthermore, the understandings children apply in mental computation can assist them in their learning of the algorithms. For example, thinking of the place-value component of a number, such as 1 hundred + 3 tens + 5 ones, when mentally solving 135×4, can establish a conceptual model for multiplying each digit in the formal algorithm. Children's choice of computational model, whether this be a mental strategy approach, an alternative written procedure, a standard algorithm, or the use of a calculator, needs to be a metacognitive one that they can justify on both conceptual and procedural grounds.

Children who use effective informal strategies are seen by Lampert (1986) as possessing "principled understanding." This understanding enables the child to invent mathematically appropriate procedures and to recognize that these can be applied in a number of different contexts. The invention of these procedures is governed by a set of formal mathematical properties and laws that Lampert (1986) terms the principles of multiplication (p. 310). A person with a principled understanding of multidigit multiplication is thus assumed to possess a knowledge of the principles of multiplication. These principles not only form the building blocks of efficient mental computation but also of the formal multiplication algorithm. We review these principles here. In addition to place value, these include:

1. *Additive composition:* Numbers are composed by addition and can be decomposed in many quantity-conserving ways. For example, 48 can be thought of as $40 + 8$, $47 + 1$, $20 + 10 + 10 + 8$, and so on.

2. *Associativity of addition:* The components of these additive compositions can be grouped and added in various quantity-conserving ways.

3. *Commutativity of addition:* The order in which additions are completed does not affect the final sum.

4. *Multiplicative composition:* Because numbers can be decomposed into equal groups, they can also be composed by multiplication. For example, 48 can be considered as $24 + 24$, which is 24×2, or as $16 + 16 + 16$ which is 16×3.

5. *Associativity of multiplication:* The components of these multiplicative compositions can be grouped and multiplied in various quantity-conserving ways. For example, $48 = (2 \times 2) \times 12 = 4 \times 12$ or $48 = 6 \times (4 \times 2) = 6 \times 8$.

6. *Commutativity of multiplication:* The order in which multiplications are done does not affect the final product.

7. *Distributive property of multiplication over addition:* Numbers to be multiplied can be decomposed additively, each of the components operated on separately, and the product obtained from recomposing the partial products. For example, $48 \times 3 = (40 + 8) \times 3 = (40 \times 3) + (8 \times 3)$ (Lampert, 1986, pp. 310–311).

There are additional understandings required here that are tied in with Lampert's place-value component. These include the patterns of multiplication by powers of ten and the process of renaming, which we addressed in the last chapter (e.g., 46 ones can be renamed as 4 tens 6 ones). The multiplication patterns are most evident in the conventional algorithm and include the following: tens × ones → tens (e.g., 3 tens [30] × 4 ones = 12 tens [120]), tens by tens → hundreds (e.g., 4 tens × 2 tens = 8 hundreds), and tens by hundreds → thousands (e.g., 6 tens × 4 hundreds = 24 thousands).

Comparable principles apply to multidigit division ("long division"). For example, the dividend and the divisor are decomposed and the operation is carried out in several steps, with the quotient being assembled from the results of these steps (Lampert, 1992). That is, we do not operate on the original dividend as a whole quantity but on a succession of one- or two-digit numbers, beginning with the digit/s in the largest place (in contrast to the other conventional algorithms where the operation begins with the ones). Operating on the dividend by a two-digit divisor requires an additional process, that of estimation. For example, in dividing 4,346 by 18, we round the divisor to 20 and use this to estimate the quotient of 43 (hundreds) divided by 18. Because the division algorithm incorporates subtraction, the renaming/regrouping processes we addressed in the last chapter also come into play.

Lampert (1992) illustrated how the conventional procedure for performing long division instantiates the mathematical concept of multiplicative structures, involving the relationships of ratio and proportion. Taking the example, 1,536 ÷ 73, Lampert adopted a quotitive interpretation of the division process that involves finding how many groups of 73 units will be needed to make a total of 1,536 units (there is also the partitive interpretation to which we will return). Rephrasing this interpretation, we have the statement, "*If 73 is 1 group, 1,536 is how many groups?*" or, "*What number will relate to 1,536 in the same way that 1 relates to 73?*" Hence in proportional terms, we have the relationship, $\frac{73}{1} = \frac{1536}{x}$, where x is the quotient to be determined. The pair of equal ratios represents a linear function that maps a group of 73 units onto each single unit (Lampert, 1992, p. 227). This approach draws upon Vergnaud's (1983) dimensional model, which we reviewed earlier, as well as Nesher's (1988) mapping rule indicating how many times the divisor will map onto a unit in the quotient.

Lampert uses these ideas as a mathematical justification for the first and subsequent steps in the conventional algorithm. For example, when beginning to divide 1,536 by 73, we consider what multiple of 7 is close to 15. We are assuming that the quotient of 153 ÷ 73 will be approximately one tenth the quotient of 1,536 ÷ 73, because 153 is about one tenth of 1,536 and the quotient of 15 ÷ 7 will be the same as that of 153 ÷ 73. Our assumptions here are based on the place-value and proportional relationships among these pairs of numbers. That is, the approximate equivalence between $\frac{153}{7}$ and $\frac{1536}{73}$

must be considered, whereas at the same time, the difference in order of magnitude between 153 and 1,536 and between 7 and 73 must be recognized. Children need to appreciate these relationships, however we suggest that these be established after children have worked the algorithm using less abstract models, such as the partititve approach. We return to this point later.

We now examine suggested approaches to developing children's mental models of the formal multiplication and division algorithms. Although we do not advocate that children perform complex examples, we nevertheless believe that they need to be exposed to these formal methods. These procedures can prove to be more powerful than informal methods in certain situations (Baroody & Ginsburg, 1986). We also recommend that the calculator be used to explore the number patterns involved in these computations.

Developing Mental Models of Multidigit Multiplication.   Because the modeling of multidigit multiplication and division is difficult, it is easy to see why the formal algorithms are frequently presented in a mechanical fashion. However the use of appropriate representational models, accompanied by meaningful explanation, can promote understanding and mastery. As we mentioned previously, it is important that children experiment with different ways of recording their procedures prior to being introduced to the conventional methods.

One approach to teaching these multidigit computations is to build an intuitive understanding of the underlying principles within the context of algorithm instruction (Lampert, 1986, 1992). In the case of multiplication, Lampert (1986) designed a curriculum to teach children that they could devise their own methods of doing multiplication if they could master the principles that constrain the possible algorithms. In all of Lampert's lessons, children were given activities in which the multiplication principles were transparent in the steps of the procedures used to derive an answer. The principles were not taught directly nor formally named. Lampert found that when students came to solve multidigit algorithms in the conventional way, they were able to explain their actions by using principled knowledge that was linked to the language of equal groups. The fact that children were able to justify their procedures by talking meaningfully about place value and the order of operations, was taken as evidence that they viewed mathematics as more than a set of procedures for finding answers.

An alternative way in which meaning can be assigned to the formal algorithm is to model simple multidigit cases with base-ten blocks, establish the basic multiplication patterns, and then use this understanding as a mental model for more complex examples. Children's initial experiences would involve representing the multiplication of tens with the base-ten blocks, such as 3 tens × 2. A knowledge of the basic fact, 3 × 2, serves as the mental model for this calculation. Children's knowledge of the multiplication of tens and the multiplication of ones (basic facts) can now be applied to simple multidigit cases involving no renaming and a single-digit multiplier (e.g., 32 × 2), as shown in Fig. 6.2A. Children need to have prior understand-

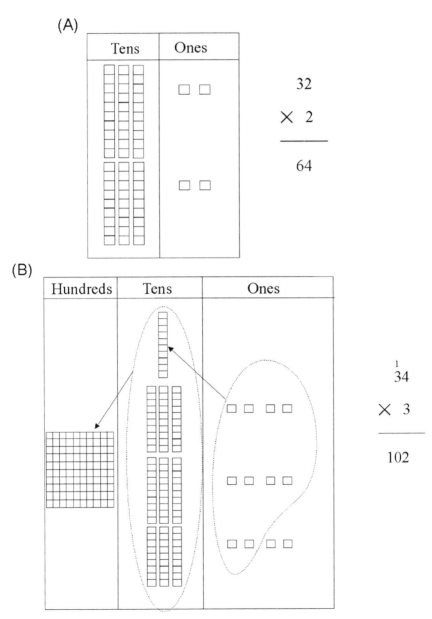

FIG. 6.2.   Modeling multidigit multiplications: (A) without renaming and (B) with renaming.

ing of the processes involved here, that is, the multiplier (ones) operates on both the tens and the ones (in contrast to the addition and subtraction algorithms), with each of these partial products combining to give the final product. This understanding should have been established previously through children's informal experiences in using the distributive property to solve such problems in meaningful contexts. Although children can begin operating with either the tens or ones in this instance, examples with renaming will require the ones to be multiplied first. Hence it seems more appropriate for children to begin with the ones first and then progress to the tens, as they have been used to doing with the addition and subtraction algorithms.

The introduction of examples involving the renaming of 10 ones as 1 ten (e.g., 34×3) can be modeled with the base-ten blocks, as shown in Fig. 6.2B. This new renaming step would have been established previously with the addition algorithm. It is important that children understand how this additional ten is derived and why it is recorded in the tens' place in the algorithm (similarly with the 1 hundred). This reduces the likelihood of the common error of adding the tens first and then multiplying. Examples in which two or more tens result from the renaming process can be introduced as parallel, although more complex, cases.

Multiplication by two-digit multipliers (e.g., 32×24) entails the coordination of a number of steps, the major new step being the multiplication by tens. Although children's mental model of multidigit multiplication by single-digit multipliers (i.e., by ones) lays the foundation for these more complex examples, children will also need a model for multiplying by tens. This can be achieved through exploring the patterns, "tens by ones give tens" and "tens by tens give hundreds" prior to tackling the two-digit by two-digit algorithm (Booker et al., 1992). An understanding of these patterns is particularly important in the multiplication of both whole numbers and decimal fractions and also fosters estimation skills. While base-ten blocks are impractical to model the algorithm, they can be used to demonstrate these patterns, as shown in Fig. 6.3. The calculator can also be used to explore these patterns. Children will need guidance in understanding that hundreds results from the multiplication of tens, because this conflicts with their previous experiences where tens have been added to, or subtracted from, tens to produce tens.

Because the two-digit by two-digit algorithm cannot be modeled effectively with base-ten blocks, the accompanying explanation for each step becomes crucial in establishing meaning for the algorithm. This explanation will need to highlight: (a) the place values of the numbers being multiplied, (b) the number patterns for multiplying by tens and ones, (c) where the product of each multiplication is recorded and why, (d) whether renaming is necessary, and (e) whether the final product is reasonable.

3 tens

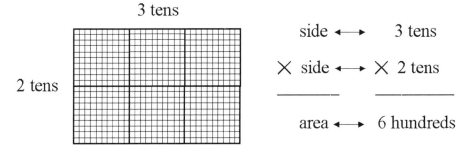

2 tens

side ←——→   3 tens

× side ←——→ × 2 tens

————————   ————————

area ←——→   6 hundreds

FIG. 6.3.   Using an area model to illustrate the pattern, tens × tens → hundreds.

Developing Mental Models of Multidigit Division.   In many ways, the division algorithm is less complex for children than the multiplication algorithm. We recommend a partitive approach using sharing with the base-ten blocks because this can be readily mapped onto children's existing knowledge of the division process. Prior to addressing our suggested approach, we review briefly an alternative method adopted by Lampert (1992).

Lampert designed a series of lessons that emphasized a "mapping rule" to relate the divisor and quotient of the algorithm, thus giving students a tool for thinking about division as a proportional relationship. Children had numerous preliminary experiences in which they divided given amounts into different groups and recorded in tabular form, the original amount, the size of the groups, the number of groups, and the quantity left over. This enabled children to observe patterns and relationships between the divisor and quotient. The chart recording this information served as a bridge between the students' informal discussions about division and the proportional nature of multiplicative structures. Children's progression to more complex examples included preliminary "sharing out" activities involving the distribution of play money, however the main focus was on making connections between reasoning about relationships and the conventional procedures of the long division algorithm.

The alternative approach we recommend involves modeling the division procedure using a partitive method with the base-ten blocks. We consider this approach to be less abstract than the one adopted by Lampert and hence more suitable for establishing an initial mental model of the algorithm. By adopting a partitive interpretation, we can build on children's earlier experiences with the division process and help them map the new algorithmic procedures onto their existing models. Furthermore, this sharing approach enables each step of the algorithm to be justified on meaningful and practical grounds. The use of a quotitive interpretation is impractical here. Modeling 522 ÷ 3, for example, would involve finding the number of groups of three that could be formed from 522. The use of quotitive-related terminology, such as, "goes into," is also inappropriate, abstract, and meaningless because it does not map onto a quotitive modeling action (i.e., groups of three would be taken out of 522, not put into).

Prior to meeting the formal algorithm, children need to have had experiences in exploring multidigit division using their own methods of manipulating materials and recording their procedures. With these experiences behind them, children are in a better position to appreciate why we decompose the dividend and operate on each of the elements separately and why we commence with the digit/s in the highest place. This latter feature is in contrast to the other algorithms where we begin operating on the digits of least value. Children also need to apply their existing understandings to the working of the division algorithm. These include place value and renaming, basic concepts of division (partition), multiplication (equal groups), subtraction (take-away) and the basic facts associated with these operations, as well as two-digit subtraction and estimation. It is easy to see why the algorithm can be difficult for children if these prerequisite understandings have not been established.

Chidren's introduction to the formal written algorithm should be within a context that enables them to manipulate the base-ten materials in a meaningful manner. Each step of the written algorithm needs to be linked with the actions on the materials. We illustrate this with a suggested questioning sequence for modeling the initial steps of an algorithm with a three-digit dividend. We take the following example:

Sam, Penny, and Annette had a paper delivery during their holidays and earned $522. They wish to share their earnings equally. How much will each person receive?

Suggested questioning sequence:
What is the problem asking us to find? How much money did the children earn?
How can we show this with our blocks? How many are sharing this amount?
What should we share first: the hundreds, tens, or ones? Why?
When you share out the hundreds, how much does each person receive? (See Fig. 6.4.)
Because each person received 1 hundred we can record this 1 hundred in the hundreds place of our answer. How many hundreds did we share out altogether?
Because each person received 1 hundred and there are 3 people, we shared out 3 hundreds. We can show this in our recording. We can also show the number of hundreds left over (See Fig. 6.5.)
Can we share these 2 hundreds as they are? What must we do to allow us to share these?

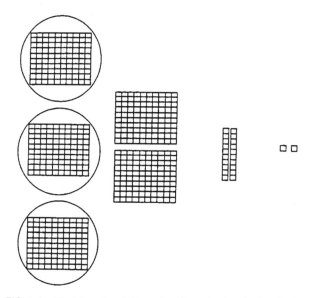

FIG. 6.4.   Modeling the division algorithm: sharing the hundreds.

If we rename the 2 hundreds as 20 tens, how many tens altogether do
   we have to share? Where should we record these? (See Fig. 6.6.)
Now share these 22 tens. What is the greatest number of tens you
   can give each person? How do you know this? We can record
   these 7 tens in the tens place of our answer.
How many tens altogether were shared out? How can you figure this
   out without counting? Record the number of tens we shared out.
   How many tens do we have left to share? Where will we record
   this? What must we do with this 1 ten so it can be shared among
   the 3 children? (Fig. 6.6).

The previous questioning would continue in the same manner for the
sharing of the ones (Fig. 6.7). It is designed to help children attach meaning
to each cycle of procedures involved in working the algorithm. By guiding

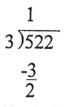

FIG. 6.5.   Modeling the division algorithm: recording the hundreds.

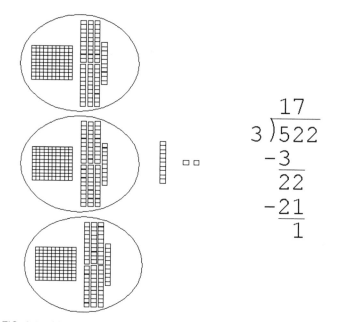

FIG. 6.6.   Modeling the division algorithm: sharing and recording the tens.

children's manipulation of the blocks and linking this with each step in the recording process, we can avoid a reliance on mechanical rules such as, "divide, multiply, subtract, bring down." Notice that each cycle of procedures focuses on the amount to be shared, the number sharing, the size of each share, and the amount remaining for further sharing.

A sound understanding of these procedures will enable children to handle "special" cases such as those with remainders, or zeros in the dividend and quotient. It also provides the base for more complex examples involving larger dividends and two-digit and decimal fraction divisors. With remainders, for example, children can extend the sharing process to rename the remaining ones as tenths and then repeat the sharing cycle. Cases involving zeros in the dividend or quotient should not present major problems if children understand the procedures they are applying. For example, when dividing 4,025 by 5, the 4 thousands cannot be shared in the form of thousands and hence must be renamed as 40 hundreds. After dividing the 40 hundreds, the resultant 8 hundreds is recorded in the hundreds' place of the quotient. Children are likely to record the 8 hundreds in the thousands' place of the quotient if they lack an understanding of these procedures.

Although the written algorithm for division by two-digit divisors is disappearing from many elementary school curricula, it is worth reviewing briefly at this point. Although calculators are frequently used for these examples,

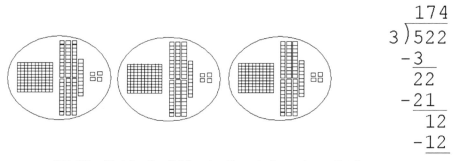

$$\begin{array}{r} 174 \\ 3\overline{)522} \\ -3 \\ \hline 22 \\ -21 \\ \hline 12 \\ -12 \end{array}$$

FIG. 6.7.   Modeling the division algorithm: sharing and recording the ones.

children still need to appreciate the processes involved and also need to interpret the quotient and check its reasonableness. The model for division by single-digit divisors provides the base for examples with two-digit divisors, that is, the same cycle of procedures is followed as each place is divided (shared) in turn. However, these examples call upon children's estimation skills because the basic multiplication and division facts do not help in determining the size of each share. By rounding the divisor to the nearest ten (or hundred) children can make an estimate of the size of the share and then check their estimate by multiplying by the divisor. In making this estimate, children may or may not use the proportional reasoning described by Lampert (1992). For example, in completing 562 ÷ 23, an estimate can be made by thinking either, "56 divided by 20" or "5 divided by 2." In the case of the former, children need to draw upon their skills in multiplying by multiples of ten to find the missing factor. The latter case requires proportional reasoning, that is, 50 is in the same relationship to 20 as 5 is to 2. Because estimating a quotient is a complex process for the child, it is advisable to sequence examples where the divisor is close to a multiple of ten (e.g., 29 or 11). This facilitates a better estimate and reduces the need for subsequent adjustments.

Developing Computational Models for the Multiplication and Division of Fractions

The special difficulties children experience with the multiplication and division of fractions have been well documented (e.g., Hiebert, 1992). Children who believe that "multiplication makes bigger," "division makes smaller," and that "the divisor must be smaller than the dividend," will have difficulty in interpreting decimal fraction situations (Bell, Swan, & Taylor, 1981; Graeber & Tirosh, 1988, 1990). It is imperative that students develop the appropriate mental models of the whole-number algorithms so that they have a strong base for the introduction of decimal fraction cases, especially when these examples are difficult to model with concrete materials. We now review a couple of approaches to establishing these additional understandings.

The new concepts to be established with decimal-fraction multiplication involve patterns similar to those for the whole number algorithms. These include multiplication of tenths and hundredths by tens, ones, and tenths. These patterns build on children's understanding of the place value of decimal fractions. Multiplication examples involving tenths by tenths (e.g., 2.4×3.2) entail the new understanding that tenths by tenths produce hundredths (rather than tenths as in addition and subtraction). Children frequently complete such examples by applying the rule, "Count the number of decimal places and insert the decimal point." However they can see why this is the case by using a calculator to explore a series of multiplications involving the "tenths by tenths" pattern. Shading squares on a 10×10 area model of one unit can also demonstrate this. It is important though, that children relate this pattern to the working of the algorithm otherwise the two activities become separate entities.

The division of decimal fractions by a whole number can be readily mapped onto the division of whole numbers. We mentioned earlier how a remainder can be expressed in tenths (and hundredths) by renaming the left-over ones as tenths and repeating the sharing cycle. If the dividend already contains a decimal fraction, then the renamed amount is simply added to the existing tenths (or hundredths) and the sharing process continued in the same manner. When the divisor contains a decimal fraction, however, the divisor must be adjusted to a whole number before the division process can commence. Proportional reasoning comes into play here. In the example, $1.5\overline{)286}$ we can adjust the divisor to 15 and the dividend to 2,860 because of the fact that 2,860 is in the same relationship to 15 as 286 is to 1.5. We can also justify this in terms of our sharing notion. That is, because the divisor must be a whole number to permit sharing, we must increase it by a power of ten. To ensure each receives the same share, the amount being shared must also be increased by that power of ten (Booker et al., 1992). Students are often unaware of this justification, relying instead on the rote procedure of "moving the decimal point" (Graeber & Tirosh, 1988).

Multiplication and division of common fractions are also less frequently used in everyday life and do not receive as much attention in elementary school curricula as they once did. They are complex operations for children because they do not map readily onto whole-number models and they are frequently difficult to represent with concrete and pictorial analogs (Taber, 1993a). However Taber (1993b) found that many children have intuitive ideas about how to solve word problems with a fraction factor and recommended that instruction begin by sharing and discussing students' strategies for solving various kinds of multiplication problems.

Of the various types, multiplication and division of a common fraction by a whole number are probably the most common in real life and the easiest to represent with concrete analogs. For example, if a recipe for four people requires $\frac{3}{4}$ of a cup of milk, then eight people would need double this amount, that is, $\frac{3}{4} \times 2$. This can be represented with cut-outs of two rectangular areas, partitioned into quarters. A fraction of a given quantity such as, $8 \times \frac{3}{4}$, can be modeled by partitioning a set of eight counters into fourths (two counters per group) and then taking three of those groups (six counters).

The way in which these examples are used in a problem situation, however, can affect the types of strategies children use to represent and solve the problem. As Taber (1993b) pointed out, an expression such as, $12 \times \frac{1}{4}$ (interpreted as "12 times $\frac{1}{4}$") can represent several different actions. For example, it can represent the action of combining 12 equal parts or the action of finding an amount that is 12 times as much as a quarter of a cup of rice. The expression, $\frac{1}{4}$, can be interpreted as the action of partitioning a starting amount of 12 items into fourths and retaining $\frac{1}{4}$ of the original amount, or finding a quantity that is $\frac{1}{4}$ as large as 12 units of a second quantity. Taber (1993b) found that children perform better on problems with fraction multipliers. However, it was noted that children were more likely to use division strategies on problems with fraction multipliers and favored multiplication strategies on problems with whole number multipliers. Children also paid attention to the action performed by the multiplier when deciding which operation to use. For example, if the word "times" was present, they tended to use multiplication, whereas division was frequently applied to problems involving the partioning of whole quantities. Taber's findings suggest that children may see multiplication by whole numbers and multiplication by fractions as very different kinds of situations.

Another approach to modeling these common fraction multiplications is one based on the operator construct that we mentioned in chapter 4. Here, the fraction is viewed as an operator acting on a natural number (G. Davis, 1991; G. Davis, Hunting, & Pearn, 1993; T. E. Kieren, 1980). Davis et al. (1993, p. 66) conceive of these examples in terms of an [m for n] operator acting on collections of discrete items that contain a multiple of n items to produce a new collection of items in which there are m items for every n items that exist in the original collection. For example, a [3 for 4] operator would act on a collection of eight items to produce ("clone") six new items. Davis et al. used a computer environment ("Copycat") to model this operator notion. Their program can be used to determine what fraction is responsible for observed numerical inputs and corresponding outputs, or to determine the numerical value of inputs or outputs for given fractions (Hunting, 1993). Hunting, Davis, and Bigelow (1991) claimed that simple versions of their tool are accessible to young children who have had no formal instruction on fractions. However, it is questionable whether these children develop a meaningful model of the operator construct or whether they simply manipulate inputs and outputs in a highly proceduralized manner.

More complex problem situations involving multiplication of a fraction by a fraction (e.g., $\frac{3}{4} \times \frac{2}{3}$) can be represented by an area model, similar to that used to illustrate tenths by tenths in decimal fraction multiplication. The example, $\frac{3}{4} \times \frac{2}{3}$, can be represented by a 4 × 3 rectangular array as shown in Fig. 6.8. By presenting children with this model already constructed, they are free to focus on the multiplicative situation being represented. Although there is merit in children constructing such models themselves, they do have difficulty in representing the starting quantity in a way that facilitates the second partitioning (Taber, 1993b). There is also the danger of the construction process becoming an end in itself.

Children will require guidance in interpreting this model. They can use their part/whole fraction understanding to identify the fraction of rows that have some shading and then the fraction of columns that are shaded. Describing the shaded rectangular region as "3 quarters by 2 thirds" reinforces the multiplicative nature of the problem being modeled. Children can then determine the product of this multiplication by identifying the fractional amount represented by the shaded region, namely, 6 shaded squares out of 12 squares altogether, giving the fraction $\frac{6}{12}$.

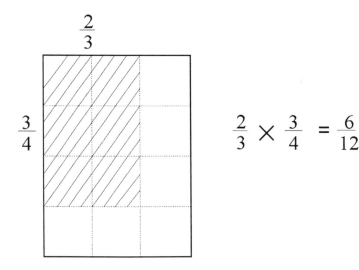

FIG. 6.8.   Use of an area/array model to represent common fraction multiplication.

Once children have formed the desired mental models of these fraction examples, they will require guidance in mapping these models onto the formal algorithmic procedures. The product of the numerators in the foregoing example (3×2) can be related to the number of shaded squares and the product of the denominators (4×3) to the total number of squares, with the final product ($\frac{6}{12}$) representing 6 shaded squares out of a total of 12 squares. Mastery of this algorithm can serve as a base for more complex examples involving multiplication of mixed numbers (e.g., $2\frac{1}{4} \times 3\frac{2}{3}$). A common error here is simply multiplying the whole numbers and then the fractions (e.g., 2×3 and $\frac{1}{4} \times \frac{2}{3}$). Because these examples are difficult to represent, we need to develop children's knowledge of improper fractions and lead them to see why we must convert the existing fractions to a form that can be readily solved with the formal algorithm. Children can then compare the response produced by the erroneous procedure with that of the correct approach. Analogy can also be drawn with whole number multiplication, for example, 24×32 is not solved by performing the operation, $(20 \times 30) + (4 \times 2)$.

Division with fractions is also difficult to model and has few real world instances. For these examples, we can apply a mathematical justification that relies on the inverse relationship between multiplication and division. Because this represents quite a complex mathematical abstraction for the child, division involving fractions is receiving less attention in elementary school curricula. Less complex examples however, where a fraction is divided by a whole number (e.g., $\frac{1}{4}$ of a cake divided between 2) can be modeled easily using a region or area model and the sharing notion of division. More difficult cases involving division by a fraction (e.g., $\frac{2}{3}$ divided by $\frac{1}{4}$) require students to apply an understanding of reciprocals. Knowing that a whole number, such as 5, can be interpreted as a fraction, $\frac{5}{1}$ (5 whole units), can help students understand that its inverse or reciprocal is $\frac{1}{5}$. Likewise, they can explore the reciprocals of fractions such as $\frac{2}{3}$, $\frac{3}{5}$, and so on, and can be encouraged to discover that the product of a number and its reciprocal is always one (e.g., $\frac{2}{3} \times \frac{2}{3} = 1$).

Once this understanding has been established, children can assign meaning to the rule, "To divide by a fraction, multiply by its reciprocal." This may be achieved by having students compare a series of paired worked examples involving division by whole numbers, then fractions, and the corresponding cases involving multiplication by the reciprocal. For example, they can compare the quotient of 9 divided by 3 with the product of 9 multiplied by $\frac{1}{3}$. This can be followed by examples involving fraction dividends and whole-number divisors, such as $\frac{3}{5}$ divided by 2 (paired with $\frac{3}{5}$ multiplied by $\frac{1}{2}$). Finally, examples comprising fraction dividends and divisors can be studied (e.g., $\frac{2}{3}$ divided by $\frac{3}{5}$ and $\frac{2}{3}$ multiplied by $\frac{5}{3}$). Given that the subjects in Taber's (1993a, 1993b) study frequently used division to solve multiplicative fraction problems, it would appear that children possess an implicit understanding of the relationship between the two problem forms. We can capitalize on this knowledge by comparing the physical modeling of examples involving whole-number divisors and the corresponding examples involving multiplication by the reciprocal.

The limitations of space prevent us from addressing the range of misconceptions children display in multiplication and division computations. However, we have addressed several of these in the course of our present discussion and have suggested instructional approaches to prevent these from developing.

SUMMARY

The key points addressed in this chapter may be summarized as follows:

1. The multiplication and division situations children meet in their computational experiences can be analyzed from three main perspectives, namely, a consideration of the semantic factors in a problem, an analysis of implicit psychological models, and a dimensional analysis. With respect to the semantic factors, differences in the nature of the quantities in a problem give rise to four main types of multiplicative situations. These are equivalent set examples, scalar problems, cross products, and rectangular area. The nature of the quantity that serves as the unknown is the semantic component that distinguishes between two types of division situations, namely, partitive division (number in each set unknown) and measurement or quotitive division (number of sets unknown).

With respect to the dimensional analyses, Vergnaud (1983) identified three main classes of multiplicative structures, namely, isomorphism of measures, product of measures, and multiple proportions. Schwartz (1988) highlighted the importance of intensive quantities.

2. Children's ability to solve multiplication and division word problems depends largely on their formation of a comprehensive problem-situation model. This is essential for the formation of a correct mathematical model.

3. The use of derived fact strategies can assist children in mastery of the basic multiplication and division facts.

4. Prior to being introduced to the formal multiplication and division algorithms, it is beneficial for children to develop efficient mental computational strategies. The understandings children apply in mental computation can assist them in the learning of the algorithms.

5. Approaches to developing the multiplication algorithm include establishing an understanding of the underlying principles within the context of algorithmic instruction (Lampert, 1986, 1992). Another approach involves

modeling simple multidigit examples with the base-ten blocks, establishing the basic multiplication patterns, and then using this understanding as a mental model for more complex examples.

6. One method of developing the division algorithm involves the use of a "mapping rule" to relate divisor and quotient. This gives students a tool for thinking about division as a proportional relationship. An alternative approach to teaching the algorithm involves modeling the procedure using a partitive method with the base-ten blocks. This approach builds on children's earlier experiences with the division process and helps them map the new algorithmic procedures onto their existing models.

7. The number patterns involved in the multiplication of tenths, hundredths, and thousandths build on children's understanding of the place value of decimal fractions. The division of decimal fractions by a whole number divisor can be readily mapped onto the division of whole numbers. When the divisor contains a decimal fraction, however, the divisor must be adjusted to a whole number before the division process can commence. Proportional reasoning comes into play here.

8. The multiplication and division of common fractions are complex operations for children because they are difficult to map onto whole-number models and they are frequently difficult to represent with concrete and pictorial analogs. However multiplication and division of a common fraction by a whole number can be modeled using real-world situations and an area or array model can be used to represent mutiplication of a fraction by a fraction. Division with fractions is difficult to model and requires a mathematical justification that relies on the inverse relationship between multiplication and division.

7

ADVANCED COMPUTATIONAL MODELS AND PROCESSES

This chapter addresses some of the advanced computational models students typically meet in their first few years of secondary school. We focus specifically on the topics of algebra and proportional reasoning, given that these domains comprise a significant component of the curriculum and present unique difficulties for students. We begin our discussion on algebra by analyzing the complexity of the domain and the sources of students' difficulties here. We then consider some ways in which we might promote students' algebraic understanding. We conclude the section on algebra by examining students' mental models of algebraic word problems.

ALGEBRA

The difficulties students experience with algebra have been highlighted in numerous research reports in the past decade (Booth, 1988, 1989a, 1989b; C. A. Brown et al., 1988; Davis, 1988, 1989a; Fey, 1989; Kieran, 1989, 1992; Kuchemann, 1981; Wagner & Kieran, 1989). The fact that a large proportion of students do not acquire the expected levels of proficiency, even after several years of study, is of grave concern to educators. We address some of the contributing factors during the course of our discussion. To appreciate why algebra is a difficult domain for students we first analyze some of its complexities.

The Complexity of Algebra

Students usually begin their study of algebra at around 12 to 13 years of age, depending of course on the country and the school curriculum. In most places, the content of the algebra curriculum has changed little over the years, with students' initial experiences usually including variables, algebraic expressions, equations, and the solving of equations. These experiences represent a whole new domain of learning for students.

The most obvious new feature is the syntax of algebra. This includes the use of letters, a different notation and convention, a focus on the manipulation of terms, and the simplification of expressions (Booth, 1989a). Although these syntactic components are necessary, they are insufficient. What is also needed and is frequently not acquired by students is the semantic component. An understanding of just what algebraic statements represent, and of why we can make certain transformations on these statements, is essential. If students comprehend the structural properties of mathematical operations and relations, they can distinguish between transformations that are permitted and those that are not (Booth, 1989a). When students lack this semantic understanding, they simply manipulate symbols with little sense of purpose or meaning.

An essential component of this structural development is acquiring a mental model of a variable, that is, an understanding of how the values of an unknown change (Kuchemann, 1981). These provide the algebraic tool for expressing generalizations. However the concept of a *variable* is more sophisticated than we often recognize and frequently blocks students' success in algebra (Leitzel, 1989). A mental model of a variable is a much more complex representation than that of a constant and initially imposes higher processing loads on the child.

A *constant* can be defined in numerous ways, as we discussed in chapter 3. Variables however, cannot be defined with respect to cardinal or ordinal reference because they have no fixed values. They can however, be defined by number system reference; for example, we can describe variable a as the sum of variables b and c ($a = b + c$). This type of definition entails understanding of the number system. Variables can also be defined by expression reference, that is, a variable is commonly defined by its relation to other terms in the expression, for example, velocity equals distance divided by time ($v = \frac{s}{t}$). Again however, ability to process the expressions is essential to understanding. We will return to these issues in subsequent discussion.

An inadequate model of a variable is one of the major sources of students' difficulties with algebra. A failure to recognize and use algebraic structure (which reflects a lack of understanding of our number system) and difficulty in handling the inconsistencies between arithmetical and algebraic conventions also contribute to students' problems in this domain (Booth, 1989a, C. Kieran, 1989). We address these difficulties in subsequent sections.

We begin with a consideration of the inconsistencies between arithmetic and algebra and the misconceptions that can arise if these are not addressed in the curriculum. Given that arithmetic can serve as an effective analog for algebra, it is particularly important that students are made aware of these differences.

Inconsistencies Between Arithmetic and Algebra

Algebra is often viewed as "generalized arithmetic" where general statements are written to represent given mathematical rules and operations (Booth, 1984). However, although arithmetic and algebra employ common symbols and signs, they interpret them differently. For example, the equal sign in arithmetic is used predominantly to connect a problem with its numerical result, although it is also used to link two processes that yield the same result or a sequence of intermediate steps leading to a final result [e.g., $3(6 + 4) = 3 \times 10 = 30$]. These statements are tautologies or universally true statements. However in algebra, the equal sign not only expresses tautologies, but also constraints (for example, $6x - 4 = 3x + 5$ is true only when $x = 3$; Matz, 1982).

In contrast to tautologies, constraint equations are not universally true statements, that is, the equal sign does not link equivalent expressions. Rather, the left-hand and right-hand side expressions are two distinct statements whose equality constrains the unknown. Incorporating these new interpretations into their arithmetic model of equality is a major shift for the child (Matz, 1982; Vergnaud, 1984). This is not easy for children because the focus of their arithmetic activities has been the finding of particular numerical answers. In algebra, however, the focus is on deriving procedures and relationships and expressing these in general, simplified form (Booth, 1988). However as Booth showed in her case studies of children's interpretation of algebraic situations, children do not realize this; they still assume that a numerical answer is required.

Another major difference between arithmetic and algebra is the use of letters. In arithmetic for example, the letters l and m can denote liters and meters respectively (i.e., 6m would mean 6 meters). In algebra however, the letters can take on an additional meaning, for example, m could indicate an unknown number of meters. Confusion over this change in usage can lead to the "lack-of-numerical referent" problem in students' interpretation of the meaning of the letters in algebra (Booth, 1988, p. 26). Here, children associate the letter with items whose name begins with that letter (e.g., $8y$ would be interpreted as 8 yams, 8 yachts etc.). This problem is exacerbated by both their arithmetic activities (e.g., "8m" is read as "8 meters") and their elementary algebraic encounters (e.g., the formula for the area of a rectangle is given as "$a = l \times w$"). Students' desire for a numerical referent is also apparent when they assign a numerical value to a letter according to its position in the alphabet, for example, a would be equal to 1, b equal to 2, and so on. This is particularly the case when students are just beginning their studies in algebra, where they show the natural tendency to interpret a new algebraic expression in terms of the only numerical frame of reference they have at the time, namely arithmetic (Chalouh & Herscovics, 1988).

A related problem here is the nature of concatenation in algebra which can present an obstacle in children's learning (Chalouh & Herscovics, 1988; Herscovics, 1989; Matz, 1979, 1982). That is, the juxtaposition of two symbols in algebra (e.g., $8y$) denotes multiplication, whereas in arithmetic, it indicates implicit addition (e.g., 94 means 90 + 4). Often both interpretations appear in the one expression, such as $52x$. Typical errors here include the response, "$4x = 46$ given that $x = 6$" (using a place-value interpretation of concatenation) and "$xy = -8$ given that $x = -3$ and $y = -5$" (implicit addition interpretation) (Matz, 1982, p.38).

The bidirectional nature of algebra, in contrast to the unidirectional nature of arithmetic, reflects a process/object difference between the two domains. Arithmetic is primarily procedural, where strings of numbers and operations are seen as processes for arriving at answers, rather than as mathematical objects in their own right. In algebra, however, written symbolic expressions are often considered as mathematical entities, not necessarily representing procedures for solving concrete problems; the procedure is actually part of the object (F. C. Kieran, 1990). As R. B. Davis (1975) commented, this makes it difficult for students to regard algebraic expressions as permissible answers. For example, in arithmetic addition, 4 + 2 is perceived as the question or problem, with 6 as the answer. However in algebraic addition, as in $x + 4$, the expression describes both the operation of adding 4 to x as well as the result that will be obtained when the operation is implemented. Hence for a student with an arithmetic frame of reference, accepting algebraic expressions as answers requires a major cognitive adjustment, that of overcoming what Davis termed the "name-process" dilemma, where the expression describes the process (adding 4 to x) and names the answer.

Collis (1974) referred to students' difficulty in holding unevaluated operations in suspension as their inability to accept the lack of closure. This difficulty was apparent in a recent study (English & Warren, in prep., 1995) in which beginning algebra students were given the problem, "*Bill has x lollies and Sue has y lollies. What can you write to show how many they have altogether?*" Although several students were content to leave their answer as, "$x + y$," many preferred to write, "$x + y =$ total," or, "$x + y = z$," or, "They have z lollies altogether."

The representation of word problems in algebra requires different reasoning processes to that of arithmetic. In arithmetic, children think of the operations they need to apply to solve the problem, whereas in algebra, they must represent the problem situation rather than the operations for solving the problem (Kieran, 1990). For example to solve a *"What is my number?"* type of problem, children have to reason in the opposite of the way they would when using arithmetic. In the example, *"When 3 is subtracted from 4 times a certain number, the result is 25; find the number,"* children would normally *add* 3 and *divide* by 4. The algebraic approach however, involves representing the problem situation with an expression such as, "$4x - 3 = 25$," which entails the operations of *subtraction* and *multiplication*. The procedures that students must implement to solve this equation also entail a new way of thinking, that is, they must apply a quantity-conserving procedure of adding 3 to each side of the equation. More complex problems, such as those with an unknown on each side of the equal sign (e.g., $ab + c = mb + d$), involve transformations that are very different from the students' previous experiences; in fact, as Kieran (1990) noted, they seem almost counterintuitive. That is, the student must operate with an unknown quantity (subtracting ab or mb from both sides). We return to these points in later discussion. We turn now to the second source of students' algebraic difficulties, namely, understanding the meaning of a variable.

Students' Mental Models of a Variable

When students are first introduced to literal symbols, they have trouble going beyond surface associations to the next level of representation (Wagner & Kieran, 1989). For example, they cannot progress beyond the superficial notion that the letter *a*, say, stands for apples to the deeper understanding that *a* is chosen mnemonically to stand for the *number* of apples. Students also have difficulty in apprehending the notion that a single symbol can represent many quantities at the same time. Because they initially work with unknowns and expressions, where only one value at a time can be substituted (e.g., $x + 3 = 5$ where x has a constant value), they have considerable difficulty in moving to relational variables. Another common misconception is that different letters must have different values (Wagner & Parker, 1993). Even students who state that any letter can be used as an unknown, may nevertheless believe that changing the letter representing the unknown can change the solution to an equation (Wagner, 1981).

In his large-scale study of students' interpretations of literal terms, Kuchemann (1981) identified six stages through which learners progress in acquiring a mental model of the variable. These are as follows:

1. *Letter evaluated*: At the outset of a problem a student assigns the letter a numerical value, without first operating on the unknown. For example, when presented with problem, $x + 3 = 11$, the child might recall any number or might recall the number fact, $8 + 3 = 11$.

2. *Letter not used*: The child ignores the letter or at best acknowledges it but does not give it any meaning. For example, if asked to find the value of $a + b + 2$ when $a + b = 27$, the student responds "29" without ever thinking about the a, the b, or $a + b$.

3. *Letter used as an object*: Here, the child regards the letter as a shorthand for an object or as an object in its own right (e.g., "$3a$" is interpreted as "3 apples.")

4. *Letter used as a specific unknown or constant*: Students perceive the letter as a specific but unknown number and can operate on it even though its value is not known. For example, Kuchemann (1981) asked children to find r when the following conditions were stated: $r = s + t$ and $r + s + t = 30$. A substantial number of children responded with r equals 10, evidently evaluating r directly from the second equation. Replacing $s + t$ by r in the second equation and then evaluating r from the expression, $r + r = 30$, is a more complex process for the child involving a system mapping. However the major difficulty here would seem to be that students just do not "see the right things in algebraic expressions" (Wenger, 1987). Here, students failed to realize that $s + t$ in the second equation should be replaced by r.

There are two probable causes of this failure. One is that the student is not aware of the goal hierachy inherent in the problem, and does not see that isolating r on the left side is a useful subgoal. Substituting r for $s + t$ represents a sub-goal embedded within the goal of achieving an expression that can be readily manipulated. The second problem is failure to see the correspondence between $r + s + t = 30$ and $r + r = 30$. In effect $s + t$ can be chunked and replaced by r, a move which is justified by the first equation. However skill in both chunking and in recognizing correspondences, based on a common relation (in this case the ternary relation of addition) between expressions, is necessary for this to be done.

5. Letter used as a generalized number: At this level the student perceives the letter as representing, or at least being able to adopt, several values rather than just one. For example, if children are asked to list all the values of x when $x + y = 12$, they will list more than one of the whole numbers that satisy the conditions rather than only one such number. However they tend not to realize that all numbers that satisfy the conditions are required. This is an example of Collis' (1978) notion of concrete generalization.

6. *Letter used as a variable*: In this final stage, the student sees the letter as representing a range of unspecified values and understands that a variable is defined by its relation to other terms in the expression.

It is often difficult to determine whether a child is operating at level 6, that is, whether the child has an understanding of how the values of an unknown change. This is because many problems can be solved by regarding the letters as specific unknowns or generalized numbers. Furthermore, we often switch from thinking in terms of a variable to thinking in terms of a less sophisticated interpretation as we solve a problem. We elaborate on this dilemma by reviewing some of the points Kuchemann (1981) raised concerning the following problem:

> Blue pencils cost 5 pence each and red pencils cost 6 pence each. I buy some blue pencils and some red pencils and altogether it costs me 90 pence.
>
> If b is the number of blue pencils bought and if r is the number of red pencils bought, what can you write down about b and r? (p. 107)

Although the statement about the number of blue and red pencils bought ($5b + 6r = 90$) can be derived by regarding the letters as specific unknowns or as generalized numbers, neither interpretation demonstrates the complete relationship that exists between b and r. We need to consider a more sophisticated interpretation. When the letters are interpreted as specific unknowns, the relationship becomes simply a statement that is true for a particular (unknown) pair of numbers. As such, this statement is static, because it involves no notion of change. When the letters are used as generalized numbers, the expression is seen as a statement that is satisfied by several pairs of numbers (e.g., [6,10], [12,5], [0,15], [18,0]) although the pairs are still basically unrelated. This interpretation acknowledges the fact that the values of b and r can change, but it does not include an awareness of how they change. This requires us to compare the values of the variables. An elementary comparison might be, "As b increases, r decreases." A more sophisticated comparison could involve a description of the degree to which b and r change, for example, "The increase in b is greater than the corresponding decrease in r." These relationships may be regarded as second-order relationships because their elements are themselves relationships (e.g., the difference in the elements of the relationship, "12 is greater than 6," is greater than the difference in the elements of the relationship, "5 is less than 10." Kuchemann considered these second-order relationships to provide a useful operational definition of variables, that is, "letters are used as variables when a second (or higher order) relationship is established between them" (1981, p. 111).

If we adopt such a definition it becomes difficult to determine whether students do, in fact, have this mental model of a variable. This necessitates designing problems where it can be assumed that such a model is required to solve them. Kuchemann (1981) used the problem, "Which is larger, $2n$ or $n + 2$?" to ascertain whether children would recognize that the relative size of the two expressions is dependent on the value of n (p. 111). Most students believed that $2n$ was the larger, giving the explanation that it involved multiplication. Few of these children quoted specific values of n and few used trial-and-error. It was hypothesized that the successful students were able to establish a second-order relationship between $2n$ and $n + 2$. That is, "as n increases, the difference between $2n$ and $n + 2$ increases," or, "the increase in $2n$ is greater than the increase in $n + 2$." For example, if we take the ordered pairs, $(6,5)$ and $(14,9)$, [corresponding to $(2n, n + 2)$], we can say that $(14 - 9 > 6 - 5)$ and $(14 - 6 > 9 - 5)$. The ability to consider the possible effects of n on the relative size of $2n$ and $n + 2$ is particularly important in solving this problem because it means the student can entertain the possibility that, for a smaller value of n, there may be no difference between $2n$ and $n + 2$ (when $n = 2$) or the difference may be reversed (when $n < 2$).

This requires a second-order relation, a difference between two differences. It also requires that the difference between $2n$ and $n + 2$ be expressed as a function of n. This is a complex set of relations, and will impose a high processing load, unless students acquire efficient chunking and serial processing strategies for handling the problem. Defining variables in terms of second-order relationships has not been emphasized in the literature, but we consider this perspective to be particularly important in establishing adequate mental models. It is all too easy to assume that students have a grasp of variables when they solve generalized arithmetic tasks. Frequently, these can be solved without an understanding of variables, that is, without considering the degree to which one set of values varies as a result of changes in another set. Students' failure to address these relationships is due largely to a lack of emphasis on the structural components in algebraic instruction.

Students' Structural Models

A knowledge of structure may be defined as "knowledge about the mathematical relationships among the elements of a mathematical expression" (Chaiklin & Lesgold, 1984). Such knowledge is crucial in performing mathematical operations on both arithmetic and algebraic expressions. Students' failure to recognize and use algebraic structure may be traced to a number of related sources. These include students' difficulty in perceiving algebra as generalized arithmetic, their lack of understanding of the semantics of algebra, their use of inappropriate arithmetic and algebraic analogies, and their lack of strategic knowledge. We address each of these in turn.

Difficulty in Perceiving Algebra as Generalized Arithmetic.   A study by Lee and Wheeler (1989) indicated that students do not seem to see algebra as generalized arithmetic. They behave as though algebra is a closed system "untroubled by arithmetic" (p. 46). Their findings suggest that students do not really believe that arithmetic can be generalized. For example, one student in Lee and Wheeler's study who was guided through a comprehensive algebraic demonstration and subsequently asked if the generalization was now true, responded, "Probably if you pick a number out of anywhere and they do work out well, there's a major chance that all the other numbers are going to work out as well" (p. 49). Even when students did believe that generalization was possible, they did not see algebra as a tool for establishing this. For example, one student commented, "You would never think or realize that you can have statements that are always true no matter what numbers you take" (p. 49).

Students who demonstrated the highest degree of algebra/arithmetic dissociation were those who were quite prepared to accept and even expected different answers in their algebraic and arithmetic solutions to a problem. These students felt no need to justify or correct these discrepancies when they were asked to use arithmetic to check their algebra. The responses of students in another study (English & Warren, in prep., 1995) also reflected this algebra/arithmetic dissociation. One student claimed that the expression, $a + b + c$, was equal to $a + f + c$ "only while you're learning algebra."

Lack of Semantic Understanding. There is substantial evidence that many students see the learning of algebra as a problem of learning to manipulate symbols in accordance with certain transformation rules (i.e. syntactically) without reference to the meaning of the expressions or transformations (i.e., the semantics; Booth, 1988, 1989a, 1989b; C. A. Brown et al., 1988; Kieran, 1989, 1992; Lesgold, Putnam, Resnick, & Sterrett, 1987; Resnick, 1986; Steinberg, Sleeman, & Ktorza, 1991; Wenger, 1987). Although Kirshner (1989a) claims that the human mind is "uniquely fashioned to learn syntax as syntax," it is nevertheless disturbing that so many students' display a poor understanding of the relations and mathematical structures that are fundamental to algebraic representation (p. 197). It is even more disturbing that these mathematical relations, which provide the justification for algebraic manipulations and simplifications, are implicitly assumed to be familiar to students from their studies in arithmetic and hence are given little attention in the curriculum. This is particularly evident in learning environments that promote meaningless manipulation of algebraic rules (Booth, 1989a; Coopersmith, 1984; R. B. Davis, 1989b; Wagner & Kieran, 1989).

In such environments, students often fail to realize that a transformed equation is equivalent to the original one. For example, some teachers direct students to begin solving an equation such as $2x + 3 = x + 8$ by thinking, "I'll move the 3 across the equal sign and change its sign." These teachers hope the student will then write, $2x = x + 8 - 3$ (R. B. Davis, 1989b, p. 270). Students thus fail to realize that 3 can be subtracted from both sides of the equation without changing its value. This is not unexpected because the procedure of transposing does not emphasize the symmetry of an equation.

Kieran (1988, 1989) documented similar findings, noting that, although transposing may be regarded as a shortened version of the procedure of forming the same operation on both sides of an equation, the two approaches are often perceived quite differently by beginning algebra students. It was found that many students who use a transposing procedure do not operate on the equation as a mathematical object but blindly apply the rule, "change side-change sign." Such blind rule following results in "sign errors" such as, "$x + 25 = 72 \rightarrow x + 25 - 25 = 72 + 25$." This may not only reflect a confusion with the transposition rule but may also reflect a belief system that attributes validity to some operations that are not mathematically valid, for example, "Whatever is taken away from one side should be added to the other" (a "fairness principle;" Kieran, 1984; Wagner & Parker, 1993).

A lack of semantic understanding is also evident in studies that have investigated students' knowledge of equivalent expressions (e.g., Cauzinille-Marmeche, Mathieu, & Resnick, 1984; Chaiklin & Lesgold, 1984). Several studies have found that students tend to compute the solutions to equivalent expressions, rather than apply their understanding of transformations. For example, Chaiklin and Lesgold (1984) found that sixth graders preferred to calculate in order to judge the equivalence of three-term arithmetic expressions with subtraction and addition operations (e.g., $685 - 492 + 947$; $947 + 492 - 685$; $947 - 685 + 492$; $947 - 492 + 685$). They displayed several different methods for judging the equivalence of these expressions and sometimes used a different method with the same expression, depending on the expression against which it was compared.

In another study, Kieran (1982, 1984) found that beginning algebra students had difficulty judging equivalent expressions involving the addition/subtraction relation. For example, they considered a case such as $x + 25 = 150$ to have the same solution as $x = 25 + 150$, suggesting that they were unsure of the structural relationships between addition and subtraction, at least when literal terms were involved.

Steinberg et al. (1991) found that, whereas eighth and ninth graders knew how to use transformations to solve simple equations, many did not use this knowledge to judge equivalence. Almost a third of the students computed the solutions, suggesting that they were not sure that a simple transformation produces an equation with the same solution or were unable to recognize when an equation has been transformed in a way that does not change the answer. For example, they used computation to solve simple pairs such as, "$x + 2 = 5$ and $x + 2 - 2 = 5 - 2$," in which the second equation is normally generated in solving the first equation. On the other hand, the students might have interpreted the task as one of proving that the two equations were equivalent, not realizing that informal methods, such as stating that a transformation was applied, were sufficient for this purpose.

A heavy dependence on calculation rules, with little principled reasoning, was also observed in a study investigating beginning algebra students' understanding of algebraic expressions and the effects of parentheses on the value of these expressions (Resnick, 1987b). Students were asked three types of questions (including justification for their responses), namely, whether two expressions are equivalent or not, whether parentheses can be placed in an expression without changing its value, and whether parentheses can be removed from an expression without changing its value. It was found that most subjects had a strong preference for reasoning in terms of rules of calculation rather than number principles or symbol manipulation rules. Although the students' calculation rules were mostly correct, they were rarely able to justify the parentheses-first calculation rule. When subjects did not calculate, they usually based their judgments of equivalence on rules for transforming expressions, however did not make reference to any principles of number. The rules were often incorrect, with most of them being systematic deviations of the formally taught algebraic rules.

Resnick (1987b) interprets these incorrect rules (algebra "malrules") as resulting from incomplete knowledge of the "permissions" and "constraints" that underlie particular formal procedures (p. 41). She contended that a rule or procedure is understood when one knows all the constraints and permissions that govern it; hence, inferences can be made about children's understanding when they construct variants of a standard procedure. If a constraint is violated, it may be inferred that the child does not know the principle justifying the constraint, or has not realized that it is appropriate to the procedure being used, or has sacrificed it to meet other constraints. According to Resnick, students ignore implicit constraints in the rules taught in school as they attempt to derive a rule that will allow them to solve a type of problem that they have not encountered before.

Inappropriate Use of Arithmetic and Algebraic Analogies. Resnick's (1987b) argument is comparable to Matz's (1982) prototype formation and extrapolation where people generate malrules by constructing prototype rules from which they extrapolate new rules. These new rules match the prototype and provide apparent justification. Matz sees this problem-solving behavior as comprising two components. The first component is a collection of "base rules" that the student has extracted from a prototype or obtained directly from a textbook. These are mainly basic rules, such as the distributive law, that form the basis of conventional algebra. The second component, the extrapolation techniques, specify ways to bridge the gap between known rules and new problems. These techniques project what the student knows either by viewing an unfamiliar problem as a familiar case (i.e., inappropriately mapping a new situation onto an existing model), or by revising a known rule so that it is applicable in an unfamiliar situation (i.e., mapping a new situation onto an inappropriately modified mental model of a known procedure).

An example of the latter case, where a prototype has been created by generalizing over the operator signs in the distributive law, is given in Fig. 7.1A. The prototype specifies that any operator can be distributed over any other operator, not that multiplication can be distributed over addition. This prototype may be regarded as the mental model the student develops from the correct rule by attending to the *pattern* of transformation of letters and operation signs. Because the focus is on the pattern of change, the constraints of the operation symbols are ignored. That is, the student perceives that a operates on b and then on c, irrespective of the type of operation. The terms of the new expression, namely a [] b and a [] c, are connected in the same way as the original terms, b and c. The student can then use this mental model as a base for any example whose surface structure corresponds with the pattern. The absence of semantic structure in this model means that malrules are easily created, as indicated in Fig. 7.1B. The fact that malrules

A. Prototype

$$a \,\square\, (b \,\triangle\, c) \;=\; (a \,\square\, b) \,\triangle\, (a \,\square\, c)$$

B. Malrules generated from prototype

$$a + (b \times c) \;=\; (a + b) \times (a + c)$$

$$\sqrt{b + c} \;=\; \sqrt{b} + \sqrt{c}$$

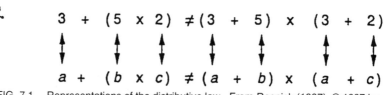

FIG. 7.1. Representations of the distributive law. From Resnick (1987). © 1987 by Lawrence Erlbaum Associates. Adapted with permission.

are not justified could be recognized by comparing them with appropriate arithmetic examples, as the structure mapping shows in Fig. 7.1C.

Several other studies have highlighted students' errors of overgeneralization as they attempt to simplify expressions (e.g., Carry, Lewis, & Bernard, 1980; Wagner & Parker, 1993). We contend that these overgeneralizations are due to students' use of inappropriate arithmetic and algebraic analogies. We agree with Wagner and Parker that the abstract nature of the field properties, especially the distributive laws, can present problems; however, when students form inappropriate analogies they often have no need to consider these properties. This is because the analogies they use either do not utilize these properties or the procedure contained in the analogy already meets the constraints of these properties. As we noted earlier, a common error in simplifying expressions is to reduce the expression to a single number, as one would in arithmetic. For example, $3 + 4x$ would be simplified to $7x$, suggesting that the example has been mapped onto the arithmetic base, $3 + 4$, and the associated arithmetic procedure applied. Students seem reluctant to have an algebraic expression with a visible operation sign as the answer and so they perform whatever operations they can on the remaining numbers to produce a single answer (Collis, 1975). On the other hand arithmetic analogs that make the logic of the problem clear are possible, as indicated in chapter 3.

The application of an inappropriate algebraic analogy is also evident in students' attempts to "cancel" a common term from the numerator and denominator of an algebraic expression, for example, $2 + \frac{x}{2}$ becomes x. Such a response may indicate a lack of understanding of the distributive law (Wagner & Partker, 1993) and a failure to understand relationships between operations. However, it is also likely that the student has encoded the source $(2 + \frac{x}{2})$ in terms of the wrong relations and considered it to be analogous with a known example, $\frac{2x}{2}$. The familiar procedure of dividing the numerator and denominator by a common factor would then be applied. In this case, the student would be unlikely to consider the distributive law because it would not be applicable to the analogous example. A similar situation exists when students convert the expression $(a + b)^2$ to $a^2 + b^2$, suggesting that they have incorrectly mapped this example onto $(ab)^2$ and applied the solution procedure, $(ab)^2 = a^2b^2$.

Other cases where students inappropriately modify their mental model of a known procedure and use it as a base for a new situation include that of "generalizing over numbers." Here students formulate a mental model from a sample problem based on the assumption that "particular numbers in sample problems are incidental rather than essential" (Matz, 1982, p. 33). For example, if students have a mental model of the procedure, $(x-3)(x-4) = 0 \rightarrow (x-3) = 0$ or $(x-4) = 0 \rightarrow x = 3$ or $x = 4$, and fail to realize that the zero is critical to the procedure itself, they will likely use this model as a base for any example conforming to this structure. The result is that they develop a generalized mental model of the form, $(x - a)(x - b) = k \rightarrow (x - a) = k$ or $(x - b) = k \rightarrow x = $ Solve $[(x - a) = k]$ or $x = $ Solve $[(x - b) = k]$ (Matz, 1982, p. 34). Matz makes the important point that skilful problem solvers attempt to rewrite a new problem so that it will match a relevant rule, whereas naive students tend to revise or extend a relevant rule.

Lack of Strategic Knowledge. The final source of difficulty we will consider in this section is students' lack of strategic knowledge in solving algebraic tasks. Students' planning processes are often defective and they frequently fail to assess their progress towards a problem goal and recognize when it has been attained. They will often perform a series of legal transformations in solving an algebraic equation but will end up with equations that are harder to solve. They often "go around in circles" and choose their next move randomly without having a specific goal in mind (Wenger, 1987); alternatively, they can fail to assess whether a rule gets them closer towards the goal and take steps that might be applicable but not productive (Matz, 1982). These situations are reflected in cases where students multiply through by a common denominator and then cancel, leaving themselves back at the original point.

Wenger (1987) maintained that students seldom look for and recognize linear patterns in algebraic expressions; this is partly due to their textbook activities where students are frequently not encouraged to focus on structure in expressions or practice using it for planning strategies. Skilled students, however, often make explicit note of such patterns as they plan a strategy of attack. Less skilled students seem reluctant to apply metacognitive strategies such as taking time initially to locate the goal variable, examine the structure of the algebraic expressions, and attempt to classify the structure as a function of the goal variable. It seems that these students do not consciously reject planning; they just do not believe it is part of "doing mathematics." Planning requires that relations within the problem be represented, and so inadequate planning may also reflect the lack of ability to represent relations between terms in an expression, and between different expressions. We revisit the issue of developing students' strategic knowledge in the next section.

Promoting Algebraic Understanding

Several instructional studies cited by Kieran (1992) indicate that students can develop structural understandings if given experiences that create a solid foundation for these concepts. These experiences include examining the field properties in both algebraic and arithmetic contexts, introducing equations containing algebraic expressions on both sides, recording numerical generalizations using clear notation, and manipulating the parameters of functional equations using computer graphing software. In this section we address some additional aspects that warrant attention in the curriculum.

From our previous discussions, we contend that algebraic instruction must address the development of appropriate analogies between arithmetic and algebraic models as well as between related algebraic models. Because a known relationship serves as the mental model for new understanding, it is imperative that students recognize the structural correspondence between algebraic expressions (Halford, 1993; see also chapter 3, this volume). This requires the source relationship to be well known and understood, which means that the relations within the source can be represented. When this is not the case, we see the creation of inappropriate analogies and various types of malrules. Students require explicit instruction in identifying structural similarities and in forming the correct analogies. They also need to be made aware of the goal hierarchies in algebraic tasks and given assistance in developing strategies for working through these. We elaborate on these points in the remainder of this section.

Students' ability to work meaningfully in an algebraic context and develop a facility with the notational conventions demands first, a semantic understanding of arithmetic (Booth, 1989a; Chaiklin & Lesgold, 1984). Students must acquire a comprehensive mental model of the arithmetical operations, including a knowledge of the "permissions" and "constraints" that underlie the formal procedures (Resnick, 1987b). They also need to know and understand the relationships between these operations. An understanding of the field properties such as commutativity, associativity, and distributivity is essential to students' proficiency with algebra. It is not sufficient that students simply manipulate the rules that instantiate these properties, they need to recognize when and why a particular rule can be applied.

If students are to apply these arithmetical understandings in establishing analogies between algebra and arithmetic, they require appropriate prealgebraic experiences (Kieran & Chalouh, 1993; National Council of Teachers of Mathematics, 1989). This is the area of mathematical learning in which students construct their algebra from their arithmetic, that is, they develop meaning for the symbols and operations of algebra in terms of their knowledge of arithmetic. Initial activities can involve children in generalizing number patterns that model and describe observed physical patterns, regularities, and problems. However, our research has shown that perceiving such patterns does not automatically lead to pattern perception in algebra and to generalizing from them (English & Warren, in press). We need to teach these patterning and generalization skills within the algebraic context.

When students are subsequently introduced to literal symbols, they can appreciate the role of these letters and become familiar with their two main uses, namely, as standing for a specific unknown, as in $x + 5 = 8$, and as a representative of a range of values, as in $4x + 8$. These prealgebraic experiences should also focus on the method or process being used instead of the answer. At the same time, students need to be aware of the nature of the operations being represented. Making the shift from thinking about the undoing or solving of operations to focusing on the forward operations needed for forming an equation is a crucial step in children's transition from arithmetic to algebra (Kieran & Chalouh, 1993). We return to this point later and focus now on the importance of developing the variable construct.

Developing the Variable Construct. We discussed earlier the importance of students acquiring a comprehensive mental model of a variable. Matz (1982) pointed out that when symbolic values, such as symbolic constants, parameters, unknowns, and arbitrary values, are all lumped together as variables, the only aspect that is highlighted is their single common feature, namely, their abstractness. This overly general model of a symbolic value obscures the important distinctions that affect how the variable is manipulated. The tasks of solving equations and simplifying expressions, for example, treat the notion of a variable in different ways. Students' initial experiences with algebraic problems usually involve a fixed numerical referent for a given symbol, such as, "If $x = 5$, what is $8 + x$?" The idea that a literal symbol can stand for a number must be established first, however. Chalouh and Herscovics (1988) describe a lesson in which children progressed from using a box as a placeholder to using a letter of their choice to denote a hidden quantity (this involved an array model, with five dots per row but with an unknown number of rows). The next lesson introduced the idea of a literal symbol representing an unknown quantity (in contrast to a hidden quantity). This entailed finding the area of a rectangle whose length and breadth were a units and 8 units respectively. Not surprisingly, students had difficulty in accepting the lack of closure in the algebraic expression, $8 \times a$, preferring to close it by writing an equal sign after the expression or by wanting to evaluate a.

As students progress to more complex problems, such as simplifying expressions, they deal with variables that act as "prototypical domain elements," capable of adopting *any* numerical value (Matz, 1982, p.39). However, to verify the results of a simplification, students must now consider the variable in terms of a particular instantiation, rather than as standing for any or all numbers. It is important though, that they realize that the instantiaton is arbitrary. A further shift in the interpretation of a variable occurs when students have to solve problems with two equations and two unknowns. Their common error here is to solve for one unknown in terms of the other. As Matz noted, students require assistance in interpreting the relationship between multiple occurrences of an unknown in an equation with one variable and between the two unknowns in a system of two equations and two unknowns.

Developing the Conventions of Syntax.   If students are to deal meaning-fully with the range of algebraic problems they will meet, they need to be made aware of the conventions of syntax. These conventions include an understanding of why concatenation in algebra (e.g., $3x$) implies multiplica-tion but not in arithemtic, and a knowledge of how to punctuate algebraic expressions, such as multiplication taking precedence over addition. As Kirshner (1989b) emphasized, even a simple expression such as, $3x^2 - 6 = 3(x^2 - 2)$, necessitates that subtraction be recognized as the dominant opera-tion of the initial expression and that $3x^2$ be interpreted as $3(x^2)$ rather than $(3x)^2$. As well, students must have an understanding of the distributive law and a mental model of the factoring transformation rule, $ab +/- ac = a(b +/- c)$, which they must apply to the given example. Their model must include the syntactic information that the dominant operation must be addition or subtraction, the next dominant must be multiplication, and there must be a common factor. This information must correspond with the structure of the given expression. Applying this model to the given expres-sion can present difficulties since there is not an immediately visible match (i.e., $3x^2 - 6$ is not identical to $ab +/- ac$). Using an arithmetic analogy can assist students in identifying the corresponding relations, as indicated in Fig. 7.2A. Applying the abstract model to the given expression involves a mul-tiple system mapping, as shown in Fig. 7.2B.

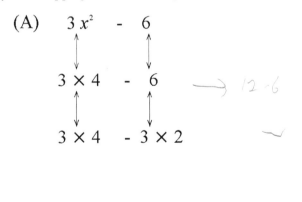

FIG. 7.2.   Mappings involved in using an arithmetic analogy and a formal rule in factoring a given expression.

Students will require explicit guidance in recognizing these corresponding structures. Students who rely on visual cues for analyzing an expression and lack such a mental model are severely disadvantaged when there is not a clear correspondence between the surface features of an algebraic expression and the factoring transformation rule. We cited evidence of this in our discussion on students' development of malrules. Recall that we also cited some examples of students extrapolating new rules from prototypes. As Matz (1982) noted, these techniques represent methods that work for students in prior mathematical experiences. For example, we replace specific numbers with arbitrary ones when we generalize from sample problems. This is fundamental to our ability to learn; without it, we could not develop a general rule from specific problems. Hence it is important that students are exposed to exceptions to the general rules they learn.

Developing an Understanding of Equivalence.   The concept of *equivalent equations* also requires explicit instruction. It is not sufficient to teach equivalence simply by referring to equivalent equations in a discussion of procedures for solving equations; they must be directly taught, with students given opportunities to reflect on their learning (Steinberg et al., 1991). Chaiklin and Lesgold (1984) liken the process of judging equivalence to that of judging the semantic equivalence of natural-language sentences. That is, a parse is made of the two expressions to be compared and meaningful units identified. The resulting units are then used as the arguments of a reasoning process that determines the equivalence of the two expressions. Providing students with guidance in parsing and judging expressions can assist them in determining equivalence. The findings of Chaiklin and Lesgold's study indicate a need to develop students' understanding of specific number properties, such as commutativity and reflexivity. In particular, students need to know for which operations these properties hold, for example, subtraction cannot be commuted.

In the process of learning equivalent equations, students require assistance in overcoming confusion between operations that are performed within a particular algebraic expression (e.g., grouping similar terms) and the transformations used in solving an equation. For example, the equation, $\frac{3x}{4} - 1 = 0$, can be transformed into $3x - 4 = 0$, and the algebraic expression, $\frac{3x}{4} - 1$ can be transformed into $\frac{3x}{4} - \frac{4}{4}$. Students can easily make an incorrect procedural mapping here and transform the expression, $\frac{3x}{4} - 1$, into $3x - 4$. It is important that students recognize and understand the differences between these two procedures.

Students' difficulties in recognizing equivalent equations can reflect basic weaknesses in their ability to solve equations. There are a number of relationships in the solution process that students need to consider, important relationships that are often not made explicit. These include the relationship between consecutive left-hand sides, between consecutive right-hand sides, and between consecutive lines of the written transformations of equations. More specifically, students must determine:

1. The nature of each transformation;
2. The relationship between two transformations that yield respectively the next consecutive left-hand and right-hand sides; and
3. The equality or inequality of consecutive corresponding sides, a judgement that is based on the determination of 1 (Matz, 1982, p. 41).

As Matz pointed out, working with equations requires facility both in interpreting the equal sign when it is explicit and in recognizing the equivalent expressions when it is implicit. This is particularly so in sample problems where several steps are often compressed into one. This makes it difficult for students to infer the scope of the transformation that has taken place. For example, given the sample solution to an equation of the form, $ax = c \rightarrow x = \frac{c}{a}$, students may form a mental model that conforms to the rule, "Divide both sides by one of the variables." When confronted with an equation such as, $ax + b = c$, they map it onto their mental model and thus make the error, $ax + b = c \rightarrow x + b = \frac{c}{a}$.

Earlier we addressed the additional interpretation of the equal sign in algebra, namely, to express constraints. However in making the transition from arithmetic to algebra, students do not begin with constraint equations but with tautologies (universally true statements). The notion of equality is the same here as in arithmetic. Matz (1982) contended that it is only when the constraint equations are introduced that real conceptual change is required. This is where students need particular guidance in distingushing between the two forms. For example, the syntactic similarity between two semantically different statements, such as $3x + 9 = 3(x + 3)$ and $3x + 9 = 2x + 12$, presents a major obstacle for students. Some students continue to work under the preconception that each individual line is a tautology, leading them to read *across* each line of the solution. They thus expect that a particular transformation has changed the left-hand expression into the right-hand expression. This naturally presents confusion for students, especially when they attempt to justify the steps of a proof.

Matz made the interesting point that facility with axioms and proofs is supposed to promote an understanding of the nature of the "legal" step. However, students who do not realize that a change in "reading styles" is required cannot even identify, in the sequence of equations, just where the axioms have been applied. Their previous experience with tautologies leads them to find an axiom that matches across each individual *line* of a solution. Because students' initial experiences in solving algebraic equations do not necessarily prepare them for the conceptual and perceptual changes required for the more difficult examples, we maintain that instruction should specifically address the issues we have outlined. This includes an understanding that statements with equal signs can be reversed and that such statements can have multiple and distinct operations on both sides of the equal sign. Understanding this concept entails representing relations in the equation as a whole. There is a quaternary relation on each side of the equals sign, so a very complex set of relations is present (equivalent to a quinary relation). Chunking and serial processing are needed, which means students must have appropriate prior concepts to bring to the task. It is probably best learned with a simpler example, such as $3x = x + 2$. Notice that even this entails a higher order relation between two ternary relations, and is equivalent to a quaternary relation.

Developing Students' Strategic Knowledge. Developing students' strategic knowledge can also help them deal with the difficulties we have addressed to date. We referred to the issue of strategic knowledge in reference to Wenger's (1987) work. We strongly support Wenger's contention that students need assistance in developing the ability to determine the features of an algebraic expression that are salient for solving a given problem. For example, they need to become aware that they can replace, by a single symbol, all factors and/or terms that contain parameters other than the goal variable [e.g., $3(2x + 4) - 7 = 17$ is equivalent to $3y - 7 = 17$]. This often involves implicit forms of equivalence that need to be made explicit if students are to apply this knowledge in specific contexts.

An important component of students' strategic knowledge is the ability to clearly identify the goal of a problem and to recognize when the goal has been attained. Students will need guidance here because algebraic directives, such as "factor" and "solve," describe only the features of the desired result and not a single method to execute, as in arithmetic (Matz, 1982). Students have to understand, for example, that "factor" means to rewrite the entire expression as a product, not just part of it. In contrast to these directives, the instruction to "simplify" is less clear. Here, students have to appreciate the aesthetic convention that one fraction is preferred to two, even if there is a complex common denominator, and that the factored form is preferred to the expanded polynomial. Students then have the task of determining whether they have attained the goal, that is, whether they can simplify the expression further.

The application of strategic knowledge can also assist students in applying their understanding of inverse operations when solving algebraic problems. This notion does not transfer readily from arithmetic to algebra (Wagner & Parker, 1993). The concept of inverse operations in arithmetic, though applicable in algebra, tends to be obscured by other complexities.

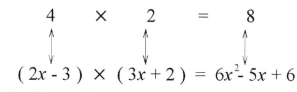

FIG. 7.3. Using an arithmetic analogy to highlight the factors of a quadratic expression.

For example, when students multiply $(2x - 3)$ by $(3x + 2)$ to produce $6x^2 - 5x + 6$, they often do not realize that $(2x - 3)$ and $(3x + 2)$ are the factors of the product, just as 4 and 2 are factors of 8 in arithmetic (the structure mapping for this analogy is shown in Fig. 7.3). This analogy needs to be made explicit. If students are asked subsequently to factorize $6x^2 - 5x + 6$, they should realize that they do not need to calculate; the original expressions provide the answer. Because the inverse relation is a more complex construct in algebra than in arithmetic, and is easily obscured by the algebraic operations themselves, students need to be explicitly shown that multiplying and factoring are inverse operations. They need to appreciate the implications of this relationship and recognize when to use this knowledge. Unfortunately, the practice of pausing to consider the higher order relations within the expressions comprising the equation does not appear to be developed effectively or explicitly enough in many textbooks. Yet this is an important form of planning or metacognitive control that can cue the recall of relevant strategies and procedures (Wenger, 1987).

Students can see more readily the link between the inverse operations in arithmetic and in algebra if they can "unitize" polynomial expressions and deal with them as single variables (Wagner & Parker, 1993). This skill is also important in factoring an expression by grouping, for example, $ax + bx + ay + by = (a + b)x + (a + b)y = (a + b)(x + y)$. This unitizing skill (which is really a form of chunking) will be slow to develop if students are used to dealing with single letters as unknowns. They thus need experience in dealing with unknowns such as $2x$ and $x + 4$. Parentheses and other bracketing symbols can serve as a perceptual aid here, however they do present difficulties for students (Booth, 1984, 1988; Kieran, 1979; Wagner & Parker, 1993). Students often ignore brackets, believing that the sequence in which the operations are written determines the order in which they should be performed. Explicit instruction in interpreting these symbols is needed, initially in an arithmetic context, as these difficulties usually stem from an incorrect perception of arithmetical representation (Booth, 1988). Students can also discuss examples where rules of thumb such as "clear the brackets first," are not the most appropriate approach to take. Such rules can often prevent students from unitizing expressions because their aim is to eliminate grouping symbols (Wagner & Parker, 1993).

Using Concrete Analogs.   To this point, we have not mentioned the use of concrete analogs in the teaching of algebraic concepts. This is largely because the complexity of this domain limits their application and the few research studies that have been conducted have not produced significant results. Concrete analogs were used in early studies by Bruner and Kenney (1965) and Dienes (1964) to justify quadratic expressions. Later studies addressing the use of concrete/pictorial analogs include those of Filloy and Rojano (e.g., 1985) where pictorial representations of a geometric situation, as well as the balance model, were used to establish an understanding of equations of the type, $ax +/- b = cx$ and $ax +/- b = cx +/- d$. The findings showed that the concrete analogs did not significantly increase most students' ability to operate at the symbolic level with equations involving two instances of the unknown. Furthermore, many students tended to fixate on the models and seemed unable to see the connections between the operations performed with the model and the corresponding algebraic operations. As a consequence, the students remained dependent on the model even when it was no longer useful.

In summary, concrete analogs do not appear as effective and as versatile in teaching algebraic concepts as they are in promoting arithmetical understanding. This means we have to rely on more abstract analogs. Existing relationships, in both arithmetic and algebra, can serve as mental models that enable the student to understand more complex ideas. For this understanding to occur, however, the base relationships must be well known and the student must recognize the structural correspondence between these and the target relationships.

Students' Mental Models of Algebraic Word Problems

As we mentioned earlier, one of the inconsistencies between arithmetic and algebra is in the solving of word problems. In contrast to arithmetic, algebraic problems require students to think in terms of the "forward" operations that represent the structure of the problem rather than in terms of the operations they used to solve it. This represents a major cognitive shift for the beginning algebraic student and demands an ability to interpret and understand the mathematical relations in these problems (Chaiklin, 1989; Kieran, 1992).

Solving agebraic word problems involves both text processing and mathematical skills (Hall, Kibler, Wenger, & Truxaw, 1989; Kaput & Sims-Knight, 1984; Nathan, Kintsch, & Young, 1992). However attention is often focussed on the manipulation of formal mathematical expressions rather than on strategies for comprehending a problem, even though problem comprehension is largely responsible for students' poor performance (Nathan et al., 1992; Willis & Fuson, 1988). The difficulties students experience in representing and solving algebraic word problems have been well documented (e.g., Greeno, 1989; Herscovics, 1989; Kieran, 1992; Nathan et al., 1992). A common finding is that students rely on a direct, syntactic approach to solving these problems, that is, they use a "phrase-by-phrase translation of the problem into variables and equations" (Chaiklin, 1989; Hinsley, Hayes, & Simon, 1977). The application of syntactic rules is usually sufficient for identifying the variables and the relations among these. However, such an approach is limited because it does not enable the student to detect irregularities or contradictions in a problem.

A commonly cited case of this limitation is the reversal error students make in solving the "Students-and-Professors" problem, namely, *"Write an equation using the variables S and P to represent the following statement: 'There are six times as many students as professors at this university"* (Clement, 1982; Clement, Lochhead, & Monk, 1981; K. M. Fisher, 1988). A significant proportion of adults make a reversal error where, instead of writing 6P = S, they write the reverse, 6S = P. One explanation for this error is the literal mapping from the symbols to words where *S* is read as *students* and *P* as *professors*, rather than S as the *number* of students and P as the *number* of professors (Clement, Lochhead, & Soloway, 1979).

MacGregor and Stacey (1993) offered an alternative explanation. They argued that students' errors on problems of this type are not due primarily to syntactic translation. They postulated that reversed equations and expressions are produced when students attempt to represent, in recorded form, cognitive models of compared unequal quantities. Information from these models can be retrieved in any order. These models simulate the semantic features of a problem situation but not the mathematical form. They are reflected in natural language, but cannot be translated directly into mathematical code. Because they are based on comparison rather than equality, the models do not possess the logical form of an equation.

To illustrate the complexity of algebraic problem solving and to provide a model for analyzing the processes involved, we revisit the three-component referential system that we advanced in chapter 5. We elaborate on these models in our present discussion and, in doing so, draw upon the work of Nathan et al. (1992) and Hall et al. (1989).

We agree with Nathan et al.'s thesis that comprehending a problem requires the student to make a correspondence between the formal equation(s) needed to solve the problem and the student's own informal understanding of the situation described in the problem. A significant component here is how the student's mental representation of the problem situation informs and constrains the formal expressions required for solution (Greeno, 1989; Hall et al., 1989). We incorporated these ideas in our own referential system where we highlighted the role of the problem-situation model in the problem-solving process. Recall that this component represents the mental model the student forms by mapping her problem-text model onto an analogous familiar situation. We consider the development of this mental model to be crucial to effective problem solving as it forms the meaningful link between the problem-text model and the remaining component, the mathematical model (cf. Hall et al.'s argument). We defined the problem-text model as the mental model that the student initially constructs as he reads the text of the problem. It is from this text model that the student must abstract propositional and situational information and make critical inferences (Nathan et al., 1992). The mathematical model comprises the formal algebraic expression that generates the solution to the problem and is formed by mapping the required algebraic expression onto the problem-situation schema. It is akin to Nathan et al.'s "problem model" the formation of which is guided by a set of algebraic problem schemas that provide "explicit, graphical cues" (p. 332).

To highlight the important role of the problem-situation model, we review a sample problem similar to that cited by van Dijk and Kintsch (1983) and Nathan et al. (1992):

> *A tourist bus leaves Sydney and travels north at 80 kilometers per hour. Two hours later, a second bus leaves Sydney on the same course and travels north at 100 hundred kilometers per hour. How long will it take the second bus to overtake the first?*

An algebraic problem such as this can be viewed from two levels of abstraction: the "quantitative structure" of the related mathematical objects and the "situational structure" of related physical objects within the problem (Hall et al., 1989, p. 227). The quantitative structure refers to the mathematical entities and relationships that are either presented or implied in the problem text. The present problem includes extensive quantities denoting a primary amount (i.e., 80 kilometers and 100 kilometers), intensive elements indicating a constant multiplicative relationship between two quantities (i.e., 80 kilometers per hour and 100 kilometers per hour), and a difference element that compares two extensives (i.e., one time interval is 2 hours longer than the other; Hall et al., 1989; Schwartz, 1988). If we adopt Hall et al.'s notion of a quantitative relation as an arithmetic operation linking three quantities, we can state that the distance, d, traveled by the slower bus is equal to 80 times the time it takes to travel that distance, that is, $d = 80 \times t$. Although students will probably have a schematic knowledge of this relationship, it will be of little assistance to them if they do not consider the situational structure of the problem.

Our sample problem may be classified as a "compound motion" problem that is assembled around related events (i.e., buses traveling in the same direction) involving an agent engaged in an activity that produces an output (distance) over a period of time. Output and time are the basic dimensions that organize this story activity (Hall et al., 1989, p. 233). In forming a problem-situation model from this problem text, the student must make some fundamental inferences. Because this problem does not tell the reader that the buses will overtake when they have traveled equal distances, the student must provide this information from her general knowledge. This is where the problem-situation model comes into play. For this model to be formed effectively, the student must have sufficient background knowlege to "read between the lines" and to draw any necessary inferences or projections. This helps provide the student with an algebraic interpretation of the text to facilitate solution and also provides situational constraints, against which she can check the formal constraints. However, this problem-situation model can only assist in the detection and correction of formal problem-schema errors when a clear mapping between it and the mathematical model has been established (Nathan et al., 1992).

In generating a mathematical model for the foregoing problem, the student must draw upon her schema that links distance, speed, and time, namely, $d = s \times t$. Two additional, supporting relations then need to be considered, namely, that the buses travel the same distance and that there is a time delay between the two. Hence, for the faster bus, we can write the equation, $d = 100 \times t$. Because the slower bus also travels the same distance we can use the same variable, d. However the slower bus has a 2-hour headstart that must be incorporated in its equation, that is, $d = 80 \times (t + 2)$. The solution-enabling equation, $100 \times t = 80 \times (t + 2)$, can then be formed.

Because the supporting relations have to be inferred from the student's problem-situation model, they can pose a considerable cognitive load. Hence, Nathan et al. hypothesized that the student will only make inferences when they seem necessary and that poor problem solvers will omit them from their solution to a problem. These poorer problem solvers tend to use a straight translation-based technique of mapping story phrases to equations. In contrast, problem solvers who form a sound problem-situation model will include inference-based equations. Nevertheless, weaker students can be taught how to form such a model by relating the characters, events, and relations in the problem text to their knowledge of formal symbols and expressions that will facilitate a solution. Reasoning with this problem-situation model serves as an effective problem-solving strategy when an algebraic problem cannot be solved by simple algebraic substitution (Hall et al., 1989).

The primary benefit of encouraging students to form sound problem-situational models however, is that it forces them to consider formal expressions with reference to a particular situation, thereby avoiding the decontextualization of their algebraic knowledge (Greeno, 1989; Hall et al., 1989; Nathan et al. 1992). As we have mentioned previously, students frequently treat symbolic representations and real-world situations as unrelated to each other, with the result that they solve symbolic expressions procedurally without any meaningful reasoning. They are then prone to performing operations on symbolic expressions that no longer map onto the situations to which the intended expressions refer (Greeno, 1989). We support Nathan et al.'s claim that a situation-based learning environment can help students' achieve the conceptual understanding needed to reason mathematically.

The ability to form an effective problem-situation model can also assist students in recognizing similarity in problem structure between a known (base) problem and a new (target) problem. This can facilitate transfer of a known solution model. Such analogical transfer involves constructing a mapping between elements in the base and target problems, and adapting the solution model from the base problem to meet the requirements of the target problem (Novick, 1992). Novick and Holyoak (1991) argued that successful mapping does not guarantee successful transfer. Mapping and procedure adaptation are seen as separate, although related, processes, with adaptation being a major source of students' difficulty in analogical problem solving with mathematical word problems.

A student may map a problem-situation model onto a target problem but fail to make the necessary adjustments to the solution model. This can occur when the problem-situation model is sufficiently adequate to recognize some structural similarities but is not sufficiently robust to accommodate new elements in the target problem and make the necessary adaptations to the base solution model. This could occur with a target problem of the form: *Two planes leave Brisbane, 2 hours apart. The first plane travels at 300 kilometers per hour and travels north. The second plane leaves 2 hours later and travels south at 350 kilometers per hour. In how many hours will they be 1900 kilometers apart?*

Both this problem and the previous example (base problem) are compound motion problems involving speed, distance, and time. Both share some surface and structural features. However, the target problem presents new conditions that the student must take into account when transferring the problem-situation and mathematical models of the base problem. Students' problem-situation models for these examples must include an appreciation of how time and distance both organize the structure of the problem and constrain the corresponding mathematical models. If students lack·this understanding, they will either not make the required adjustments when transferring these models or will have difficulty in doing so.

Successful transfer to the target problem can lead to the induction of more general models encompassing the source and target problems; these models can facilitate solution of subsequent analogous problems (Gick & Holyoak, 1983; Novick, 1992; Novick & Holyoak, 1991). However, students will require particular assistance in detecting the underlying structural similarities between problems, that is, the commonalities in the relations among the elements in the problems rather than the specific elements themselves. This will enable them to retrieve an appropriate base problem when faced with a new target problem. The skill of adapting existing problem-situation models and associated mathematical models to target problems needs particular attention. Instruction could begin by using specific examples to address some different types of adaptations that students might encounter in solving algebraic word problems (Novick, 1992). Students also need help in recognizing when particular base models should be used in solving these problems. We return to the issue of analogical transfer in our disussion on problem solving in the next chapter. We turn now to a consideration of proportional reasoning that represents another complex domain for children.

PROPORTIONAL REASONING

The attainment of proportional reasoning is regarded as a milestone in students' cognitive development (Cramer & Post, 1993; Hoffer & Hoffer, 1992; Lesh, Post, & Behr, 1988). It may be viewed as both the "capstone of children's elementary school arithmetic" and the "cornerstone of all that is to follow" (Lesh et al., pp. 93–94). That is, proportional reasoning is one of the highest level elementary understandings and one of the most basic "higher order" understandings.

There are varying perspectives on what constitutes proportional reasoning. According to Piaget (Piaget & Inhelder, 1975), the essential feature of proportional reasoning is the involvement of a second-order relationship (i.e., a relationship betwen two relationships) rather than just a relationship between two directly perceivable quantities. The Piagetian perspective argues that an early phase in children's proportional reasoning involves "additive reasoning" of the form, $a - b = c - d$. However, as Lesh et al. (1988) pointed out, the reasoning paradigm a child uses often varies within a task and from one task to another. Hence, tasks that can be characterized by additive equations (i.e., $a - b = c - d$ or $a + b = c + d$), should not be referred to as proportional reasoning tasks. Even some multiplicative tasks, such as the beam balance, that are characterized by the equation $a.b = c.d$, may be poor indicators of true proportional reasoning, especially when an algorithmic solution, or a lower level rule, is applied. Lesh et al. thus contended that only those tasks that can be characterized by a relationship between two rational expressions, that is, $\frac{a}{b} = \frac{c}{d}$, should be regarded as proportional reasoning tasks.

We adopt the view that proportional reasoning deals with multiplicative relationships between two rational expressions such as ratios, rates, quotients, and fractions (Lesh et al., 1988; we addressed this multiplicative relationship in the last chapter when we reviewed Vergnaud's, 1983, notion of multiplicative structures). As discussed in chapter 3, proportional reasoning is a quaternary relation, and entails four-way relations between the relevant variables. This is necessary if proportion is to be distinguished from superficially similar situations, such as $a - b = c - d$, and if correspondences between different instances of a proportion are to be recognized. Representation of a quaternary relation is necessary if all the questions that can be reasonably asked about a proportion are to be answered, as we will see.

We might note in passing that there is a subtle, but crucially important, difference between analogy and proportion. Consider analogies based on binary relations, of the form, A is to B as C is to D (A:B::C:D). There are four variables here, but they can be processed as two binary relations. The four-way relation between A,B,C, and D does not need to be processed, whereas in proportion it does.

Assessing Proportional Reasoning

Three main types of problem situations have been used to assess students' proportional reasoning, namely, numerical comparison, missing value, and qualitative prediction and comparison (Cramer & Post, 1993; Heller, Post, Behr, & Lesh, 1990; Post et al., 1988; Vergnaud, 1988). We review each of these types and students' approaches to solving them. We also consider a couple of alternative approaches to classifying proportional situations.

In numerical comparison problems, the student has to compare two given, complete rates. A numerical answer is not required. Noelting's (1980) orange juice problem is a commonly used example of this problem type. In one instance, students are shown an illustration of two pitchers (A and B) and two sets of shaded and unshaded glasses representing orange juice mix and water respectively. One set comprises two shaded glasses and three unshaded glasses. The other set contains three shaded and four unshaded glasses. Students are to imagine that each set of orange juice mixture and water is poured into a pitcher and must determine which pitcher (A or B) would have the stronger-tasting orange juice, or whether the mixtures would taste the same. Noelting varied the numbers used in this task to include integer and noninteger relationships within and between measure spaces. As would be expected, students found the noninteger relationships more difficult (e.g., three cups of juice to seven cups of water and four cups of juice to nine cups of water).

In missing value problems, three items of numerical information are given with one piece to be found. A commonly used task of this type is the tall-man-short-man problem (E. F. Karplus, Karplus, & Wollman, 1974). Students are given a chain of six paper clips and told that it represents Mr.

Short's height in paper clips. They are also told that Mr. Short measures four large buttons tall. It is then explained that Mr. Tall is similar to Mr. Short but is six large buttons tall (students are not shown this). Students are asked to find Mr. Tall's height in paper clips and explain their answer.

The information in missing-value problems can be represented as rates, that is, 6 paper clips/4 buttons is a complete rate and x paper clips/6 buttons is an incomplete rate. Using Vergnaud's notation, the problem can be depicted as follows:

	Height (buttons)	Height (paper clips)
Mr. Short	4	6
Mr. Tall	6	x

There are three main approaches to solving numerical-comparison and missing-value problems (Cramer & Post, 1993; Cramer, Post, & Currier, 1993). The first approach, the unit rate strategy, involves finding the constant factor that relates the quantities between the measure spaces. This can be achieved in the Mr. Short/Mr. Tall example by finding the number of paper clips that equal one button, $\frac{6}{4} = \frac{3}{2}$ (paper clips per one button; the "how many for one" strategy), and then multiplying this by the quantity, six buttons. The other approach is a factor-of-change method ("times as many" strategy) where the multiplicative relationship among the elements within each measure space is found. This approach is easy to use when the factor relating the numbers within the button measure space is an integer (e.g., if, in the above Mr. Short/Mr. Tall example, Mr. Tall were 8 buttons high). The reasoning here is that, if the number of buttons is doubled, then the number of paper clips must also be doubled.

Recognizing the within and between relationships in the data of the Mr. Short/Mr. Tall table enables students to choose between the two strategies. However when these relationships are noninteger, students have more difficulty and often resort to incorrect additive strategies. For example, if Mr. Short were three buttons and seven paper clips high, and Mr. Tall, five buttons high, students might reason that $x = 9$ because $3 + 4 = 7$ and hence, $5 + 4 = 9$, or because $3 + 2 = 5$ so $7 + 2 = 9$. A reluctance or inability to deal with the noninteger relationships ("avoidance of fractions"), coupled with the high processing loads involved, is the likely cause of this error (R. Karplus, Pulos, & Stage, 1983, p. 83).

The third approach to solving these problems is the cross-product algorithm. This is an extremely efficient procedure but is mechanical and devoid of meaning (Cramer & Post, 1993). It is poorly understood by students (Post et al., 1988), is rarely generated naturally (Hart, 1984), and is often used as a means of avoiding proportional reasoning rather than facilitating it (Lesh et al., 1988). Indeed, the procedure does not involve proportional reasoning per se. To apply this procedure to the Mr. Short/Mr. Tall problem, the student would set up a proportion, form the cross product, and solve the resulting equation by division: $\frac{4}{6} = \frac{6}{x} \rightarrow 4x = 36 \rightarrow x = 9$. The results of the Rational Number Project (Post et al., 1988; Heller et al., 1990) showed that the unit-rate strategy was favored by seventh graders in solving these problems whereas the cross-product method was used most often by eighth graders who had been specifically taught this algorithm.

The third type of problem used to assess proportional reasoning is the qualitative prediction and comparison example. These problems require students to make comparisons that are not dependent on specific numerical values. This can be seen in the following problem involving qualitative comparison of density:

> *Two friends hammered a line of nails into different boards. Bill hammered more nails than Greg. Bill's board was shorter than Greg's. On which board are the nails hammered closer together? (a) Bill's board (b) Greg's board (c) Their nails are spaced the same (d) Not enough information to tell* (Cramer & Post, 1993, p. 405).

In contrast to the previous two problem types where a memorized skill may be used, qualitative prediction and comparison problems require students to understand the meaning of proportions. The qualitative thinking demanded by these problems allows students to check the feasibility of their answers and establish appropriate parameters for problem situations (Cramer & Post, 1993). Given the importance of this type of thinking, qualitative prediction and comparison problems should have a recognized place in the mathematics curriculum.

Singer and Resnick (1992) adopted a different means of classifying proportional problems by making use of the part/whole and part–part schemas. Numerical comparison problems would be classified as "For Every" situations where two like quantities, defined on the same measure space (with a common superset), are set up in correspondence to each other.

Lamon (1993a, 1993b) offered a third way in which proportional reasoning problems may be classified for assessment purposes. She identified four semantic problem types: well-chunked measures, part–part–whole, associated sets, and stretchers and shrinkers. The well-chunked measures type involves the comparison of two extensive measures, producing an intensive measure or rate that is a well-known entity (e.g., kilometers per hour). In part–part–whole examples, the extensive measure (cardinality) of a subset of a whole is given in terms of the cardinalities of two or more subsets, such as classes with a ratio of x boys to y girls. Associated-sets problems refer to examples in which the relationship between two elements is unknown or ill-defined unless their relationship is defined within the problem situation. A typical problem of this type asks the student to identify who will get more pizza in a situation in which three pizzas are shared among seven girls and one pizza is shared among three boys. Stretchers-and-shrinkers problems refer to scaling examples such as comparing the rate of growth of two trees over a period of time.

We will revisit Lamon's study briefly when we examine the development of children's proportional reasoning. At present we simply note that the assessments for proportionality, taken collectively, would require processing of a quaternary relation. That is, although some tests individually could be performed using lower rank relations, an understanding of the four-way relation is necessary to devise an answer for all of them. We turn now to the complexity of proportional reasoning and highlight some of the difficulties it presents for students.

The Complexity of Proportional Reasoning

Research has shown that proportional thinking skills emerge slowly and are often not acquired by a large segment of society (Cramer et al., 1993; Heller et al., 1990; Hoffer & Hoffer, 1992; Resnick & Singer, 1993). As Cramer et al. (1993) noted, we cannot define a proportional reasoner as simply one who knows how to set up and solve a proportion. Proportional reasoning involves the ability to discriminate proportional from nonproportional situations. For example, Cramer et al. cited a case in which 32 out of 33 preservice elementary teachers interpreted a simple addition problem as a proportional problem: *Sue and Julie were running equally fast around a track. Sue started first. When she had run 9 laps, Julie had run 3 laps. When Julie completed 15 laps, how many laps had Sue run?* (Cramer et al., 1993, p. 159). These prospective teachers assumed that a multiplicative relationship exists between the quantities in the problem (i.e., "9 laps for every 3 laps") and solved it by applying the traditional proportion algorithm.

Not only must students discriminate between proportional and nonproportional situations, they must also recognize structural similarity (Lesh et al., 1988). That is, in dealing with a proportional expression such as $\frac{a}{b} = \frac{c}{d}$, students must recognize that both sides of the equation involve the same pattern of relations or operations and that the components are multiplicatively related. An equation such as $\frac{8}{2} = 5 - 1$ is obviously not a proportion, because its two sides are not structurally similar even though they are equal. Lesh et al. make the important point that tasks which involve a multiplicative relationship ($\frac{a}{b} = \frac{c}{d}$ or $a.b = c.d$) do not necessarily entail proportional reasoning. If the student cannot demonstrate a recognition of the structural similarity of the two sides of the equation, then there is no evidence of proportional reasoning. For example, in a task that corresponds to the form, $a.b = c.d$, with a.b corresponding directly to a perceivable quantity, the student may transform it to $Y = c.d$ where Y is a "new" element in the system. When this happens, the student ignores the structural similarity and hence does not need to use proportional reasoning. Being able to give the correct answer to problems of the form $a.b = c.d$ clearly does not guarantee that proportional reasoning is being used. If the quaternary relation is represented, it should be possible to recognize whether proportion is involved.

Recognizing the invariance of certain types of transformations on mathematical objects, whether these transformations be qualitative or quantitative, is another significant component of proportional reasoning (Heller et al., 1990). In a study by Behr et al. (1984), students were shown the equality, $\frac{3}{4} = \frac{6}{8}$, and then a given number was subtracted from one of the four numbers. Students were to change one of the remaining three numbers to restore equality (e.g., $\frac{3-1}{4} = \frac{6-?}{8}$. It is not surprising that students typically increased or decreased the corresponding numbers by the same amount on both sides (i.e., $\frac{3-1}{4} = \frac{6-1}{8}$). Presumably, they were applying their mental model of solving equations by adding or subtracting the same amount from both sides. The students were simply operating on the numbers as if they were distinct entities and not considering the proportions involved.

This problem provides a good example of how four-way relations are needed to understand proportion. To understand the problem, it is necessary to contrast $\frac{3}{4} = \frac{6}{8}$ with $\frac{2}{4} = \frac{5}{8}$, (the latter being the incorrect solution to the problem in the last paragraph). In the first proportion, the second numerator is twice the first (6 is twice 3); similarly for the denominators. However in the proposed (incorrect) solution ($\frac{2}{4} = \frac{5}{8}$), the relation between the numerators is not preserved (5 is not twice 2), though the relation between denominators is preserved. Also the relation between numerator and denominator in the two ratios is not maintained ($\frac{2}{4}$ vs. $\frac{5}{8}$). In the correct solution (i.e., $\frac{2}{4} = \frac{4}{8}$), all relations are maintained. Thus the whole set of relations between the four variables has to be processed to distinguish the valid from an invalid answer.

In a related study, Heller et al. (1990) examined the relationship between junior high school students' directional reasoning about rates and their numerical reasoning on proportion-related word problems. The directional questions included types such as, "What will happen to the fraction $\frac{7}{8}$ if the top number gets smaller and the bottom number gets bigger?" (p. 391). Their findings revealed that only about one fifth of the seventh graders and one fourth of the eighth graders possessed a functional understanding of proportionality. The remaining students could not recognize that both the numerator and denominator of a rate can decrease or increase proportionally or nonproportionally.

Heller et al.'s findings also showed that determining the effect of directional changes on the value of a given fraction does not appear to be

substantially related to deciding what happens to a rate i
Likewise, deciding which of two given fractions is smaller
be related to the skill of deciding which of two rates .
problems. Given that these fraction exercises and rate word problem.
the same level of structural (relational) complexity, Heller et al. concluded
that students must be using different reasoning processes in solving the two
types of problems. The presence of a context may be responsible here. That
is, students may have difficulty in forming an adequate problem-situation
model from the given data. The fact that students are not capitalizing on the
structural similarities involved, even when the numerical quantities remain
constant, suggests weaknesses in the mathematics curriculum. It seems that
students are not being taught to apply their rational number skills to obvious
areas of application, such as proportionality. A comprehensive mental model
of rational number can serve as a valuable base for the introduction of
proportional relationships. We also need to capitalize on children's intuitive
understanding of proportional reasoning, which we examine in the next
section.

Children's Development of Proportional Reasoning

Resnick and Singer (1993) presented an interesting analysis of the origins of
children's proportional reasoning. They maintain that, at an early age,
children appear to be sensitive to patterns of covariation between two series
of quantities. For example, preschoolers learn that, as they grow larger, the
clothes and shoes they wear must also become larger. They also see that
larger and older people eat larger portions of food. Resnick and Singer
viewed the inferences children make here as adopting the form of simple
direct proportions of the type: Daddy size/My size = Daddy dinner size/My
dinner size. That is, children are perceiving the relationship between Daddy
and them as covarying directly with the relationship between Daddy's
dinner and their dinner. This relationship is seen as general across all fathers
and all children.

An understanding of direct covariation appears to precede an understanding of inverse covariation. Understanding that things can increase and
decrease in the same direction is less complex for children than understanding that things change in opposite directions. Several studies have demonstrated that, by about 6 years, children can make inferences based on direct
covariation but cannot do so for inverse covariation until about 9 years of
age (Acredolo, Adams, & Schmid, 1984; Kun, 1977; Strauss & Stavy, 1982).

Covariation is a binary relation, because it entails only two variables, and
is therefore simpler than proportion. It is therefore quite plausible that
understanding covariation would be a precursor to proportion. Indirect

covariation is also a binary relation, but is probably harder to observe, which could explain its later attainment. Proportion entails the four-way relation between four variables, as we have seen.

A recognized development in children's relational reasoning involves coordinating two numerically quantified series, without constructing a single ratio to express the relationship (Resnick & Singer, 1993). For example, consider the problem, *"Jack saves $5 each week while Sue saves $8. When Jack has saved $20, how many dollars will Sue have saved?"* Children can solve this by forming two independent series, one for Jack (5, 10, 15, 20) and one for Sue (8, 16, 24, 32), and keeping them coordinated by aligning them in tabular format. Children can then determine that Sue will have saved $32 when Bill has saved $20. Such a procedure however, does not require children to establish a ratio between Jack and Sue's rate of saving. Furthermore, it does not demand the use of a covariation schema where the same relationship is applied to both components. Rather, it simply involves the application of two different relations, one to Jack and one to Sue.

Resnick and Singer (1993) raised an interesting issue regarding children's preference for additive strategies in solving proportional problems. When they are very young, children are sensitive to patterns of covariation between two series of quantities. Yet they appear to abandon these schemas, in favor of familiar and "comfortable" additive strategies, once they start to quantify proportional situations. Resnick and Singer posited two contributing factors to children's preference for additive over multiplicative relationships. First, protoquantitative multiplicative relations develop considerably more slowly than additive ones. Second, when children begin to quantify patterns of covariation, they know a great deal more about the additive composition properties of numbers than about their multiplicative composition. The findings of several studies support these conjectures, indicating that children do not utilize the multiplicative properties of number until around grade 6 (Campbell & Graham, 1985; Cuneo, 1982; Miller & Gelman, 1983).

Even beyond this age, students seem to avoid multiplication when dealing with proportion examples, preferring to use an additive strategy. This involves "building up" to an answer by dealing with small segments of a problem and then adding together their answers (K. Hart, 1981). This entails serial processing, and would impose smaller processing loads. Although this strategy might work for simple cases, it is cumbersome for more complex examples. When the additive strategy becomes difficult or impossible, students frequently switch to considering the difference between the components instead of the ratio (i.e., $a - b$ instead of a:b). The fact that most of the students in Hart's study were unable to complete these more complex examples suggests that they conceived of ratio as an additive operation and hence, replaced multiplication by repeated addition. As we commented in the last chapter, an overemphasis on the repeated addition approach to multiplication limits children's facility with multiplicative situations.

Lamon (1993b) noted in her study that the emergence of relative thinking appeared as the signal that a student was beginning to bridge the gap between additive and multiplicative structures. Being able to make relative comparisons is essential to students' ability to understand the functional and scalar relationships inherent in a proportion. The ability to view a ratio as a unit appears as a natural extension of the process of composing extensive (cardinal) units.

Given the inherent difficulty of proportional reasoning, it is particularly important that educators take the complexity of the domain into account when designing student learning experiences. In the next section, we consider ways in which we might foster the development of proportional reasoning.

Fostering Students' Proportional Reasoning

The Curriculum and Evaluation Standards (National Council of Teachers of Mathematics, 1989) recommended that students experience problem situations that can be modeled and then solved through proportional reasoning. Unfortunately, the literature is not prolific in offering ideas on how to foster this reasoning. The findings of the studies we have cited here however, point to some areas in need of attention.

One area in which children require a great deal more experience is with situations involving invariance of a product and a ratio (Harel, Behr, Post, & Lesh, 1992). As Harel et al. stressed, when children are acquiring an understanding of the four operations, instruction should not be limited to a static perspective of finding the answer when problem components are given (e.g., finding the product when factors are given). Instruction should include the dynamic perspective of determining whether a given product or quotient (or sum or difference) changes or is invariant when transformations are made to the problem components. Children's experiences here should also include determining the direction of change, the magnitude of change, and what is needed to compensate for a change so that invariance can be achieved.

Students' difficulties with transformations in proportional reasoning problems also reflect a lack of awareness of the structural similarities between fraction and ratio constructs. The findings of Heller et al.'s (1990) study indicate that students are not using their existing understanding of rational number as a base for their learning of ratio and proportion ideas. The standard mathematics curriculum appears to introduce the latter concepts in isolation from related ideas such as the equivalence of fractions (Streefland, 1985). Furthermore, given children's early intuitive understanding of ratio and proportion, it would appear that the introduction of these concepts is being left too late. We need to build on this initial understanding and explore the ideas of ratio and proportion as natural extensions of children's experiences with both whole and rational numbers. Fractions can be explored before proportion, because each fraction entails only a binary relations. Fractions are the building blocks for proportions.

The use of ratio tables (Streefland, 1985) can contribute to this development. For example, consider a recipe example (cf. Hart, 1981) where two stock cubes are needed to make soup for four people. To find how many cubes are needed for 16 people, we can construct a ratio table as follows:

| soup cubes | 2 | 4 | 6 | 8 |
| people | 4 | 8 | 12 | 16 |

A table of this nature provides an effective means of organizing the problem data and enables children to detect more readily all of the relations displayed, both within and between, the series. It is important that children do not just focus on the additive relations within each series. Cases in which each series does not entail equal increments from one number to the next, such as 2, 5, 7, 12 and 4, 10, 14, 24, should be included. Another benefit of such a table is that it serves as a permanent record of proportion as an equivalence relation and, in this way, can contribute to children's acquisition of the correct concept. The table is also seen as a unifying model for a variety of ratio contexts and can assist children in discovering and applying properties that characterize ratio-preserving mappings.

One of the findings of Lamon's (1993b) study was that children's conceptual and procedural competencies were greater than their symbolic ability. Because the students did not use the traditional symbolism for a proportion, their prior knowledge and general problem-solving skills enabled them to generate creative solutions to problems involving ratio and proportion. Indeed, children should be encouraged to find their own ways of solving such problems prior to being introduced to formal symbolism. Included here should be examples in which ratio and proportion occur in a wide variety of everyday contexts. Such contexts serve a dual role: they can act as both a source for concept development and as a domain for applying these concepts.

SUMMARY

The points we raised in this chapter may be summarzied as follows:

1. The syntax of algebra opens up a new area of learning. Students must now deal with the use of letters, a different notation and convention system, an emphasis on the manipulation of terms, and the simplification of algebraic expressions.

2. The semantic aspect of algebra is an equally important component for students. They must understand what algebraic statements represent and why certain transformations can be made on these statements. This requires an understanding of the structural properties of mathematical operations and relations.

3. Students' difficulties with algebra include: an inadequate model of a variable, problems in handling the inconsistencies between arithmetic and algebraic conventions, a failure to perceive algebra as generalized arithmetic, a lack of understanding of the semantics of algebra, the use of inappropriate arithmetic and algebraic analogies, and a lack of strategic knowledge in solving algebraic problems.

4. Arithmetic can serve as an effective analog for algebraic learning. However, there are inconsistencies between the two domains that need to be addressed in the curriculum.

5. Students have been observed to progress through a number of stages in their development of a mental model of a variable. These stages range from simply assigning any numerical value to a letter, to the most sophisticated interpretation where a variable is seen as representing a range of unspecified values and defined by its relation to other terms in an expression.

6. Instruction which addresses the development of appropriate analogies between arithmetic and algebraic models, as well as between related algebraic models, can foster structural understandings. Students also need to be made aware of the goal hierarchies in algebraic tasks and given assistance in developing strategies for working through these.

7. An ability to interpret and understand the mathematical relations in algebraic word problems is a significant component of students' development. The construction of an appropriate problem-situation model which informs and constrains the formal expressions required for solution is crucial here.

8. Proportional reasoning entails reasoning about the four-way relations between two rational expressions such as ratios, rates, quotients, and fractions.

9. Three different types of problem situations have been used to assess students' proportional reasoning, namely, numerical comparison, missing value, and qualitative prediction and comparison.

10. Proportional reasoning involves not only being able to set up and solve a proportion, but also to discriminate proportional from nonproportional situations and to recognize structural similarity. It also involves recognizing the invariance of certain types of transformations on mathematical objects, whether these transformations be qualitative or quantitative.

8

PROBLEM SOLVING, PROBLEM POSING, AND MATHEMATICAL THINKING

Solving a problem means finding a way out of a difficulty, a way around an obstacle, attaining an aim which was not immediately attainable.
—Polya, 1962, p. v

Problem solving was selected as the major focus of mathematics education for the 1980s (National Council of Teachers of Mathematics, 1980). This was largely a reaction to the failure of the back-to-basics movement of the 1970s. With the emphasis on rote mechanical skills during that decade, students were given little opportunity to engage in problem solving and reasoning. As a result, they performed poorly in these areas and, furthermore, did not demonstrate significant improvements in the basic skills. The decade of the 1980s was thus pronounced the era of problem solving.

There are mixed views however, on the success of this problem-solving decade. Schoenfeld (1992) remarked that the rhetoric of problem solving is more prevalent than its substance, with the terms *problem solving*, and *metacognition* being the "two most overworked and least understood buzzwords of the 1980s" (p. 336). Likewise, Stanic and Kilpatrick (1988) claimed that the term *problem solving* has become "a slogan encompassing different views of what education is, of what schooling is, of what mathematics is, and of why we should teach mathematics in general and problem solving in particular" (p. 1).

On the positive side however, the last decade has made us more knowledgeable about the nature of mathematical learning, thinking, and problem solving. It has also left us with multiple meanings for these terms. In the first section of this chapter, we review some of the different perspectives on the nature of problem solving, problem posing, and mathematical thinking. We then review the key cognitive factors involved in mathematical problem solving and posing. To illustrate how these components operate, we consider some studies addressing children's solutions to novel combinatorial and deductive reasoning problems. We conclude the chapter with a discussion on instructional issues.

PERSPECTIVES ON PROBLEM SOLVING, PROBLEM POSING, AND MATHEMATICAL THINKING

Traditionally, problem solving has not been seen as a goal in itself, but as a means of achieving other goals, such as providing practice on a newly taught mathematical procedure. Such routine sets of exercises provided little scope for any divergent or creative thinking. In more recent times, the notion of problem solving has expanded to encompass problem posing, mathematical thinking, and reasoning in novel contexts.

Problem posing is an important companion to problem solving and lies at the heart of mathematical activity (Kilpatrick, 1987a). As Moses, Bjork, and Goldenberg (1990) remarked, "We learn mathematics particularly well when we are actively engaged in creating not only the solution strategies but the problems that demand them" (p. 90). Furthermore, wherever a problem originates, the problem solver is always obliged to reformulate it (Kilpatrick, 1987a). Despite its role in children's problem-solving development, problem posing is significantly underrepresented in both the research and curriculum domains. Little attention has been given to children's ability to solve open-ended problems or to generate their own problems to solve (Kilpatrick, 1987a; Silver & Mamona, 1989a, 1989b).

The importance of problem solving and reasoning is evident in the goals for mathematics education articulated by the Curriculum and Evaluation Standards for School Mathematics (National Council of Teachers of Mathematics, 1989). Of their five goals, two relate to problem solving and reasoning. The *Standards* considers mathematical reasoning to be fundamental to knowing and doing mathematics. The ultimate aim is for students to gain "mathematical power." This refers to an individual's abilities to "explore, conjecture, and reason logically, as well as the ability to use a variety of mathematical methods effectively to solve nonroutine problems" (National Council of Teachers of Mathematics, p. 5).

The increased focus on mathematical thinking and reasoning reflects changing views on what consitutes mathematics and mathematics learning. The traditional focus has been on the mastery of mathematics content comprising facts, rules, and procedures. When problem solving is characterized by sets of routine exercises in which there is only one right way to solve a given problem, students adopt the view that mathematics requires one to have a ready-made solution procedure and that such a procedure should produce an answer as efficiently as possible (Schoenfeld, 1988, 1989). The current focus has moved away from this content perspective to one of process. Although not denying the importance of domain knowledge, students need to acquire the mathematical modes of thinking that will enable them to utilize this knowledge effectively.

There are differing opinions, however, on what consititutes mathematical thinking. The National Research Council (1989) referred to "modeling, abstraction, optimization, logical analysis, inference from data, and use of symbols" in its discussion on mathematical modes of thought (p. 31). An alternative perspective is given by Schoenfeld (1992), where learning to think mathematically means "developing a mathematical point of view." This involves "developing competence with the tools of the trade, and using these tools in the service of the goal of understanding structure—mathematical sense making" (Schoenfeld, in press). In a similar vein, Greeno (1992) perceived mathematical and scientific thinking to be "activities in which concepts and methods of a mathematical or scientific discipline are used in understanding, including understanding involved in solving a problem" (p. 41).

Burton (1984, 1992) adopted a somewhat broader perspective on mathematical thinking. She preferred to use the term, *thinking mathematically*, in preference to *mathematical thinking*, which she claimed is usually interpreted in terms of the content of mathematics (e.g., thinking about patterns and relationships in the number system). Thinking mathematically is seen as "the style of processing which supports an enquiry which might ultimately lead to the learning of some mathematics but equally might lead to learning in other subject areas" (p. 58). The processes that Burton claimed constitute mathematical thinking, especially for young children, include strategies such as classifying, ordering, enumerating, testing, conjecturing, and generalizing.

We return to this important area of mathematical thinking when we consider a number of higher order thinking skills that play a significant role in problem solving/posing and in mathematics learning in general.

COGNITIVE COMPONENTS OF MATHEMATICAL PROBLEM SOLVING

Although different terminology may be used, there nevertheless appears to be general agreement on the broad aspects of cognition that play a critical role in mathematical problem solving. We address these here in terms of problem models (mental models comprising problem representation and problem-solving heuristics), strategic processes (goal-directed operations to facilitate problem solution), metaprocesses (comprising analogical reasoning, higher order thinking skills, and metacognitive processes), and affective models (beliefs, attitudes, and emotions). These components are represented in diagrammatic form in Fig. 8.1. We review each of these components in turn, and consider ways in which they interact to facilitate problem solution.

Problem Models: Problem Representation and Knowledge of Heuristics

Problem Representation. We addressed the role of mental models in representing computational problems in chapters 5 to 7. In this section we focus specifically on their role in formulating and solving novel problems.

Recall that mental models are representations that are active while solving a particular problem and that provide the workspace for inference and mental operations (Halford, 1993). During problem solving, learners modify or extend their existing mental models by connecting new information to their present knowledge structures and constructing new relationships among those structures (Silver & Marshall, 1990). We elaborate on this process in a subsequent section.

The type of mental models that we construct profoundly influences the expectations we have about the world, the way we go about solving problems, and the way we acquire new knowledge. To illustrate the way in which mental models influence our ability to solve problems, we consider the well-known problem about the car and the bird:

> A car makes a journey from town A to town B, 100 miles apart, and travels at 25 miles per hour. At the moment the car leaves A, a bird leaves B, flies towards the car at 50 miles per hour and, on reaching the car, returns to B. Then it flies out to meet the car again, returns to B, and so on until the car reaches B. How far does the bird fly?

Attempts to solve the problem by calculating the time of each out-and-return journey, then summing the times, leads to a very complex series, with cumbersome calculations. A more effective problem-situation model is to realize that, since the car will take 4 hours to travel from A to B, and the bird flies at 50 miles per hour, then the bird flies 200 miles.

The importance of effective mental models has been emphasized in numerous studies of expert problem solvers. One of the most commonly cited examples is the knowledge representation of expert chess players (Chase & Chi, 1981; Chase & Simon, 1973; deGroot, 1965;). They demon-

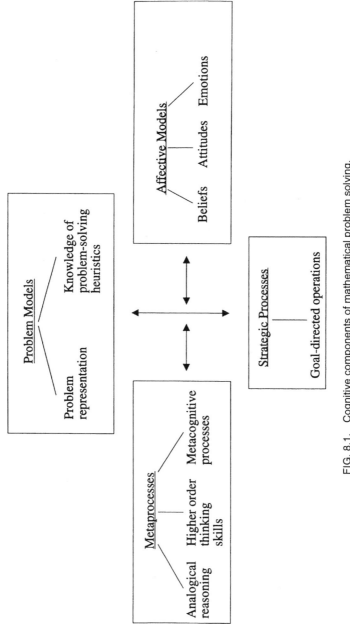

FIG. 8.1. Cognitive components of mathematical problem solving.

strate superior performance because of their ability to rapidly recognize meaningful patterns on the chess board.

Highly competent problem solvers in the scientific domain develop mental models that focus on the principles of the domain, rather than on the superficial features of the problem (Larkin, McDermott, Simon, & Simon, 1980; Silver & Marshall, 1990). These experts spend a proportionately greater amount of time than novices in building this principled representation before they implement their solution plan. In contrast, novices form a problem-situation model that is more loosley organized and lacking in information about related principles and their application (Chi, Glaser, & Rees, 1982; Lesgold, 1988). Their models reflect a superficial understanding of the problem and largely comprise the data of their problem-text model (the model formed from their initial reading of the problem text). Novices in the scientific domain also frequently construct explanations for commonly observed phenomena that are inconsistent with formal, scientific theories (McCloskey, 1983).

Silver's (1979) study also documented the superior mental representations of effective problem solvers. Junior high school students were asked to sort a set of 24 mathematics problems into groups of problems that were mathematically related. He found that the more successful students were those who sorted the problems on the basis of their underlying similarities in mathematical structure. The less successful students relied on surface similarities in problem setting or context or on the nature of the question being asked in the problem. Silver and Marshall (1990) concluded that successful students search for, and find, structural information in their problem-solving experiences, whereas unsuccessful students do not.

As we have shown, the adequacy of the problem-situation model largely determines problem-solving success. The formation of this model may be likened to the first stage of Polya's (1957) four-phase guide for solving problems, namely, understand the problem. It follows that students who do not understand a given problem fail to construct an adequate problem-situation model and hence do not solve the problem. The second and third phases of Polya's model, namely, devise a plan and carry it out, require students to draw upon specific problem-solving heuristics.

Problem-Solving Heuristics.   Polya (1957) is usually given credit for demonstrating the value of specific problem-solving heuristics. There are a large number of heuristics that appear in problem-solving texts, including techniques such as drawing a diagram, making a physical model of the problem, making a table of facts, looking for a pattern, guessing and checking, thinking of a related problem, and solving a simpler problem. These heuristic processes do not guarantee a correct solution. However they may suggest useful directions in which the solution might proceed (Silver & Marshall, 1990).

Research addressing the effects of instruction in the use of heuristics has presented mixed results. In a compilation of dissertation studies in problem solving during the 1970s, Harvey and Romberg (1980) noted that the teaching of problem-solving strategies was "promising" but had yet to produce overall significant results. In a more recent meta-analysis of experiments and relational studies in problem solving, Hembree (1992) found that students who were taught to use heuristics displayed higher scores than students who simply practiced problems.

Hembree's analysis of studies, which focused on only a limited number of specific heuristics, found that instruction in using diagrams and translating verbal statements yielded the greatest mean effects on problem-solving performance. However, this only occurred when explicit training was given; without direct intervention and teacher oversight, practice in using these skills did not produce better performance. Providing children with physical materials to use in modeling problems also produced large gains in performance. These findings highlight the importance of helping children form an effective problem-situation model from the outset. The construction of a diagram or physical model of the problem is particularly worthwhile here because it can help the student represent the explicit relations in the problem and subsequently recognize the implied relationships. Furthermore, these visual records can overcome processing limitations in dealing with several relations at once (Bauer & Johnson-Laird, 1993).

Hembree further noted that instruction in handling extraneous data produced a large effect, whereas more modest effects were identified for instruction in guess-and-check procedures, in composing original problems, in verbalizing concepts, and in improving mathematics vocabulary. His analysis also indicated that simultaneous instruction in multiple skills appears less effective than instruction in a particular skill.

Instructing students in the use of heuristic processes without attending also to domain-general processes is inadequate (Lester, 1989). Having a knowledge of heuristics is of little avail if students are not discriminatory in their use of these, if they do not monitor their application, and do not reflect on the results of their actions. We address the important role played by such metaprocesses in a subsequent section. We turn now to a consideration of the strategic processes that facilitate problem solution.

Strategic Processes

Although there are diverse opinions on what constitutes a strategy (Bisanz & LeFevre, 1990), there is nevertheless some agreement on its key features. It is usually accepted that strategies are "goal-directed operations employed to facilitate task performance" (Harnishfeger & Bjorklund, 1990, p. 1). They are frequently seen as domain specific (Pressley, Borkowski, & Schneider,

1987) and designed to facilitate both knowledge acquisition and utilization (Prawat, 1989). Some view strategies as necessarily involving a choice of procedures (Siegler & Jenkins, 1989), with the procedure being invoked in a "flexible, goal-directed manner ... that influences the selection and implementation of subsequent procedures" (Bisanz & LeFevre, 1990, p. 236). Procedures that create new procedures or alter old ones in flexible ways are also considered strategic (Bisanz & LeFevre, 1990). There are others who emphasize the "potentially conscious and controllable" nature of strategies (Bjorklund, Muir-Broaddus, & Schneider, 1990; Pressley et al., 1987), as well as the dynamic interaction of strategies, one's knowledge of the strategies, and one's monitoring of their implementation (Pressley, Forrest-Pressley, Elliott-Faust, & Miller, 1985).

Research in the last decade has presented convincing evidence that children behave strategically, are able to direct their own learning, and acquire a knowledge of the domain in which they are working (e.g., DeLoache, Sugarman, & Brown, 1985; English, 1991a; Gelman & Brown, 1986; Gelman & Greeno, 1989; Karmiloff-Smith, 1984). For children to behave strategically in solving problems, they must first realize that their actions influence their progress toward a goal and then keep the goal in mind as they solve the problem. As children become more aware of the outcomes of their actions in problem-solving situations, they give more attention to the behaviors they use to achieve the goal. This results in enhanced awarenesss of the connection between their actions and the goal. As this awareness improves, children will be more likely to monitor their progress towards the goal, resulting in heightened consciousness of their actions and increased effectiveness of their strategy (Bjorklund & Harnishfeger, 1990).

The work of DeLoache et al. (1985), involving children's free play with a set of nested cups, indicated that children progress from trial-and-error behavior to a careful consideration of the relationships among elements of the problem as a whole. Other studies have revealed this general progression from immature to mature activities, where children create and modify solutions, detect and correct their errors, and develop more mature strategies on their own own (e.g., Burton, 1992; Gelman & Brown, 1986; Karmiloff-Smith, 1979). This progression reflects "a general learning mechanism" that characterizes cross-age descriptions of children's initial attacks on a problem (Gelman & Brown, 1986, p. 188). This general learning mechanism becomes increasingly effective with age, due mainly to underlying changes in children's knowledge base, their processing efficiency, and their self-monitoring skills (e.g., Bjorklund & Harnishfeger, 1990; A. L. Brown & Kane, 1988). We address these monitoring processes during the course of the next section.

Metaprocesses

Analogical Reasoning.   In 1954, Polya produced a volume on the use of analogy and induction in mathematics. Although he demonstrated how analogies can provide a fertile source of new problems and can enhance problem-solving performance, his ideas on analogy were not as widely adopted as some of his other work, largely because they were descriptive rather than prescriptive (Schoenfeld, 1992). More recent studies however, have given greater attention to analogical reasoning in problem solving and transfer, particularly within the context of science (e.g., Clement, 1993; Duit, 1991; Gentner & Gentner, 1983; Stavy & Tirosh, 1993), cognitive science, and cognitive development (e.g., Halford, 1992, 1993; Holyoak, 1985; Robins & Mayer, 1993). Several studies have also addressed analogical reasoning in mathematical problem solving (e.g., Catrambone & Holyoak, 1990; Novick, 1992; Novick & Holyoak, 1991; Reed, 1987). However, the research in the mathematical domain is in its infancy and has been confined mainly to algebraic and general problems solved by high school and university students.

Analogical reasoning plays a significant role in students' construction of ideas during problem solving. As we mentioned in the last chapter, the ability to access a known problem (base or source problem) that has an identical goal structure to the new problem to be solved (target problem) can enhance problem-solving performance (Holyoak & Koh, 1987; Novick, 1988, 1992; Novick & Holyoak, 1991). This analogical transfer involves constructing a mapping between elements in the base and target problems, and adapting the solution model from the base problem to account for the unique aspects of the target problem (i.e., those not shared with the source problem; Novick, 1992). However as Novick pointed out, it will only make sense to adapt the solution from the source problem into a similar procedure

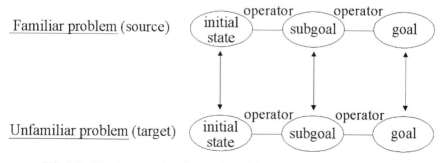

FIG. 8.2.   Structure-mapping diagram for solving analogous problems. From Halford (1993). © 1993 by Lawrence Erlbaum Associates. Reprinted by permission.

for solving the target problem if a sufficiently detailed and coherent mapping is constructed between the elements of the two problems, that is, if the two problems are very similar structurally. The adaptation process is considered important, because transfer of the solution from the source to target problem is not a natural consequence of a successful mapping (Holyoak, Novick, & Melz, 1994; Novick & Holyoak, 1991). Mapping and adaptation are thus viewed as separate components of analogical transfer in the solution of complex arithmetic word problems, with adaptation being a major source of difficulty (Novick & Holyoak, 1991).

We can represent the use of analogy in problem solving by a conventional structure-mapping diagram (Halford, 1993) as shown in Fig. 8.2. The source is the problem-solving process used previously on a now-familiar problem. The elements of the structure-mapping are states and goals, and the relations are operators that effect changes from the initial state to one or more subgoals and then to the final goal. The target is a novel problem. The use of analogical reasoning entails mapping the states, goals, and operators of the novel problem into the familiar one.

Before children can make use of analogical transfer, however, they must notice the correspondence between the target problem and the base problem and retrieve the base in terms of its generalizable structure (Gholson, Morgan, Dattel, & Pierce, 1990). Studies have shown though, that novice problem solvers often have difficulty in detecting structural similarities between problems that have different surface features (Novick, 1988). This is largely because, as we mentioned previously, novices tend to focus on salient surface features such as the specific objects and terms mentioned, rather than the structural features, such as how the entities in the problem are causally interrelated (Chi, Feltovich, & Glaser, 1981; Gholson et al., 1990; Novick, 1988, 1992; Silver, 1981; Stavy & Tirosh, 1993). This means that the surface features in a novice's model of a target problem will likely serve as retrieval cues for a related problem in memory. On the other hand, studies have shown that similarity among surface details, or superficial similarity, promotes "reminding," that is, assists novices to notice a correspondence between their mental model of a base problem and the new target problem (Gentner & Landers, 1985; Reed, 1987; B. H. Ross, 1984, 1987). Although surface similarity can facilitate children's retrieval of the base problem, its usefulness for analogical transfer is governed by their ability to detect the structural correspondences between the base and target problems (Gentner & Landers, 1985).

Although children may be particularly dependent on surface cues for the retrieval of a base problem, there is some evidence that even preschoolers can overcome similarity in appearance in categorizing objects if they are given relevant information, including age-appropriate materials and procedures (Carey, 1985; Gelman & Markman, 1986).

Evidence that children can use analogical transfer in solving more complex problems has been provided in a series of studies by Gholson and his colleagues (Gholson, Eymard, Long, Morgan, & Leeming, 1988; Gholson, Dattel, Morgan, & Eymard, 1989; Pierce & Gholson, 1994). They used the well-known farmer's dilemma, the missionaries and cannibals, and the three-disk tower-of-Hanoi puzzles, together with a number of isomorphs, with children aged 4-10 years. There was a sequence of moves that was common to each type of problem, that can be illustrated with the farmer's dilemma. A farmer has to move a fox, a goose, and some corn in a wagon that will only transport one thing at a time. The problem is to move all three things without ever leaving the fox with the goose, or the goose with the corn, because in either case the former would eat the latter. The solution is to take the goose first, then go back, take the fox, then take the goose back, then take the corn, then go back, then take the goose again. The structure of this task is similar to the tower-of-Hanoi puzzle, in that both involve a sequence of forward and backward moves. Excellent isomorphic transfer was shown, even by the youngest children. Gholson et al. (1989) suggested this might have been because extensive experience with the source tasks gave the children plenty of opportunity to acquire a high quality representation of the source.

The use of analogy can also enhance students' ability to pose new problems (Kilpatrick, 1987a). However, as Kilpatrick (1987a) and Gentner (1982) pointed out, not every analogy is productive. The key to using analogical reasoning in formulating new problems is the ability to "see below the surface of a fuzzy notion of similarity to the relationship that can yield new problems for investigation" (Kilpatrick, 1987a, p. 137). The challenge facing the classroom teacher is to help students develop a constructive attitude towards problem posing, one that encourages them to seek out analogies that might generate interesting new problems. This requires students to be discerning in their selection of analogies and to evaluate the appropriateness and effectiveness of their choice. It is here that students need to utilize their metacognitive processes.

Metacognitive Processes.   The importance of metacognitive processes in mathematical problem solving has been well documented (e.g., Garofalo, Kroll, & Lester, 1987; L. C. Hart, 1993; Lester & Garofalo, 1982; A. Schoenfeld, 1992; Silver, 1985; Silver & Marshall, 1990). Although the notions of monitoring and control have appeared in numerous cognitive models over the past few decades, comparatively little research on these processes has been done in mathematical problem solving.

The plethora of articles addressing metacognition has resulted in numerous interpretations and considerable confusion over what is and what is not metacognitive (Campione, Brown, & Connell, 1989). In his pioneering work, Flavell (1976) emphasized the learner's knowledge about person, task, and strategy variables in order to identify components of metacognitive knowledge that might be relevant to memory. Around the same time, Brown (1978) emphasized the executive aspects of cognition such as planning, monitoring, evaluating, and revising one's thinking. More recent perspectives on the topic usually combine both perspectives into a definition that emphasizes first, knowledge about cognitive states and processes and second, control or executive aspects of metacognition (Campione et al., 1989; Lester, 1989; Paris & Winograd, 1990; Schoenfeld, 1987, 1992). The first component addresses students' conscious and stateable knowledge about cognition, about themselves as learners, about the cognitive resources they have available to them, and about the structure of the domain knowledge with which they are dealing (Campione et al., 1989). The second aspect focuses on students' self-regulation, their monitoring, evaluating, and general orchestration of their own cognitive resources. It also includes students' ability to reflect on their knowledge states and their self-management skills. Schoenfeld (1987) included a third component of metacognition, namely, beliefs and intuitions (e.g., the ideas about mathematics and problem solving that we bring to our work in mathematics and how this shapes the way in which we do mathematics). We will address this third category in the next section.

It is well established that successful students possess powerful strategies for dealing with novel problems, can reflect on their problem-solving actions, and can monitor and regulate those strategies efficiently and effectively (Campione et al., 1989; English, 1992a, 1992c; Flavell, 1979; Lawson, 1990; Peterson, 1988). In her naturalistic studies of elementary mathematics classrooms, Peterson found students' abilities to diagnose and monitor their own understanding to be a significant predictor of their mathematics achievement. Students who were able to provide a good explanation of which particular mathematics problem or lesson component they were unable to understand and why, tended to have significantly higher scores on a test of mathematics achievement. Giving a good explanation of their lack of understanding was also significantly related to students' reported use of specific cognitive strategies, their reports of mathematics concepts and procedures, and their reported checking of their answers against an external criterion.

Positive effects of self-monitoring training have been obtained in intervention studies. In Delclos and Harrington's (1991) study, fifth- and sixth-grade children were given extensive proactive instruction on the content of a computer-based problem-solving game. Children who received both problem-solving and self-monitoring instruction solved more complex problems and took less time to do so than children who were given no training or training in problem solving only.

In another intervention study at the middle-school level, Lester, Garofalo, and Kroll (1989) attempted to foster seventh graders' metacognitive processes in mathematical problem solving. This was accomplished by having the teacher serve as an external monitor during problem-solving sessions. The teacher would also encourage discussion of behaviors considered important for the development of metacognitive processes and would model effective executive behaviors. Lester concluded that metacognitive processes evolve over time in domain-specific contexts and that there exists a dynamic interaction between mathematical concepts and metacognitive processes used to solve problems involving those concepts. The research of English (e.g., 1988, 1992a) also supports this argument as we now indicate.

The research we have cited to date has focused on intervention and naturalistic studies in middle-grade classrooms. Little research appears to have been conducted on young children's use of metacognitive processes in novel mathematical problem solving. Studies by English (e.g., 1988, 1991a, 1992a), however, have demonstrated that 4-to 9-year-olds spontaneously monitor their actions when solving novel, hands-on combinatorial problems.

In these studies, children were individually administered a set of combinatorial problems involving the dressing of toy bears in all possible combinations of colored T-shirts and pants (or identically colored T-shirts and pants comprising varying numbers of buttons for the final two problems). Because the problem domain was novel, the children had to rely on their exisiting informal combinatorial knowledge, together with their metacognitive processes, to solve the problems. Analyses of the children's responses revealed a series of increasingly sophisticated solution strategies (reflecting domain-specific knowledge), plus a number of scanning actions serving primarily in a monitoring capacity (reflecting an application of metacognitive processes). Significant associations were found between children's solution strategies and their scanning actions on each problem, with the children changing the nature of their scanning as they adopted more complex solution strategies.

Because the children initially used trial-and-error strategies to solve the problems, they had to carefully monitor their actions if they were to be successful. These monitoring processes differed in their degree of thoroughness and efficiency and, when coupled with a trial-and-error strategy, determined the extent of problem success. For example, children who used a trial-and-error strategy and checked *only after* they had acted were naturally more error prone and less successful in goal attainment. In contrast, children who checked *prior to acting* or who checked *continuously* throughout problem execution, were less error prone and more successful in solving the problems.

The children's initial monitoring actions may be regarded as compensatory, that is, they compensated for children's lack of efficient domain knowledge (Garner, 1990). From here, children adjusted their monitoring in one

of three main ways. For some children, self-monitoring became unnecessary; they relied on the generative nature of their solution strategy (i.e.,
holding one item constant while systematically varying the others) to secure
goal attainment. They were confident that their strategy would generate the
required solution and hence did not bother to monitor the results of their
actions. Other children changed their monitoring from a compensatory form
to one that regulated procedural implementation rather than goal attainment. That is, their focus of attention was on their pattern of item selection
(i.e., the order in which they chose the T-shirts and pants) rather than on the
uniqueness of the combinations formed. Like the previous group, these
children knew that their strategy would generate problem solution, but they
nevertheless monitored its implementation.

Another group of children displayed highly effective monitoring processes. They monitored both the implementation of their procedure and
their attainment of the problem goal. These particular children were the
most effective problem solvers and were the only ones who could solve a
problem that comprised a hidden constraint on goal attainment. In this
particular problem, each combination of T-shirt and pants had to have a
unique total number of buttons. However, it was possible to form combinations that were different in terms of items, but not in terms of totals (e.g., a 2-
button T-shirt combined with 5-button pants yields the same total as a
3-button T-shirt combined with 4-button pants). No amount of sophisticated
domain knowledge would help those children who did not monitor the
results of their actions.

Higher Order Thinking Skills.   There has been increasing emphasis over
the last decade on the importance of fostering students' higher order thinking
skills in all areas of the curriculum (e.g., Beyer, 1987; Halpern, 1992; Jones &
Idol, 1990; Lesgold, 1988; Paul, 1990; Peterson, 1988; Resnick, 1987b; Splitter,
1988, 1991). As Fennema and Peterson (1985) noted, higher order thinking
skills enable an individual to learn more mathematics, to apply mathematics
to other disciplines, and to solve mathematical problems throughout life.

It is not an easy task to define these thinking skills. Several interpretations exist, ranging from the idea that higher order thinking "includes all
tasks that call for more than information retrieval" to specific intellectual
processes that are unique to particular domains (e.g., the use of approriate
rhetorical structure in written composition) (Baker, 1991). There is some
concern however, over the use of the term, *higher order.* It can be misleading
in that it implies that such skills can only be addressed after "lower order"
facts and skills have been mastered (Lesh, 1991). However as Resnick
(1987) stressed, higher order thinking is the "hallmark of successful learning
at all levels—not only the advanced (levels)" (p. 45). Likewise, Splitter
(1991) contended that thinking skills are basic because they are the founda-

tion of all disciplines and subject domains. We agree with these sentiments and refer to such thinking skills as "higher order" only in an effort to highlight the important role they play in mathematical problem solving and learning. Indeed, a failure to address these so-called higher order thinking skills in the course of developing basic skills may be a major source of learning difficulties in elementary mathematics.

In an effort to clarify the nature of these skills, we refer to the features that Resnick (1987) cited as suggestive of higher order thinking:

> Higher order thinking involves a cluster of elaborative mental activities requiring nuanced judgment and analysis of complex situations according to multiple criteria. Higher order thinking is effortful and depends on self-regulation. The path of action or correct answers are not fully specified in advance. The thinker's task is to construct meaning and impose structure on situations rather than to expect to find them already apparent. (p. 44)

Splitter (1988) was more explicit in defining what he considers to be some of the features that exemplify an adequate list of thinking competencies:

> It must reflect the extraordinary flexibility of the human mind by incorporating such diverse areas as inference and consistency, formulating questions and active listening, identifying assumptions and predicting consequences, understanding cause and effect, constructing hypotheses and criteria, using analogies, resolving problems and dilemmas, understanding the nature of value judgements, suggesting alternatives and possibilities, and thinking creatively and imaginatively. (p. 40)

There is a plethora of texts addressing a wide range of thinking skills and the many ways in which these might be taught (e.g., Beyer, 1987; Brandt, 1989; Costa & Lowery, 1989; Nickerson, Perkins, & Smith, 1985; Halpern, 1992; Narode, Heiman, Lochhead, & Slomianko, 1987; Norris & Ennis, 1989). It is generally assumed that students can learn to recognize and use these thinking skills appropriately, and when they do so, should become more effective thinkers (Halpern, 1992). It is beyond the scope of this book to address the range of thinking skills and programs cited in the literature. Rather, we cite a selection of thinking skills and processes that we consider to be essential to mathematical learning and problem solving/posing. We divide these into two broad strands: modes of thinking and reasoning, and modes of communicating.

Modes of Thinking and Reasoning.   We include the following skills in this category and define each in turn:

- flexible and creative thinking

- inductive and deductive reasoning
- spatial and visual thinking, and pattern perception
- critical thinking

Students often have difficulty in considering alternative points of view or in dealing with several sources of information at once (Costa & Lowery, 1989). Being flexible in one's thinking is particularly important in problem solving. By changing their point of view, or by examining a problem from more than one perspective, students can avoid the tunnel vision syndrome and are less likely to get "bogged down" in solving a problem. Flexible thinking is also a necessary component of creative thinking. This includes applying novel and original ideas to the solution of a problem, as well as generating a number of different solutions to an open-ended problem (English, 1986, 1990b, 1990c).

Induction and deduction play a significant role in problem solving and in mathematics learning in general (National Council of Teachers of Mathematics, 1989). Induction involves drawing inferences in order to generate hypotheses that extend our knowledge (Holyoak & Nisbett, 1988). Induction is often used to solve a problem, often through the use of analogical reasoning. As we indicated earlier, analogical reasoning is a powerful means of problem solving/posing and mathematics learning in general.

Deduction is a systematic process in which the goal is to draw a valid consequence from given statements. Deductive reasoning is fundamental to many tasks. For example, deduction is used to interpret and formulate instructions, plans of action, rules, and general principles. It is also used to assess data, to determine the consequences of assumptions and hypotheses, and to decide between competing ideas. Deductive reasoning is the method by which the validity of a mathematical assertion is established (National Council of Teachers of Mathematics, 1989). In essence, "a world without deduction would be a world without science, technology, laws, social conventions, and culture" (Johnson-Laird & Byrne, 1991, p. 3).

The significant contribution of spatial thinking to mathematical performance is well documented (e.g., Kirshner, 1989b; Koltz, 1991; National Council of Teachers of Mathematics, 1989; Presmeg, 1992; Tarte, 1990). Spatial thinking may be viewed in terms of two distinct components, namely spatial visualization and spatial orientation (Tarte, 1990). Spatial visualization involves the skill of mentally manipulating, rotating, twisting, or inverting a pictorially presented stimulus object. By contrast, spatial orientation involves the skill of understanding a representation or comprehending a change that has taken place between two representations. Effective spatial thinkers are better able to interpret, visualize, construct, transform, and classify geometric shapes, patterns, and diagrams.

Being able to identify, analyze, describe, and generalize patterns is fundamental to mathematical problem solving and to mathematics learning in general. As with deduction, it is difficult to imagine a world without patterns. Relating patterns in numbers, geometry, and measurement helps children understand connections among mathematical topics. These connections foster the type of mathematical thinking that serves as a foundation for more abstract mathematical ideas (National Council of Teachers of Mathematics, 1989). *patterns are abstractions*

Critical thinking takes place within a problem-solving context and may be defined as reasonable and reflective thinking that is focussed upon deciding what to believe or do (Norris & Perkins, 1989). Such thinking incorporates aspects of metacognition that we examined in the previous section. Effective problem solvers are reflective in their actions and focussed in their thinking, that is, their thinking is consciously directed towards the goal in question and the appropriateness of their actions.

Critical thinking involves making inferences based on the problem data and one's existing knowledge and judging the soundness of these inferences. It also involves the ability to maintain clarity (Norris & Perkins, 1989). That is, one must clearly determine which questions are being asked, what data are to be used, what assumptions might exist, and what decision is to be reached. Unfortunately, these important critical thinking skills are often not evident in students' behavior (Byrnes, 1993).

Modes of Communicating. Greeno (1992) maintained that several important features of mathematical or scientific thinking are evident in students' ability to participate in mathematical or scientific discourse. Such discourse involves ways of formulating conjectures, claims, and counterclaims, and ways of supporting conclusions. Learning to participate in the discourse of a discipline is considered a major aspect of learning in that discipline (Pea & Greeno, 1990). Students can be involved in conversations where they offer their understandings of a question or idea, discuss each others' views and identify the assumptions that underlie alternative opinions, and work to resolve conflicts of opinion.

Developing a classroom "community of inquiry" (Sharp, 1987; Splitter, 1988) can foster the development of mathematical communication. Here, students identify, discover, and invent questions and problems and, in so doing, engage in self-corrective inquiry through explicit metacognitive behavior. Engaging in higher order thinking with others can help students realize that they have "the ability, the permission, and even the obligation" to be critial in their thinking, to not always accept a given problem formulation, and to challenge an accepted position (Resnick, 1987b, p. 41). The dialogue or "connected talking" among students (and the teacher) can become the primary tool for constructing mathematical and scientific ideas, thoughts, and opinions (Splitter, 1988, p. 45). We revisit these ideas in the final section of this chapter.

Affective Models

We conclude this section on the cognitive components of mathematical problem solving with a consideration of students' affective models. Given that there is a vast literature on students' (and teachers') beliefs in, and attitudes towards, mathematical problem solving and mathematics in general, we will offer only a brief review here. We refer the reader to additional sources such as Schoenfeld (1985a, 1987, 1992), McLeod (1985, 1992), and McLeod & Adams (1989).

As a result of instruction, many students develop erroneous beliefs about the nature of mathematics that can have a strong negative effect on their mathematical behavior (Schoenfeld, 1987). A commonly held view is that "ordinary" students cannot expect to understand mathematics and must therefore resort to memorization techniques and mechanized procedures in solving mathematics problems (Lampert, 1990). Mathematics is perceived as a closed subject where there is only one (right) answer and only one way of getting it, and where divergent thinking is unnecessary (Carpenter, Lindquist, Matthews, & Silver, 1983; Lampert, 1990; Silver & Marshall, 1990). Solving problems in school is seen as a solitary activity and unrelated to solving problems in the real world. It is believed that a solution should depend on recently taught techniques and that every problem should conform to some model that has been taught previously (Silver & Marshall, 1990). There is also the commonly held view that all problems can be solved in less than 10 minutes, with the result that students do not devote the required time to problem formulation and solution (Schoenfeld, 1987; Lampert, 1990). Other students display greater concern for the way in which they record their problem-solving responses than for the appropriateness of these responses or for their level of understanding of a problem.

Beliefs about one's self also have a significant impact on students' mathematical performance. These beliefs are related to the metacognitive components of self-regulation and self-awareness that we addressed earlier. Results from the National Assessment data (Dossey, Mullis, Lindquist, & Chambers, 1988) revealed a decline in students' levels of confidence in mathematics as they progress through school. Substantial gender differences have also been widely recorded (e.g., Leder, 1992; Meyer & Fennema, 1988). In general, females tend to be less confident than males even when their performance indicates they should be more confident. Females are also less likely than males to attribute their success in mathematics to ability; females see their success as the result of extra effort. Males tend to attribute their failures to a lack of effort more than females do (McLeod, 1992).

Other components of students' affective models include their attitudes towards mathematics and mathematical problem solving and their emotional reactions to these domains. Research on students' attitudes has been extensive, whereas studies examining their emotional responses to mathematics have been less prominent. In general, there is a positive correlation between attitude and achievement (Dossey et al., 1988; Foxman, Martini, & Mitchell, 1982), with a decline in positive attitudes towards mathematics as children progress through the grades. Peterson's (1988) research indicated that students with positive attitudes may persist longer in the face of weak understanding than their counterparts with negative attitudes.

McLeod (1992) reported on a selection of the few studies that have addressed emotional responses to mathematics. For example, Wagner, Rachlin, & Jensen (1984) found that algebra students who experienced difficulties would sometimes become upset and would grab at any response that would get them past the blockage, no matter how irrational that response might be. More positive responses have been documented on students' satisfaction in mathematical problem solving (the "Aha!" experience; Mason, Burton, & Stacey, 1982) and on moments of insight when children see the connections between important ideas (Lawler, 1981).

This ability to draw connections between ideas is an important component of problem solving (R. B. Davis, 1984; English, 1994; Maher & Martino, 1991). In the next section we illustrate how elementary school children achieve this during the course of solving novel combinatorial and deductive reasoning problems. We focus here on children's use of strategic processes and their application of metaprocesses in constructing mental models of these domains.

Children's Models and Processes in Solving Novel Combinatorial and Deductive Reasoning Problems

Children's Construction of Mathematical Models During Problem Solving. Children's construction of mathematical ideas during problem solving is reflected in their strategy development as they attempt to master a challenging problem situation (English, 1992a, 1994; Ericsson & Oliver, 1988; Martino & Maher, 1991). Children are thought to cycle through various steps as they build representations of those situations (R. B. Davis, 1984). As we have mentioned previously, children must first examine the problem for cues or clues that might guide the retrieval from memory of a relevant mental model of a related problem or situation. After retrieving a model that might be useful in solving or in trying to solve the problem, children attempt to map the model onto the problem data. If the mapping appears adequate, that is, if there is a correspondence between the elements of the mental model and

the problem, the model can be used to commence the solution
owever, retrieving an appropriate mental model may not be
automatic or easy for children, especially when the problem presents a novel
situation. Children's attempts at making a suitable mapping may involve
rejecting, modifying, or extending the retrieved model or perhaps replacing
it with another model. This necessitates frequent checking of the correspondence between the model and the problem data. When a suitable mental
model of the problem situation has been constructed, other techniques (e.g.,
setting subgoals) may be brought into play to assist in the solution process. As
children progress on the problem, they may recycle through the previous
steps in an effort to construct a more powerful model of the problem situation
and its solution process. This construction process is considered responsible
for children's development of new mathematical ideas.

Children's use of metaprocesses that we reviewed earlier play a significant role in this knowledge construction (Alexander & Judy, 1988; English,
1992a; Kuhn, Amsel, & O'Loughlin, 1988). As we mentioned previously, the
process of knowledge construction and the application of appropriate
metaprocesses are seen to occur simultaneously during the problem-solving
episode, with the nature of their interaction determining the extent of goal
attainment. The fact that, in the absence of instruction, children do modify
their ideas and actions in their efforts to solve a novel problem highlights the
important contribution of these processes (Kuhn & Phelps, 1982; Kuhn et
al., 1988; Pressley, Borkowski, & Schneider, 1987). Through problem experience, children acquire not only knowledge about the particular problem
domain, but also knowledge about their own strategies as they apply to the
problem.

We now illustrate some of these points in our analysis of children's
responses to novel combinatorial and deductive problems.

---

1. Tim has a green bucket, a red bucket, and a blue bucket. He also has
an orange spade, a purple spade, and a blue spade. How many different
spade and bucket sets can he make?

2. Marianne has a yellow T-shirt and a white T-shirt. She also has a
green skirt and a red skirt. With these, she can wear orange sandals or
blue sandals. How many different outfits can she make with these items?

3. The Select-A-Card company plans to make new boxes of greeting cards.
In each box there will be greeting cards that are:
    either GREEN or YELLOW, and have
    either CHRISTMAS greetings or BIRTHDAY greetings or EASTER
    greetings, and have either GOLD LETTERING or SILVER LETTERING.
How many different greeting cards will there be in each box?

FIG. 8.3. Written combinatorial problems.

Studies of Children's Combinatorial and Deductive Reasoning. The studies we address in this section utilized problems involving combinatorial and deductive reasoning, these being significant components of mathematical thinking (English, 1988, 1991b, 1992a, 1993a, 1993b, 1994) The problems incorporated both "hands-on" and written examples and represented novel situations for the elementary school children participating in the studies. Because the children lacked a knowledge of these domains, they had to make considerable use of various metaprocesses.

Approximately 420 children, ranging in age from 4 to 12 years, have been involved in the studies. The problems have been presented to the children on an individual basis but could be administered easily in group situations within the classroom context. The children were not given any assistance in solving the problems and had not been taught previously how to solve them. Where appropriate, children were asked to describe or explain their actions.

The hands-on combinatorial problems required children to dress toy bears in all possible combinations of colored tops and pants (two-dimensional examples, $X \times Y$) or colored tops, pants, and tennis rackets (three-dimensional examples, $X \times Y \times Z$). The bears were made of thin wood and were placed on a stand so that the children could see clearly their completed combinations. Several variations of these problems, including the addition of hidden constraints on goal attainment, have been incorporated in the

---

Hands-on deductive reasoning problem

Here are some playing cards. Follow the clues to see how you are to arrange the cards in front of you.

* The jack is immediately to the right of the queen.
* The king is to the right of the ace.
* The queen is somewhere between the ten and the ace.
* The ten is immediately to the left of the queen.

Four famous people entered a television studio. One was a tennis player, one was a swimmer, one was a golfer, and the other was a chess player. Use the clues to find out who played what sport:
* Mr. Bowler is not good at chess.
* Both Mr. Big's and Ms. Ace's sports involve a ball.
* Ms. Fish can't swim at all.
* Neither Ms. Ace nor Ms. Fish play tennis.

FIG. 8.4. Examples of deductive reasoning problems.

studies. The written combinatorial problems were isomorphs of the hands-on examples, as indicated in Fig. 8.3.

The deductive problems also incorporated hands-on problems as well as isomorphic written examples. Samples of these appear in Fig. 8.4.

In the next section, we review the strategies children use in solving the combinatorial problems. These strategies represent the responses of children across all of the studies. We have used tree diagrams to represent these strategies because they provide an effective visual representation of the generation of combinations (DeGuire, 1991; Graham, 1991). Following a review of these strategies, we examine two case studies of children (one low achiever and one high achiever in school mathematics) who participated in one of the recent studies (English, in press).

Children's Combinatorial Strategies.   Children's strategies in solving the two-dimensional and three-dimensional problems reflect three main stages of development, as indicated in Figs. 8.5 and 8.6. The first stage (non-planning) entails random, trial-and-error procedures that are devoid of any global planning components. In the second stage, children display transitional strategies where they adopt an identifiable pattern in their selection of items to combine. However the pattern is not the most efficient for task solution. For the two-dimensional strategies (Fig. 8.5 ii & iii), the pattern is of an alternating or cyclic nature and is usually confined to items of the one type. At the beginning of this transitional stage however, children do not continue their pattern throughout problem execution and revert to a trail-and error approach (as indicated by the final three combinations of Fig. 8.5 ii). The three-dimensional strategies (Fig. 8.6 ii & iii) also display both a systematic and trial-and-error apporach in this transitional phase. We return to these later. In the final phase, children develop "odometer" (or "almost odom-eter") strategies. These are so named because of their similarity to the odometer in a vehicle (English, 1988; Scardamalia, 1977). They are the most efficient for problem solution because of their generative nature, that is, they provide an organizational structure for generating all possible combinations.

These odometer strategies involve the repeated selection of an item (referred to here as, "holding an item constant") and systematically matching it with each of the other, "varying" items. These latter items are varied in a cyclic fashion, as shown in Fig. 8.5 v (X_1 matched with Y_1, Y_2, Y_3, then X_2 matched with Y_1, Y_2, Y_3). In the case of the two-dimensional problems ($X \times Y$) there is only one item to be held constant at any one time, as indicated by items X_{1-3} in Fig. 8.5 v. For the three-dimensional problems however, there are two items (X_{1-2} and Y_{1-3}) that are held constant at any one time. The item that is changed least often (X_{1-2}), that is, the slowest moving dimension, is referred to here as the *major constant item*; the item that is changed more frequently (Y_{1-3}), the faster moving dimension, is termed the *minor constant item* (refer to Fig. 8.6 v).

X_1-Y_1
X_2-Y_2
X_1-Y_2
X_3-Y_1
X_2-Y_3
X_1-Y_3
X_3-Y_2
X_2-Y_1
X_3-Y_3

(i)

Non-planning stage

X_1-Y_1
X_2-Y_2
X_3-Y_3
X_1-Y_3
X_2-Y_1
X_3-Y_2
X_2-Y_3
X_3-Y_1
X_1-Y_2

(ii)

Transitional stage

X_1-Y_1
X_2-Y_2
X_3-Y_2
X_1-Y_2
X_2-Y_2
X_3-Y_1
X_1-Y_3
X_2-Y_1
X_3-Y_2

(iii)

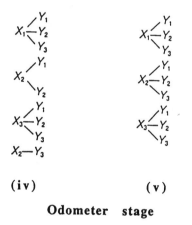

(iv)   **(v)**

Odometer stage

FIG. 8.5. Three stages in children's construction of two-dimensional combinatorial strategies. From English (1993a). © 1993 by National Council of Teachers of Mathematics. Reprinted by permission.

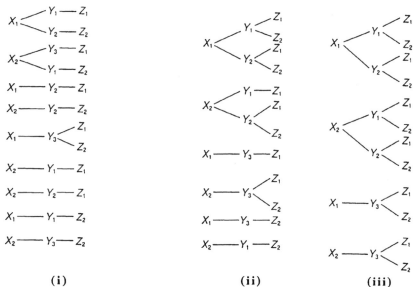

(i)

Non-planning stage

(ii)　　　　(iii)

Transitional stage

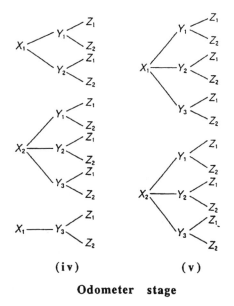

(iv)　　　　(v)

Odometer stage

FIG. 8.6.　Three stages in children's construction of three-dimensional combinatorial strategies. From English (1993a). © 1993 by National Council of Teachers of Mathematics. Reprinted by permission.

The extent to which children exhaust these minor and major items distinguishes the transitional and odometer three-dimensional strategies. In the early transitional phase (Fig. 8.6 ii), children do not exhaust all of the minor constant items but do so later in the phase (Fig. 8.6 iii). They do not exhaust either of the major constant items. In the odometer phase, children initially exhaust only one of the major items, as indicated in Fig. 8.6 iv. They finally master the exhaustion of both constant items, as shown in Fig. 8.6 v. We turn now to our case studies.

James' Development of Combinatorial Models and Processes.   Our first case study, James, age 9 years 4 months, was in his fourth year of elementary school. His school was situated in a middle to upper socioeconomic suburb of a major Australian city. He was considered a high-achieving student in school mathematics. James was administered the written problems prior to the hands-on problems.

Like several of the other high achievers in the larger sample, James did not use any notation to represent his ideas in solving the written problems, preferring instead to determine the combinations mentally. Given the number of combinations to be formed, it is of no surprise that he failed to generate the correct combinations for each of the written problems. His response to the first written combinatorial problem (refer to Fig. 8.3) was as follows: "O.K., let's see. Two. . . . no, that is not exactly right because you can make much more. I like to do these in my head. I'm counting up each one. I'm going 2, 4, like that. Green and orange, red and purple, green and purple, that's 6." When asked how many sets he had made, James repeated his existing sets and then continued to generate a further eight sets, retaining all in memory. Although James applied some general monitoring procedures in an effort to keep track of his combinations, he nevertheless had difficulty in generating all of the possible sets.

James' performance on the remaining two written (3-D) problems was not significantly better, although he did progress towards the transitional stage in the second problem where he exhausted a few of the minor constant items (but not all). He demonstrated quite an amazing mental capacity in his effort to generate and monitor 14 combinations without the aid of notation. Because he duplicated combinations, James produced nearly double the number required. Had he been able to exhaust more of his items, James would have been better able to keep track of his combinations.

James adopted an unusual approach to the third written problem. He read the problem silently to himself, pondered for a few minutes, and then stated: "Forty-nine. I squared it. I counted up each type. I counted up green, yellow, Christmas, birthday, Easter, gold lettering and silver lettering, and I squared it. My answer is forty-nine."

James gave a rather confused reply when asked why he squared the seven, making reference to the previous problem, which he said reminded him of squaring and "square roots." The fact that James linked the squaring of a number with the generation of all possible combinations could mean that he had met the formal combinatorial rule some time in his informal experiences with number (he had not been taught combinatorics in school). However, his mental model of such a rule was clearly erroneous.

James' lack of significant improvement on the second set of problems (dressing the bears) suggests that he simply mapped some of his procedures for solving the written examples onto these hands-on problems, without building on these existing strategies. His strategy for solving the first hands-on problem (3 sets of tops × 3 sets of pants; 9 combinations in all) was basically one of trial-and-error, although there was an emerging awareness of the efficiency of repeating the selection of an item. When asked to explain his strategy for solving this first hands-on problem, James simply recalled his selection of items for the first four combinations. When he reached the fifth outfit (blue top and blue pants), he explained:

> When I got to this one, I thought, O.K., maybe I should just put the whole lot on like a tracksuit. I thought when I got to the fifth one, I thought I might as well not waste my patterns here. I thought I might as well put in a matching thing (pointing to the blue top of the fourth bear) and the same with this one (pointing to the orange pants of the seventh bear and indicating it was also used to dress the sixth bear).... every time I finished one, I'd check up on all the others. If I did find a pattern to be the same, then I'd take that one off and think hard about the next one. You may have noticed when I was stuck a bit, I went like that (putting his hand to his head). I thought of the pattern.

James' reference to a "pattern" in the above explanation involved repeating the selection of an item to generate a new combination. He seemed aware of the need to develop some form of generative procedure, suggesting that he was beginning to construct some knowledge of the combinatorial domain. However he did not build on these ideas as he worked the remaining two problems (3-D examples comprising 8 and 12 combinations respectively). The increase in problem complexity could have been a contributing factor here, although our next case study, Kerry, moved into the final odometer stage on a complex, $2 \times 3 \times 2$ example.

James monitored his actions in the first hands-on problem by checking each combination after he had formed it. He obviously considered it important to use such thorough checking; in fact, without it, he would not have solved the problem. This highlights the important role of metacognitive processes in the absence of a strong body of domain knowledge.

In solving the second hands-on problem (3-D example comprising eight combinations), James again used a trial-and-error approach in forming the first four outfits. He then repeated the selection of two items in forming the fifth and sixth combinations. After the seventh outfit, he stated that he had solved the problem. James' explanation of his strategy was similar to the previous problem and indicated that he was aware of the value of repeating an item selection. However he did not appreciate the need to exhaust an item. When he had difficulty in constructing a new combination, he just looked back at an outfit that he had formed earlier and used it again with modification (e.g., changed the tennis racket). He was clearly still at the beginning of the transitional stage in his construction of combinatorial ideas.

The final hands-on problem (comprising 12 combinations) was considerably more difficult for James; in fact, he reverted to the non-planning stage in solving this. He duplicated combinations in constructing the first six outfits but soon corrected these. In forming the remaining combinations, James spent considerable time in making trial combinations and checking them against the previous outfits. He managed to form all but one of the remaining outfits. His explanation of his approach reflected a reliance on trial-and-error and efficient checking.

On completing all of the problems, James was asked whether he noticed similarities in the two problem sets and whether solving the first written set helped him with the second hands-on set. It is interesting to note that he commented on the usefulness of the hands-on materials in the second problem set, especially since he did not use any form of notation to represent his ideas in the written problems. It may be that he had not been encouraged to do so in school or more likely, he felt that he had no need to use notation because of his confidence in his mental computation.

In reflecting on problem similarity, James could see the parallel between the clothing problem in the written set and those of the hands-on set. This is not surprising, given that the resemblance between the problem items would create a high-transparency mapping condition for the child (Gentner, 1989). This similarity in surface features appeared to alert James to their structural correspondence, which he saw in terms of matching items. He did not comment though, on the idea of all possible different matchings. Nevertheless, his responses here support our earlier discussion on how superficial similarity can help novices notice a correspondence between their mental model of a base problem and a new target problem. It is clear that the third written problem, in which James "guessed" and constructed his "own theory of squaring," did not assist him in solving the hands-on problems.

Our second case study, Kerry, a low achiever in school mathematics, provides an interesting contrast to James.

Kerry's Development of Combinatorial Models and Processes.   Kerry, age 9 years 5 months, was also in her fourth year of school. She attended a different school from James, one situated in a lower socioeconomic suburb of a major Australian city. She was considered a low-achieving student in mathematics. Kerry was administered the hands-on problems prior to the written examples.

In contrast to James, Kerry was not as vocal in her discussion of her actions, yet made greater progress in her strategy construction. She commenced the hands-on combinatorial problems at the non-planning stage where she relied on a trial-and-error procedure to solve the first problem. When asked to describe the method she used, Kerry stated, "I just kept on checking back to the last one so that I knew I didn't do the same." This checking procedure however, was not sufficiently thorough for her to detect all of the duplicated combinations.

Kerry also duplicated outfits in the second and third hands-on problems and again, was unable to make all of the required modifications. However, she demonstrated a distinct improvement in her solution strategy. She was now working in the transitional stage where she reduced her number of new item selections by repeating the selection of several minor items. Although she was unable to exhaust all of these minor items, she nevertheless adopted an efficient dressing procedure that assisted her progress. Instead of completing the dressing of a bear prior to moving onto the next one, she dressed the bears in pairs (or occasionally in threes). She accomplished this by placing two identical items on both bears (e.g., two green tops), followed by another two identical items (e.g., two orange pants), and finally, changed the third item in an alternating fashion (e.g., orange tennis racket, blue tennis racket, orange tennis racket). It appeared that Kerry was aware, at least implicitly, of her decision to dress two or three bears in the same two items and vary the third.

Although Kerry attempted to correct her duplicated combinations, she was unable to make all the necessary modifications. She was apparently unaware that there were still corrections to be made for she claimed that all of the outfits were different and that she had solved the problem. Her explanation of how she constructed her combinations was simply, "I just kept on changing the clothes every time I went and kept on looking back."

Kerry's response to the first written combinatorial problem (refer to Fig. 8.7) was interesting. After reading the problem, she stated immediately that there were three combinations. When asked whether there were any more possible combinations, Kerry began to use the clothing items from the hands-on tasks to represent the problem data. She tried to match the colors of the clothing items to the colors of the buckets and spades. However she became very confused when she attempted to use the tennis rackets for spades because she did not have the correct colors. When asked if there was another way in which she could solve the problem, Kerry replied, "I could do it in my head but I can't work it out that way." She then decided to use notation to represent the problem data, as indicated in Fig. 8.7. Her use of a uniform cyclic pattern in selecting the spades assisted her here.

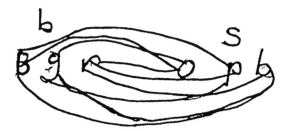

FIG. 8.7.   Kerry's notation for the first written problem.

Kerry remained in this transitional stage as she solved the second written problem. Although she repeated the selection of each T-shirt, she did not exhaust these items and was unable to generate all eight combinations. Kerry applied a procedure similar to that of Fig. 8.7 for representing the problem data.

It was on the third written problem that Kerry demonstrated the greatest progress in her construction of combinatorial knowledge. Kerry again represented the problem data by listing the first letter of each item, one under the other. As before, she drew lines to link the different items and verbalized her actions as she proceeded. Kerry had now progressed to the third stage where she was employing a complete odometer strategy to solve the problem. That is, she chose the gold and silver lettering as her major constant items and used them repeatedly until they were exhausted. She did the same with the minor constant items (the colors), while systematically cycling through the remaining items (the greetings).

Kerry's progress from her initial nonplanning stage through to this final stage reflects considerable growth in her construction of combinatorial ideas. Her commencing mental model of problem solution was simply one of joining items and ensuring that each new combination was different from all preceding combinations. Although her general monitoring strategies were not as effective as James', she nevertheless continued to modify and extend her model as she worked through the problems.

We return to Kerry's construction of combinatorial knowledge but will first refer to her comments on the similarities between the two problem sets. She claimed that the sets were similar because they "have all got colors." She was unable to suggest any other ways in which the problems were similar. Given Kerry's limited explanations throughout the problem session, it is not surprising that she was unable to comment further. However, it seems that the transparency feature of the problems, that is, the similarity in the nature of the problem items, had a greater impact on Kerry than the systematicity component, that is, the similarity in relational structure (Gentner & Toupin, 1986). This contrasts with James' ability to detect the structural correspondences as well as similarities and differences in surface features.

Reflecting on the Two Case Studies

It is interesting to speculate on why Kerry was better able to construct combinatorial ideas than James, given that neither child had met these problems in school. The fact that Kerry worked the hands-on problems prior to the written examples may have contributed to her progress. On the other hand, unlike James, Kerry did not seem to perceive the structural correspondence between the two problem sets. She was also not as efficient in her use of monitoring processes.

What Kerry did demonstrate though, was an active search for more efficient methods of problem solution and, in so doing, was able to modify and extend her initial mental model of the problem. The studies of Miller-Jones (1991) also demonstrated that low achievers display increasing systematicity as aspects of a problem's rule structure become apparent. Being aware of the limitations of generating a solution mentally, Kerry appreciated the value of concrete and diagrammatic representations in formulating her ideas and made effective use of these. Kerry's efforts at streamlining the solution process were particularly evident in the second and third hands-on problems (3-D) where she formed two or three outfits simultaneously by holding two item pairs constant and varying the third pair. Her preoccupation with this procedure however, meant a decline in her monitoring processes with the result that she could not correct all of her errors. Her acquisition of the expert odometer strategy alleviated this difficulty. However, Kerry could not rely solely on such a procedure if she were presented with a similar problem that comprised a hidden constraint on goal attainment.

James presents a particularly interesting case. He was rated as a high achieving student in mathematics, had an effective command of language, was skilled in monitoring his actions, and demonstrated insight into his own thought processes. In contrast to Kerry, he had confidence in his mental capacity and relied on this to solve the written problems. Although he did an admirable job of keeping track of his combinations, James nevertheless was unable to solve the problem. His reluctance to use some form of written assistance was a major stumbling block. His reluctance could be due to perceived or actual constraints of formal schooling. In his search for an efficient method of solving the most difficult written problem, James reflected on the data of the previous problem. This prompted him to retrieve a formal mathematical "theory" which he inappropriately mapped onto the data of this final written problem. It is tempting to speculate that James viewed problem solving in terms of retrieving an (apparently) appropriate rule and applying it to the problem at hand. The studies of Miller-Jones (1991) support this conjecture, indicating that high achievers have a greater expectation of rule-regulated structure than low achievers. Nevertheless, James did see the value of concrete representation after solving the hands-on problems. It is difficult to say whether James would have made better progress if he had been given these hands-on problems initially. Although he did recognize the structural similarity between the problems, he did not appear to use this to facilitate solution of the hands-on problems. This suggests that he might not have been as successful as Kerry.

Children's Reasoning in Solving the Deductive Problems

In this section, we review James and Kerry's responses to the written deductive reasoning problem of Fig. 8.4 ("sports" problem). To appreciate the complexity of such problems, we first analyze the reasoning processes entailed in solving the sports example. *assumed to be fixed*

Complexity of Deductive Reasoning. The structural complexity of these deductive reasoning problems would obviously have a significant bearing on children's ability to solve them. In chapter 2 we considered the dimensionality of a representation, which we defined as the number of independent sources of variation processed in parallel. In solving the sports problem, the minimum number of dimensions that must be active when making a deduction is two. However, a consideration of three dimensions is frequently needed. Unless an efficient form of recording is used, such as a matrix, this problem can pose considerable processing loads for the child.

We now illustrate the problem's complexity by working through the clues without the assistance of a matrix because the children in our case studies did not use a matrix. The first clue is not a useful starting point as it only provides one item of information. The second clue provides sufficient information to make a decision about the sports played by Mr. Big and Ms. Ace. However, we need to take into account three dimensions in making this decision. We need to consider the sports people, Mr. Big and Ms. Ace, the fact that their sports involve a ball, and the fact that the sports that involve a ball are golf and tennis. This enables us to conclude that Mr. Big plays either tennis or golf and Ms. Ace plays either tennis or golf. Knowing these facts, it is wise to move to the last clue that provides related information, namely, that Ms. Ace does not play tennis. By considering this item in conjunction with our previous two facts (three dimensions now being taken into account), we can conclude that Ms. Ace must play golf and Mr. Big must play tennis. This leaves us with the remaining items, namely, Mr. Bowler, Ms. Fish, chess, and swimming. We must examine the two remaining clues together to decide who plays what sport. Because Ms. Fish cannot swim, she must be the chess player and Mr. Bowler must be the swimmer (we actually did not need the first clue).

Deductive reasoning problems of this nature are essentially three dimensional, the dimensions being people (Ace, Big, Fish, Bowler), games (tennis,

	Tennis	Golf	Chess	Swimming
Ms. Ace	-	+	-	-
Mr. Big	+	-	-	-
Ms. Fish	-	-	+	-
Mr. Bowler	-	-	-	+

FIG. 8.8.   A matrix representation for a deductive reasoning problem.

golf, chess, swimming) and the assignment of games to people. In solving this problem, a mental model equivalent to a ternary relation is constructed out of a combination of premises two and four, and another mental model of the same kind is constructed out of the inferences drawn from this first model, plus premise three. The use of a matrix to solve this problem facilitates the drawing of inferences from the premises because it clearly shows the relations between the dimensions, as indicated in Fig. 8.8.

James' Reasoning on the Sports Problem.   James initially had difficulty in working this problem because he was attempting to deduce his answers mentally, as he did for the combinatorial problems. He commenced the problem by considering the two most appropriate clues, namely, the second and last clues. His initial comments were, "That means Mr. Big plays tennis because it's got here Mr. Big and Ms. Ace's sports involve a ball and neither Ms. Ace nor Ms. Fish play tennis." However he then indicated that this was "only a possibility." James then reread all of the clues and concluded that Ms. Fish plays chess: "Ms. Fish does the chess because Mr. Bowler's not good at chess and both Mr. Big and Ms. Ace's sports involve a ball and chess doesn't. Ms. Fish can't swim at all and neither Ms. Ace nor Ms. Fish plays tennis, so that means Ms. Fish plays chess." Notice how James considered all the related clues to justify why Ms. Fish plays chess.

James reread the clues for some time and then proceeded to eliminate some of the players: "It can't be Ms. Fish. It can't be Ms. Ace because of tennis, so it's now Mr. Big and Mr. Bowler. Ah!" James again read the clues and stated, "That means Mr. Big and Ms. Ace could be the ones that do swimming." He then decided against this, stating that either of these two could be the golfer and that Mr. Big was his "prime suspect for tennis." James displayed his frustration at this point, claiming, "It's very hard. I don't get this." It was at this point that he decided to record his answers, using a listing format rather than the more effective matrix.

James wrote the four sports on his sheet and then eliminated certain sports as he reviewed the clues. However, he did not recall all of the deductions he had made previously and virtually started from scratch. His efforts to deduce the sports of Ms. Ace and Ms. Bowler appear to have been hampered by his notion of a female golfer. Many of the children in this study questioned the appropriateness of a female golfer and were reluctant to assign golf to Ms. Ace. As James commented, "If a lady plays golf, is she a golfer too?" He went on to conclude that Ms. Ace is the swimmer, apparently forgetting that Ms. Ace's sport involves a ball.

One of the interesting features of James' response was his concern for checking the accuracy of his deductions during the course of problem solution. However, he did not check his overall finished product. By reviewing several of the clues as he worked the problem, James was confident that he had made correct deductions, such as concluding that Mr. Big played tennis. However, the fact that he was considering several dimensions at once meant an increased processing load. He failed to use efficient reprsentations, such as a matrix mentioned earlier, which would have enabled him to chunk the premises into the minimum number of dimensions. This meant that he had insufficient capacity to process all the relevant information, and this contributed to his final two incorrect deductions.

As was the case for the combinatorial problems, Kerry displayed quite a different response to James.

Kerry's Reasoning on the Sports Problem.   In contrast to James, Kerry completed the problem in a minimum number of steps, but only made one correct deduction. She brought preconceived ideas to the problem that prevented her from solving it. She assumed that the male players must play chess and golf and the female players, swimming and tennis. She used this assumption along with the first clue in drawing her initial deduction: "Mr. Big plays chess because it says Mr. Bowler is no good at chess, so he misses out on chess. And Mr. Big must play chess because he's the only other man and the two women must play tennis."

Kerry proceeded to reread the clues and then made a list of the players on her sheet. As she recorded the sports against the players, she commented: "Ms. Ace plays tennis because the other woman can't play tennis. Mr. Bowler plays golf because Ms. Ace plays tennis and Mr. Big plays chess and Ms. Fish swims. No, Ms. Fish plays tennis and Ms. Ace must swim."

Unlike James, Kerry did not bother to check her deductions. In fact, she did not monitor her responses in any of the deductive problems. She appeared quite confident in her conclusions for the sports problem, largely because of her beliefs about chess players and golfers. It is a sad fact that children's stereotyped views of gender roles can hinder their mathematical problem solving.

When asked if solving one set of problems helped them solve the other and whether they could see any similarity between the problem sets, James stated that the problems were "all puzzles, just like, 'Who dunnits'," yet claimed their similarity did not assist him. Kerry maintained that the similarity did help her but could not explain why. She could recognize some similarity between the problems involving arrangements, stating, "In the books' problem, you had to stack them (clues were given for stacking a set of books) and in the cards' problem you had to do them (arrange them) across." The comments of other children in this study suggest that children often do not attempt to look for relational correspondence in their mathematical activities. For example, when 12-year-old Natalie was asked if solving one set of deductive reasoning problems helped her solve the other, she claimed: "I did each (set of problems) separately. I didn't relate them." When questioned on the similarities between the combinatorial problem sets, she commented, "You've got to match stuff up with other stuff but otherwise I don't relate problems as I don't really look at that sort of thing."

The children's responses to both the combinatorial and deductive reasoning problems demonstrate that they can construct important mathematical ideas and can reason mathematically in solving novel problems set within meaningful contexts. The role of children's metaprocesses is particularly important here. They just need opportunities to develop these processes and to ascribe them into meaningful strategies, as we indicate in the next section.

Fostering Children's Problem Solving, Problem Posing, and Mathematical Thinking

We conclude this chapter with some suggestions for developing students' problem solving, problem posing, and mathematical thinking processes. It is beyond the scope of this book to provide a comprehensive coverage of all the issues that need to be addressed. We concentrate therefore on issues pertaining to the teaching of heuristics, the fostering of students' metacognitive processes and higher order thinking skills, and the development of problem posing processes.

Teaching Heuristics.   Schoenfeld (1992) noted that many texts contain "problem-solving" sections in which students are given drill-and-practice activities on simple versions of the strategies they were taught in a previous section. When strategies are taught in this way, they are no longer heuristics in Polya's sense, that is, they become mere algorithms. As we stressed at the beginning of this chapter, problem solving involves grappling with a novel situation in the absence of an "expert" solution strategy. When students are drilled in particular procedures and simply apply these to a given problem, they no longer engage in the mathematical thinking that novel situations encourage.

Students need to acquire a repertoire of general heuristics and should know not only how to apply them appropriately but also when to apply them. The research of Novick and Francis (1993) has highlighted the difficulties problem solvers experience in discriminating situations for which various representations, such as a matrix or a tree diagram, would be most appropriate. As we mentioned in a previous section, applying an heuristic can help students represent the explicit relations in a problem and subsequently recognize the implied relationships. Students need to appreciate how an appropriately used heuristic can help them refine their mental model of a problem.

These heuristics can also alleviate processing difficulties in dealing with several relations at once. We saw this in James' case when he turned to a recorded procedure in solving the first deductive example, after becoming confused in his initial mental attempts. However, James' recording format was not the most effective for the problem. He probably would have been more successful had he known how to use a matrix. This representational format is particularly beneficial for deductive reasoning problems (Novick, 1990; Polich & Schwartz, 1974). Similarly, tree diagrams are an effective means of solving combinatorial problems because they provide a visual organizational structure to the generation of combinations. Children should be exposed to these specialized diagrams after they have had prior experiences with less formal methods.

The usefulness of a heuristic will depend on, among other things, the clarity of the student's problem-situation model. If the student fails to form an adequate mental representation of the problem, it will be reflected in the heuristic she employs. This is evident in the diagram a seventh-grade student drew to solve the problem shown in Fig. 8.9 (English & Warren, in press, 1995). Notice how the student's drawing reflects surface, rather than structural, features of the problem. In this instance, the diagram provides little assistance in solving the problem. We can assist students in using heuristics effectively by first guiding them in forming a comprehensive problem-situation model. This may be achieved by directing students towards the structural features of a new problem, rather than its superficial details. This approach also increases the likelihood that students will retrieve a useful base (i.e., a known problem of similar structure) to assist them in solving a target problem (Gholson et al., 1990).

Fostering Students' Metacognitive Processes and Higher Order Thinking Skills.   Campione et al. (1989) claimed that attention to metacognitve aspects of learning can play a central role in improving instructional programs

A saw in a sawmill saws long logs, each 16 meters long, into short logs, each 2 meters long. If each cut takes 2 minutes, how long will it take for the saw to produce eight short logs from one long log?

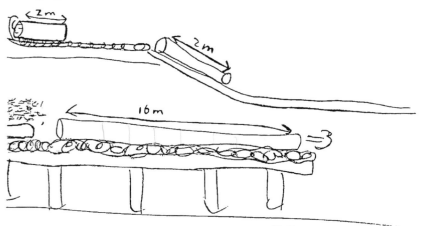

FIG. 8.9.   Inappropriate use of a diagram to solve a novel problem.

and methods of assessment. They expressed concern over the fact that many students do not have a strong conceptual grasp of the goal of their activities, are not provided with opportunities to apply their knowledge and strategies in a flexible manner, and are not encouraged to monitor, regulate, and control their own learning.

Students require explicit instruction in the use of different metacognitive strategies. However as Campione et al. (1989) remarked, just because a student has a strategy avaliable does not mean that it will be accessed appropriately when it is needed, nor executed optimally when accessed. Campione et al. have designed alternative approaches that incorporate metacognitive factors within both instruction and assessment. This involves students and adults working collaboratively to solve problems, where the adult models and monitors appropriate problem-solving strategies. In the initial stages, the adult does the bulk of the cognitive work but this contribution decreases as the students become progressively more able to manage the problem-solving processes themselves. A set of domain-appropriate strategies is used to scaffold the discussion, although these strategies are not practiced independently of the problem context. The teacher models and the students practice the metacognitive processes associated with the flexible use of these strategies. This permits "critiquing and shaping of thinking" because the processes of thinking, as well as the products, become visible (Resnick & Nelson-Le Gall, 1987, p. 216).

Schoenfeld (1992) used a related approach in his efforts to develop students' metacognitive processes during problem-solving classes. This involves an instructor acting as a "roving consultant" while students work in small groups. As the instructor circulates through the room, she poses questions such as:

What (exactly) are you doing? (Can you describe it precisely?)

Why are you doing it? (How does it fit into the solution?)

How does it help you? (What will you do with the outcome when you obtain it?) (p. 356).

Questions of this nature can assist students in adopting a more reflective approach to problematic situations (Kilpatrick, 1987a). Likewise, Mason et al. (1982) noted that learning to solve problems involves becoming your own questioner, this being an important component of the ability to think mathematically.

An alternative approach to fostering students' metacognitive and mathematical thinking processes is to design collaborative problem-solving sessions that incorporate ideas from the program, *Philosophy for Children* (Lipman, 1984). The basic rationale of the program is that through structured discussion of philosophical (or conceptual) issues and ideas, children of all ages and ability levels will improve their thinking and learning skills. By utilizing questions adapted from the program, we can broaden children's understanding of thinking in general and mathematical thinking in particular. These questions provide excellent starting points for collaborative problem solving because they help students become more aware of their own thinking and problem-solving processes, as well as their approaches to mathematics learning in general. Some sample questions follow. These are adapted from Lipman, Sharp, and Oscanyan (1984), and Lipman and Sharp (1982a, 1982b) and are addressed in English (1992b, 1993c):

- What is thinking? Do you ever think about your thinking?
- In your "everyday thinking," do you think in pictures?. . . in color? . . . in black and white? . . . in isolated words? . . . in sentences?
- How do you think in mathematics? Do you think in words? . . . in pictures? . . . in diagrams? . . . in symbols? . . . in rules?
- How would you describe a good mathematics thinker? a good "everyday" thinker? Are they necessarily different?
- How would you describe your thinking when you're solving a mathematics problem? Is this different from your thinking in solving an everyday problem?

Students' discussions on these issues can also help them develop alternative formulations of problems as well as discover and create their own mathematics problems. These activities ought to be a component of every student's education (Kilpatrick, 1987a). We turn now to a consideration of ways in which we might foster these skills.

Fostering Students' Problem Posing Processes.   School mathematics curricula usually present students with problems that have well-specified goals. As a consequence, students have little opportunity to generate novel results because these have already been specified in advance by the teacher (Silver & Mamona, 1989b). This is not surprising, given the paucity of curricular and instructional attention on problem posing; there is also little research on the cognitive components. However S. I. Brown and Walter's 1983 text, *The Art of Problem Posing*, and their more recent volume, *Problem Posing: Reflections and Applications* (1993) offer some worthwhile suggestions for developing students' problem posing processes. We refer to a couple of their examples.

One effective problem-posing strategy offered in their texts is the use of the "what-if-not" question. We cite one of the examples in which Brown and Walter (1983) considered the attributes of a geoboard (comprising 25 nails arranged in a square array). If we look at the attributes of a geoboard as being variable, we can generate a range of new possibilities. For example, "What if the geoboard were not square? What could it be?" If we were to consider a circular goeboard with the spacing of the nails unchanged, then we could raise the question: "How many nails would be eliminated if we were to cut the largest circular board out of a square one" (S. I. Brown & Walter, 1983, p. 37). Using the "what-if-not" strategy can highlight new attributes that were not previously considered. For example, "What if the board were not finite and bounded? How might an infinite board be drawn?"

In addition to the use of this strategy, Silver and Mamona (1989b) advocated the use of "open" problems where students must "add structure," as a means of promoting problem posing (Silver & Adams, 1987). One such problem could be to draw a five-sided irregular polygon with a perimeter of 30 units. Students could generate many different responses to this problem, with each answer checked against set criteria for an acceptable solution. The typical closed problems in textbooks can be readily modified to become open problems by using the "what-if-not" strategy. Even the common problems presented to children in first grade can be easily modified to become open problems. For example, consider the problem, "Jack has 45 cents. He wants to buy some gumballs from the gumball machine. If they cost 5 cents each, how many can he buy?" Several open problems can be created from this case, such as, "What if the gumball machine only took 5-cent coins, . . how many gumballs might Jack be able to get then?"

Other approaches to problem posing include "what-is-the-problem?" and "create a related problem" activities. When given the answer to a problem without the problem data, children can search for a variety of possibilities. For example, "The answer to a problem is 54, what might the problem have been?" The answer does not necessarily have to be numerical. For example, "Sue's answer to a problem was, 'The dictionary is on the second shelf.' What might the problem have been?" Such problems are simple to devise and serve as a valuable source of problem-posing experiences. Group work provides a constructive environment for these activities because children often identify problems that would be missed if they were working in isolation. Such a setting also enables students to clarify their ideas (Kilpatrick, 1987a).

Encouraging children to create their own problem that is similar to a given example not only develops their problem-posing skills but also fosters recognition of problem structure and develops analogical reasoning skills. Activities of this type can help students appreciate how problem structure can be retained while contextual features are altered. They can also alert students to the dangers of relying on surface features as an aid to problem solution.

SUMMARY

We summarize our main points as follows:

1. The important components of problem solving, problem posing, and mathematical thinking include problem models, strategic processes, metaprocesses, and affective models.

2. Skilled problem solvers develop comprehensive mental models that focus on the principles of a domain, rather than on the superficial features of a problem.

3. During problem solving, learners modify or extend their existing mental models by connecting new information to their present knowledge structures and constructing new relationships among those structures. Children can construct important mathematical ideas and can reason mathematically in solving novel problems set within meaningful contexts. Their use of metaprocesses is particularly important here.

4. Heuristic processes, such as drawing a diagram or making a physical model, can provide useful directions in which the solution to a problem might proceed. However, a knowledge of such heuristics is of little avail if students do not form a meaningful problem-situation model from the outset, if they do not know when to apply the heuristic, if they do not monitor its application, and do not reflect on the results of their actions. We need to ensure that children develop these processes within a positive and rich learning environment.

5. Metacognition incorporates knowledge about cognitive states and one's cognitive processes, together with the "executive" components of planning, monitoring, evaluating, and revising one's thinking. Collaborative problem activities, incorporating the use of "thinking" programs such as *Philosophy for Children,* can be effective in developing children's metacognitive and higher order thinking processes.

6. Analogical reasoning plays a significant role in problem solving and problem posing. However, children must be able to detect the corresponding problem structures, especially in the face of distracting surface cues. Children need to be aware of when and how they can make use of these structures.

9

REFLECTIONS AND RECOMMENDATIONS

In this chapter, we attempt to provide an overview of the main arguments presented in the book and offer some recommendations for mathematics instruction. One of the major issues in mathematics education is the need for children to see connections and relationships between mathematical ideas and to apply this understanding to the solution of new problems. Young children bring to school a substantial body of knowledge about number and informal problem-solving processes and can successfully solve a range of problems by directly representing or modelling the actions or relationships described in the problem (Carpenter et al., 1993; Fuson, 1992a, 1992b; Ginsburg & Baron, 1993; Resnick, 1992). However, as children progress through the grade levels, for many of them their perception of mathematics as a meaningful domain appears to deteriorate and they have difficulty linking what they already know and understand to the symbols and rules they use (Fuson, 1992a, 1992b; Greeno, 1989; Onslow, 1991; Wearne & Hiebert, 1985). This is clearly evident by the middle grades (Wearne & Hiebert, 1988b).

If we consider learning to involve an active construction process based on recognizing similarities between new and existing ideas (Baroody & Ginsburg, 1990; Davis, Maher, & Noddings, 1990; Duit, 1991), then we must ensure that children develop meaningful and cohesive knowledge structures from the outset. We have addressed these structures in terms of mental models. These are representations that are active while solving a particular problem and provide the workspace for inference and mental operations. Mental models are typically analogs that can deal with both concrete and abstract understandings. To be effective, the mental models children develop must focus on the underlying relations between ideas, not on superficial surface details. Effective mathematics learning necessitates the formation of relational connections between important ideas. The complexity of the relations we expect children to grasp however, is critically important. If children are required to process too much information simultaneously, their processing capacity is likely to be exceeded and they will fail to make the desired learnings. Complexity analysis of the mathematical concepts we present to children is essential to designing good pedagogy.

We have argued that children's development of mental models involves a process of analogical reasoning, in which something new is understood by recognizing the structural correspondence with something that is known. Such reasoning appears to be one of the most important mechanisms underlying human thought and may be defined as a mapping of relations from one structure, the base or source, to another structure, the target (Gentner, 1983, 1989; Halford, 1993; Holyoak & Thagard, 1989, 1995). Analogies can make learning and transfer more efficient, and can foster the development of appropriate procedures. Given that analogical reasoning processes of some kind are certain to be used by children, it is best for educators to provide good analogies and ensure they are used appropriately.

The main uses of analogy in mathematics are, first, in concrete teaching aids that, as we have shown, are technically analogs, and their analysis in terms of analogy theory sheds considerable light on their strengths and weaknesses. Second, analogy is used when correspondences are seen between one domain and another. An important example of this is where relations between constants in arithmetic are used to justify, or illustrate, algebraic relations. This is essentially what happens when sets of arithmetic examples are used to make algebraic concepts, such as the distributive law, meaningful. Third, analogy is involved when correspondences are seen between two algebraic expressions. The importance of analogy in mathematics is not new, and was well recognized by Polya (1954). However, we have used contemporary theory of analogy developed by cognitive scientists to provide deeper insights into the processes entailed in analogy, with the result that its benefits and pitfalls, as well as its role as a fundamental process of thought, can be more clearly seen.

Analogical reasoning, however, is far from being the only process responsible for children's mathematical development. Also of importance are the strategic, goal-directed processes involved in problem solving and the numerous metaprocesses, such as higher order thinking skills and metacognition, that underlie effective mathematical thinking. Indeed, all of these reasoning processes should permeate the entire curriculum from the beginning school years.

Learning mathematics depends partly on acquiring adequate mental models of concepts, including relations between the elements of which a concept is composed. However, it also depends on acquisition of strategies and procedures for performing mathematics. Autonomous development of strategies depends on adequate mental models. Strategies can be learned by rote, without understanding, but students will lack flexibility in using strategies learned in this way, and they may degenerate into malrules. Once acquired, strategies and procedures need to be strengthened through practice. Efficient performance will require key components to become automatic. Understanding, in the form of adequate mental models, can make the acquisition process more efficient, more meaningful, and more enjoyable, but cannot completely replace practice.

We now give greater consideration to these cognitive components of mathematical learning as we review their roles in children's development of number sense, algebraic and proportional reasoning, and problem solving (including problem posing and mathematical thinking).

Developing Children's Number Sense

A considerable proportion of this book has been devoted to the development of children's understanding of number (including arithmetic properties), numeration, and computation. Our ultimate aim here is to promote children's number sense. Sowder (1988) defined number sense as "a well organized conceptual network that enables a person to relate number and operation properties" (p. 183). Number sense includes the ability to use number magnitude, to make qualitative and quantitative judgements, to recognize inappropriate results of calculations, and to use nonalgorithmic procedures to compute mentally. A person who has number sense is able to solve number problems in flexible and creative ways.

Children's development of number sense begins with their early numerical experiences with concrete analogs that mirror important numerical relations. Because we want children to use the structure of the analog to construct a mental model of the numerical idea, it is important that the analog be an appropriate one and be manipulated in a way that mirrors the targeted concept. The structure of the analog must be sufficiently clear and robust to allow unambiguous mappings to be formed between the source and the target. We need to assess carefully the analogs we use in our teaching to ensure that they do meet this criterion. As indicated in chapter 4, some analogs may be structurally simple, such as colored counters, but prove to be complex learning aids when applied to target concepts that comprise inherently complex relations, such as fractions. When an analog is used in this way, children are faced with an additional processing load as they attempt to interpret the arbitrary structure imposed on the analog.

In promoting children's early development of number sense, we need to be cognizant of the complexities that our number system presents them.

Cardinal value involves a basic unary relation, yet children face the difficulty of mapping number concepts onto number words that do not refer to individual items or to properties of items, but to properties of sets of items. The difficulty here is that our counting routine assigns a number word to each item being counted. This means that children must come to the realization that our number words refer to properties of sets of items, not individual items. Children's development of this understanding may be likened to an "accumulator" model that fills up in equal increments, one for each entity counted. The entire fullness of the accumulator, not the final increment alone, represents the numerosity of the items counted. This is a more complex concept because it entails a ternary relation, as shown in chapter 3, and therefore will be harder for young children to acquire. In establishing cardinality, we need to ensure that children focus on the "entire fullness" of the sets they count and that they perceive each new set as comprising all previous sets.

The mental models children construct of two-digit numbers provide the foundation for their mastery of multidigit numeration. Because of the irregularities in the two-digit number names, we need to structure children's learning experiences according to appropriate psychological principles, not according to mathematical logic. Introducing children to the numeration of teen numbers prior to the other two-digit numbers is not desirable because there is not a clear and direct mapping from the analog representation of the teens to their number names. An understanding of the "regular" numbers, in which there is a direct link from the analog representation to the number name, forms the mental model that provides the scaffolding for the learning of the "irregular" numbers. The importance of establishing such mental models is also evident in children's mastery of large numbers where concrete analog representation is cumbersome and inappropriate. Here, children's mental models of the place-value relationships in our number system provide an essential foundation.

In introducing rational number, we need to take into account the complexities involved in both their interpretation and their representation in analog form. The increased processing load resulting from the need to consider a number of relations jointly means children are susceptible to interpreting fractions as isolated digits. This is compounded by the various meanings that can be assigned to a fraction. We thus need to introduce children initially to the least complex meaning, via an analog whose structure clearly conveys the intended construct. The part/whole notion of a fraction can be illustrated effectively with an area analog because the concept of parts to a whole can be discerned clearly. In contrast, a set analog is a more complex representation because the relationship between the parts and the whole is not readily apparent.

The part/whole construct serves as a foundation for the development of decimal-fraction understanding. It is important that children develop a cohesive model of rational number where decimal and common fractions are seen to be derived from the same construct but recorded in different formats. This understanding can be fostered through the use of a common analog, such as the area model. Some educators prefer to use the base-ten blocks where the whole-number values are replaced by decimal-fraction values. This practice entails a higher processing load for children as they attempt to accommodate the new values. As a consequence, children can default to viewing the decimal fraction representation in terms of familiar whole-number relationships. When recording, comparing, and sequencing decimal fractions however, children do need to draw on their understanding of whole-number relationships. However working with fractions entails more complex relations, and children require guidance in mapping the appropriate relations from one number system to the other. If children simply transport whole-number relations to decimal fractions, without considering the special features of these fractions, their understanding of rational number will be impaired.

The foundation for children's computational understanding lies in their early experiences with increasing, decreasing, and sharing sets of items, as well as in their activities involving comparison and part/whole ideas. These early experiences must be meaningful and extensive if children are to handle the range of problem situations presented by the four operations. It is important that children recognize the relational correspondence between the concrete, pictorial, and symbolic representations of these elementary computations. The explanation used in linking these corresponding structures is crucial here (Leinhardt, 1987).

It is also important that children form interrelated computational models that draw upon established understandings, including elementary operations and numeration concepts and processes. Fragmented mental models result when children do not see that uniform computational processes are applied to different number systems. For example, children often see addition with whole numbers as quite distinct from addition of common fractions. Likewise, the renaming/regrouping processes applied in the addition and subtraction of whole numbers are often seen as unrelated to those applied in computations with fractions.

Children's facility with computation should also include effective cognitive strategies that enable them to be creative and flexible in their calculations. These strategies include a repertoire of derived fact procedures, used in the mastery of the basic facts, as well as a number of strategies that both facilitate effective mental computation and enable children to explore alternative ways of working the formal written algorithms. Also of importance are metacognitive strategies. Children need to assess whether mental computation or written procedures (or both) are appropriate for solving a given problem and then need to monitor their actions as they proceed. They also have to recognize when renaming/regrouping processes are required and must assess whether these have been carried out correctly. The reasonableness of the solution also needs to be assessed.

Children's computational skills alone, however, are inadequate for solving word problems. When faced with such a problem, children need to first form a problem-text model. This is the initial mental model children construct from reading or listening to a given problem. They must then map this model onto an analogous familiar situation in order to construct a meaningful interpretation of the problem; we refer to this as the problem-situation model. We can assist children in constructing this model by helping them identify the relevant data and the logical conditions and relationships in the problem. An effective problem-situation model will enable children to subsequently construct the correct mathematical model that represents the solution to the problem. The appropriate mapping between each of these models plays a crucial role in children's competence in solving computational word problems.

In addition to the learnings we have reviewed are the important arithmetic properties and relations such as commutativity, associativity, and distributivity. These provide the foundation for children's understanding of algebra. We turn now to this area of study.

Developing Students' Algebraic and Proportional Reasoning

Algebraic and proportional reasoning are complex processes for children because of the higher order relations they entail. Proportion is a quaternary relation, comprising a higher order relation between two rational numbers. Algebra involves relations between variables, which, unlike constants, must be defined by number system reference or expression reference. Algebra thus depends on an understanding of relations between numbers, which can be understood using arithmetic relations as analogs. This means that we must ensure that children establish adequate mental models of arithmetic relations and can recognize the correspondence between arithmetic and algebraic expressions. At the same time, students need to be aware of the inconsistencies between the arithmetic and algebraic domains, which we addressed in chapter 7.

An important component of students' algebraic development is the understanding that algebraic expressions and equations are entities in their own right and that it is these that are being operated on, not numbers or constants. Students who lack this understanding are reluctant to consider algebraic expressions, such as $x + 4$, as permissible answers to a problem and attempt to close the expression, as they would in arithmetic.

A sound mental model of a variable is essential when dealing with algebraic expressions. Children's understanding of this construct is often inadequate and stops at interpreting the letter as standing for a specific constant or, at best, as a generalized number able to adopt several values rather than just one. We need to assist children in acquiring a complete understanding of a variable, namely, that it can represent a range of unspecified values and is defined by its relation to other terms in the expression. Unfortunately, many of the common algebraic tasks that children are presented can be solved without considering the degree to which one set of values varies as a result of changes in another.

The ability to recognize and apply algebraic structure is fundamental to students' algebraic development. Studies have shown that students frequently prefer to compute the solutions to equivalent equations instead of applying their understanding of structural transformations. Students are also prone to using inappropriate arithmetic and algebraic analogies, such as in reducing the expression, $3 + 4x$ to $7x$. On the other hand appropriate arithmetic analogies can make it clear to students why this answer is incorrect, as shown in chapter 3. Instruction thus needs to address the development of appropriate analogies between arithmetic and algebraic models, as well as between algebraic models themselves. Because a known relationship serves as the mental model for new understanding, it is important that students know the relationship well and can recognize this structural correspondence between algebraic expressions. Explicit instruction in identifying these structural similarities and in forming the correct analogies is needed. This must be coupled with the development of students' strategic and metastrategic knowledge.

In solving algebraic word problems, students require guidance in forming an appropriate problem-situation model that informs and constrains the formal expressions required for solution. Because students tend to rely on a direct, syntactic approach to solving these problems, they need assistance in applying a mathematical principle to comprehend and organize the problem variables. The construction of an effective problem-situation model not only reduces the detextualization of algebraic knowledge but can also assist students in recognizing similarity in problem structures. This can then foster the transfer of a known solution procedure and the subsequent induction of more general problem models. Once again, students require guidance in detecting the common relations among the elements in problems and in recognizing when a known solution model can be applied to a new problem.

The complexities of proportional reasoning also demand attention in the curriculum. Such reasoning deals with multiplicative relationships between rational expressions such as ratios, rates, quotients, and fractions. Because proportions involve four-dimensional concepts, they impose higher processing loads for children. The different types of problem situations involving proportional relationships also add to the complexity. Qualitative prediction and comparison problems for example, require students to make comparisons that are not dependent on specific numerical values. They demand an understanding of the meaning of proportions and hence should receive considerable attention in the curriculum.

In fostering students' proportional reasoning ability, we need to guide them not only in setting up and solving a proportion, but also in discriminating proportional from nonproportional situations. Recognizing structural similarity is another crucial component. Students need to recognize that both sides of the equation, $\frac{a}{b} = \frac{c}{d}$, involve the same pattern of relations or operations and that the components are multiplicatively related. Tied in with this is the ability to recognize the invariance of certain types of transformations on these components, whether these transformations be qualitative or quantitative. Students' problem-solving experiences should include situations in which they must determine whether a given problem solution changes or is invariant when the problem components are transformed.

Developing Competence in Problem Solving, Problem Posing, and Mathematical Thinking

Problem solving, problem posing, and mathematical thinking are key elements of the curriculum. For a number of years, problem solving has received a good deal of attention in the literature and in curriculum documents. However mathematical thinking, and problem posing in particular, have not been given the emphasis they deserve. Problem posing can enhance children's mathematical development because it actively involves children in devising their own problems, in solving open-ended problems, and in testing and verifying conjectures. Problem-posing activities also encourage children to focus on the underlying structures of problems and to use these as a source for the construction of new problems. Mathematical thinking has been interpreted in various ways in the literature and encompasses a range of processing styles and specific thinking skills. Children do engage in a significant amount of mathematical and scientific thinking in their everyday activities; we need to capitalize on this and provide activities to strengthen and refine these processes.

There are a number of key cognitive components that need to be addressed in the development of children's problem-solving and problem-posing skills. These were examined in chapter 8 and include problem models, strategic processes, metaprocesses, and affective models. Successful students look for, and find, structural information in their problem-solving experiences. It is important that we assist children in forming problem-situation models that focus on the underlying principles of the problem domain, not on the superficial features of the problem itself. In addition to forming a meaningful problem-situation model, students need to draw on a repertoire of problem-solving heuristics. Techniques such as drawing a diagram or constructing a physical model can help students represent the explicit relations in a problem and subsequently recognize the implied relationships. However, students do require explicit instruction in the use of these heuristics; without direct teacher intervention and oversight, practice in using these skills is unlikely to improve problem-solving performance (Hembree, 1992).

We also need to foster the development of children's strategic processes as well as their metaprocesses. Young children do behave strategically in solving problems and are able to direct and monitor their own learning. This ability must be nurtured throughout the school years. We may achieve this by presenting children with a range of novel problems (both numerical and nonnumerical) for which they do not have a ready-made solution procedure but have sufficient informal knowledge to begin working the problem. Several studies have shown how, during the course of working a problem, children construct more powerful models of the problem and its solution process; this results in the growth of new mathematical ideas. Children's metaprocesses come into play here. In the absence of instruction, children have been shown to plan, predict, self-monitor, reflect, and use related ideas in solving novel problems.

The metaprocesses that we addressed in chapter 8 include analogical reasoning, metacognitive processes, and higher order thinking skills. As previously discussed, analogical reasoning plays a significant role in problem solving and problem posing. Being able to access a known problem that has an identical structure to a target problem can both enhance problem-solving performance as well as foster the construction of new ideas and new problems. This requires us to guide children in detecting corresponding problem structures, especially in the face of distractors. Children also need assistance in analogical transfer involving adaptation of a solution procedure from a source problem to a similar procedure for solving a target problem.

For analogical reasoning to be effective however, metacognitive processes must be utilized. For example, students need to be aware of when it is appropriate to access a known problem and need to assess the extent of correspondence between the two problem structures; this in turn will assist them in determining the extent of procedural adaptation required. In addition to the "executive" components of metacognition is knowledge about one's cognitive states and cognitive processes, as well as one's beliefs and intuitions. Studies have found positive effects of intervention on students' metacognitive development, with their metacognitive processes evolving over time in domain-specific contexts under teacher guidance. Studies have also found a dynamic interaction between children's metacognitive growth and their mathematical concept development.

Higher order thinking skills also contribute significantly to problem solving and problem posing. Although termed higher order, these skills are fundamental to all learning. Skills such as deduction, induction, spatial and visual thinking, creative and flexible thinking, and critical analysis can be enhanced through designing specific activities as well as through emphasizing these skills during routine mathematical tasks. Developing a classroom atmosphere of inquiry as a mode of student/student and student/teacher communication can encourage the growth of these skills. Such a community of inquiry can foster the construction of mathematical and scientific ideas as well as the growth of positive attitudes towards problem solving and mathematics learning in general. Indeed, we would argue that engaging students in constructive mathematical discourse can be one of the most powerful means of fostering the development of desired mathematical models and processes.

In this book, we have adopted an approach that is more specifically related to cognitive science than to any school or ideology. We have done this because, as noted in chapter 1, we believe cognitive science provides the most accurate account so far of the actual processes that people use in mathematics and offers the best potential for genuine increases in efficiency. However, it also entails an attitude of scientific enquiry. All the tenets we propose in this book are subject to verification in further research, both in the laboratory and in the classroom. Our aim has been to offer a foundation set of principles that can guide further development, rather than to provide the last word on any issue.

However, we also suggest that cognitive science can subsume many of the most important contributions from earlier approaches. For example, modern theories of learning, induction, and strategy development have a clear role for active construction by the child. The concepts of complexity and capacity have been given new meaning, and clearer explanations are offered for some Piagetian observations of typical ages at which complex concepts are acquired. Some of the chief tenets of the constructivist position are therefore incorporated, but in a form that makes their underlying processes explicit and open to scrutiny. Concepts such as *schema*, and even the all important concept of *understanding*, are given explicit treatment within this approach.

The role of associative learning is also recognized, but not as a universal set of learning principles as proposed by the early learning theorists, but as a means of strengthening automatic processes, after the higher level cognitive processes have done their work. Although associative processes can influence the strengthening of automatic procedures, they cannot account for

mathe… strategies and
proced…

We … y in mathemat-
ics ed… …tic accounts of
the p… …d positive atti-
tudes… …aking students'
learr… …ts will be able to
use … …now the very real
sati… …ning and reason-
ing … …thematics educa-
tio… …e with educational
res… …rit of constructive
en… …or further develop-
m… …ed.

REFERENCES

Acredolo, C., Adams, A., & Schmid, J. (1984). On the understanding of the relationships between speed, duration, and distance. *Child Development, 55*, 2151–2159.

Af Ekenstam, A., & Greger, K. (1983). Some aspects of children's ability to solve mathematical problems. *Educational Studies in Mathematics, 14*, 369–384.

Alexander, P. A., & Judy, J. E. (1988). The interaction of domain-specific and strategic knowledge in academic performance. *Review of Educational Research, 58*(4), 375–404.

Allport, D. A. (1980). Patterns and actions: Cognitive mechanisms are content-specific. In G. Claxton (Ed.), *Cognitive psychology* (pp. 26–64). London: Routledge & Kegan Paul.

Anderson, J. R. (1985). *Cognitive psychology and its implications.* New York: W. H. Freeman.

Anderson, J. R. (1987). Skill acquisition: Compilation of weak-method problem solutions. *Psychological Review, 94*, 192–210.

Anderson, J. R. (1990). *The adaptive character of thought.* Hillsdale, NJ: Lawrence Erlbaum Associates.

Anghileri, J. (1989). An investigation of young children's understanding of multiplication. *Educational Studies in Mathematics, 20*, 367–385.

Ashcraft, M. H. (1990). Strategic processing in children's mental arithmetic: A review and proposal. In D. F. Bjorklund (Ed.), *Children's strategies: Contemporary views of cognitive development* (pp. 185–211). Hillsdale, NJ: Lawrence Erlbaum Associates.

Ashcraft, M. H., Donley, R. D., Halas, M. A., & Vakali, M. (1992). Working memory, automaticity, and problem difficulty. In J. I. D. Campbell (Ed.), *The nature and origins of mathematical skills* (pp. 301–329). Amsterdam: Elsevier.

Ashlock, R. B. (1992). *Error patterns in computation: A semi-programmed approach.* New York: Macmillan.

Ashlock, R., Johnson, M., Wilson, J., & Jones, W. (1983). *Guiding each child's learning of mathematics: A diagnostic approach to instruction.* Columbus, OH: Merrill.

Australian Education Council. (1990). *A national statement on mathematics for Australian schools.* Victoria, Australia: Curriculum Corporation.

Baddeley, A. D. (1986). *Working memory.* Oxford: Clarendon.

Baddeley, A. D. (1990). *Human memory: Theory and practice.* Needham Heights, MA: Allyn & Bacon.

Baker, E. L. (1991). Developing comprehensive assessments of higher order thinking. In G. Kulm (Ed.), *Assessing higher order thinking in mathematics* (pp. 7–20). Washington, DC: American Association for the Advancement of Science.

Ball, D. (1992). Manipulatives and the reform of math education. *American Educator,* Summer, 14–18, 46–47.

Ball, D. (1993). Halves, pieces, and twoths: Constructing and using representational contexts in teaching fractions. In T. P. Carpenter, E. Fennema, & T. A. Romberg (Eds.), *Rational numbers: An integration of research* (pp. 157–196). Hillsdale, NJ: Lawrence Erlbaum Associates.

Baroody, A. J. (1984). Children's difficulties in subtraction: Some causes and questions. *Journal for Research in Mathematics Education, 15,* 203–213.

Baroody, A. J. (1987). The development of counting strategies for single-digit addition. *Journal for Research in Mathematics Education, 18,* 141–157.

Baroody, A. J. (1990). How and when should place-value concepts and skills be taught? *Journal for Research in Mathematics Education, 21*(4), 281–286.

Baroody, A. J., & Ginsburg, H. P. (1986). The relationship between initial meaningful and mechanical knowledge of arithmetic. In J. Hiebert (Ed.), *Conceptual and procedural knowledge: The case of mathematics* (pp. 75–112). Hillsdale, NJ: Lawrence Erlbaum Associates.

Baroody, A. J., & Ginsburg, H. P. (1990). Children's learning: A cognitive view. In R. B. Davis, C. A. Maher, & N. Noddings (Eds.), *Constructivist views on the teaching and learning of mathematics* (pp. 51–64). Reston, VA: National Council of Teachers of Mathematics.

Baroody, A. J., Ginsburg, H. P., & Waxman, B. (1983). Children's use of mathematical structure. *Journal for Research in Mathematics Education, 14*(3), 156–168.

Baturo, A. R., & English, L. D. (1985). *Sunshine maths: Year 5.* Melbourne: Longman Cheshire.

Bauer, M. I., & Johnson-Laird, P. N. (1993). How diagrams can improve reasoning. *Psychological Science, 4*(6), 372–378.

Bednarz, N., & Janvier, B. (1982). The understanding of numeration in primary school. *Educational Studies in Mathematics, 13,* 33–57.

Behr, M. (1976). *Teaching experiment: The effect of manipulatives in second graders' learning of mathematics* (PMDC Tech. Rep. No. 11). Tallahassee: Florida State University. (ERIC Document Reproduction Service No. ED 144809)

Behr, M. J., Harel, G., Post, T., & Lesh, R. (1992). Rational number, ratio, and proportion. In D. A. Grouws (Ed.), *Handbook of research on mathematics teaching and learning* (pp. 296–333). New York: Macmillan.

Behr, M. J., Harel, G., Post, T., & Lesh, R. (1993). Rational numbers: Toward a semantic analysis—Emphasis on the operator construct. In T. Carpenter, E.

Fennema, & T. A. Romberg (Eds.), *Rational numbers: An integration of research* (pp. 13–47). Hillsdale, NJ: Lawrence Erlbaum Associates.

Behr, M. J., Lesh, R., Post, T., & Silver, E. (1983). Rational number concepts. In R. Lesh & M. Landau (Eds.), *Acquisition of mathematical concepts and processes* (pp. 92–127). New York: Academic Press.

Behr, M. J., Wachsmuth, I., & Post, T. (1988). Rational number learning aids: Transfer from continuous models to discrete models. *Focus on Learning Problems in Mathematics, 10*(4), 1–18.

Behr, M., Wachsmuth, I., Post, T., & Lesh, R. (1984). Order and equivalence of rational numbers: A clinical teaching experiment. *Journal for Research in Mathematics Education, 15*(5), 323–341.

Beishuizen, M. (1993). Mental strategies and materials or models for addition and subtraction up to 100 in Dutch second grades. *Journal for Research in Mathematics Education, 24*(4), 294–323.

Bell, A., Fischbein, E., & Greer, B. (1984). Choice of operation in verbal arithmetic problems: The effects of number size, problem structure and context. *Educational Studies in Mathematics, 15*, 129–147.

Bell, A., Greer, B., Grimison, L., & Mangan, C. (1989). Children's performance on multiplicative word problems: Elements of a descriptive theory. *Journal for Research in Mathematics Education, 20*(5), 434–449.

Bell, A., Swan, M., & Taylor, G. (1981). Choice of operations in verbal problems with decimal numbers. *Educational Studies in Mathematics, 12*, 399–420.

Bergeron, J. C., & Herscovics, N. (1990). Psychological aspects of learning early arithmetic. In P. Nesher & J. Kilpatrick (Eds.), *Mathematics and cognition: A research synthesis by the International Group for the Psychology of Mathematics Education* (pp. 31–52). Cambridge, England: Cambridge University Press.

Bernstein, A. (1988, September). Where the jobs are is where the skills aren't. *Business Week*, 104–108.

Best, J. B. (1992). *Cognitive psychology*. New York: West Publishing.

Beyer, B. K. (1987). *Practical strategies for the teaching of thinking*. London: Allyn & Bacon.

Bezuk, N. S., & Bieck, M. (1993). Current research on rational numbers and common fractions: Summary and implications for teachers. In D. T. Owens (Ed.), *Research ideas for the classroom: Middle grade mathematics* (pp. 118–136). National Council of Teachers of Mathematics Research Interpretation Project. New York: Macmillan.

Bialystok, E. (1992). Symbolic representation of letters and numbers. *Cognitive Development, 7*(3), 301–316.

Bigelow, J. C., Davis, G., & Hunting, R. (1989, April). *Some remarks on the homology and dynamics of rational number learning*. Paper presented at the research presession, annual meeting of National Council of Teachers of Mathematics, Orlando.

Bisanz, J., & LeFevre, J. (1990). Strategic and nonstrategic processing in the development of mathematical cognition. In D. F. Bjorklund (Ed.), *Children's strategies: Contemporary views of cognitive development* (pp. 213–244). Hillsdale, NJ: Lawrence Erlbaum Associates.

Bjorklund, D. F., & Harnishfeger, K. K. (1990). Children's strategies: Their definition and origins. In D. F. Bjorklund (Ed.), *Children's strategies: Contemporary views of cognitive development* (pp. 309–322). Hillsdale, NJ: Lawrence Erlbaum Associates.

Bjorklund, D. F., Muir-Broaddus, E., & Schneider, W. (1990). The role of knowledge in the development of strategies. In D. F. Bjorklund (Ed.), *Children's strategies: Contemporary views of cognitive development* (pp. 93–128). Hillsdale, NJ: Lawrence Erlbaum Associates.

Booker, G., Briggs, J., Davey, G., & Nisbet, S. (1992). *Teaching primary mathematics.* Melbourne: Longman Cheshire.

Boole, G. (1951). *An investigation of the laws of thought, on which are founded the mathematical theories of logic and probabilities.* New York: Dover. (Original work published 1854)

Booth, L. R. (1984). *Algebra: Children's strategies and errors.* Windsor, Berkshire: NFER-Nelson.

Booth, L. R. (1988). Children's difficulties in beginning algebra. In A. F. Coxford & A. P. Shulte (Eds.), *The ideas of algebra, K–12* (pp. 20–32). Reston, VA: National Council of Teachers of Mathematics.

Booth, L. R. (1989a). A question of structure. In S. Wagner & C. Kieran (Eds.), *Research issues in the learning and teaching of algebra* (pp. 57–59). Reston, Virginia: National Council of Teachers of Mathematics; Hillsdale, NJ: Lawrence Erlbaum Associates.

Booth, L. R. (1989b). The research agenda in algebra: A mathematics education perspective. In S. Wagner & C. Kieran (Eds.), *Research issues in the learning and teaching of algebra* (pp. 238–246). Reston, Viginia: National Council of Teachers of Mathematics; Hillsdale, NJ: Lawrence Erlbaum Associates.

Brainerd, C. J. (1978). The stage question in cognitive developmental theory. *The Behavioral and Brain Sciences, 2,* 173–213.

Brainerd, C. J. (1985). Model-based approaches to storage and retrieval development. In C. J. Brainerd & M. Pressley (Eds.). *Basic processes in memory development* (pp. 143–208). New York: Springer-Verlag.

Brandt, R. S. (Ed.). (1989). *Readings from Educational Leadership: Teaching thinking.* Alexandria, VA: Association for Supervision and Curriculum Development.

Briars, D. J., & Larkin, J. H. (1984). An integrated model of skills in solving elementary word problems. *Cognition and Instruction, 1,* 245–296.

Briars, D. J., & Siegler, R. S. (1984). A featural analysis of preschoolers' counting knowledge. *Developmental Psychology, 20,* 607–618.

Bright, G. W., Behr, M., Post, T. R., & Wachmuth, I. (1988). Identifying fractions on the number line. *Journal for Research in Mathematics Education, 19*(3), 215–233.

Broadbent, D. E. (1975). *The magic number seven after fifteen years.* London: Wiley.

Brown, A. L. (1978). Knowing when, where, and how to remember: A problem of metacognition. In R. Glaser (Ed.), *Advances in instructional psychology* (Vol. 1, pp. 77–165). Hillsdale, NJ: Lawrence Erlbaum Associates.

Brown, A. L., & Kane, M. J. (1988). Preschool children can learn to transfer: Learning to learn and learning from example. *Cognitive Psychology, 20,* 493–523.

Brown, A. L., Kane, M. J., & Echols, C. H. (1986). Young children's mental models determine analogical transfer across problems with a common goal structure. *Cognitive Development, 1,* 103–121.

Brown, C. A., Carpenter, T. P., Kouba, V. L., Lindquist, M. M., Silver, E. A., &

Swafford, J. O. (1988). Secondary school results for the fourth NAEP mathematics assessment: Algebra, geometry, mathematical methods, and attitudes. *Mathematics Teacher, 81*, 337–347.

Brown, C. A., Carpenter, T. P., Kouba, V. L., Lindquist, M. M., Silver, E. A., & Swafford, J. O. (1989). *Results of the fourth mathematics assessment: National assessment of educational progress.* Reston, VA: National Council of Teachers of Mathematics.

Brown, J. S., & Burton, R. R. (1978). Diagnostic models for procedural bugs in basic mathematical skills. *Cognitive Science, 2*, 155–192.

Brown, J. S., & VanLehn, K. (1980). Repair theory: A generative theory of bugs in procedural skills. *Cognitive Science, 4*, 379–426.

Brown, J. S., & VanLehn, K. (1982). Toward a generative theory of "bugs." In T. P. Carpenter, J. M. Moser, & T. A. Romberg (Eds.), *Addition and subtraction: A cognitive perspective* (pp. 117–135). Hillsdale, NJ: Lawrence Erlbaum Associates.

Brown, S. (1992). Second-grade children's understanding of the division process. *School, Science and Mathematics, 92*(2), 92–95.

Brown, S. I., & Walter, M. I. (1983). *The art of problem posing.* Philadelphia: Franklin Institute Press.

Brown, S. I., & Walter, M. I. (1993). *Problem posing: Reflections and applications.* Hillsdale, NJ: Lawrence Erlbaum Associates.

Brownell, W. A. (1935). Psychological considerations in the learning and teaching of arithmetic. In W. D. Reeve (Ed.), *The teaching of arithmetic: Tenth Yearbook of the National Council of Teachers of Mathematics* (pp. 1–31). New York: Teachers College, Columbia University.

Brownell, W. A. (1945). When is arithmetic meaningful? *Journal of Educational Research, 38*(3), 481–498.

Brownell, W. A. (1947). The place of meaning in the teaching of arithmetic. *Elementary School Journal, 47*(1), 256–265.

Brownell, W. A., & Moser, H. E. (1949). Meaningful vs. mechanical learning: A study in grade 3 subtraction. *Duke University Research Studies in Education, No. 8* (pp. 1–207). Durham: Duke University Press.

Bruner, J. S. (1960). *The process of education.* Cambridge, MA: Harvard University Press.

Bruner, J. S., & Kenny, H. J. (1965). Representation and mathematics learning. In *Society for Research in Child Development, Cognitive development in children: Five monographs* (pp. 485–494). Chicago: Chicago University Press.

Bryant, P. E. (1972). The understanding of invariance by very young children. *Canadian Journal of Psychology, 26*, 78–96.

Bryant, P. E. (1989). Commentary on Halford (1989). *Human Development, 32*(6), 369–374.

Bryant, P. E., & Trabasso, T. (1971). Transitive inferences and memory in young children. *Nature, 232*, 456–458.

Burton, L. (1984). Mathematical thinking: The struggle for meaning. *Journal for Research in Mathematics Education, 15*(1), 35–49.

Burton, L. (1992). Do young children think mathematically? *Early Childhood Care and Development Journal. Special Edition on Young Children and Mathematics, 82*, 55–63.

REFERENCES

Burton, L. (1993). Implications of constructivism for achievement in mathematics. In J. A. Malone & P. C. Taylor (Eds.), *Constructivist interpretations of teaching and learning mathematics*. Perth, Western Australia: Science and Mathematics Education Center, Curtin University.

Byrnes, J. P. (1993). Analyzing perspectives on rationality and critical thinking: A commentary on the *Merrill-Palmer Quarterly* Invitational Issue. *Merrill-Palmer Quarterly, 39*(1), 159–171.

Campbell, J. I. D., & Graham, D. J. (1985). Mental multiplication skill: Structure, process, and acquisition. *Canadian Journal of Psychology, 39*, 338–366.

Campione, J. C., Brown, A. L., & Connell M. L. (1989). Metacognition: On the importance of understanding what you are doing. In R. I. Charles & E. A. Silver (Eds.), *The teaching and assessing of mathematical problem solving* (Vol. 3, pp. 93–114). Hillsdale, NJ: Lawrence Erlbaum Associates; Reston, VA: National Council of Teachers of Mathematics.

Carey, S. (1985). *Conceptual change in childhood*. Cambridge, MA: Bradford Press.

Carey, S. (1986). *Are children fundamentally different kinds of thinkers and learners than adults?* Hillsdale, NJ: Lawrence Erlbaum Associates.

Carey, S. (1990). *Cognitive development*. Cambridge, MA: MIT Press.

Carpenter, T. P. (1985). Learning to add and subtract: An exercise in problem solving. In E. A. Silver (Ed.), *Teaching and learning mathematical problem solving: Multiple research perspectives* (pp. 17–40). Hillsdale, NJ: Lawrence Erlbaum Associates.

Carpenter, T. P., Ansell, E., Franke, M. L., Fennema, E., & Weisbeck, L. (1993). Models of problem solving: A study of kindergarten children's problem-solving processes. *Journal for Research in Mathematics Education, 24*(5), 428–441.

Carpenter, T. P., Fennema, E., & Romberg, T. A. (Eds.). (1993). *Rational numbers: An integration of research*. Hillsdale, NJ: Lawrence Erlbaum Associates.

Carpenter, T. P., Hiebert, J., & Moser, J. M. (1981). Problem structure and first-grade children's initial solution processes for simple addition and subtraction problems. *Journal for Research in Mathematics Education, 12*, 27–39.

Carpenter, T. P., Lindquist, M. M., Matthews, W., & Silver, E. A. (1983). Results of the third NAEP Mathematics Assessment: Secondary school. *Mathematics Teacher, 76*, 652–659.

Carpenter, T. P., & Moser, J. M. (1982). The development of addition and subtraction problem-solving skills. In T. P. Carpenter, J. M. Moser, & T. A. Romberg (Eds.), *Addition and subtraction: A cognitive perspective* (pp. 9–24). Hillsdale, NJ: Lawrence Erlbaum Associates.

Carpenter, T. P., & Moser, J. M. (1983). The acquisition of addition and subtraction concepts. In R. Lesh & M. Landau (Eds.), *Acquisition of mathematics concepts and processes* (pp. 7–44). New York: Academic Press.

Carpenter, T. P., & Moser, J. M. (1984). The acquisition of addition and subtraction concepts in grades one through three. *Journal for Research in Mathematics Education, 15*, 179–202.

Carpenter, T. P., Moser, J. M., & Romberg, T. A. (Eds.). (1982). *Addition and subtraction: A cognitive perspective*. Hillsdale, NJ: Lawrence Erlbaum Associates.

Carr, M., & Jessup, D. (1993, March). *Cognitive and metacognitive predictors of decomposition strategy use.* Paper presented at the sixtieth anniversary meeting of the Society for Research in Child Development, New Orleans.

Carry, L. R., Lewis, C., & Bernard, J. (1980). *Psychology of equation solving: An information processing study* (Final Tech. Rep.). Austin: University of Texas at Austin, Department of Curriculum and Instruction.

Case, R. (1985). *Intellectual development: Birth to adulthood.* New York: Academic Press.

Catrambone, R., & Holyoak, K. J. (1990). Learning subgoals and methods for solving probability problems. *Memory & Cognition, 18*(6), 593–603.

Cauzinille-Marmeche, E., Mathieu, J., & Resnick, L. B. (1984, April). *Children's understanding of algebraic and arithmetic expressions.* Paper presented at the annual meeting of the American Educational Research Association, New Orleans, LA.

Chaiklin, S. (1989). Cognitive studies of algebra problem solving and learning. In S. Wagner & C. Kieran (Eds.), *Research issues in the learning and teaching of algebra* (Vol. 4, pp. 93–114). Hillsdale, NJ: Lawrence Erlbaum Associates; Reston, VA: National Council of Teachers of Mathematics.

Chaiklin, S., & Lesgold, S. (1984, April). *Prealgebra students' knowledge of algebraic tasks with arithmetic expressions.* Paper presented at the annual meeting of the American Educational Research Association, New Orleans, LA.

Chalouh, L., & Herscovics, N. (1988). Teaching algebraic expressions in a meaningful way. In F. Coxford & A. P. Shulte (Eds.), *The ideas of algebra, K-12* (pp. 33–42). Reston, VA: National Council of Teachers of Mathematics.

Chapman, M. (1987). Piaget, attentional capacity, and the functional limitations of formal structure. *Advances in Child Development and Behaviour, 20,* 289–334.

Chapman, M. (1990). *Cognitive development and the growth of capacity: Issues in neo-Piagetian theory.* Amsterdam: North Holland.

Chase, W. G., & Chi., M. T. H. (1981). Cognitive skill: Implications for spatial skill in large-scale environment. In J. Harvey (Ed.), *Cognition, social behaviors, and the environment* (pp. 111–136). Hillsdale, NJ: Lawrence Erlbaum Associates.

Chase, W. G., & Simon, H. A. (1973). Perception in chess. *Cognitive Psychology, 4,* 55–81.

Chi, M. T. H. (1978). Knowledge structures and memory development. In R. S. Siegler (Ed.), *Children's thinking: What develops?* (pp. 73–96). Hillsdale, NJ: Lawrence Erlbaum Associates.

Chi, M. T. H., Feltovich, P. J., & Glaser, R. (1981). Categorization and representation of physics problems by experts and novices. *Cognitive Science, 5,* 121–152.

Chi, M. T. H., Glaser, R., & Farr, M. J. (1988). *The nature of expertise.* Hillsdale, NJ: Lawrence Erlbaum Associates.

Chi, M. T. H., Glaser, R., & Rees, E. (1982). Expertise in physics problem solving. In R. J. Sternberg (Ed.), *Advances in the psychology of human problem solving* (Vol. 1, pp. 7–75). Hillsdale, NJ: Lawrence Erlbaum Associates.

Clement, J. (1982). Algebra word problem solutions: Thought processes underlying a common misconception. *Journal for Research in Mathematics Education, 13,* 16–30.

Clement, J. (1993). Using bridging analogies and anchoring intuitions to deal with students' preconceptions in physics. *Journal of Research in Science Teaching, 30*(10), 1241–1257.

Clement, J., Lochhead, J., & Monk, G. (1981). Translation difficulties in learning mathematics. *American Mathematical Monthly, 88*, 286–290.

Clement, J., Lochhead, J., & Soloway, E. (1979). *Translating between symbol systems: Isolating a common difficulty in solving algebra word problems.* Unpublished manuscript, University of Massachusetts at Amherst, Department of Physics and Astronomy.

Cobb, P., Wood, T., & Yackel, E. (1990). Classrooms as learning environments for teachers and researchers. In R. B. Davis, C. A. Maher, & N. Noddings (Eds.), *Constructivist views on the teaching and learning of mathematics* (pp. 125–146). Reston, VA: National Council of Teachers of Mathematics.

Cobb, P., Yackel, E., & Wood, T. (1988). Curriculum and teacher development: Psychological and anthropological perspectives. In E. Fennema, T. P. Carpenter, & S. L. Lamon (Eds.), *Integrating research on teaching and learning mathematics* (pp. 92–130). Madison: Wisconsin Center for Education Research.

Collis, K. F. (1974, June). *Cognitive development and mathematics learning.* Paper presented at the Psychology of Mathematics Workshop, Centre for Science Education, Chelsea College, London.

Collis, K. F. (1975). *The development of formal reasoning.* Newcastle, Australia: University of Newcastle.

Collis, K. F. (1978). Implications of the Piagetian model for mathematics teaching. In J. A. Keats, K. F. Collis, & G. S. Halford (Eds.), *Cognitive development: Research based on a neo-Piagetian approach* (pp. 249–283). London: Wiley.

Confrey, J. (1990). What constructivism implies for teaching. In R. B. Davis, C. A. Maher, & N. Noddings (Eds.), *Constructivist views on the teaching and learning of mathematics* (pp. 107–124). Reston, VA: National Council of Teachers of Mathematics.

Coombs, C. H., Dawes, R. M., & Tversky, A. (1970). *Mathematical psychology: An elementary introduction.* Englewood Cliffs, NJ: Prentice-Hall.

Cooney, J. B., Swanson, H. L., & Ladd, S. F. (1988). Acquisition of mental multiplication skill: Evidence for the transition between counting and retrieval strategies. *Cognition and Instruction, 5*(4), 323–345.

Cooney, T. (1985). A beginning teacher's view of problem solving. *Journal for Research in Mathematics Education, 16*(5), 324–336.

Coopersmith, A. (1984). Factoring trinomials: Trial and error? Hardly ever! *Mathematics Teacher, 77*, 194–195.

Copeland, R. W. (1974). *How children learn mathematics: The implications of Piaget's research.* New York: Macmillan.

Costa, A. L., & Lowery, L. F. (1989). *Techniques for teaching thinking.* Pacific Grove, CA: Midwest Publications.

Cramer, K., & Post, T. (1993). Connecting research to teaching: Proportional reasoning. *Mathematics Teacher, 86*(5), 404–407.

Cramer, K., Post, T., & Currier, S. (1993). Learning and teaching ratio and proportion: Research implications. In D. T. Owens (Ed.), *Research ideas for the classroom: Middle grades mathematics* (pp. 159–178). New York: Macmillan.

Cummins, D. D. (1991). Children's interpretations of arithmetic word problems. *Cognition and Instruction, 8*(3), 261–283.

Cummins, D. D., Kintsch, W., Reusser, K., & Weimer, R. (1988). The role of understanding in solving word problems. *Cognitive Psychology, 20*, 405–438.

Cuneo, D. (1982). Children's judgments of numerical quantity: A new view of early quantification. *Cognitive Psychology, 14*, 13–44.

Davis, G. (1991). Fractions as operators and as cloning machines. In R. P. Hunting & G. Davis (Eds.), *Early fraction learning: Recent research in psychology* (pp. 91–102). New York: Springer-Verlag.

Davis, G., Hunting, R. P., & Pearn, C. (1993). What might a fraction mean to a child and how would a teacher know? *Journal of Mathematical Behavior, 12*, 63–76.

Davis, G., & Pepper, K. (1992). Mathematical problem solving by pre-school children. *Educational Studies in Mathematics, 23*, 397–415.

Davis, R. B. (1975). Cognitive processes involved in solving simple algebraic equations. *Journal of Children's Mathematical Behavior, 1*(3), 7–35.

Davis, R. B. (1983). Complex mathematical cognition. In H. B. Ginsburg (Ed.), *The development of mathematical thinking* (pp. 253–290). New York: Academic Press.

Davis, R. B. (1984). *Learning mathematics: The cognitive science approach to mathematics education*. London: Croom Helm.

Davis, R. B. (1988). The interplay of algebra, geometry, and logic. *Journal of Mathematical Behavior, 7*, 9–28.

Davis, R. B. (1989a). Three ways of improving cognitive studies in algebra. In S. Wagner & C. Kieran (Eds.), *Research issues in the learning and teaching of algebra* (Vol. 4, pp. 115–119). Hillsdale, NJ: Lawrence Erlbaum Associates; Reston, VA: National Council of Teachers of Mathematics.

Davis, R. B. (1989b). Research studies in how humans think about algebra. In S. Wagner & C. Kieran (Eds.), *Research issues in the learning and teaching of algebra* (Vol. 4, pp. 266–274). Hillsdale, NJ: Lawrence Erlbaum Associates; Reston, VA: National Council of Teachers of Mathematics.

Davis, R. B., Maher, C. A., & Noddings, N. (1990). (Eds.). *Constructivist views on the teaching and learning of mathematics*. Reston, VA: National Council of Teachers of Mathematics.

Davydov, V. V., & Tsvetkovich, Z. H. (1991). On the objective origin of the concept of fractions. *Focus on Learning Problems in Mathematics, 13*(1), 13–64.

De Corte, E., & Verschaffel, L. (1987). The effect of semantic structure on first-graders' strategies for solving addition and subtraction word problems. *Journal for Research in Mathematics Education, 18*, 363–381.

De Corte, E., Vershaffel, L., & De Win, L. (1985). The influence of rewording verbal problems on children's problem representations and solutions. *Journal of Educational Psychology, 77*, 460–470.

De Corte, E., Verschaffel, L., & Van Coillie, H. (1988). Influence of number size, problem structure, and response mode on children's solutions of multiplication word problems. *Journal of Mathematical Behavior, 7*, 197–216.

de Groot, A. D. (1965). *Thought and choice in chess*. The Hague: Mouton.

DeGuire, L. (1991). Permutations and combinations: A problem-solving approach for middle school students. In M. J. Kenny & C. R. Hirsch (Eds.), *Discrete mathematics across the curriculum, K–12* (1991 yearbook, pp. 59–66). Reston, VA: National Council of Teachers of Mathematics.

Delclos, V. R., & Harrington, C. (1991). Effects of strategy monitoring and proactive instruction on children's problem-solving performance. *Journal of Educational Psychology, 83*(1), 53–42.

Dellarosa, D. (1988). A history of thinking. In R. J. Sternberg & E. E. Smith (Eds.), *The psychology of human thought* (pp. 1–18). Cambridge: Cambridge University Press.

DeLoache, J. S., Sugarman, S., & Brown, A. L. (1985). The development of error correction strategies in young children's manipulative play. *Child Development, 56,* 928–939.

Dienes, Z. P. (1960). *Building up mathematics.* London: Hutchinson Education.

Dienes, Z. P. (1963). *An experimental study of mathematics learning.* New York: Hutchinson & Co., Ltd.

Dienes, Z. P. (1964). *Mathematics in the primary school.* Melbourne: Macmillan.

Dienes, Z. P., & Golding, E. W. (1971). *Approach to modern mathematics.* New York: Herder & Herder.

Dossey, J. (1992). The nature of mathematics: Its role and influence. In D. A. Grouws (Ed.), *Handbook of research on mathematics teaching and learning* (pp. 39–48). New York: Macmillan; Reston, VA: National Council of Teachers of Mathematics.

Dossey, J. A., Mullis, I. V. S., Lindquist, M. M., & Chambers, D. L. (1988). *The mathematics report card: Trends and achievement based on the 1986 National Assessment.* Princeton: Educational Testing Service.

Dufour-Janvier, B., Bednarz, N., & Belanger, M. (1987). Pedagogical considerations concerning the problem of representation. In C. Janvier (Ed.), *Problems of representation in the teaching and learning of mathematics* (pp. 109–122). Hillsdale, NJ: Lawrence Erlbaum Associates.

Duit, R. (1991). On the role of analogies and metaphors in learning science. *Science Education, 75*(6), 649–672.

Duncker, K. (1945). On problem solving. *Psychological Monographs, 58,* 1–110.

Engelhardt, J. M., & Usnick, V. (1991). When should we teach regrouping in addition and subtraction? *School Science and Mathematics, 91*(1), 6–9.

English, L. D. (1986). Fostering mathematical thinking during the early school years. In K. Swinson (Ed.), *Proceedings of the Eleventh Biennial Conference of the Australian Association of Mathematics Teachers* (pp. 68–75). Brisbane, Australia: Brisbane College of Advanced Education.

English, L. D. (1988). *Young children's competence in solving novel combinatorial problems.* Unpublished doctoral dissertation, University of Queensland.

English, L. D. (1990a). Children's competence in forming combinations. In L. Steffe & T. Wood (Eds.), *International perspectives on transforming early childhood mathematics education* (pp. 174–180). Hillsdale, NJ: Lawrence Erlbaum Associates.

English, L. D. (1990b). Little people solve big problems. In P. Jeffery (Ed.), *SET: Research information for teachers (No. 2).* Melbourne: Australian Council for Educational Research.

English, L. D. (1990c). Mathematical power in early childhood. *The Australian Journal of Early Childhood, Special Edition on Mathematics, 15*(1), 37–42.

English, L. D. (1991a). Young children as independent learners. In G. Evans (Ed.), *Learning and teaching cognitive skills* (pp. 70–86). ACER [Monograph Series on Cognitive Processes and Education]. Melbourne: Australian Council for Educational Research.

English, L. D. (1991b). Young children's combinatoric strategies. *Educational Studies in Mathematics, 22,* 451–474.

English, L. D. (1992a). Children's use of domain-specific knowledge and domain-general strategies in novel problem solving. *British Journal of Educational Psychology, 62,* 31–45.

English, L. D. (1992b). *Philosophy for Children* and mathematics education. *Thinking: The Journal of Philosophy for Children, 10*(1), 15–17.

English, L. D. (1992c). Problem solving with combinations. *Arithmetic Teacher, 40*(2), 72–77.

English, L. D. (1993a). Children's strategies in solving two- and three-dimensional combinatorial problems. *Journal for Research in Mathematics Education, 24*(3), 255–273.

English, L. D. (1993b). *Development of children's strategic and metastrategic knowledge in a novel mathematical domain.* (ERIC Clearinghouse for Science, Mathematics, and Environmental Education, Document No. ED 365 514).

English, L. D. (1993c). Using philosophical inquiry to enhance mathematical communication. *Critical and Creative Thinking: The Australasian Journal of Philosophy for Children, 1*(2), 57–61.

English, L. D. (in press). Children's construction of mathematical knowledge in solving novel isomorphic problems in concrete and written form. *Journal of Mathematical Behavior.*

English, L. D., & Warren, E. (1995). *Students' reasoning processes in solving novel and routine algebraic problems.* Manuscript in preparation.

English, L. D., & Warren E. (in press). General reasoning processes and elementary algebraic understanding: Implications for initial instruction. *Focus on Learning Problems in Mathematics.*

Ericsson, K. A., & Oliver, W. (1988). Methodology for laboratory research on thinking: Task selection, collection of observations, and data analysis. In R. J. Sternberg (Ed.), *The psychology of human thought* (pp. 392–428). New York: Cambridge University Press.

Ernest, P. (1985). The philosophy of mathematics and mathematics education. *International Journal of Mathematics, Education, Science, and Technology, 16*(5), 603–612.

Fehr, H. F. (1953). Theories of learning related to the field of mathematics. In H. F. Fehr (Ed.), *The learning of mathematics: Its theory and practice. Twenty-first Yearbook of the National Council of Teachers of Mathematics* (pp. 1–41). Washington, DC: National Council of Teachers of Mathematics.

Fennema, E., & Peterson, P. L. (1985). Autonomous learning behavior: A possible explanation of gender-related differences in mathematics. In L. C. Wilkinson & C. B. Marrett (Eds.), *Gender influences in classroom interaction* (pp. 17–35). Orlando, FL: Academic Press.

Fey, J. T. (1989). School algebra for the year 2000. In S. Wagner & C. Kieran (Eds.), *Research issues in the learning and teaching of algebra* (Vol. 4, pp. 199–213).

Hillsdale, NJ: Lawrence Erlbaum Associates; Reston, VA: National Council of Teachers of Mathematics.

Filloy, E., & Rojano, T. (1985). Obstructions to the acquisition of elemental algebraic concepts and teaching strategies. In L. Streefland (Ed.), *Proceedings of the Ninth International Conference for the Psychology of Mathematics Education* (Vol. 1, pp. 154–158). Utrecht, The Netherlands: State University of Utrecht.

Fischbein, E. (1990). Introduction to text, *Mathematics and cognition*. Cambridge: Cambridge University Press.

Fischbein, E., Deri, M., Nello, M. S., & Marino, M. S. (1985). The role of implicit models in solving verbal problems in multiplication and division. *Journal for Research in Mathematics Education, 16*(1), 3–17.

Fischer, K. W. (1987). Relations between brain and cognitive development. *Child Development, 58*, 623–632.

Fisher, C. (1990). The Research Agenda Project as prologue. *Journal for Rsearch in Mathematics Education, 21*, 81–89.

Fisher, D. L. (1984). Central capacity limits in consistent mapping, visual search tasks: Four channels or more? *Cognitive Psychology, 16*(4), 449–484.

Fisher, K. M. (1988). The students-and-professors problem revisited. *Journal for Research in Mathematics Education, 19*(3), 260–262.

Flavell, J. H. (1963). *The developmental psychology of Jean Piaget*. New York: Van Nostrand.

Flavell, J. H. (1972). An analysis of cognitive developmental sequence. *Genetic Psychology Monographs, 86*, 279–350.

Flavell, J. H. (1976). Metacognitive aspects of problem solving. In L. Resnick (Ed.), *The nature of intelligence* (pp. 231–236). Hillsdale, NJ: Lawrence Erlbaum Associates.

Flavell, J. H. (1977). *Cognitive development*. Englewood Cliffs, NJ: Prentice Hall.

Flavell, J. H. (1979). Metacognition and cognitive monitoring: A new era of cognitive developmental inquiry. *American Psychologist, 34*, 906–911.

Flavell, J. H. (1984). Cognitive development during the post-infancy years. In H. W. Stevenson & J. Qicheng (Eds.), *Issues in cognition: Proceedings of a joint conference in psychology* (pp. 1–17). Washington, DC: National Academy of Science, American Psychological Association.

Foxman, D. D., Martini, R. M., & Mitchell, P. (1982). *Mathematical development: Secondary survey report No. 3*. London: Her Majesty's Stationery Office.

Foxman, D. D., Ruddock, G., McCallum, & Schagen, P. (1991). *APU mathematics monitoring (phase 2)*. Slough, Berkshire: National Foundation for Educational Research.

Freudenthal, H. (1983). *A didactical phenomenology of mathematics*. Dordrecht, Netherlands: Reidel.

Frye, D., Braisby, N., Lowe, J., Maroudas, C., & Nicholls, J. (1989). Children's understanding of counting and cardinality. *Child Development, 60*, 1158–1171.

Fuson, K. C. (1988a). *Children's counting and concepts of number*. New York: Springer-Verlag.

Fuson, K. C. (1988b). Summary comments: Meaning in middle grade number concepts. In J. Hiebert & M. Behr (Eds.), *Number concepts and operations in the middle grades* (pp. 260–264). Hillsdale, NJ: Lawrence Erlbaum Associates; Reston, VA: National Council of Teachers of Mathematics.

Fuson, K. C. (1990a). Conceptual structures for multiunit numbers: Implications for learning and teaching multidigit addition, subtraction, and place value. *Cognition and Instruction, 7*(4), 343–403.

Fuson, K. C. (1990b). Issues in place-value and multi-digit addition and subtraction learning and teaching. *Journal for Research in Mathematics Education, 21*(4), 273–280.

Fuson, K. C. (1992a). Research on learning and teaching addition and subtraction of whole numbers. In G. Leinhardt, R. T. Putnam, & R. Hattrup (Eds.), *Analysis of arithmetic for mathematics teaching.* Hillsdale, NJ: Lawrence Erlbaum Associates.

Fuson, K. C. (1992b). Research on whole number addition and subtraction. In D. A. Grouws (Ed.), *Handbook of research on mathematics teaching and learning* (pp. 243–275). New York: Macmillan; Reston, VA: National Council of Teachers of Mathematics.

Fuson, K. C., & Briars, D. J. (1990). Using a base-ten blocks learning/teaching approach for first- and second-grade place-value and multidigit addition and subtraction. *Journal for Research in Mathematics Education, 21,* 180–206.

Fuson, K. C., & Burghardt, B. H. (1993, April). *Children's invented multidigit addition solutions and teacher support of problem solving and reflection.* Paper presented at the annual meeting of the American Educational Research Association, Atlanta.

Fuson, K. C., Fraivillig, J. L., & Burghardt, B. H. (1992). Relationships children construct among English number words, multiunit base-ten blocks, and written multidigit addition. In J. I. D. Campbell (Ed.), *The nature and origins of mathematical skills* (pp. 39–112). North Holland: Elsevier.

Fuson, K. C., & Hall, J. W. (1983). The acquisition of early number word meanings. In H. Ginsburg (Ed.), *The development of children's mathematical thinking* (pp. 49–107). New York: Academic Press.

Fuson, K. C., & Kwon, Y. (1992). Korean children's single-digit addition and subtraction: Numbers structured by ten. *Journal for Research in Mathematics Education, 23*(2), 148–165.

Fuson, K. C., Richards, J., & Briars, D. J. (1982). The acquisition and elaboration of the number word sequence. In C. Brainerd (Ed.), *Progress in cognitive development research: Vol. 1. Children's logical and mathematical cognition* (pp. 33–92). New York: Springer-Verlag.

Fuson, K. C., & Willis, G. B. (1989). Second graders' use of schematic drawings in solving addition and subtraction word problems. *Journal of Educational Psychology, 81,* 514–520.

Gallistel, C. R. (1990). *The organization of learning.* Cambridge, MA: MIT Press.

Garner, R. (1990). When children and adults do not use learning strategies: Toward a theory of settings. *Review of Educational Research, 60*(4), 517–530.

Garofalo, J., Kroll, D. L., & Lester, F. K. (1987, July). *Metacognition and mathematical problem solving: Preliminary research findings.* Paper presented at the annual meeting of the International Group for the Psychology of Mathematics Education, Montreal.

Gelman, R. (1977). How young children reason about small numbers. In N. J.

Castellan, D. B. Pisoni, & G. R. Potts (Eds.), *Cognitive theory* (Vol. 2, pp. 219–238). New York: Springer-Verlag.

Gelman, R. (1990). First principles organize attention to and learning about relevant data: Number and the animate-inanimate distinction. *Cognitive Science, 14*, 79–106.

Gelman, R. (1991). Epigenetic foundations of knowledge structures: Initial and transcendent constructions. In S. Carey & R. Gelman (Eds.), *The epigenesis of mind: Essays on biology and cognition* (pp. 293–322). Hillsdale, NJ: Lawrence Erlbaum Associates.

Gelman, R., & Brown, A. L. (1986). Changing views of competence in the young. In N. J. Smelser & D. R. Gerstein (Eds.), *Behavioral and social science: Fifty years of discovery* (pp. 175–207). Washington, DC: National Academy Press.

Gelman, R., & Gallistel, C. R. (1978). *The child's understanding of number.* Cambridge, MA: Harvard University Press.

Gelman R., & Greeno, J. G. (1989). On the nature of competence: Principles for understanding in a domain. In L. B. Resnick (Ed.), *Knowing, learning, and understanding* (pp.125–186). Hillsdale, NJ: Lawrence Erlbaum Associates.

Gelman, R., & Markman, E. (1986). Categories and induction in young children. *Cognition, 23*, 183–209.

Gelman, R., & Meck, E. (1986). The notion of principle: The case of counting. In J. Hiebert (Ed.), *The relationship between procedural and conceptual competence* (pp. 29–57). Hillsdale, NJ: Lawrence Erlbaum Associates.

Gentner, D. (1982). Are scientific analogies metaphors? In D. S. Miall (Ed.), *Metaphor: Problems and perspectives* (pp. 106–132). Atlantic Highlands, NJ: Humanities Press.

Gentner, D. (1983). Structure mapping: A theoretical framework for analogy. *Cognitive Science, 7*, 155–170.

Gentner, D. (1988). Metaphor as structure mapping: The relational shift. *Child Development, 59*(1), 47–59.

Gentner, D. (1989). The mechanisms of analogical learning. In S. Vosniadou & A. Ortony (Eds.), *Similarity and analogical reasoning* (pp. 199–241). Cambridge: Cambridge University Press.

Gentner, D., & Gentner, D. R. (1983). Flowing waters or teaming crowd: Mental models of electricity. In D. Gentner & A. L. Stevens (Eds.), *Mental models* (pp. 99–129). Hillsdale, NJ: Lawrence Erlbaum Associates.

Gentner, D., & Landers, R. (1985, November). Analogical reminding: A good match is hard to find. *Proceedings of the International Conference on Systems,* Tucson, AZ.

Gentner, D., & Toupin, C. (1986). Systematicity and surface similarity in the development of analogy. *Cognitive Science, 10*, 277–300.

Gholson, B., Dattel, A. R., Morgan, D., & Eymard, L. A. (1989). Problem solving, recall, and mapping relations in isomorphic transfer and non-isomorphic transfer among preschoolers and elementary school children. *Child Development, 60*(5), 1172–1187.

Gholson, B., Eymard, L. A., Long, D., Morgan, D., & Leeming, F. C. (1988). Problem solving, recall, isomorphic transfer, and nonisomorphic transfer among third-grade and fourth-grade children. *Child Development, 3*, 37–53.

Gholson, B., Morgan, D., Dattel, A. R., & Pierce, K. A. (1990). The development of analogical problem solving: Strategic processes in schema acquisition and transfer. In D. F. Bjorklund (Ed.), *Children's strategies: Contemporary views of cognitive development* (pp. 269–308). Hillsdale, NJ: Lawrence Erlbaum Associates.

Gick, M. L., & Holyoak, K. J. (1983). Schema induction and analogical transfer. *Cognitive Psychology, 15*, 1–38.

Gilbert, R. K., & Bush, W. S. (1988). Familiarity, availability, and use of manipulative devices in mathematics at the primary level. *School Science and Mathematics, 88*(6), 459–469.

Ginsburg, H. P. (1985). Piaget and education. In N. Entwistle (Ed.), *New directions in educational psychology* (pp. 45–60). London: The Falmer Press.

Ginsburg, H. P., & Baron, J. (1993). Cognition: Young children's construction of mathematics. In R. J. Jensen (Ed.), *Research ideas for the classroom: Early childhood mathematics* (pp. 3–21). National Council of Teachers of Mathematics Research Interpretation Project. New York: Macmillan.

Ginsburg, H. P., Posner, J. K., & Russell, R. L. (1981). The development of mental addition as a function of schooling and culture. *Journal of Cross-Cultural Psychology, 12*, 163–178.

Glaser, R. (1990). The re-emergence of learning theory within instructional research. *American Psychologist, 45*(1), 29–39.

Goswami, U. (1991). Analogical reasoning: What develops? *Child Development, 62*(1), 1–22.

Goswami, U. (1992). *Analogical reasoning in children.* Hillsdale, NJ: Lawrence Erlbaum Associates.

Goswami, U., & Brown, A. L. (1990). Melting chocolate and melting snowmen: Analogical reasoning and causal relations. *Cognition, 35*(1), 69–95.

Graeber, A. O., & Baker, K. M. (1991). Curriculum materials and misconceptions concerning multiplication and division. *Focus on Learning Problems in Mathematics, 13*(3), 25–38.

Graeber, A. O., & Tanenhaus, E. (1993). Multiplication and division: From whole numbers to rational numbers. In D.T. Owens (Ed.), *Research ideas for the classroom: Middle grade mathematics* (pp. 99–126). National Council of Teachers of Mathematics Research Interpretation Project. New York: Macmillan.

Graeber, A. O., & Tirosh, D. (1988). Multiplication and division involving decimals: Preservice elementary teachers' performance and beliefs. *Journal of Mathematical Behavior, 7*, 263–280.

Graeber, A. O., & Tirosh, D. (1990). Insights fourth and fifth graders bring to multiplication and division with decimals. *Educational Studies in Mathematics, 21*, 565–588.

Graeber, A. O., Tirosh, D., & Glover, R. (1989). Preservice teachers' misconceptions in solving verbal problems in multiplication and division. *Journal for Research in Mathematics Education, 20*(1), 95–102.

Graham, C. Z. (1991). Strengthening a K–8 mathematics program. In M. J. Kenny & C. R. Hirsch (Eds.), *Discrete mathematics across the curriculum, K–12* (1991 yearbook, pp. 18–29). Reston, VA: National Council of Teachers of Mathematics.

Gray, E. M. (1991). An analysis of diverging approaches to simple arithmetic: Preference and its consequences. *Educational Studies in Mathematics, 22*, 551–574.

Greeno, J. G. (1989). Situation models, mental models, and generative knowledge. In D. Klahr & K. Kotovsky (Eds.), *Complex information processing: The impact of Herbert Simon*. Hillsdale, NJ: Lawrence Erlbaum Associates.

Greeno, J. G. (1991). Number sense as situated knowing in a conceptual domain. *Journal for Research in Mathematics Education, 22*(3), 170–218.

Greeno, J. G. (1992). Mathematical and scientific thinking in classrooms and other situations. In D. F. Halpern (Ed.), *Enhancing thinking skills in the sciences and mathematics* (pp. 39–61). Hillsdale, NJ: Lawrence Erlbaum Associates.

Greeno, J. G., & Johnson, W. (1985). Competence for solving and understanding problems. In G. d'Ydewalle (Ed.), *Cognition, information processing and motivation*. Amsterdam: Elsevier.

Greeno, J. G., Riley, M. S., & Gelman, R. (1984). Conceptual competence and children's counting. *Cognitive Psychology, 16*, 94–143.

Greer, B. (1988). Nonconservation of multiplication and division involving decimals. *Journal for Research in Mathematics Education, 18*(1), 37–45.

Greer, B. (1992). Multiplication and division as models of situations. In D. A. Grouws (Ed.), *Handbook of research on mathematics teaching and learning* (pp. 276–295). New York: Macmillan; Reston, VA: National Council of Teachers of Mathematics.

Grieve, R., & Garton, A. (1981). On the young child's comparison of sets. *Journal of Experimental Child Psychology, 32*, 443–458.

Groen, G.J., & Kieran, C. (1983). In search of Piagetian Mathematics. In H. P. Ginsburg (Ed.), *The development of mathematical thinking* (pp. 351–375). New York: Academic Press.

Groen, G. J., & Parkman, J. M. (1972). A chronometric analysis of simple addition. *Psychological Review, 79*, 329–343.

Grover, B., Hojnacki, S. K., Paulson, D., & Matern, C. (1994). Legs + heads + 1,000,000,000 floor tiles = thinking mathematics. In C. A. Thornton & N. S. Bley (Eds.), *Windows of opportunity: Mathematics for students with special needs* (pp. 337–351). Reston, VA: National Council of Teachers of Mathematics.

Halford, G. S. (1982). *The development of thought*. Hillsdale, NJ: Lawrence Erlbaum Associates.

Halford, G. S. (1984). Can young children integrate premises in transitivity and serial order tasks? *Cognitive Psychology, 16*, 65–93.

Halford, G. S. (1987). A structure-mapping approach to cognitive development. *International Journal of Psychology, 22*, 609–642.

Halford, G. S. (1989). Reflections on 25 years of Piagetian cognitive developmental psychology, 1963–1988. *Human Development, 32*, 325–387.

Halford, G. S. (1992). Analogical reasoning and conceptual complexity in cognitive development. *Human Development, 35*(4), 193–217.

Halford, G. S. (1993). *Children's understanding: The development of mental models*. Hillsdale, NJ: Lawrence Erlbaum Associates.

Halford, G. S., & Boulton-Lewis, G. M. (1992). Value and limitations of analogs in mathematics teaching. In A. Demetriou, A. Efkliades, & M. Shayer (Eds.), *The modern theories of cognitive development go to school* (pp. 183–209). London: Routledge.

Halford, G. S., & Boyle, F. M. (1985). Do young children understand conservation of number? *Child Development, 56*, 165–176.

Halford, G. S., & Leitch, E. (1989). Processing load constraints: A structure-mapping approach. In M. A. Luszcz & T. Nettelbeck (Eds.), *Psychological development: Perspectives across the life-span* (pp. 151–159). Amsterdam: North-Holland.

Halford, G. S., Maybery, M. T., & Bain, J. D. (1986). Capacity limitations in children's reasoning: A dual task approach. *Child Development, 57*, 616–627.

Halford, G. S., Maybery, M. T., & Bain, J. D. (1988). Set-size effects in primary memory: An age-related capacity limitation? *Memory and Cognition, 16*(5), 480–487.

Halford, G. S., Maybery, M. T., Smith, S. B., Bain, J. D., Dickson, J. C., & Kelly, M. E. (1992). *Acquisition of reasoning: A computational model of strategy development in transitive inference.* University of Queensland, Australia: Department of Psychology, Centre for Human Information Processing and Problem Solving.

Halford, G. S., Smith, S. B., Dickson, J. C., Maybery, M. T., Kelly, M. E., Bain, J. D., & Stewart, J. E. M. (1995). Modeling the development of reasoning strategies: The roles of analogy, knowledge, and capacity. In T. Simon & G. S. Halford (Eds.), *Developing cognitive competence: New approaches to cognitive modeling.* Hillsdale, NJ: Lawrence Erlbaum Associates.

Halford, G. S., Wiles, J., Humphreys, M. S., & Wilson, W. H. (1993). Parallel distributed processing approaches to creative reasoning: Tensor models of memory and analogy. In T. Dartnall, S. Kim, R. Levinson, & D. Subramanian (Eds.), *Artificial intelligence and creativity. Papers from the 1993 Spring Symposium.* Technical Report SS-93-01. Menlo Park, CA: AAAI Press.

Halford, G. S., & Wilson, W. H. (1980). A category theory approach to cognitive development. *Cognitive Psychology, 12*, 356–411.

Halford, G. S., & Wilson, W. H. (1993). Creativity and capacity for representation: Why are humans so creative? *Newsletter of the Society for the Study of Artificial Intelligence and Simulation of Behaviour. Special Theme: AI and Creativity, 85*, 32–41.

Halford, G. S., & Wilson, W. H. (1994). *Processing capacity defined by relational complexity: Implications for comparative, developmental, and cognitive psychology.* Manuscript submitted for publication.

Halford, G. S., Wilson, W. H., Guo, J., Gayler, R. W., Wiles, J., & Stewart, J. E. M. (1994). Connectionist implications for processing capacity limitations in analogies. In K. J. Holyoak & J. Barnden (Eds.), *Advances in connnectionist and neural computation theory: Vol. 2. Analogical connections* (pp. 363–415). Norwood, NJ: Ablex.

Hall, R., Kibler, D., Wenger, E., & Truxaw, C. (1989). Exploring the episodic structure of algebra story problem solving. *Cognition and Instruction, 6*(3), 223–283.

Halpern, D. (1992). A cognitive approach to improving thinking skills in the sciences and mathematics. In D. Halpern (Ed.), *Enhancing thinking skills in the sciences and mathematics* (pp. 1–14). Hillsdale, NJ: Lawrence Erlbaum Associates.

Harel, G., Behr, M., Post, T., & Lesh, R. (1992). The blocks task: Comparative analyses of the task with other proportion tasks and qualitative reasoning skills of seventh-grade children in solving the task. *Cognition and Instruction, 9*(1), 45–96.

Harnishfeger, K. K., & Bjorklund, D. (1990). Children's strategies: A brief history. In D. F. Bjorklund (Ed.), *Children's strategies: Contemporary views of cognitive development* (pp.1–22). Hillsdale, NJ: Lawrence Erlbaum Associates.

Hart, K. (1981). Ratio and proportion. In K. M. Hart, M. L. Brown, D. E. Kuchemann, D. Kerslake, G. Ruddock, & M. McCartney (Eds.), *Children's understanding of mathematics 11–16* (pp. 88–101). London: John Murray.

Hart, K. (1984). *Ratio: Children's strategies and errors.* Windsor, England: NFER-Nelson Publishing Company.

Hart, L. C. (1993). Some factors that impede or enhance performance in mathematical problem solving. *Journal for Research in Mathematics Education, 24*(2), 167–171.

Harvey, J. G., & Romberg, T. A. (1980). *Problem-solving studies in mathematics.* Madison, WI: Wisconsin Research and Development Center Monograph Series.

Hayes, N. A., & Broadbent, D. E. (1988). Two models of learning for interactive tasks. *Cognition, 28,* 249–276.

Heege, H. ter. (1985). The acquisition of basic multiplication skills. *Educational Studies in Mathematics, 16,* 375–388.

Heller, P. M., Post, T. R., Behr, M., & Lesh, R. (1990). Qualitative and numerical reasoning about fractions and rates by seventh- and eighth-grade students. *Journal for Research in Mathematics Education, 21*(5), 388–402.

Hembree, R. (1992). Experiments and relational studies in problem solving: A meta-analysis. *Journal for Research in Mathematics Education, 23*(3), 242–273.

Herscovics, N. (1989). Cognitive obstacles encountered in the learning of algebra. In S. Wagner & C. Kieran (Eds.), *Research issues in the learning and teaching of algebra* (pp. 60–86). Reston, VA: National Council of Teachers of Mathematics; Hillsdale, NJ: Lawrence Erlbaum Associates.

Hersh, R. (1986). Some proposals for revising the philosophy of mathematics. In T. Tymoczko (Ed.), *New directions in the philosophy of mathematics* (pp. 9–28). Boston: Birkhauser.

Hiebert, J. (1992). Mathematical, cognitive, and instructional analyses of decimal fractions. In G. Leinhardt, R. T. Putnam, & R. Hattrup (Eds.), *Analysis of arithmetic for mathematics teaching* (pp. 283–322). Hillsdale, NJ: Lawrence Erlbaum Associates.

Hiebert, J., & Behr, M. (1988). Introduction: Capturing the major themes. In J. Hiebert, & M. Behr (Eds.), *Number concepts and operations in the middle grades* (pp. 1–18). Hillsdale, NJ: Lawrence Erlbaum Associates; Reston, VA: National Council of Teachers of Mathematics.

Hiebert, J., & Carpenter, T. P. (1992). Learning and teaching with understanding. In D. A. Grouws (Ed.), *Handbook of research on mathematics teaching and learning* (pp. 65–97). New York: Macmillan.

Hiebert, J., & Wearne, D. (1985). A model of students' decimal computation procedures. *Cognition and Instruction, 2,* 175–205.

Hiebert, J., & Wearne, D. (1986). Procedures over concepts: The acquisition of decimal number knowledge. In J. Hiebert (Ed.), *Conceptual and procedural knowledge: The case of mathematics* (pp. 199–223). Hillsdale, NJ: Lawrence Erlbaum Associates.

Hiebert, J., & Wearne, D. (1988). Instruction and cognitive change in mathematics. *Educational Psychologist, 23,* 105–117.

Hiebert, J., & Wearne, D. (1992). Links between teaching and learning place value with understanding in first grade. *Journal for Research in Mathematics Education, 23*(2), 98–122.

Hiebert, J., & Wearne, D. (1993). Instructional tasks, classroom discourse, and students' learning in second-grade arithmetic. *American Educational Research Journal, 30*(2), 393–425.

Hiebert, J., Wearne, D., & Taber, S. (1991). Fourth graders' gradual construction of decimal fractions during instruction using different physical representations. *The Elementary School Journal, 91*(4), 321–341.

Hinsley, D. A., Hayes, J. R., & Simon, H. A. (1977). From words to equations: Meaning and representation in algebra word problems. In M. A. Just & P. A. Carpenter (Eds.), *Cognitive processes in comprehension* (pp. 88–106). Hillsdale, NJ: Lawrence Erlbaum Associates.

Hoffer, A. R., & Hoffer, S. A. K. (1992). Ratios and proportional reasoning. In T. R. Post (Ed.), *Teaching mathematics in grades K-8: Research-based methods* (pp. 303–330). Sydney: Allyn & Bacon.

Holland, J. H., Holyoak, K. J., Nisbett, R. E., & Thagard, P. R. (1986). *Induction: Processes of inference, learning and discovery.* Cambridge, MA: Bradford Books/MIT Press.

Holyoak, K. J. (1985). The pragmatics of analogical transfer. In G. H. Bower (Ed.), *The psychology of learning and motivation* (Vol. 19, pp. 59–87). San Diego, CA: Academic Press.

Holyoak, K. J. (1991). *Symbolic connectionism: Towards third-generation theories of expertise.* Cambridge, UK: Cambridge University Press.

Holyoak, K. J., & Koh, K. (1987). Surface and structural similarity in analogical transfer. *Memory & Cognition, 15,* 332–340.

Holyoak, K. J., Koh, K., & Nisbett, R. E. (1989). A theory of conditioning: Inductive learning within rule-based hierarchies. *Psychological Review, 96*(2), 315–340.

Holyoak, K. J., & Nisbett, R. E. (1988). Induction. In R. J. Sternberg & E. E. Smith (Eds.), *The psychology of human thought* (pp. 50–91). Cambridge: Cambridge University Press.

Holyoak, K. J., Novick, L. R., & Melz, E. (1994). Component processes in analogical transfer: Mapping, pattern completion, and adaptation. In K. J. Holyoak & J. A. Barnden (Eds.), *Connectionist approaches to analogy, metaphor, and case-based reasoning* (Vol. 2, pp. 113–180). Norwood, NJ: Ablex.

Holyoak, K. J., & Thagard, P. (1989). A computational model of analogical problem solving. In S. Vosniadou & A. Ortony (Eds.), *Similarity and analogical reasoning* (pp. 242–266). New York: Cambridge University Press.

Holyoak, K. J., & Thagard, P. (1995). *Mental leaps: Analogy in creative thought.* Cambridge, MA: MIT Press.

Hope, J. A. (1987). A case study of a highly skilled mental calculator. *Journal for Research in Mathematics Education, 18*(5), 331–342.

Hope, J. A., & Owens, D. T. (1987). An analysis of the difficulty of learning fractions. *Focus on Learning Problems in Mathematics, 9*(4), 25–40.

Hope, J. A., & Sherrill, J. M. (1987). Characteristics of unskilled and skilled mental calculators. *Journal for Research in Mathematics Education, 18,* 98–111.

Howard, A. C. (1991, December). Addition of fractions: The unrecognized problem. *Mathematics Teacher,* 710–713.

Howe, M. L., & Rabinowitz, F. M. (1990). Resource panacea? Or just another day in the developmental forest. *Developmental Review, 10,* 125–154.

Howe, R. W., Blosser, P. E., & Warren, C. R. (1990). *Trends and issues in mathematics education: Curriculum and instruction.* Columbus, OH: ERIC Clearinghouse for Science, Mathematics, and Environmental Education (ED 335 231).

Hudson, T. (1983). Correspondences and numerical differences between disjoint sets. *Child Development, 54,* 84–90.

Hunting, R. P. (1991). The interaction of thought, words, and deeds in children's early fraction learning. In R. P. Hunting & G. Davis (Eds.), *Early fraction learning.* New York: Springer-Verlag.

Hunting, R. P. (1993, July). *On the role of didactic materials in teaching and learning mathematics.* Paper presented at the Sixteenth Annual Conference of the Mathematics Education Research Group of Australasia. Brisbane, Australia.

Hunting, R. P., Davis, G., & Bigelow, J. C. (1991). Higher order thinking in young children's engagements with a fraction machine. In R. P. Hunting & G. Davis (Eds.), *Early fraction learning* (pp. 73–90). New York: Springer-Verlag.

Hutchings, B. (1975). Low-stress subtraction. *Arithmetic Teacher, 22, 226–232.*

Janvier, C. (1987). Translation processes in mathematics education. In C. Janvier (Ed.), *Problems of representation in the teaching and learning of mathematics* (pp. 27–32). Hillsdale, NJ: Lawrence Erlbaum Associates.

Johnson-Laird, P. N. (1983). *Mental models.* Cambridge: Cambridge University Press.

Johnson-Laird, P. N., & Byrne, R. M. J. (1991). *Deduction.* Hillsdale, NJ: Lawrence Erlbaum Associates.

Jones, B. F., & Idol, L. (1990). Introduction. In B. F. Jones & L. Idol (Eds.), *Dimensions of thinking and cognitive instruction* (pp. 1–13). Hillsdale, NJ: Lawrence Erlbaum Associates.

Jones, G. A., & Thornton, C. A. (1993). Children's understanding of place value: A framework for curriculum development and assessment. *Young Children, 48*(5), 12–18.

Jones, G. A., Thornton, C. A., & Putt, I. J. (1994). A model for nurturing and assessing multidigit number sense among first grade children. *Educational Studies in Mathematics, 27,* 117–143.

Kahneman, D. (1973). *Attention and effort.* Englewood Cliffs, NJ: Prentice-Hall.

Kahneman, D., & Tversky, A. (1973). On the psychology of prediction. *Psychological Review, 80*(4), 237–251.

Kail, R. (1986). Sources of age differences in speed of processing. *Child Development, 57,* 969–987.

Kail, R. (1988). Developmental functions for speeds of cognitive processes. *Journal of Experimental Child Psychology, 45,* 339–364.

Kail, R. (1991). Processing time declines exponentially during childhood and adolescence. *Developmental Psychology, 27*(2), 259–266.

Kallio, K. D. (1982). Developmental change on a five-term transitive inference. *Journal of Experimental Child Psychology, 33,* 142–164.

Kamii, C., & Joseph, L. (1988). Teaching place value and double-column addition. *Arithmetic Teacher, 35*(6), 48–52.

Kamii, K., & DeClark, G. (1985). *Young children reinvent arithmetic: Implications of Piaget's theory.* New York: Teachers College Press.

Kamin, L. (1968). *Predictability, surprise, attention and conditioning.* New York: Appleton-Century-Crofts.

Kaput, J. J. (1985). Representation and problem solving: Methodological issues related to modeling. In E. A. Silver (Ed.), *Teaching and learning mathematical problem solving: Multiple research perspectives* (pp. 381–398). Hillsdale, NJ: Lawrence Erlbaum Associates.

Kaput, J. J. (1987). Representation systems and mathematics. In C. Janvier (Ed.), *Problems of representation in the teaching and learning of mathematics* (pp. 19–26). Hillsdale, NJ: Lawrence Erlbaum Associates Associates.

Kaput, J. J. (1989). Supporting concrete visual thinking in multiplicative reasoning: Difficulties and opportunities. *Focus on Learning Problems in Mathematics, 11*(1), 35–47.

Kaput, J. J., & Sims-Knight, J. (1984). Errors in translations to algebraic equations: Roots and implications. In M. Behr & G. Bright (Eds.), Special issue on mathematics learning problems of the postsecondary student. *Focus on Learning Problems in Mathematics.*

Karmiloff-Smith, A. (1979). Problem-solving construction and representations of closed railway circuits. *Archives of Psychology, 47*, 37–59.

Karmiloff-Smith, A. (1984). Children's problem solving. In M. Lamb, A. L. Brown, & B. Rogoff (Eds.), *Advances in educational psychology* (Vol. 3, pp. 39–90). Hillsdale, NJ: Lawrence Erlbaum Associates.

Karmiloff-Smith, A. (1986). From meta-processes to conscious access: Evidence from children's metalinguistic and repair data. *Cognition, 23*, 95–147.

Karmiloff-Smith, A. (1990). Constraints on representational change: Evidence from children's drawing. *Cognition, 34*(1), 57–83.

Karplus, E. F., Karplus, R., & Wollman, W. (1974). Intellectual development beyond elementary school IV: Ratio, the influence of cognitive style. *School Science and Mathematics, 74*, 476–482.

Karplus, R., Pulos, S., & Stage, E. K. (1983). Proportional reasoning of early adolescents. In R. Lesh & M. Landau (Eds.), *Acquisition of mathematics concepts and processes* (pp. 45–90). New York: Academic Press.

Kaye, D. B. (1986). The development of mathematical cognition. *Cognitive Development, 1*, 157–170.

Kaye, D. B., deWinstanley, P., Chen, Q., & Bonnefil, V. (1989). Development of efficient arithmetic computation. *Journal of Educational Psychology, 81*(4), 467–480.

Keil, F. C. (1981). Constraints on knowledge and cognitive development. *Psychological Review, 88*, 197–227.

Keil, F. C. (1990). Constraints on constraints: Surveying the epigenetic landscape. *Cognitive Science, 14*(1), 135–168.

Kennedy, L. M. (1986). A rationale. *Arithmetic Teacher, 33*(6), 6–7, 32.

Kieran, C. (1979). Children's operational thinking within the context of bracketing and the order of operations. In D. Tall (Ed.), *Proceedings of the Third International Conference for the Psychology of Mathematics Education* (pp. 128–133). Coventry, England: Warwick University, Mathematics Education Research Centre.

Kieran, C. (1982, March). *The learning of algebra: A teaching experiment.* Paper presented at the annual meeting of the American Educational Research Association, New York.

Kieran, C. (1984). A comparison between novice and more-expert algebra students on tasks dealing with the equivalence of equations. In J. M. Moser (Ed.), *Proceedings of the Sixth Annual Meeting of the North American Chapter of the International*

Group for the Psychology of Mathematics Education (pp. 83–91). Madison: University of Wisconsin.

Kieran, C. (1988). Two different approaches among algebra learners. In A. F. Coxford & A. P. Shulte (Eds.), *The ideas of algebra, K–12* (pp. 91–96). Reston, VA: National Council of Teachers of Mathematics.

Kieran, C. (1989). The early learning of algebra: A structural persepctive. In S. Wagner & C. Kieran (Eds.), *Research issues in the learning and teaching of algebra* (pp. 33–56). Reston, VA: National Council of Teachers of Mathematics; Hillsdale, NJ: Lawrence Erlbaum Associates.

Kieran, C. (1990). Cognitive processes involved in learning school algebra. *Mathematics and cognition: A research synthesis by the International Group for the Psychology of Mathematics Education* (pp. 96–112). Cambridge: Cambridge University Press.

Kieran, C. (1992). The learning and teaching of school algebra. In D. A. Grouws, (Ed.), *Handbook of research on mathematics teaching and learning* (pp. 390–419). New York: Macmillan.

Kieran, C., & Chalouh, L. (1993). Prealgebra: The transition from arithmetic to algebra. In D.T. Owens (Ed.), *Research ideas for the classroom: Middle grade mathematics* (pp. 179–198). National Council of Teachers of Mathematics Research Interpretation Project. New York: Macmillan.

Kieren, T. E. (1976). On the mathematical, cognitive, and instructional foundations of rational numbers. In R. Lesh (Ed.), *Number and measurement* (pp. 125–149). Columbus, OH: ERIC/SMEAC.

Kieren, T. E. (1980). The rational number construct: Its elements and mechanisms. In T. E. Kieren (Ed.), *Recent research on number learning* (pp. 125–150). Columbus: ERIC/SMEAC.

Kieren, T. E. (1983). Axioms and intuition in mathematical knowledge building. In J. Bergeron & N. Herscovics (Eds.), *Proceedings of the Fifth Annual PME-NA Meeting* (pp. 67–73). Montreal: PME:NA.

Kieren, T. E. (1988). Personal knowledge of rational numbers: Its intuitive and formal development. In J. Hiebert, & M. Behr (Eds.), *Number concepts and operations in the middle grades,* (pp. 162–181). Hillsdale, NJ: Lawrence Erlbaum Associates; Reston, VA: National Council of Teachers of Mathematics.

Kieren, T. E. (1993). Rational and fractional numbers: From quotient fields to recursive understanding. In T. Carpenter, E. Fennema, & T. A. Romberg (Eds.), *Rational numbers: An integration of research* (pp. 49–84). Hillsdale, NJ: Lawrence Erlbaum Associates.

Kilpatrick, J. (1987a). Problem formulating: Where do good problems come from? In A. H. Schoenfeld, (Ed.), *Cognitive science and mathematics education* (pp. 123–147). Hillsdale, NJ: Lawrence Erlbaum Associates.

Kilpatrick, J. (1987b). What constructivism might be in mathematics education. In J. C. Bergeron (Ed.), *Proceedings of the Eleventh International Conference of the International Group for the Psychology of Mathematics Education* (Vol. 1, pp. 3–27).

Kilpatrick, J. (1992). A history of research in mathematics education. In D. A. Grouws (Ed.), *Handbook of research on mathematics teaching and learning* (pp. 3–38). New York: Macmillan; Reston, VA: National Council of Teachers of Mathematics.

Kintsch, W. (1986). Learning from text. *Cognition and Instruction, 3*(2), 87–108.

Kintsch, W., & Greeno, J. G. (1985). Understanding and solving word arithmetic problems. *Psychological Review, 92*, 109–129.

Kirshner, D. (1989a). Critical issues in current representation system theory. In S. Wagner & C. Kieran (Eds.), *Research issues in the learning and teaching of algebra* (pp. 195–198). Reston, VA: National Council of Teachers of Mathematics; Hillsdale, NJ: Lawrence Erlbaum Associates.

Kirshner, D. (1989b). The visual syntax of algebra. *Journal of Research in Mathematics Education, 20*(3), 274–287.

Klahr, D. (1984). *Transition processes in quantitative development*. New York: Freeman.

Koltz, E. (1991). Visualization in geometry: A case study of a multimedia mathematics education project. In W. Zimmermann & S. Cunningham (Eds.), *Visualization in teaching and learning mathematics* (pp. 95–104). Mathematical Association of America.

Kouba, V. L. (1989). Children's solution strategies for equivalent set multiplication and division word problems. *Journal for Research in Mathematics Education, 20*(2), 147–158.

Kouba, V. L., Brown, C. A., Carpenter, T. P., Lindquist, M. M., Silver, E. A., & Swafford, J. O. (1988). Results of the fourth NAEP assessment of mathematics: Number, operations, and word problems. *Arithmetic Teacher, 35*(8), 10–16.

Kouba, V. L., & Franklin, K. (1993). Multiplication and division: Sense making and meaning. In R. J. Jensen (Ed.), *Research ideas for the classroom: Early childhood mathematics* (pp. 103–126). National Council of Teachers of Mathematics Research Interpretation Project. New York: Macmillan.

Kroll, D. L. (1989). Connections between psychological learning theories and the elementary mathematics curriculum. In P. Trafton & A. Shulte (Eds.), *New directions for elementary school mathematics* (pp. 199–211). Reston, VA: National Council of Teachers of Mathematics.

Kuchemann, D. E. (1981). Algebra. In K. Hart (Ed.), *Children's understanding of mathematics: 11–16* (pp. 102–119). London: John Murray.

Kuhn, D., Amsel, E., & O'Loughlin (1988). *The development of scientific thinking skills*. Orlando, FL: Academic Press.

Kuhn, D., & Phelps, E. (1982). The development of problem-solving strategies. In H. W. Reese (Ed.), *Advances in child development and behavior* (pp. 2–43). New York: Academic Press.

Kun, A. (1977). Development of the magnitude-covariation and compensation schemata in ability and effort attributions of performance. *Child Development, 48*, 862–873.

Labinowicz, E. (1985). *Learning from children: New beginnings for teaching numerical thinking*. Menlo Park, CA: Addison-Wesley.

Lamon, S. J. (1993a). Ratio and proportion: Children's cognitive and metacognitive processes. In T. Carpenter, E. Fennema, & T. A. Romberg (Eds.), *Rational numbers: An integration of research* (pp. 131–156). Hillsdale, NJ: Lawrence Erlbaum Associates.

Lamon, S. J. (1993b). Ratio and proportion: Connecting content and children's thinking. *Journal for Research in Mathematics Education, 24*(1), 41–61.

Lampert, M. (1986). Knowing, doing, and teaching multiplication. *Cognition and Instruction, 3*(4), 305–342.

Lampert, M. (1990). When the problem is not the question and the solution is not the answer: Mathematical knowing and teaching. *American Educational Research Journal, 27*, 29–63.

Lampert, M. (1992). Teaching and learning long division for understanding in school. In G. Leinhardt, R. T. Putnam, & R. Hattrup (Eds.), *Analysis of arithmetic for mathematics teaching* (pp. 221–282). Hillsdale, NJ: Lawrence Erlbaum Associates.

Larkin, J. H., McDermott, J., Simon, D. P., & Simon, H. A. (1980). Expert and novice performance in solving physics problems. *Science, 208*, 1335–1342.

Larson, S. Behr, M., Harel, G., Post, T., & Lesh, R. (1989). Proportional reasoning in young adolescents: An analysis of strategies. In C. A. Maher, G. A. Goldin, & R. B. Davis (Eds.), *Proceedings of the Eleventh Annual Meeting of the American Chapter of the International Group for the Psychology of Mathematics Education* (pp. 181–197), New Brunswick, NJ.

Lawler, R. W. (1981). The progressive construction of mind. *Cognitive Science, 5*, 1–30.

Lawson, M. J. (1990). The case for instruction in the use of general problem-solving strategies in mathematics teaching: A comment on Owen and Sweller. *Journal for Research in Mathematics Education, 21*(5), 403–410.

LeBlanc, J. F. (1976). (Ed.). *Numeration.* Reading, MA: Addison-Wesley.

Leder, G. C. (1992). Mathematics and gender: Changing perspectives. In D. A. Grouws (Ed.), *Handbook of research on mathematics teaching and learning* (pp. 597–622). New York: Macmillan.

Lee, L., & Wheeler, D. (1989). The arithmetic connection. *Educational Studies in Mathematics, 20*(1), 41–45.

Leinhardt, G. (1987). The development of an expert explanation: An analysis of a sequence of subtraction lessons. *Cognition and Instruction, 4*, 225–282.

Leinhardt, G. (1988). Getting to know: Tracing students' mathematical knowledge from intuition to competence. *Educational Psychologist, 23*(2), 119–144.

Leitzel, J. R. (1989). Critical considerations for the future of algebra instruction. In S. Wagner & C. Kieran (Eds.), *Research issues in the learning and teaching of algebra* (Vol. 4, pp. 25–32). Hillsdale, NJ: Lawrence Erlbaum Associates; Reston, VA: National Council of Teachers of Mathematics.

Lesgold, A. (1988). Problem solving. In R. J. Sternberg & E. E. Smith (Eds.), *The psychology of human thought* (pp. 188–213). Cambridge: Cambridge University Press.

Lesgold, S. B., Putnam, R. T., Resnick, L. B., & Sterrett, S. G. (1987, April). *Referents and understanding of algebraic transformations.* Paper presented at the annual meeting of the American Educational Research Association, Washington, DC.

Lesh, R. (1991). Computer-based assessment of higher order understandings and processes in elementary mathematics. In G. Kulm (Ed.), *Assessing higher order thinking in mathematics* (pp. 81–110). Washington, DC: American Association for the Advancement of Science.

Lesh, R., Post, T., & Behr, M. (1987). Representations and translations among representations in mathematics learning and problem solving. In C. Janvier (Ed.),

Problems of representation in the teaching and learning of mathematics (pp. 33–40). Hillsdale, NJ: Lawrence Erlbaum Associates.

Lesh, R., Post, T., & Behr, M. (1988). Proportional reasoning. In J. Hiebert & M. Behr (Eds.), *Number concepts and operations in the middle grades* (pp. 93–118). Hillsdale, NJ: Lawrence Erlbaum Associates; Reston, VA: National Council of Teachers of Mathematics.

Lester, F. (1989). Reflections about mathematical problem-solving research. In R. I. Charles & E. A. Silver (Eds.), *The teaching and assessing of mathematical problem solving* (pp. 115–124). Hillsdale, NJ: Lawrence Erlbaum Associates.

Lester, F. K., & Garofalo, J. (1982, March). *Metacognitve aspects of elementary school students' performance on arithmetic tasks.* Paper presented at the annual meeting of the American Educational Research Association, New York.

Lester, F. K., Garofalo, J., & Kroll, D. (1989). *The role of metacognition in mathematical problem solving: A study of two grade seven classes* (Final report to the National Science Foundation, NSF project MDR 85-50346).

Lewis, A. B. (1989). Training students to represent arithmetic word problems. *Journal of Educational Psychology, 81*(4), 521–531.

Lewis, A. B., & Mayer, R. E. (1987). Students' miscomprehension of relational statements in arithmetic word problems. *Journal of Educational Psychology, 79,* 363–371.

Lindquist, M. M. (1989). *Results from the fourth mathematics assessment of the National Asessment of Educational Progress.* Reston, VA: National Council of Teachers of Mathematics.

Lipman, M. (1984). Philosophy and the cultivation of reasoning. *Thinking: The Journal of Philosophy for Children, 5*(4), 33–41.

Lipman, M., & Sharp, A. (1982a). *Looking for meaning: An instructional manual to accompany Pixie.* New York: University Press of America.

Lipman, M., & Sharp, A. (1982b). *Wondering at the world: An instructional manual to accompany Kio and Gus.* New York: University Press of America.

Lipman, M., Sharp, A., & Oscanyan, F. (Eds.). (1984). *Philosophical inquiry: An instructional manual to accompany Harry Stottlemeier's Discovery. 2nd Edition.* New York: University Press of America.

Logan, G. D. (1979). On the use of a concurrent memory load to measure attention and automaticity. *Journal of Experimental Psychology: Human Perception and Performance, 5,* 189–207.

MacGregor, M., & Stacey, K. (1993). Cognitive models underlying students' formulation of simple linear equations. *Journal for Research in Mathematics Education, 24*(3), 217–232

Mack, N. K. (1990). Learning fractions with understanding: Building on informal knowledge. *Journal for Research in Mathematics Education, 21*(1), 16–32.

Mack, N. K. (1993). Learning rational numbers with understanding: The case of informal knowledge. In T. P. Carpenter, E. Fennema, & T. A. Romberg (Eds.), *Rational numbers: An integration of research* (pp. 85–106). Hillsdale, NJ: Lawrence Erlbaum Associates.

Maher, C., & Martino, A. M. (1991). The construction of mathematical knowledge by individual children working in groups. In P. Boero (Ed.), *Proceedings of the*

Fifteenth Annual Conference of the International Group for the Psychology of Mathematics Education (pp. 365–372). Assissi, Italy: PME.

Markman, E. M., & Seibert, J. (1976). Classes and collections: Internal organization and resulting holistic properties. *Cognitive Psychology, 8*, 561–577.

Martino, A., & Maher, C. (1991). An analysis of Stephanie's justifications of problem representations in small group interactions. In R. Underhill (Ed.), *Proceedings of the Thirteenth Annual Meeting for the North American Chapter for the Psychology of Mathematics Education* (pp. 70–76). Blacksburg, VA: Virginia Polytechnic University.

Mason, J., Burton, L., & Stacey, K. (1982). *Thinking mathematically.* London: Addison-Wesley.

Matz, M. (1979). *Towards a process model for high school algebra errors.* (Working Paper 181). Cambridge: Massachusetts Institute of Technology, Artificial Intelligence Laboratory.

Matz, M. (1982). Towards a process model for high school algebra errors. In D. Sleeman & J. S. Brown (Eds.), *Intelligent tutoring systems* (pp. 25–50). New York: Academic Press.

Maybery, M. T., Bain, J. D., & Halford, G. S. (1986). Information processing demands of transitive inference. *Journal of Experimental Psychology: Learning, Memory, & Cognition, 12*, 600–613.

Mayer Committee (1992). *Employment-related key competencies: A proposal for consultation.* Canberra, Australia: Ministry of Education and Training.

Mayer, R. E., Lewis, A. B., & Hegarty, M. (1992). Mathematical misunderstandings: Qualitative reasoning about quantitative problems. In J. I. D. Campbell (Ed.), *The nature and origins of mathematical skills* (pp. 137–154). Amsterdam: Elsevier.

McClelland, J. L., & Rumelhart, D. E. (1986). (Eds.). *Parallel distributed processing, Vol. 2.* Cambridge, MA: MIT Press.

McCloskey, M. (1983). Naive theories of motion. In D. Gentner & A. L. Stevens (Eds.), *Mental models* (pp. 299–324). Hillsdale, NJ: Lawrence Erlbaum Associates.

McCloskey, M., & Lindemann, A. M. (1992). MATHNET: Preliminary results from a distributed model of arithmetic fact retrieval. In J. I. D. Campbell (Ed.), *The nature and origins of mathematical skills* (pp. 365–409). Amsterdam: Elsevier.

McCoy, L. P. (1990, April). *Correlates of mathematics anxiety.* Paper presented at the annual meeting of the American Educational Research Association, Boston.

McGarrigle, J., & Donaldson, M. (1975). Conservation accidents. *Cognition, 3*, 341–350.

McGarrigle, J., Grieve, R., & Hughes, M. (1978). Interpreting inclusion: A contribution to the study of the child's cognitive and linguistic development. *Journal of Experimental Child Psychology, 26*, 528–550.

McKnight, C. C., Crosswhite, F. J., Dossey, J. A., Kifer, E., Swafford, J. O., Travers, K. J., & Cooney, T. J. (1987). *The underachieving curriculum: Assessing U.S. school mathematics from an international perspective.* Champaign, IL: Stipes.

McLeod, D. B. (1985). Affective issues in research on teaching mathematical problem solving. In E. A. Silver (Ed.), *Teaching and learning mathematical problem solving: Multiple research perspectives* (pp. 267–279). Hillsdale, NJ: Lawrence Erlbaum Associates.

McLeod, D. B. (1992). Research on affect in mathematics education: A reconceptualization. In D. A. Grouws, (Ed.), *Handbook of research on mathematics teaching and learning* (pp. 575–596). New York: Macmillan.

McLeod, D. B., & Adams, V. M. (Eds.). (1989). *Affect and mathematical problem solving: A new perspective.* New York: Springer-Verlag.

Mechmandarov, I. (1987). *The role of dimensional analysis in teaching multiplicative word problems.* Unpublished manuscript, Center for Educational Technology, Tel-Aviv.

Meck, W. H., & Church, R. M. (1983). A mode control model of counting and timing processes. *Journal of Experimental Psychology: Animal Behavior Processes, 9,* 320–334.

Meyer, M. R., & Fennema, E. (1988). Girls, boys, and mathematics. In T. R. Post (Ed.), *Teaching mathematics in grades K–8: Research-based methods* (pp. 406–425). Boston: Allyn & Bacon.

Michie, S. (1985). Development of absolute and relative concepts of number in preschool children. *Developmental Psychology, 21*(2), 247–252.

Miller, G. A. (1956). The magical number seven, plus or minus two: Some limits on our capacity for processing information. *Psychological Review, 63,* 81–97.

Miller, K., & Gelman, R. (1983). The child's representation of number: A multidimensional scaling analysis. *Child Development, 54,* 1470–1479.

Miller-Jones, D. (1991). Informal reasoning in inner-city children. In J. F. Voss, D. N. Perkins, & J. W. Segal (Eds.), *Informal reasoning and education* (pp. 107–130). Hillsdale, NJ: Lawrence Erlbaum Associates.

Minor, L. H. (1988). Factoring twins as a teaching tool. In A. F. Coxford & A. P. Shulte (Eds.), *The ideas of algebra, K–12* (pp. 192–198). Reston, VA: National Council of Teachers of Mathematics.

Miura, I. T., Okamoto, Y., Kim, C. C., Steere, M., & Fayol, M. (1993). First graders' cognitive representation of number and understanding of place value: Cross-national comparisons: France, Japan, Korea, Sweden, and the United States. *Journal of Educational Psychology, 85*(1), 24–30.

Miwa, T. (1992). School mathematics in Japan and the U.S.: Focusing on recent trends in elementary and lower secondary school. In I. Wirszup & R. Streit (Eds.), *Developments in school mathematics education around the world* (Vol. 3, pp. 405–427). Reston VA: National Council of Teachers of Mathematics.

Moses, B., Bjork, E., & Goldenberg, E. P. (1990). Beyond problem solving: Problem posing. In T. J. Cooney & C. R. Hirsch (Eds.), *Teaching and learning mathematics in the 1990s* (pp. 82–91). Reston, VA: National Council of Teachers of Mathematics.

Mulligan, J. T. (1992). Children's solutions to multiplication and division word problems: A longitudinal study. *Mathematics Education Research Journal, 4*(1), 24–42.

Mulligan, J. T. (1993, July). *Sixth graders' understanding of multiplicative structures: A five year follow-up study.* Paper presented at the *Sixteenth Annual Conference of the Mathematics Education Research Group of Australasia,* Brisbane, Australia.

Narode, R., Heiman, M., Lochhead, J., & Slomianko, J. (1987). *Teaching thinking skills: Science.* Washington, DC: National Education Association.

Nathan, M. J., Kintsch, W., & Young, E. (1992). A theory of algebra word-problem comprehension and its implications for the design of learning environments. *Cognition and Instruction 9*(4), 329–391.

National Assessment of Educational Progress (1983). *The third mathematics assessment of the national assessment of educational progress: Results, trends, and issues.* Denver, CO: Education Commission of the States.

National Council of Teachers of Mathematics (1980). *An agenda for action: Recommendations for school mathematics of the 1980s.* Reston, VA: Author.

National Council of Teachers of Mathematics (1989). *Curriculum and evaluation standards for school mathematics.* Reston, VA: Author.

National Council of Teachers of Mathematics (1991). *Professional standards for teaching mathematics.* Reston, VA: Author.

National Research Council (1989). *Everybody counts: A report to the nation on the future of mathematics education.* Washington, DC: National Academy Press.

National Research Council (1990). *Reshaping school mathematics: A philosophy and framework for curriculum.* Washington, DC: National Academy Press.

Nesher, P. (1988). Multiplicative school word problems: Theoretical approaches and empirical findings. In J. Hiebert & M. Behr (Eds.), *Number concepts and operations in the middle grades* (pp. 19–40). Hillsdale, NJ: Lawrence Erlbaum Associates; Reston, VA: National Council of Teachers of Mathematics.

Nesher, P. (1989). Microworlds in mathematics education: A pedagogical realism. In L. B. Resnick (Ed.), *Knowing, learning, and instruction: Essays in honor of Robert Glaser.* Hillsdale, NJ: Lawrence Erlbaum Associates.

Nesher, P. (1992). Solving multiplication word problems. In G. Leinhardt, R. T. Putnam, & R. Hattrup (Eds.), *Analysis of arithmetic for mathematics teaching* (pp. 189–220). Hillsdale, NJ: Lawrence Erlbaum Associates.

Nesher, P., & Peled, I. (1986). Shifts in reasoning. *Educational Studies in Mathematics, 17,* 67–79.

Newell, A., & Simon, H. A. (1972). *Human problem solving.* Englewood Cliffs, NJ: Prentice-Hall.

Nickerson, R. S., Perkins, D. N., & Smith, E. E. (1985). *The teaching of thinking.* Hillsdale, NJ: Lawrence Erlbaum Associates.

Nik Pa, N. A. (1986). Meaning in arithmetic from four different perspectives. *For the Learning of Mathematics, 6*(1), 11–16.

Noddings, N. (1990). Constructivism in mathematics education. In R. B. Davis, C. A. Maher, & N. Noddings (Eds.), *Constructivist views on the teaching and learning of mathematics* (pp. 7–18). Reston, VA: National Council of Teachers of Mathematics.

Noelting, G. (1980). The development of proportional reasoning and the ratio concept: Part 1. Differentiation of stages. *Educational Studies in Mathematics, 11,* 217–253.

Norman, D. A. (1986). *Reflections on cognition and parallel distributed processing.* Cambridge, MA: MIT Press.

Norris, S. P., & Ennis, R. H. (1989). *Evaluating critical thinking.* Pacific Grove, CA: Midwest Publications.

Norris, S. P., & Perkins, D. N. (1989). *Teaching thinking: Issues and approaches.* Pacific Grove, CA: Midwest Publications.

Novick, L. R. (1988). Analogical transfer, problem similarity, and expertise. *Journal of Experimental Psychology: Learning, Memory, and Cognition, 14,* 510–520.

Novick, L. R. (1990). Representational transfer in problem solving. *Psychological Science, 1*(2), 128–133.

Novick, L. R. (1992). The role of expertise in solving arithmetic and algebra word problems by analogy. In J. I. D. Campbell (Ed.), *The nature and origins of mathematical skills* (pp. 155–188). Amsterdam: Elsevier.

Novick, L. R., & Francis M. (1993, November). *Assessing students' knowledge and use of symbolic representations in problem solving.* Paper presented at the 34th meeting of the Psychonomic Society, Washington, DC.

Novick, L. R., & Holyoak, K. J. (1991). Mathematical problem solving by analogy. *Journal of Experimental Psychology: Learning, Memory, and Cognition, 17,* 398–415.

Novillis, C. G. (1976). An analysis of the fraction concept into a hierarchy of selected subconcepts and the testing of the hierarchical dependencies. *Journal for Research in Mathematics Education, 7,* 131–144.

Ohlsson, S. (1988). Mathematical learning and applicational meaning in the semantics of fractions and related concepts. In J. Hiebert & M. Behr (Eds.), *Number concepts and operations in the middle grades* (pp. 55–92). Hillsdale, NJ: Lawrence Erlbaum Associates; Reston, VA: National Council of Teachers of Mathematics.

Ohlsson, S., & Rees, E. (1988). *An information processing analysis of the function of conceptual understanding in the learning of arithmetic procedures* (Tech. Rep. No. KUL 88–03). Pittsburgh: University of Pittsburgh, Learning Research and Development Center.

Ohlsson, S., & Rees, E. (1991). The function of conceptual understanding in the learning of arithmetic procedures. *Cognition and Instruction, 8*(2), 103–179.

Onslow, B. (1991). Linking reality and symbolism: A primary function of mathematics. *For the Learning of Mathematics, 11*(1), 33–37.

Paivio, A. (1971). *Imagery and verbal processes.* New York: Holt, Rinehart & Winston.

Paris, S., & Winograd, P. (1990). How metacognition can promote academic learning and instruction. In B. F. Jones & L. Idol (Eds.), *Dimensions of thinking and cognitive instruction* (pp. 15–52). Hillsdale, NJ: Lawrence Erlbaum Associates.

Pascual-Leone, J. A. (1970). A mathematical model for the transition rule in Piaget's developmental stages. *Acta Psychologica, 32,* 301–345.

Pascual-Leone, J. A. (1984). *Attention, dialectic and mental effort: Towards an organismic theory of life stages.* New York: Plenum.

Paul, R. (1990). Critical and reflective thinking: A philosophical perspective. In B. F. Jones & L. Idol (Eds.), *Dimensions of thinking and cognitive instruction* (pp. 445–493). Hillsdale, NJ: Lawrence Erlbaum Associates.

Payne, J. N., & Huinker, D. M. (1993). Early number and numeration. In R. J. Jensen (Ed.), *Research ideas for the classroom: Early childhood mathematics* (pp. 343–71) (National Council of Teachers of Mathematics Research Interpretation Project). New York: Macmillan.

Pea, R., & Greeno, J. G. (1990, April). *Reflections on directions of reform in mathematics education.* Paper presented at the annual meeting of the American Educational Research Association, Boston.

Peck, D. M., & Jencks, S. M. (1981). Conceptual issues in the teaching and learning of fractions. *Journal for Research in Mathematics Education, 12*(5), 339–348.

Peled, I., Mukhopadhyay, S., & Resnick, L. B. (1988, November). *Formal and informal sources of mental models for negative numbers.* Paper presented at the 29th annual meeting of the Psychonomic Society, Chicago.

Peterson, P. L. (1988). Teaching for higher order thinking in mathematics: The challenge for the next decade. In D. A. Grouws, T. J. Cooney, & D. Jones (Eds.), *Perspectives on research on effective mathematics teaching* (Vol.1, pp. 2–26). Hillsdale, NJ: Lawrence Erlbaum Associates; Reston, VA: National Council of Teachers of Mathematics.

Petitto, A. L., & Ginsburg, H. P. (1981). Mental arithmetic in Africa and America: Strategies, principles, and explanations. *International Journal of Psychology, 17*, 81–102.

Piaget, J. (1950). *The psychology of intelligence* (M. Piercy & D. E. Berlyne, Trans.). London: Routledge & Kegan Paul. (Original work published 1947)

Piaget, J. (1970). *Genetic epistemology*. New York: Columbia University Press.

Piaget, J. (1971). *Science of education and the psychology of the child*. New York: Viking.

Piaget, J. (1973). Comments on mathematical education. In A. G. Howson (Ed.), *Developments in mathematical education: Proceedings of the Second International Congress on Mathematics Education*. Cambridge: Cambridge University Press.

Piaget, J. (1980). The psychogenesis of knowledge and its epistemological significance. In M. Piatelli-Palmarini (Ed.), *Language and learning: The debate between Jean Piaget and Noam Chomsky*. Cambridge, MA: Harvard University Press.

Piaget, J., & Inhelder, B. (1975). *The origin of the idea of chance in children*. London: Routledge & Kegan Paul.

Pierce, K. A., & Gholson, B. (1994). Surface similarity and relational similarity in the development of analogical problem solving: Isomorphic and nonisomorophic transfer. *Developmental Psychology, 30*(5), 724–737.

Pirie, S., & Kieren, T. (1992). Creating constructivist environments and constructing creative mathematics. *Educational Studies in Mathematics, 23*, 505–528.

Polich, J. M., & Schwartz, S. H. (1974). The effect of problem size on representation in deductive problem solving. *Memory & Cognition, 2*, 683–686.

Pollak, H. (1987, May). Notes from a talk presented at the Mathematical Sciences Education Board, Frameworks Conference, Minneapolis. (Cited in National Council of Teachers of Mathematics, 1989, Curriculum and Evaluation Standards for School Mathematics.)

Polya, G. (1954). *Mathematics and plausible reasoning, Vol.1: Induction and analogy in mathematics*. Princeton, NJ: Princeton University Press.

Polya, G. (1957). *How to solve it* (2nd ed.). New York: Doubleday.

Polya, G. (1962). *Mathematical discovery: On understanding, learning, and teaching problem solving (Vol.1)*. New York: Wiley.

Polya, G. (1971). *How to solve it: A new aspect of mathematical method (2nd ed.)*. Princeton, NJ: Princeton University Press.

Post, T., Behr, M., & Lesh, R. (1988). Proportionality and the development of pre-algebra understandings. In A. F. Coxford & A. P. Shulte (Eds.), *The ideas of algebra, K–12* (pp. 78–90). Reston, VA: National Council of Teachers of Mathematics.

Post, T. R., Cramer, K. A., Behr, M., Lesh, R., & Harel, G. (1993). Curriculum implications of research on the learning, teaching, and assessing of rational number concepts. In T. Carpenter, E. Fennema, & T. A. Romberg (Eds.), *Rational numbers: An integration of research* (pp. 327–362). Hillsdale, NJ: Lawrence Erlbaum Associates.

Post, T. R., Wachsmuth, E., Lesh, R., & Behr, M. (1985). Order and equivalence of rational number: A cognitive analysis. *Journal for Research in Mathematics Education, 15*, 18–36.

Pothier, Y., & Sawada, D. (1983). Partitioning: The emergence of rational number ideas in young children. *Journal for Research in Mathematics Education, 14*, 307–317.

Prawat, R. S. (1989). Promoting access to knowledge, strategy, and disposition in students: A research synthesis. *Review of Educational Research, 59*(1), 1–41.

Premack, D. (1983). The codes of man and beasts. *The Behavioral and Brain Sciences, 6*, 125–167.

Presmeg, N. (1992). Prototypes, metaphors, metonymies, and imaginative rationality in high school mathematics. *Educational Studies in Mathematics, 23*, 595–610.

Pressley, M., Borkowski, J. G., & Schneider, W. (1987). Cognitive strategies: Good strategy users coordinate metacognition and knowledge. *Annals of Child Development*, 89–129.

Pressley, M., Forrest-Pressley, D. L., Elliott-Faust, D., & Miller, G. (1985.) Children's use of cognitive strategies, how to teach strategies, and what to do if they can't be taught. In M. Pressley & C. J. Brainerd (Eds.), *Cognitive learning and memory in children* (pp. 1–47). New York: Springer-Verlag.

Putnam, R. T., deBettencourt, L. U., & Leinhardt, G. (1990). Understanding of derived-fact strategies in addition and subtraction. *Cognition and Instruction, 7*(3), 161–195.

Putnam, R. T., Lampert, M., & Peterson, P. L. (1990). Alternative perspectives on knowing mathematics in elementary schools. In C. B. Cazden (Ed.), *Review of Research in Education, 16* (pp. 57–150). Washington, DC: American Educational Research Association.

Quintero, A. (1985). Conceptual understanding of multiplication: Problems involving combination. *Arithmetic Teacher, 33*(3), 36–39.

Rathmell, E. C. (1978). Using thinking strategies to teach the basic facts. In M. Suydam & R. Reys (Eds.), *Developing computational skills* (1978 yearbook, pp. 31–38). Reston, VA: National Council of Teachers of Mathematics.

Reber, A. S. (1989). Implicit learning and tacit knowledge. *Journal of Experimental Psychology: General, 118*(3), 219–235.

Reed, S. (1987). A structure-mapping model for word problems. *Journal of Experimental Psychology: Learning, Memory, and Cognition, 13*, 124–139.

Rescorla, R. A. (1988). Pavlovian conditioning: It's not what you think it is. *American Psychologist, 43*(3), 151–160.

Resnick, L. B. (1982). Syntax and semantics in learning to subtract. In T. P. Carpenter, J. M. Moser, & T. A. Romberg (Eds.), *Addition and subtraction: A cognitive perspective* (pp. 136–155). Hillsdale, NJ: Lawrence Erlbaum Associates.

Resnick, L. B. (1983). A developmental theory of number understanding. In H. P. Ginsburg (Ed.), *The development of mathematical thinking* (pp. 109–151). New York: Academic Press.

Resnick, L. B. (1986). The development of mathematical intuition. In M. Perlmutter

(Ed.), *Perspectives on intellectual development: The Minnesota Symposia on Child Psychology* (Vol. 19, pp. 159–194). Hillsdale, NJ: Lawrence Erlbaum Associates.

Resnick, L. B. (1987a). Constructing knowledge in school. In L. S. Liben (Ed.), *Development and learning: Conflict or congruence?* (pp. 19–50). Hillsdale, NJ: Lawrence Erlbaum Associates.

Resnick, L. B. (1987b). *Education and learning to think.* Washington, DC: National Academy Press.

Resnick, L. B. (1992). From protoquantities to operators: Building mathematical competence on a foundation of everyday knowledge. In G. Leinhardt, R. T. Putnam, & R. Hattrup (Eds.), *Analysis of arithmetic for mathematics teaching* (pp. 373–430). Hillsdale, NJ: Lawrence Erlbaum Associates.

Resnick, L. B., Bill, V., & Lesgold, S. (1992). Developing thinking abilities in arithmetic class. In A. Demetriou, M. Shayer, & A. Efklides (Eds.), *Neo-Piagetian theories of cognitive development* (pp. 210–230). London: Routledge.

Resnick, L. B., & Ford, W. W. (1984). *The psychology of mathematics for instruction.* Hillsdale, NJ: Lawrence Erlbaum Associates.

Resnick, L. B., & Greeno, J. G. (1990). *Conceptual growth of number and quantity.* Unpublished manuscript, University of Pittsburgh, PA.

Resnick, L. B., & Nelson-Le-Gall, S. (1987). Meaning construction in mathematical problem solving. In J. C. Bergeron, N. Herscovics, & C. Kieran (Eds.), *Proceedings of the Eleventh Annual Conference of the International Group for the Psychology of Mathematics Education* (Vol. 3, pp. 215–221). Montreal: International Group for the Psychology of Mathematics Education.

Resnick, L. B., Nesher, P., Leonard, F., Magone, M., Omanson, S., & Peled, I. (1989). Conceptual bases of arithmetic errors: The case of decimal fractions. *Journal for Research in Mathematics Education, 20,* 8–27.

Resnick, L. B., & Omanson, S. F. (1987). Learning to understand arithmetic. In R. Glaser (Ed.), *Advances in instructional psychology* (Vol. 3, pp. 41–95). Hillsdale, NJ: Lawrence Erlbaum Associates.

Resnick, L. B., & Resnick, D. P. (1992). Assessing the thinking curriculum: New tools for educational reform. In B. R. Gifford & M. C. O'Connor (Eds.), *Changing assessments: Alternative views of aptitude, achievement and instruction* (pp. 37–75). Boston: Kluwer.

Resnick, L. B., & Singer, J. (1993). Protoquantitative origins of ratio reasoning. In T. Carpenter, E. Fennema, & T. A. Romberg (Eds.), *Rational numbers: An integration of research* (pp. 107–130). Hillsdale, NJ: Lawrence Erlbaum Associates.

Reusser, K. (1990). From text to situation to equation: Cognitive simulation of understanding and solving mathematical word problems. In H. Mandl, E. De Corte, N. Bennett, & H. F. Friedrich (Eds.), *Learning and instruction: Vol. 2. Analysis of complex skills and complex knowledge domains* (pp. 477–498). Elmsford, NY: Pergamon Press.

Reys, R. E. (1992). Mental computation: Some ideas and directions for teaching. In C. J. Irons (Ed.), *Challenging children to think when they compute.* Brisbane, Australia: Centre for Mathematics and Science Education.

Reys, R. E., Suydam, M., & Lindquist, M. (1984). *Helping children learn mathematics.* Englewood Cliffs, NJ: Prentice-Hall.

Riley, M. S., & Greeno, J. G. (1988). Developmental analysis of understanding language about quantities and of solving problems. *Cognition and Instruction, 5*(1), 49–101.

Robins, S., & Mayer, R. E. (1993). Schema training in analogical reasoning. *Journal of Educational Psychology, 85*(3), 529–538.

Robitaille, D. F., & Garden, R. A. (1989). *The IEA study of mathematics II: Contexts and outcomes of school mathematics.* Oxford: Pergamon Press.

Ross, B. H. (1984). Remindings and their effects in learning a cognitive skill. *Cognitive Psychology, 16*, 371–416.

Ross, B. H. (1987). This is like that: The use of earlier problems and the separation of similarity effects. *Journal of Experimental Psychology: Learning, Memory, and Cognition, 13*, 629–639.

Ross, S. H. (1986, April). *The development of children's place-value numeration concepts in grades two through five.* Paper presented at the annual meeting of the American Educational Research Association, San Francisco.

Ross, S. H. (1989). Parts, wholes, and place value: A developmental view. *Arithmetic Teacher, 36*(6), 47–51.

Rudy, J. W. (1991). Elemental and configural associations, the hippocampus and development. *Developmental Psychobiology, 24*(4), 221–236.

Sato, S. (1984, August). *Measurement division is easier than partitive division.* Paper presented at the Fifth International Congress on Mathematical Education, Adelaide, Australia.

Saxe, G. B. (1991). *Culture and cognitive development: Studies in mathematical understanding.* Hillsdale, NJ: Lawrence Erlbaum Associates.

Scandura, J. M. (1970). Role of rules in behavior: Toward an operational definition of what (rule) is learned. *Psychological Review, 77*, 516–533.

Scardamalia, M. (1977). Information processing capacity and the problem of horizontal decalage: A demonstration using combinatorial reasoning tasks. *Child Development, 48*, 28–37.

Schneider, W., & Detweiler, M. (1987). A connectionist/control architecture for working memory. *The Psychology of Learning and Motivation, 21*, 53–119.

Schoenfeld, A. H. (1982). Some thoughts on problem-solving research and mathematics education. In F. K. Lester, Jr., & J. Garofalo (Eds.), *Mathematical problem solving: Issues and research* (pp. 27–37). Philadelphia: Franklin Institute Press.

Schoenfeld, A. H. (1985a). *Mathematical problem solving.* Orlando: Academic Press.

Schoenfeld, A. H. (1985b). Psychology and mathematical method: A capsule history and a modern view. *Education and Urban Society, 17*, 387–403.

Schoenfeld, A. H. (1986). On having and using geometric knowledge. In J. Hiebert (Ed.), *Conceptual and procedural knowledge: The case of mathematics* (pp. 225–264). Hillsdale, NJ: Lawrence Erlbaum Associates.

Schoenfeld, A. H. (1987). What's all the fuss about metacognition? In A. H. Schoenfeld (Ed.), *Cognitive science and mathematics education* (pp. 189–215). Hillsdale, NJ: Lawrence Erlbaum Associates.

Schoenfeld, A. H. (1988). When good teaching leads to bad results: The disasters of "well taught" mathematics classes. *Educational Psychologist, 23*, 145–166.

Schoenfeld, A. H. (1989). Explorations of students' mathematical beliefs and behavior. *Journal for Research in Mathematics Education, 20*, 338–355.

Schoenfeld, A. H. (1992). Learning to think mathematically: Problem solving, metacognition, and sense making in mathematics. In D. A. Grouws (Ed.), *Handbook of research on mathematics teaching and learning* (pp. 334–370). New York: Macmillan.

Schoenfeld, A. H. (1994). Reflections on doing and teaching mathematics. In A. H. Schoenfeld (Ed.), *Mathematical thinking and problem solving*. Hillsdale, NJ: Lawrence Erlbaum Associates.

Schwartz, J. L. (1988). Intensive quantity and referent transforming arithmetic operations. In J. Hiebert & M. Behr (Eds.), *Number concepts and operations in the middle grades* (pp. 41–52). Hillsdale, NJ: Lawrence Erlbaum Associates; Reston, VA: National Council of Teachers of Mathematics.

Schwarz, B. B., Kohn, A. S., & Resnick, L. B. (1992). Bootstrapping mental constructions: A learning system about negative numbers. *ITS 92 Proceedings of the Second International Conference on Intelligence Tutoring Systems*, Montreal.

Schwarz, B. B., Kohn, A. S., & Resnick, L. B. (in press). Positives about negatives. *Journal for the Learning Sciences*.

Secada, W. G., Fuson, K., & Hall, J. W. (1983). The transition from counting-all to counting-on in addition. *Journal for Research in Mathematics Education, 14*(1), 47–57.

Shaklee, H. (1979). Bounded rationality and cognitive development: Upper limits on growth? *Cognitive Psychology, 11*, 327–345.

Sharp, A. (1987). What is a community of inquiry? *Analytic Teaching, 8*(1), 13–18.

Shepard, R. N., & Metzler, J. (1971). Mental rotation of three-dimensional objects. *Science, 171*, 701–703.

Sheppard, J. L. (1978). *A structural analysis of concrete operations*. London: Wiley.

Shiffrin, R. M., & Schneider, W. (1977). Controlled and automatic human information processing: II. Perceptual learning, automatic attending, and a general theory. *Psychological Review, 84*, 127–190.

Shuard, H. (1991). *Calculators, children and mathematics*. London: Menthuen.

Siegler, R. S. (1981). Developmental sequences within and between concepts. *Monographs of the Society for Research in Child Development, 46*, 1–84.

Siegler, R. S., & Campbell, J. (1990). Diagnosing individual differences in strategy choice procedures. In N. Frederiksen, R. Glaser, A. Lesgold, & M. G. Shafto (Eds.), *Diagnostic monitoring of knowledge and skill acquisition* (pp. 113–139). Hillsdale, NJ: Lawrence Erlbaum Associates.

Siegler, R. S., & Jenkins, E. A. (1989). *How children discover new strategies*. Hillsdale, NJ: Lawrence Erlbaum Associates.

Siegler, R. S., & Robinson, M. (1982). *The development of numerical understanding*. London: Academic Press.

Siegler, R. S., & Shipley, C. (in press). Variation, selection, and cognitive change. In T. Simon & G. S. Halford (Eds.), *Developing cognitive competence: New approaches to process modeling*. Hillsdale, NJ: Lawrence Erlbaum Associates.

Siegler, R. S., & Shrager, J. (1984). Strategy choices in addition and subtraction: How do children know what to do? In C. Sophian (Ed.), *Origins of cognitive skills* (pp. 229–293). Hillsdale, NJ: Lawrence Erlbaum Associates.

Sigel, I. E. (1984). *Distancing theory: Its implications for the development of representational thought*. Dusseldorf: Schwann.

Silver, E. A. (1979). Student perceptions of relatedness among mathematical verbal problems. *Journal for Research in Mathematics Education, 10*, 195–210.

Silver, E. A. (1981). Recall of mathematical problem formulation: Solving related problems. *Journal for Research in Mathematics Education, 12*(1), 54–64.

Silver, E. A. (1985). Research on teaching mathematical problem solving: Some underrepresented themes and needed directions. In E. A. Silver (Ed.), *Teaching and learning mathematical problem solving: Multiple research perspectives* (pp. 247–266). Hillsdale, NJ: Lawrence Erlbaum Associates.

Silver, E. A., & Adams, V. M. (1987). Using open-ended problems. *Arithmetic Teacher, 34*, 34–35.

Silver, E. A., & Mamona, J. (1989a). Problem posing by middle school mathematics teachers. In C. A. Maher, G. A. Goldin, & R. B. Davis (Eds.), *Proceedings of the eleventh annual meeting of the North American Chapter of the International Group for the Psychology of Mathematics Education* (pp. 263–269). New Brunswick, NJ: PME.

Silver, E. A., & Mamona, J. (1989b). Stimulating problem posing in mathematics instruction through open problems and "what-if-nots." In G. W. Blume & M. K. Heid (Eds.), *Implementing new curriculum and evaluation standards* (pp. 1–7). University Park, PA: Pennsylvania Council of Teachers of Mathematics.

Silver, E. A., & Marshall, S. P. (1990). Mathematical and scientific problem solving: Findings, issues, and instructional implications. In B. F. Jones & L. Idol (Eds.), *Dimensions of thinking and cognitive instruction* (pp. 265–290). Hillsdale, NJ: Lawrence Erlbaum Associates.

Silver, E. A., Mukhopadhyay, S., & Gabriele, A. J. (1992). Referential mappings and the solution of division story problems involving remainders. *Focus on Learning Problems in Mathematics, 14*(3), 29–39.

Silver, E. A., Shapiro, L. J., & Deutsch, A. (1993). Sense making and the solution of division problems involving remainders: An examination of middle school students' solution processes and their interpretations of solutions. *Journal for Research in Mathematics Education, 24*(2), 117–135.

Simon, H. (1978). Information-processing theory of human problem solving. In W. K. Estes (Ed.), *Handbook of learning and cognitive processes* (Vol. 5, pp. 271–295). Hillsdale, NJ: Lawrence Erlbaum Associates.

Simon, T., & Klahr, D. (in press). A computational theory of children's learning about number conservation. In T. Simon & G. S. Halford (Eds.), *Developing cognitive competence: New approaches to process modeling.* Hillsdale, NJ: Lawrence Erlbaum Associates.

Singer, J. A., & Resnick, L. B. (1992). Representations of proportional relationships: Are children part-part or part-whole reasoners? *Educational Studies in Mathematics, 23*, 231–246.

Sowder, J. T. (1988). Mental computation and number comparison: Their roles in the development of number sense and computational estimation. In J. Hiebert & M. Behr (Eds.), *Number concepts and operations in the middle grades* (Vol. 2, pp. 182–197). Hillsdale, NJ: Lawrence Erlbaum Associates; Reston, VA: National Council of Teachers of Mathematics.

Sowder, J. T. (1989). *Setting a research agenda, Vol. 5.* Hillsdale, NJ: Lawrence Erlbaum Associates; Reston, VA: National Council of Teachers of Mathematics.

Sowder, J. T. (1990). Mental computation and number sense. *Arithmetic Teacher, 37*(7), 18–20.

Sowder, J. T. (1992). Estimation and number sense. In D. A. Grouws (Ed.), *Handbook of research on mathematics teaching and learning* (pp. 371–389). New York: Macmillan.

Sowder, J. T., & Kelin, J. (1993). Number sense and related topics. In D. T. Owen (Ed.), *Research ideas for the classroom: Middle grades mathematics* (pp. 41–57). New York: Macmillan.

Sowell, E. (1989). Effects of manipulative materials in mathematics. *Journal for Research in Mathematics Education, 20*(5), 498–505.

Splitter, L. (1988). On teaching children to be better thinkers. *Unicorn, 14*(1), 40–47.

Splitter, L. (1991). *Philosophy for children: The community of inquiry and thinking about thinking.* Unpublished manuscript, Australian Council for Educational Research, Centre for Philosophy for Children, Melbourne.

Squire, L. R. (1992). Memory and the hippocampus: A synthesis from findings with rats, monkeys and humans. *Psychological Review, 99*(2), 195–231.

Stanic, G. M. A., & Kilpatrick, J. (1988). Historical perspectives on problem solving in the mathematics curriculum. In R. Charles & E. Silver (Eds.), *The teaching and assessing of mathematical problem solving* (pp. 1–22). Reston, VA: National Council of Teachers of Mathematics.

Stanic, G. M. A., & McKillip, W. D. (1989). Developmental algorithms have a place in elementary school mathematics instruction. *Arithmetic Teacher, 36*(5), 14–16.

Starkey, P., Spelke, E. S., & Gelman, R. (1990). Numerical abstraction by young infants. *Cognition, 36*, 97–128.

Stavy, R., & Tirosh, D. (1993) When analogy is perceived as such. *Journal of Research in Science Teaching, 30*(10), 1229–1239.

Steffe, L. P. (1988). Children's construction of number sequences and multiplying schemes. In J. Hiebert & M. Behr (Eds.), *Number concepts and operations in the middle grades* (Vol. 2, pp. 119–140). Hillsdale, NJ: Lawrence Erlbaum Associates; Reston, VA: National Council of Teachers of Mathematics.

Steffe, L. P. (1989). *Children's construction of the rational numbers of arithmetic* (Proposal to the National Science Foundation). Washington, DC: National Science Foundation.

Steffe, L. P., & Cobb, P. (1988). *Construction of arithmetical meanings and strategies.* New York: Springer-Verlag.

Steinberg, R. M. (1985). Instruction on derived facts strategies in addition and subtraction. *Journal for Research in Mathematics Education, 16*(5), 337–355.

Steinberg, R. M., Baroody, A. J., & Fuson, K. C. (1984). From counting to recall of number facts. In J. M. Moser (Ed.), *Proceedings of the sixth annual meeting of the North American Chapter of the International Group for the Psychology of Mathematics Education* (pp. 253–262). Madison: University of Wisconsin, Wisconsin Centre for Education Research.

Steinberg, R. M., Sleeman, D. H., & Ktorza, D. (1991). Algebra students' knowledge of equivalence of equations. *Journal for Research in Mathematics Education, 22*(2), 112–121.

Stern, E. (1989, September). *The role of arithmetic in solving word problems.* Paper presented at the third conference of the European Association of Research in Learning and Instruction, Madrid.

Stern, E. (1993). What makes certain arithmetic word problems involving the comparison of sets so difficult for children? *Journal of Educational Psychology, 85*(1), 7–23.

Sternberg, R. J. (1980a). The development of linear syllogistic reasoning. *Journal of Experimental Child Psychology, 29*, 340–356.

Sternberg, R. J. (1980b). Representation and process in linear syllogistic reasoning. *Journal of Experimental Psychology: General, 109*, 119–159.

Stigler, J. W., & Baranes, R. (1988). Culture and mathematics learning. In E. Z. Rothkopf (Ed.), *Review of Research in Education* (pp. 253–306). Washington, DC: American Educational Research Association.

Stigler, J. W., Fuson, K. C., Ham, M., & Kim, M. S. (1986). An analysis of addition and subtraction word problems in American and Soviet elementary mathematics textbooks. *Cognition and Instruction, 3*, 153–171.

Stigler, J. W. Lee, S. Y., & Stevenson, H. W. (1990). *The mathematical knowledge of Japanes, Chinese, and American elementary school children.* Reston, VA: National Council of Teachers of Mathematics.

Stillings, N. A., Feinstein, M. H., Garfield, J. L., Rissland, E. L., Rosenbaum, D. A., Weisler, S., & Baker-Ward, L. (1987). *Cognitive Science: An introduction.* Cambridge, MA: MIT Press.

Strauss, S., & Stavy, R. (1982). U-shaped behavioral growth: Implications for theories of development. In W. Hartup (Ed.), *Review of child development research* (Vol. 6, pp. 547–599). Chicago: University of Chicago Press.

Streefland, L. (1985). Basic principles for teaching and learning fractions. In A. Bell, B. Low, & J. Kilpatrick (Eds.), *Theory, research, and practice in mathematical education.* Nottingham, England: Shell Centre for Mathematical Education, University of Nottingham.

Streefland, L. (1985). Search for the roots of ratio: Some thoughts on the long term learning process (towards ... a theory), Part II. *Educational Studies in Mathematics, 16*, 75–94.

Suppes, P. (1965). On the behavioural foundations of mathematical concepts. *Monographs of the Society for Research in Child Development, 30*, 60–96.

Suydam, M. N. (1984). Research report: Learning the basic facts. *Arithmetic Teacher, 32*(1), 15.

Sweller, J. (1989). Cognitive technology: Some procedures for facilitating learning and problem solving in mathematics and science. *Journal of Educational Psychology, 81*, 457–466.

Taber, S. B. (1993a, April). *Cognitive obstacles in developing an understanding of multiplication of fractions.* Paper presented at the annual meeting of the American Education Research Association, Atlanta, GA.

Taber, S. B. (1993b, April). *Dividing to multiply: The interface of students' knowledge about multiplication and fractions.* Paper presented at the annual meeting of the American Education Research Association, Atlanta, GA.

Tarte, L. (1990). Spatial orientation skill and mathematical problem solving. *Journal for Research in Mathematics Education, 21*(3), 216–229.

Thompson, P. W. (1992). Notations, conventions, and constraints: Contributions to effective uses of concrete materials in elementary mathematics. *Journal for Research in Mathematics Education, 23*(2), 123–147.

Thompson, P. W. (1994). Concrete materials and teaching for mathematical understanding. *Arithmetic Teacher, 41*(9), 556–558.

Thorndike, E. L., (1922). *The psychology of arithmetic.* New York: Macmillan.

Thornton, C. A. (1990). Solution strategies: Subtraction number facts. *Educational Studies in Mathematics, 21*, 241–263.

Thornton, C. A., Jones, G. A., & Toohey, M. A. (1983). A multisensory approach to thinking strategies for remedial instruction in basic addition facts. *Journal for Research in Mathematics Education, 14*(3), 198–203.

Thornton, C. A., & Toohey, M. (1985). Basic math facts: Guidelines for teaching and learning. *Learning Disabilities Focus, 1*, 44–57.

Tirosh, D., & Graeber, A, O. (1990). Inconsistencies in preservice elementary teachers' beliefs about multiplication and division. *Focus on Learning Problems in Mathematics, 12*(3 & 4), 65–74.

Travers, K. J., & Westbury, I. (1990). *The IEA study of mathematics: I. Analysis of mathematics curricula.* Oxford: Pergamon Press.

van Dijk, T. A., & Kintsch, W. (1983). *Strategies of discourse comprehension.* New York: Academic Press.

Van Engen, H. (1949). An analysis of meaning in arithmetic. *Elementary School Journal, 49*, 321–329, 395–400.

Van Engen, H. (1953). The formation of concepts. In H. F. Fehr (Ed.), *The learning of mathematics: Its theory and practice. Twenty-first Yearbook of the National Council of Teachers of Mathematics* (pp. 69–98). Washington, DC: National Council of Teachers of Mathematics.

Van Engen, H. (1993). Twentieth century mathematics for the elementary school. *Arithmetic Teacher, 41*(2), 92–96. (Original work published in 1958)

VanLehn, K. (1990). *Mind bugs: The origins of procedural misconceptions.* Cambridge, MA: MIT Press.

VanLehn, K., & Brown, J. S. (1980). Planning nets: A representation for formalizing analogies and semantic models of procedural skills. In R. E. Snow, P. A. Federico, & W. E. Montague (Eds.), *Aptitude learning and instruction: Vol. 2. Cognitive process analyses of learning and problem solving* (pp. 95–137). Hillsdale, NJ: Lawrence Erlbaum Associates.

Vergnaud, G. (1983). Multiplicative structures. In R. Lesh & M. Landau (Eds.), *Acquisition of mathematics concepts and processes* (pp. 127–174). New York: Academic Press.

Vergnaud, G. (1984). Understanding mathematics at the secondary-school level. In A. Bell, B. Low, & J. Kilpatrick (Eds.), *Theory, research and practice in mathematical education* (Report of ICME 5 Working Group on Research in Mathematics Education, pp. 27–35). Nottingham, UK: Shell Centre for Mathematical Education.

Vergnaud, G. (1988). Multiplicative structures. In J. Hiebert & M. Behr (Eds.), *Number concepts and operations in the middle grades* (pp. 141–161). Hillsdale, NJ: Lawrence Erlbaum Associates; Reston, VA: National Council of Teachers of Mathematics.

von Glasersfeld, E. (1990). Environment and communication. In L. P. Steffe & T. Wood (Eds.), *Transforming children's mathematics education: International perspectives* (pp. 30–38). Hillsdale, NJ: Lawrence Erlbaum Associates.

Vygotsky, L. S. (1962). *Thought and language.* Cambridge, MA: MIT Press. (Original work published 1934)

Wagner, S. (1981). Conservation of equation and function under transformations of variable. *Journal for Research in Mathematics Education, 12*(2), 107–118.

Wagner, S., & Kieran, C. (1989). An agenda for research on the learning and teaching of algebra. In S. Wagner & C. Kieran (Eds.), *Research issues in the learning and teaching of algebra* (Vol. 4, pp. 220–237). Hillsdale, NJ: Lawrence Erlbaum Associates; Reston, VA: National Council of Teachers of Mathematics.

Wagner, S., & Parker, S. (1993). Advancing algebra. In P. S. Wilson (Ed.), *Research ideas for the classroom: High school mathematics* (pp. 119–139). New York: Macmillan.

Wagner, S., Rachlin, S. L., & Jensen, R. J. (1984). *Algebra learning project: Final report.* Athens, GA: University of Georgia.

Wallas, G. (1926). *The art of thought.* New York: Harcourt Brace Jovanovich.

Wang, M. C., Haertel, G. D., & Walberg, H. J. (1993). Toward a knowledge base for school learning. *Review of Educational Research, 63*(3), 249–294.

Watson, J. M., Campbell, K. F., & Collis, K. (1993). Multimodal functioning in understanding fractions. *Journal of Mathematical Behavior, 12*, 45–62.

Wearne, D. (1990). Acquiring meaning for decimal fraction symbols: A one year follow-up. *Educational Studies in Mathematics, 21*, 545–564.

Wearne, D., & Hiebert, J. (1985). Teaching for thinking in mathematics. *Curriculum Review*, 25(1), 65–68.

Wearne, D., & Hiebert, J. (1988a). A cognitive approach to meaningful mathematics instruction: Testing a local theory using decimal numbers. *Journal for Research in Mathematics Education, 19*(5), 371–384.

Wearne, D., & Hiebert, J. (1988b). Constructing and using meaning for mathematical symbols: The case of decimal fractions. In J. Hiebert, & M. Behr (Eds.), *Number concepts and operations in the middle grades* (pp. 220–235). Hillsdale, NJ: Lawrence Erlbaum Associates; Reston, VA: National Council of Teachers of Mathematics.

Wenger, R. H. (1987). Cognitive science and algebra learning. In A. Schoenfeld (Ed.), *Cognitive science and mathematics education* (pp. 115–135). Hillsdale, NJ: Lawrence Erlbaum Associates.

Werner, H. (1948). *Comparative psychology of mental development.* Chicago: Follet.

Wertheimer, M. (1959). *Productive thinking.* New York: Harper & Row.

Wheeler, R. H. (1935). The new psychology of learning. In W. D. Reeve (Ed.), *The teaching of arithmetic. Tenth yearbook of the National Council of Teachers of Mathematics* (pp. 233–250). New York: Teachers College, Columbia University.

Whitehead, A. N., & Russell, B. (1927). *Principia mathematica* (2nd ed.). Cambridge: Cambridge University Press.

Wickens, C. D. (1974). Temporal limits of human information processing. *Psychological Bulletin, 81*, 739–755.

Widaman, K. F., & Little, T. D. (1992). The development of skill in mental arithmetic: An individual differences perspective. In J. I. D. Campbell (Ed.), *The nature and origins of mathematical skills* (pp. 189–253). Amsterdam: Elsevier.

Williams, J. P. (1984). Psychology and education. In M. H. Bornstein (Ed.), *Psychology and its allied disciplines: Vol. 2. The social sciences* (pp. 89–121). Hillsdale, NJ: Lawrence Erlbaum Associates.

Willis, G. B., & Fuson, K. (1988). Teaching children to use schematic drawings to solve addition and subtraction word problems. *Journal of Educational Psychology, 80,* 192–201.

Wolters, M. A. D. (1983). The part-whole schema and arithmetical problems. *Educational Studies in Mathematics, 14,* 127–138.

Wood, T., Cobb, P., Yackel, E., & Dillon, D. (1993). (Eds.). *Rethinking elementary school mathematics: Insights and issues.* Reston, VA: National Council of Teachers of Mathematics.

Wynn, K. (1989, April). *Children's understanding of counting.* Paper presented at the biennial meeting of the Society for Research in Child Development, Kansas City, KS.

Wynn, K. (1990). Children's understanding of counting. *Cognition, 36,* 155–193.

Wynn, K. (1992a). Addition and subtraction by human infants. *Nature, 358,* 749–750.

Wynn, K. (1992b). Evidence against empirical accounts of the origins of numerical knowledge. *Mind and Language, 7*(4), 315–332.

Younger, B. (1993). Understanding category members as "the same sort of thing": Explicit categorization in ten month infants. *Child Development, 64*(1), 309–320.

Zweng, M. (1964). Division problems and the concept of rate. *Arithmetic Teacher, 11*(8), 43–47.

Author Index